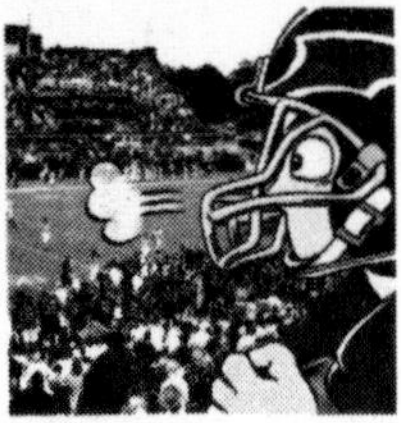

稲垣理一郎

Riichiro Inagaki

While we were in America, we went to see a college football game. The fans' passion was really amazing. For every play, it seemed like there were equal amounts of cheering and jeering.
The stands were packed. Everyone from the area was there, and it seemed like all of them were wearing the team's colors to show which side they supported.
It was a very productive fact-finding trip, even though a big, burly policeman confiscated my film. But I guess that was exciting too.

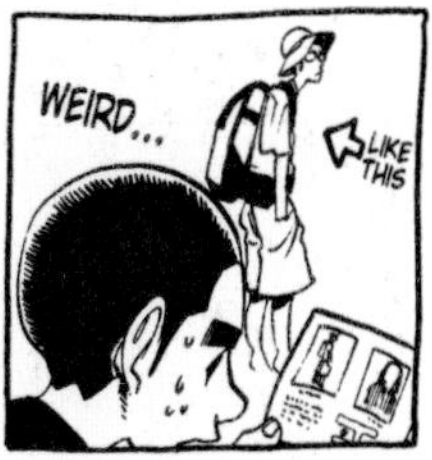
LIKE THIS
WEIRD...

村田雄介

Yusuke Murata

The other day, the weirdest thing happened. I saw a flier for some guy's one-man show, and the guy's picture looked just like me.
It wasn't just his face, but even his body type and the way he was dressed was the same...it was totally a case of a chance resemblance between strangers.

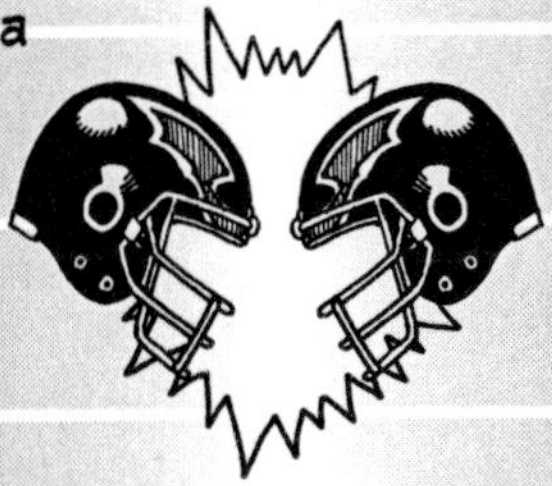

Eyeshield 21 is the hottest gridiron manga to hit the scene. A collaborative effort between writer Riichiro Inagaki and artist Yusuke Murata, ***Eyeshield 21*** was originally serialized in Japan's ***Weekly Shonen Jump***. An OAV created for Shueisha's Anime Tour is available in Japan, and the ***Eyeshield 21*** hit animated TV series debuted in spring 2005!

EYESHIELD 21

Vol 9: Hell Is for Devil Bats

The SHONEN JUMP ADVANCED Manga Edition

STORY BY RIICHIRO INAGAKI
ART BY YUSUKE MURATA

Translation & English Adaptation/Allison Markin Powell
Touch-up Art & Lettering/James Gaubatz
Cover and Graphic Design/Sean Lee
Editor/Frances E. Wall

Managing Editor/Frances E. Wall
Editorial Director/Elizabeth Kawasaki
VP & Editor in Chief/Yumi Hoashi
Sr. Director of Acquisitions/Rika Inouye
Sr. VP of Marketing/Liza Coppola
Exec. VP of Sales & Marketing/John Easum
Publisher/Hyoe Narita

Printed in the U.S.A.

Published by VIZ Media, LLC
P.O. Box 77010
San Francisco, CA 94107

SHONEN JUMP ADVANCED Manga Edition
10 9 8 7 6 5 4 3 2
First printing, August 2006
Second printing, August 2006

www.viz.com

RATED T+ FOR OLDER TEEN

PARENTAL ADVISORY
EYESHIELD 21 is rated T+ for Older Teen and is recommended for ages 16 and up. It contains graphic fantasy violence and crude humor.

EYESHIELD 21™

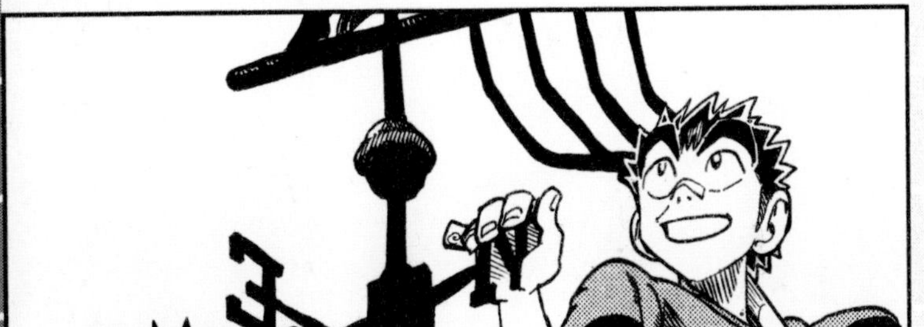

Vol. 9
Hell Is for Devil Bats

Story by Riichiro Inagaki Art by Yusuke Murata

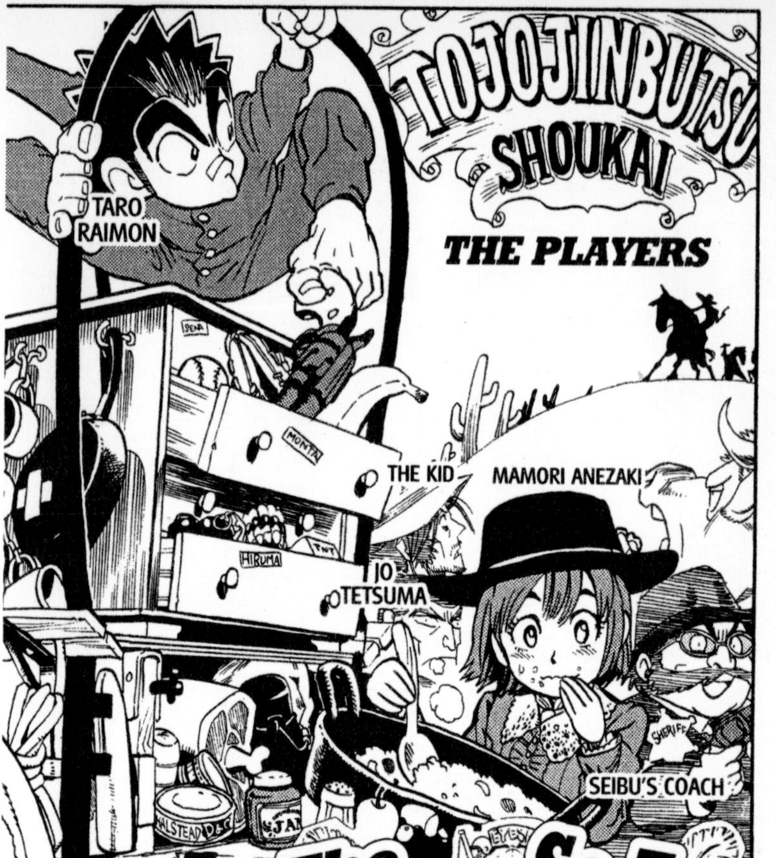
TOJOJINBUTSU SHOUKAI
THE PLAYERS
TARO RAIMON
THE KID
MAMORI ANEZAKI
JO TETSUMA
SEIBU'S COACH

The Story So Far

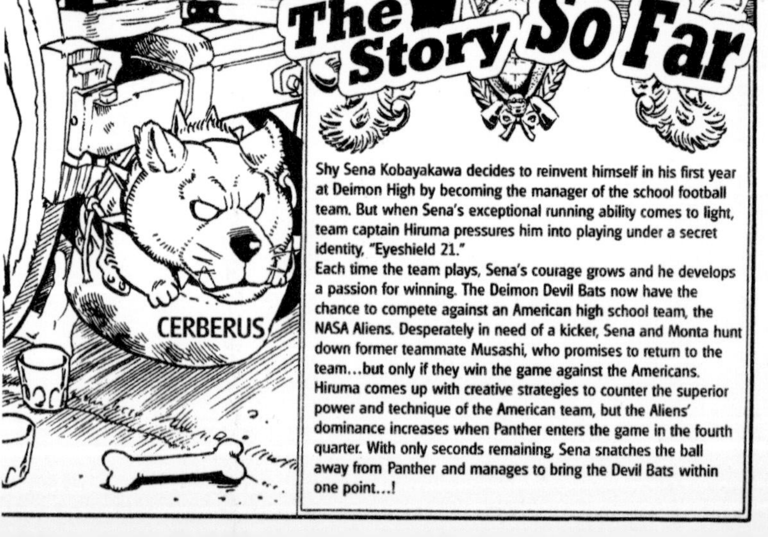
CERBERUS

Shy Sena Kobayakawa decides to reinvent himself in his first year at Deimon High by becoming the manager of the school football team. But when Sena's exceptional running ability comes to light, team captain Hiruma pressures him into playing under a secret identity, "Eyeshield 21."

Each time the team plays, Sena's courage grows and he develops a passion for winning. The Deimon Devil Bats now have the chance to compete against an American high school team, the NASA Aliens. Desperately in need of a kicker, Sena and Monta hunt down former teammate Musashi, who promises to return to the team…but only if they win the game against the Americans. Hiruma comes up with creative strategies to counter the superior power and technique of the American team, but the Aliens' dominance increases when Panther enters the game in the fourth quarter. With only seconds remaining, Sena snatches the ball away from Panther and manages to bring the Devil Bats within one point…!

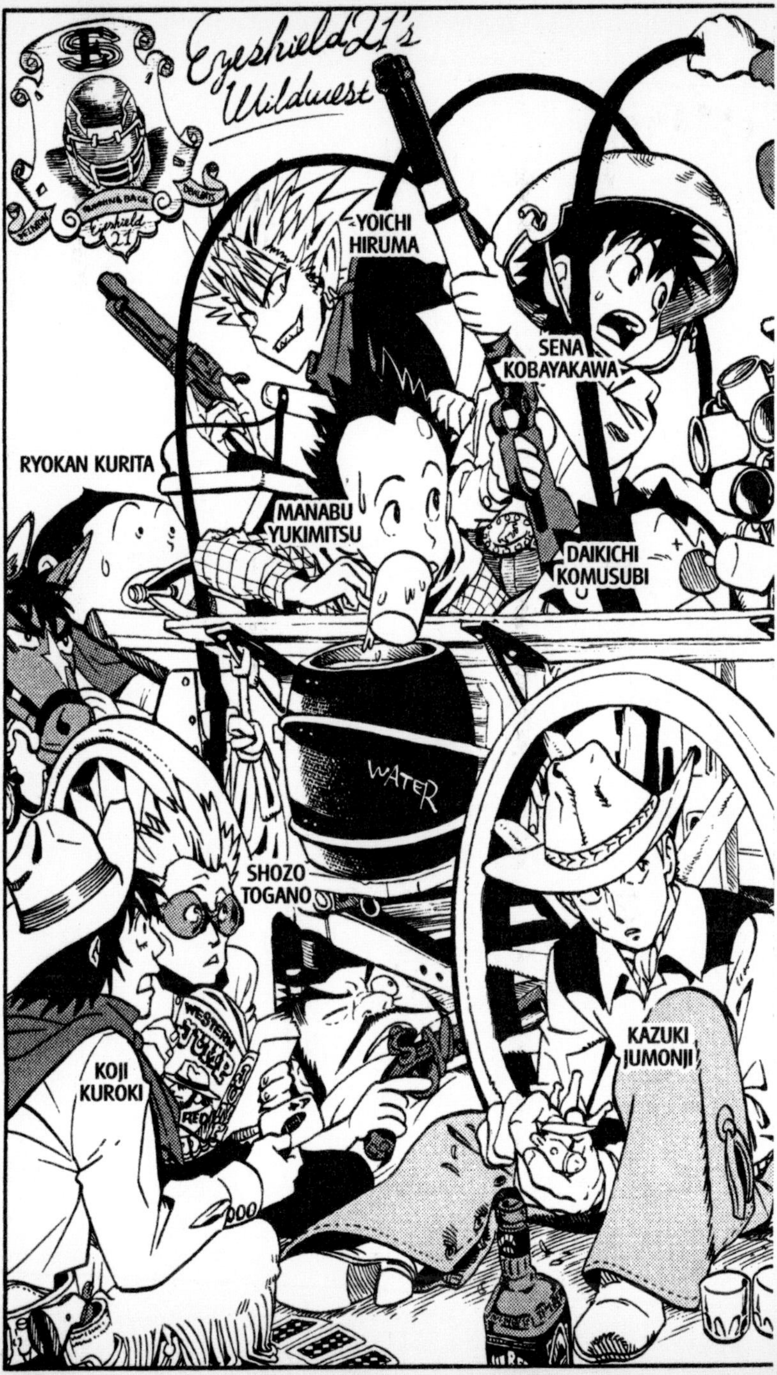
Eyeshield 21's Wildwest
YOICHI HIRUMA
SENA KOBAYAKAWA
RYOKAN KURITA
MANABU YUKIMITSU
DAIKICHI KOMUSUBI
WATER
SHOZO TOGANO
KAZUKI JUMONJI
KOJI KUROKI
WESTERN

Vol. 9
Hell Is for Devil Bats

CONTENTS

Chapter 71
No Way! USA?

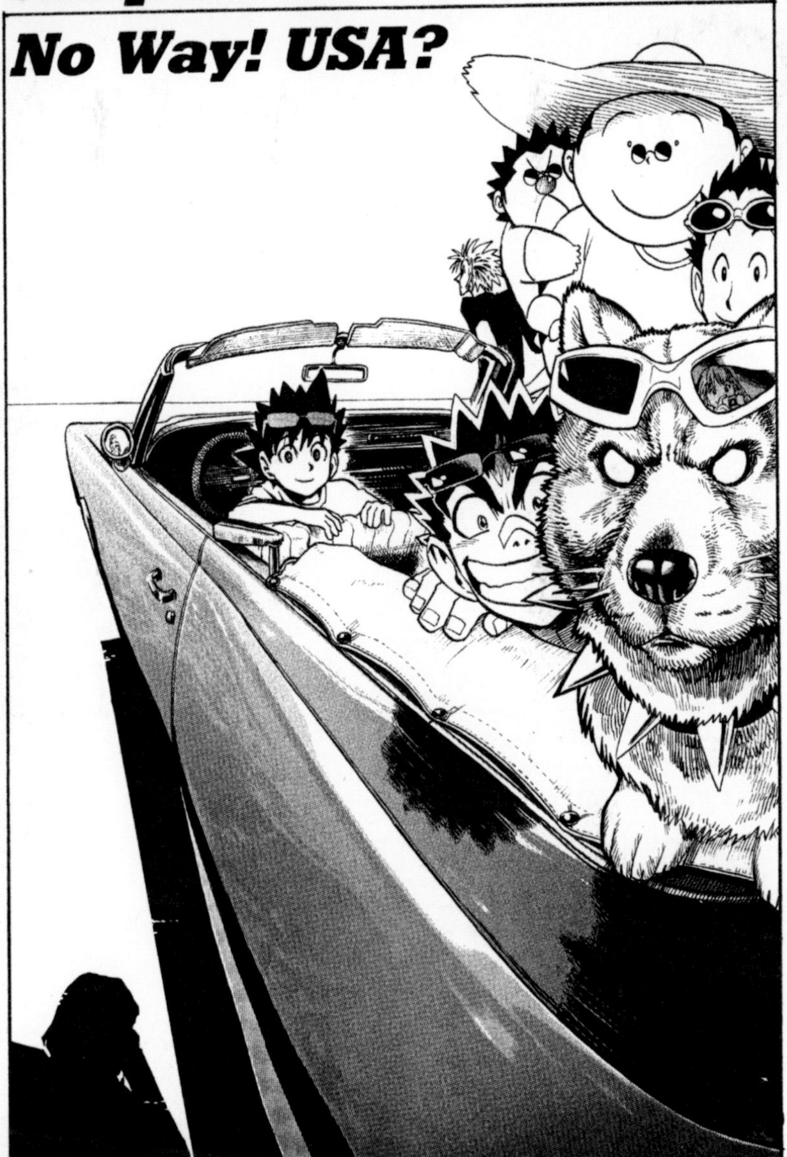

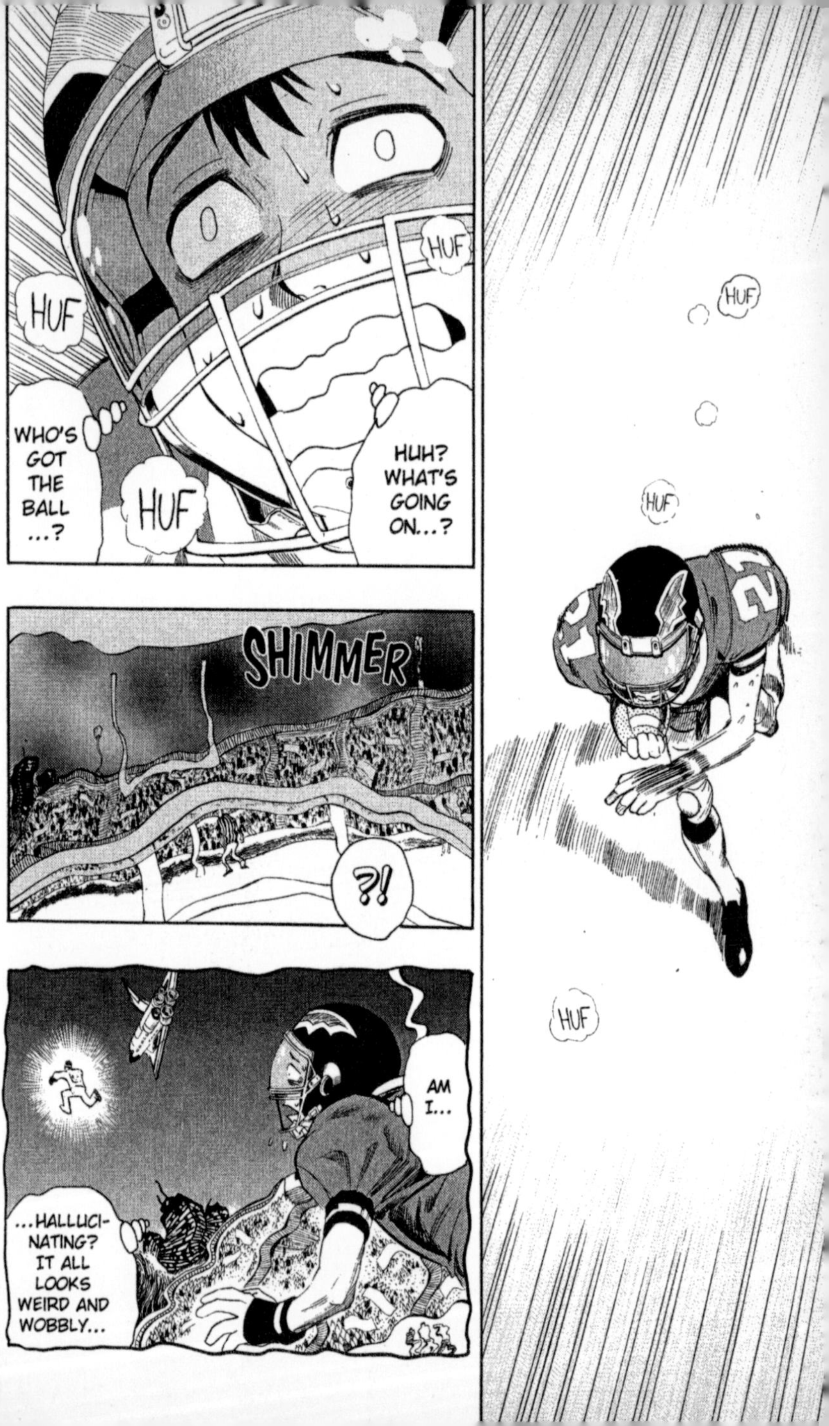

HUF
HUF
HUF
HUF
HUF
HUH? WHAT'S GOING ON...?
WHO'S GOT THE BALL ...?
HUF
SHIMMER
?!
AM I...
...HALLUCINATING? IT ALL LOOKS WEIRD AND WOBBLY...

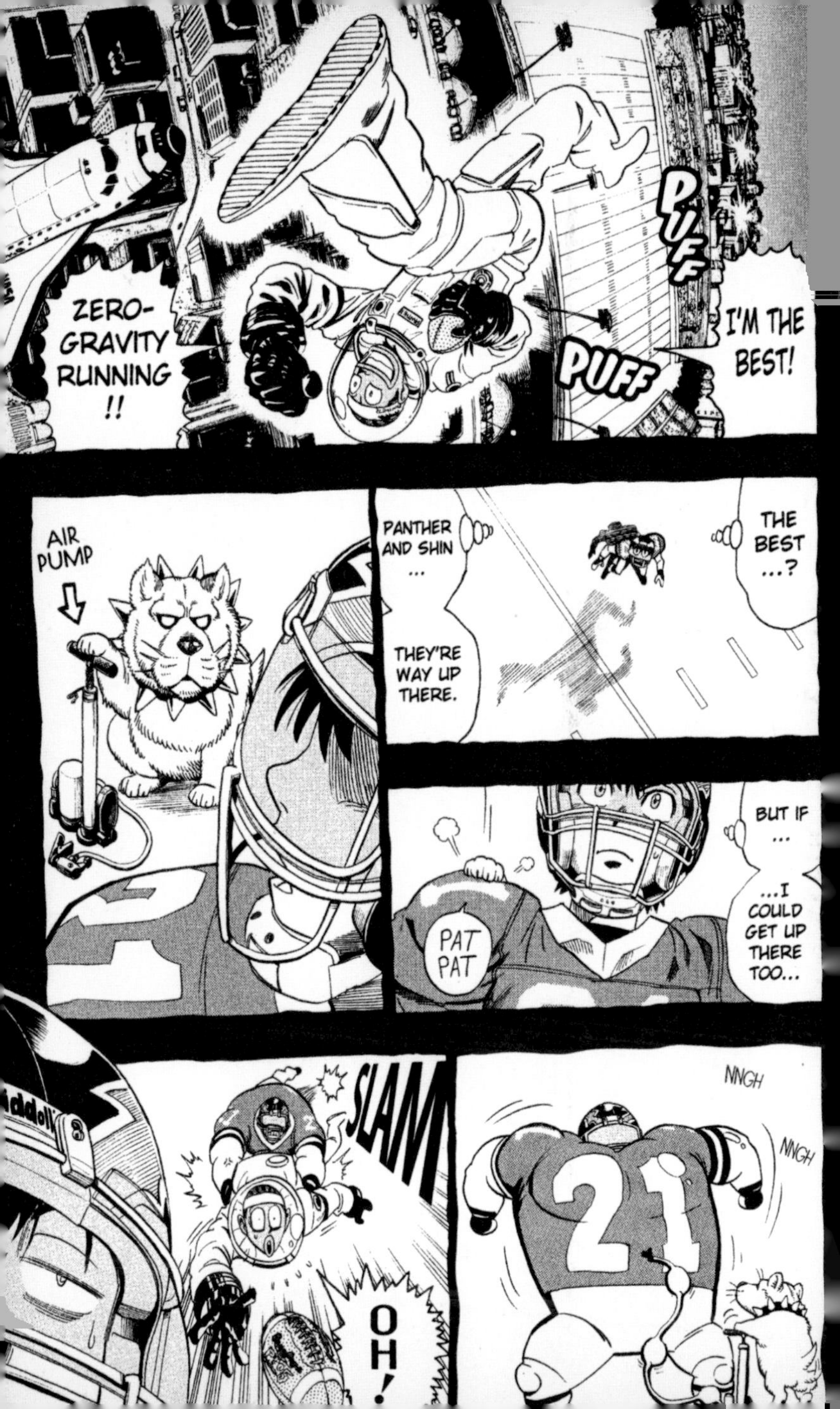
I'M THE BEST!
PUFF
PUFF
ZERO-GRAVITY RUNNING!!
THE BEST ...?
PANTHER AND SHIN ...
THEY'RE WAY UP THERE.
BUT IF ...
...I COULD GET UP THERE TOO...
PAT PAT
AIR PUMP
NNGH
NNGH
SLAM
OH!

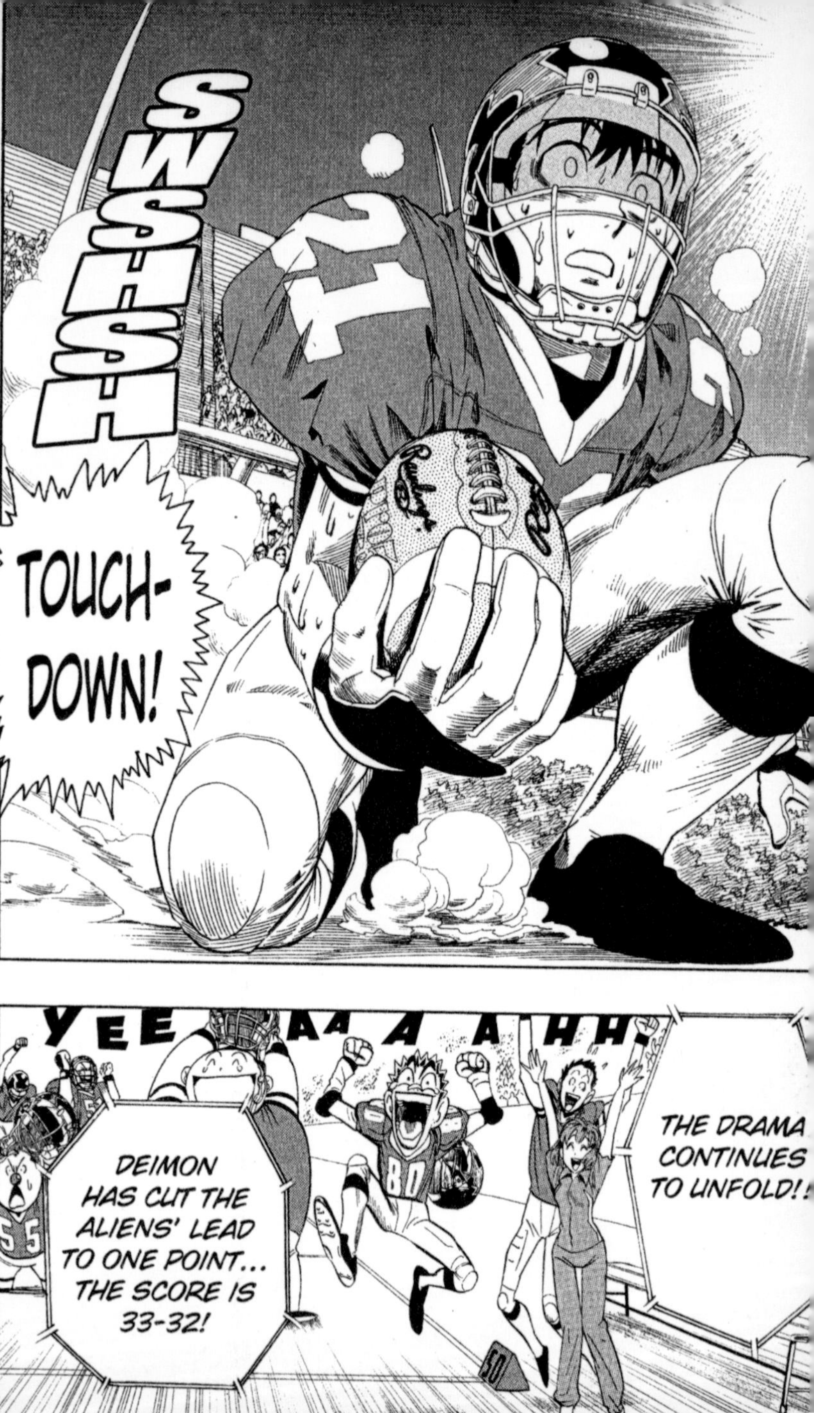
SWSHSH
TOUCH-DOWN!
YEEAAAAHH
THE DRAMA CONTINUES TO UNFOLD!!
DEIMON HAS CUT THE ALIENS' LEAD TO ONE POINT... THE SCORE IS 33-32!

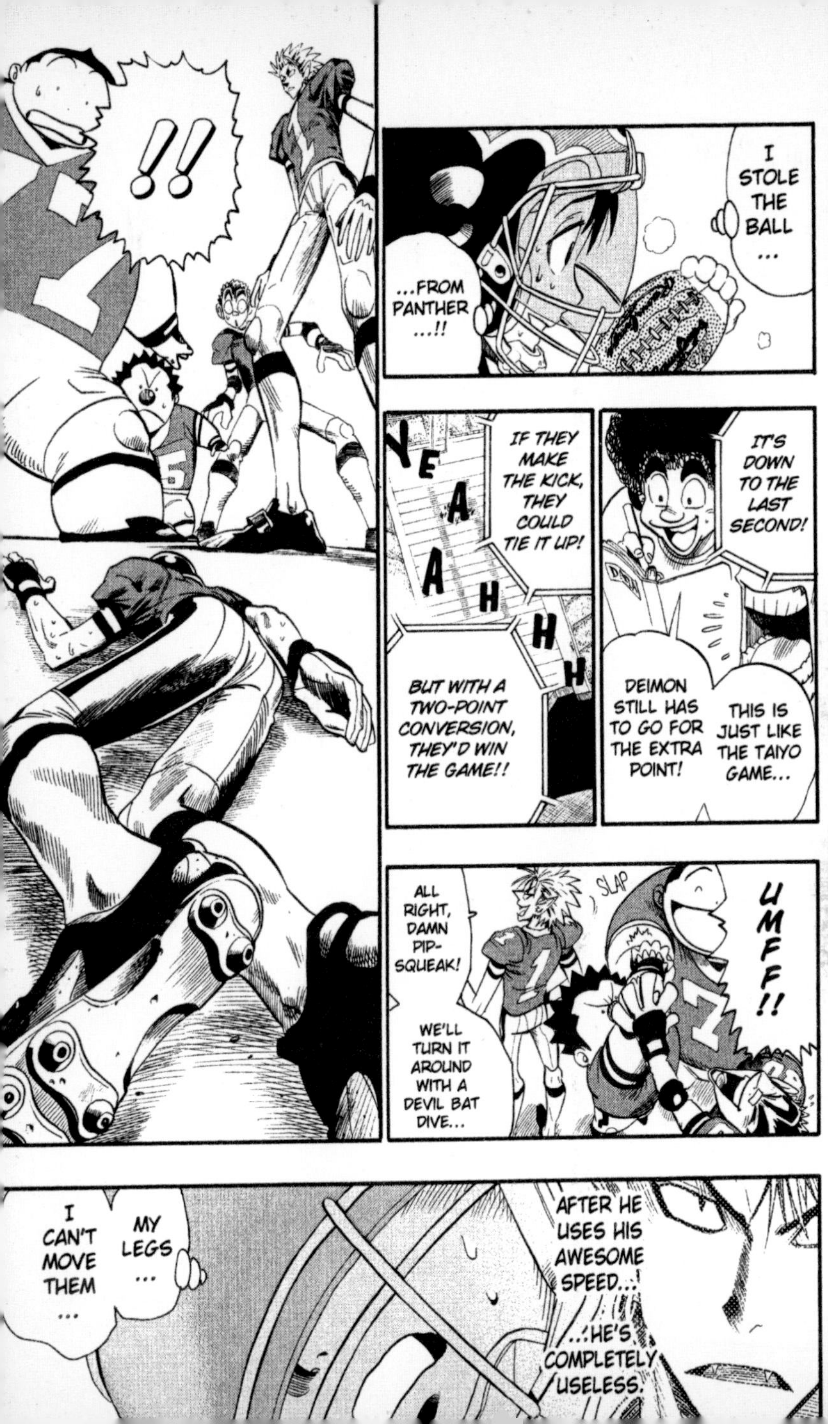
I STOLE THE BALL...
...FROM PANTHER...!!
IT'S DOWN TO THE LAST SECOND!
DEIMON STILL HAS TO GO FOR THE EXTRA POINT!
THIS IS JUST LIKE THE TAIYO GAME...
YEAAHHHH
IF THEY MAKE THE KICK, THEY COULD TIE IT UP!
BUT WITH A TWO-POINT CONVERSION, THEY'D WIN THE GAME!!
UMFF!!
SLAP
ALL RIGHT, DAMN PIP-SQUEAK!
WE'LL TURN IT AROUND WITH A DEVIL BAT DIVE...
!!
AFTER HE USES HIS AWESOME SPEED...
...HE'S COMPLETELY USELESS.
MY LEGS...
I CAN'T MOVE THEM...

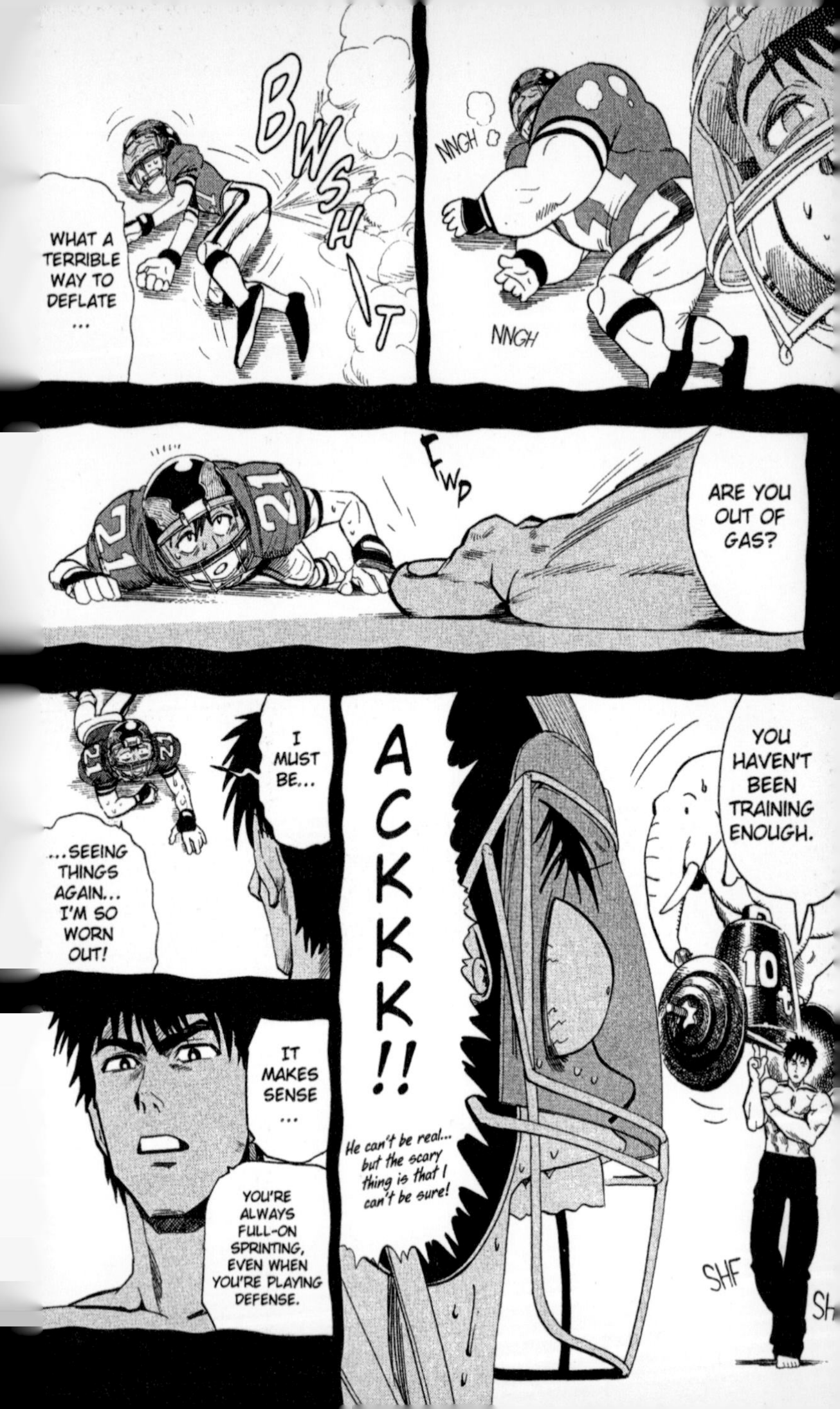
NNGH
NNGH
BWSHIT
WHAT A TERRIBLE WAY TO DEFLATE...
ARE YOU OUT OF GAS?
FWP
YOU HAVEN'T BEEN TRAINING ENOUGH.
10t
SHF
SH
ACKKK!!
He can't be real... but the scary thing is that I can't be sure!
I MUST BE...
...SEEING THINGS AGAIN... I'M SO WORN OUT!
IT MAKES SENSE...
YOU'RE ALWAYS FULL-ON SPRINTING, EVEN WHEN YOU'RE PLAYING DEFENSE.

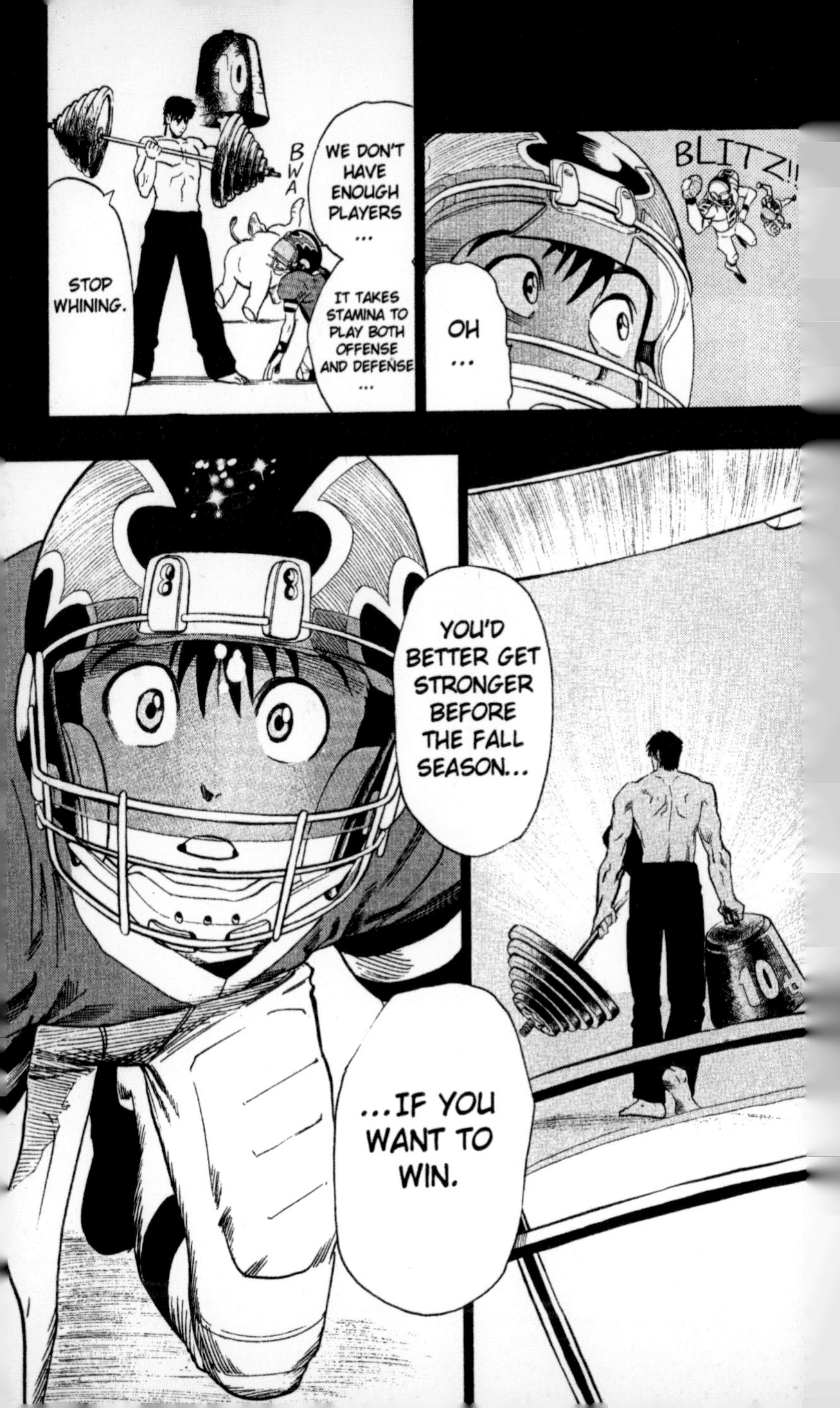
BLITZ!!
OH...
WE DON'T HAVE ENOUGH PLAYERS...
BWA
IT TAKES STAMINA TO PLAY BOTH OFFENSE AND DEFENSE...
STOP WHINING.
YOU'D BETTER GET STRONGER BEFORE THE FALL SEASON...
...IF YOU WANT TO WIN.

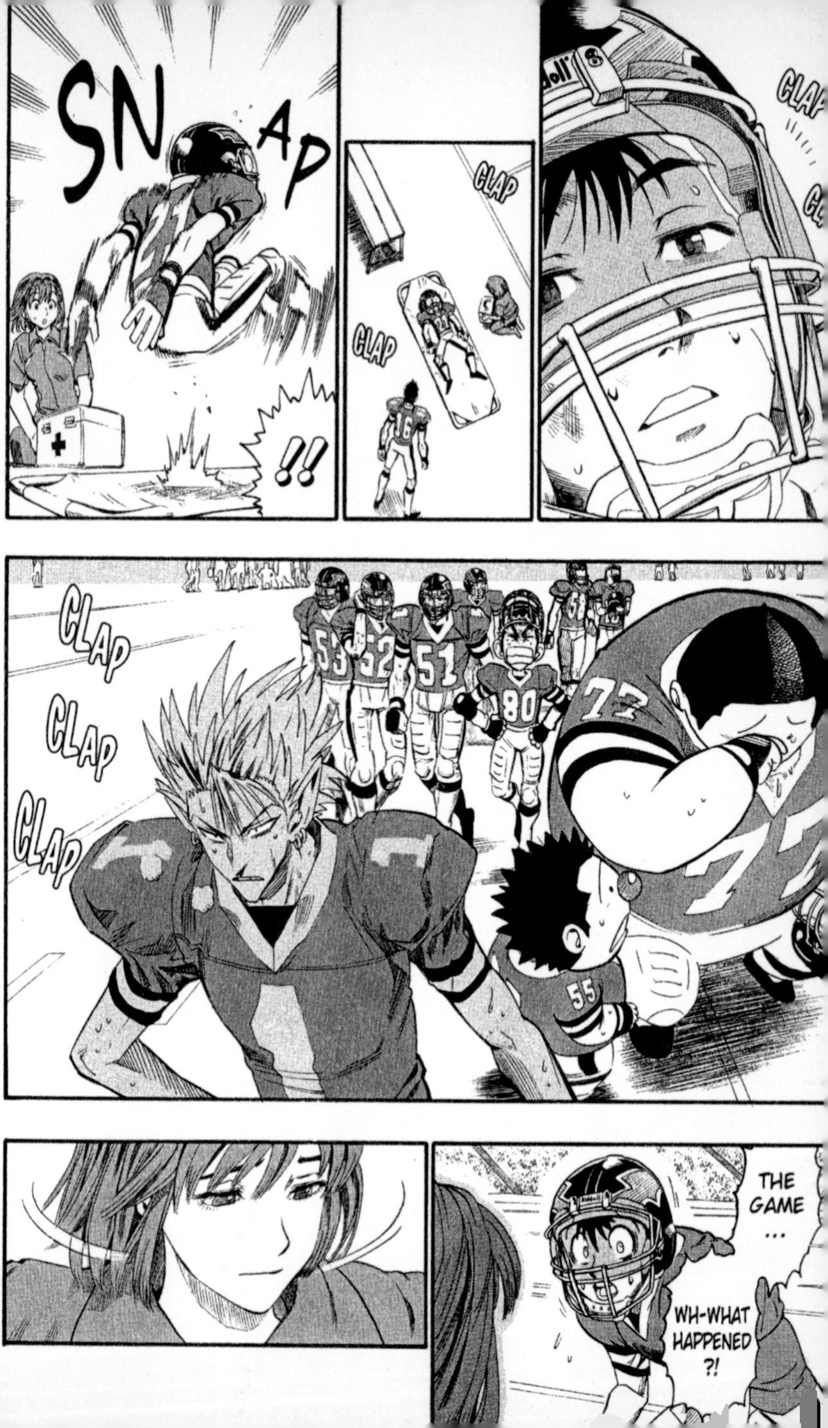
CLAP
CLAP
CLAP
SNAP
!!
CLAP
CLAP
CLAP
THE GAME ...
WH-WHAT HAPPENED ?!

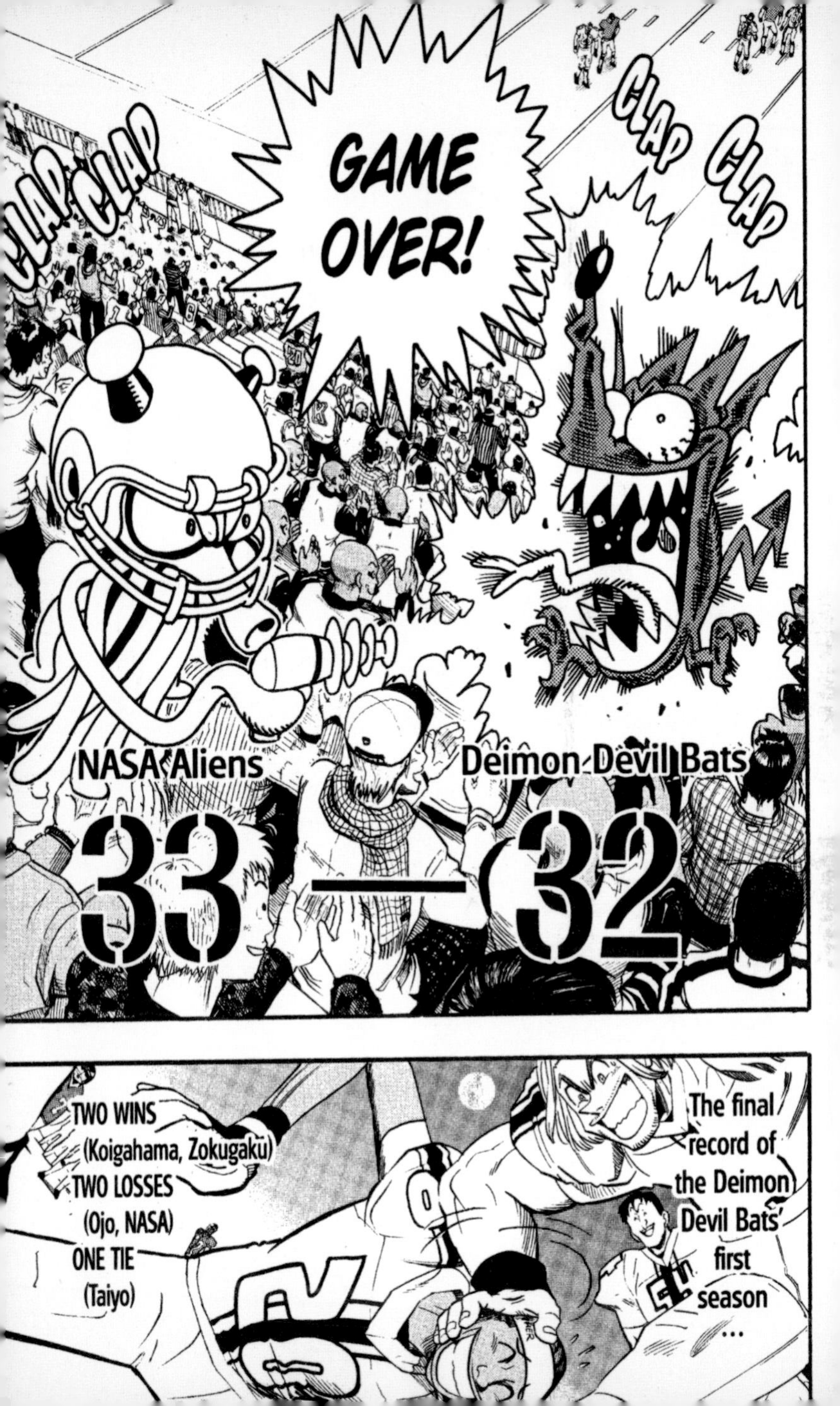
CLAP CLAP
GAME OVER!
CLAP CLAP
Deimon Devil Bats
NASA Aliens
33 — 32
The final record of the Deimon Devil Bats' first season...
TWO WINS (Koigahama, Zokugaku)
TWO LOSSES (Ojo, NASA)
ONE TIE (Taiyo)

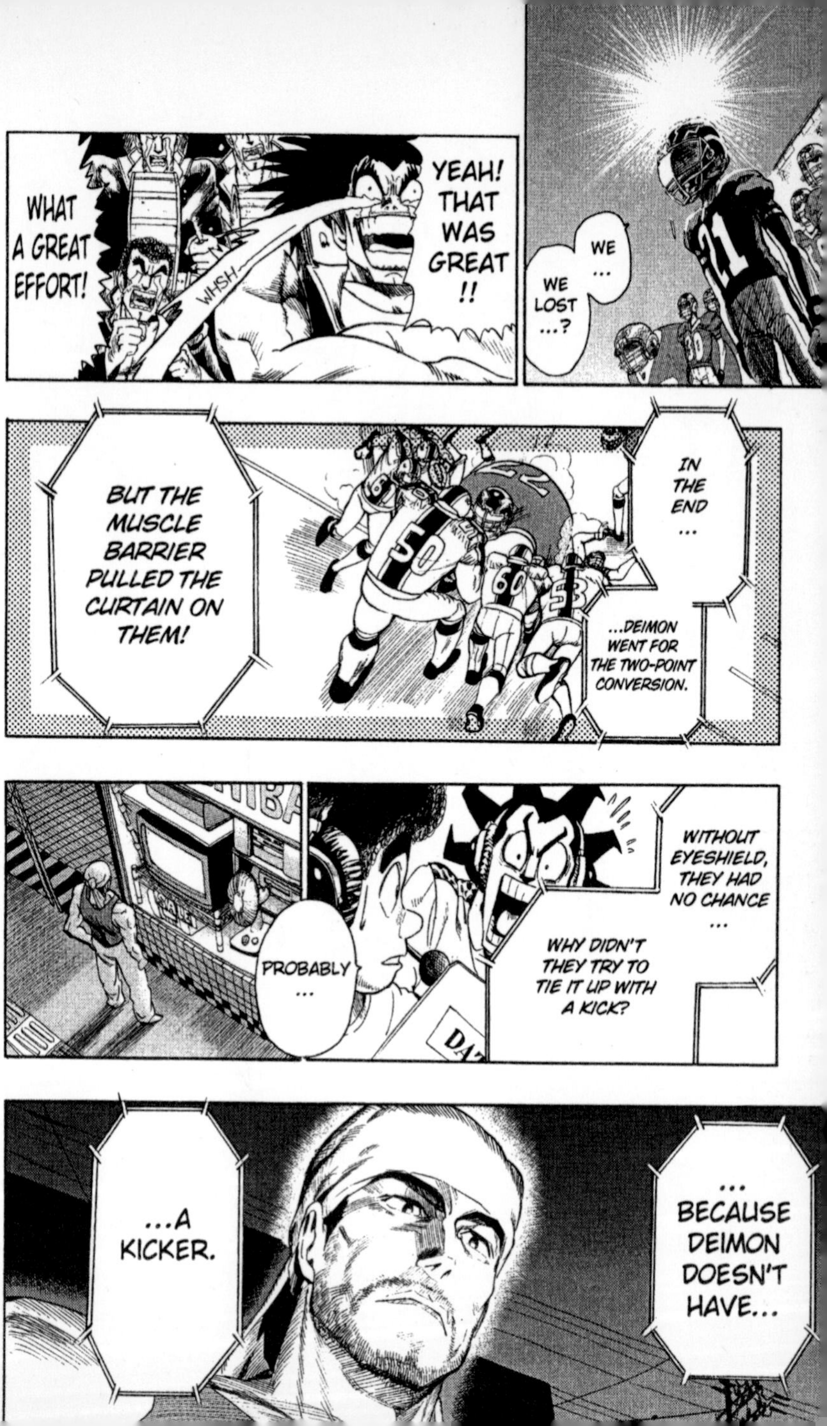

WE ...
WE LOST ...?
YEAH! THAT WAS GREAT !!
WHAT A GREAT EFFORT!
WHSH
IN THE END ...
...DEIMON WENT FOR THE TWO-POINT CONVERSION.
BUT THE MUSCLE BARRIER PULLED THE CURTAIN ON THEM!
WITHOUT EYESHIELD, THEY HAD NO CHANCE ...
WHY DIDN'T THEY TRY TO TIE IT UP WITH A KICK?
PROBABLY ...
... BECAUSE DEIMON DOESN'T HAVE...
...A KICKER.

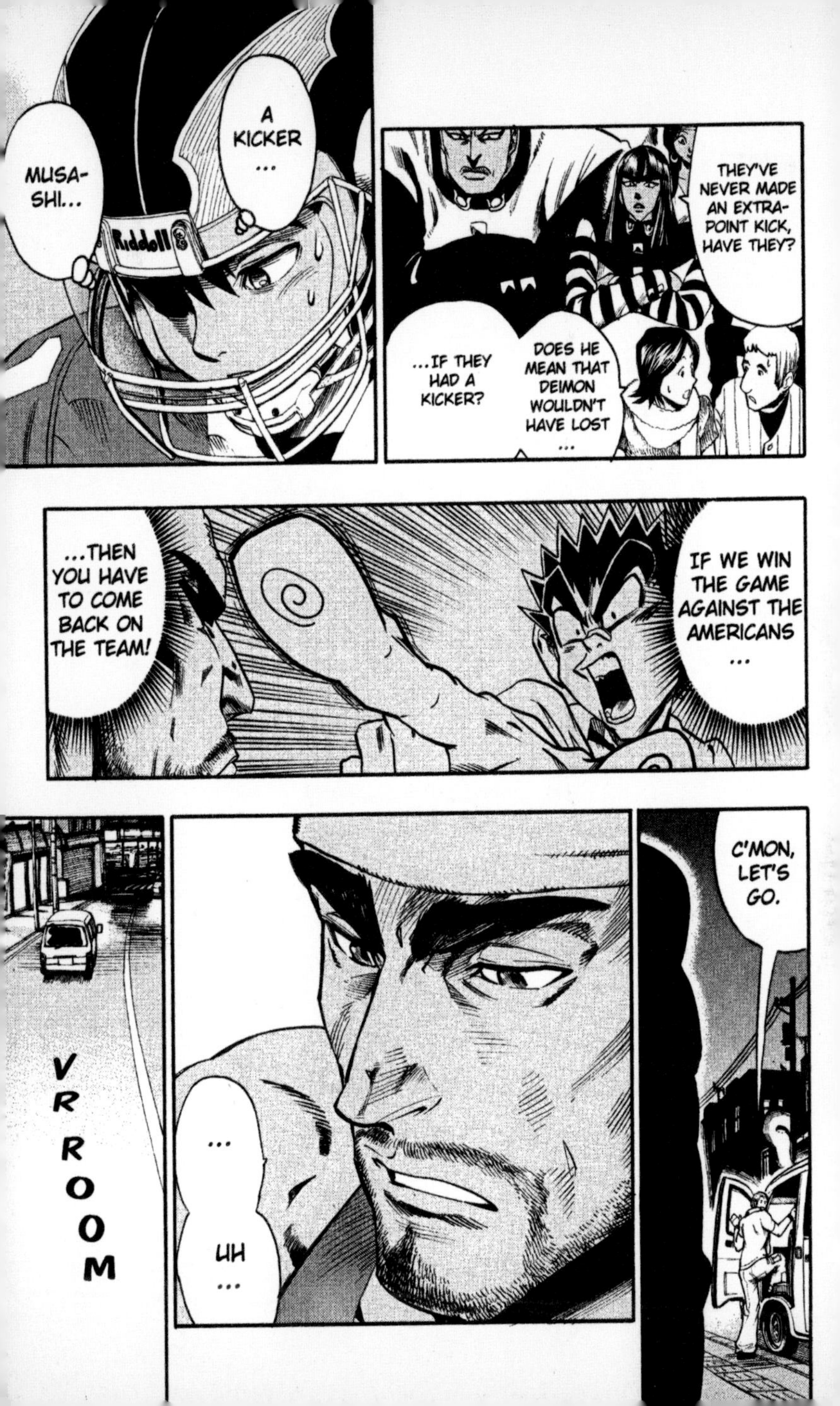
THEY'VE NEVER MADE AN EXTRA-POINT KICK, HAVE THEY?
DOES HE MEAN THAT DEIMON WOULDN'T HAVE LOST ...
...IF THEY HAD A KICKER?
A KICKER ...
MUSA-SHI...
IF WE WIN THE GAME AGAINST THE AMERICANS ...
...THEN YOU HAVE TO COME BACK ON THE TEAM!
C'MON, LET'S GO.
...
UH ...
VR ROOM

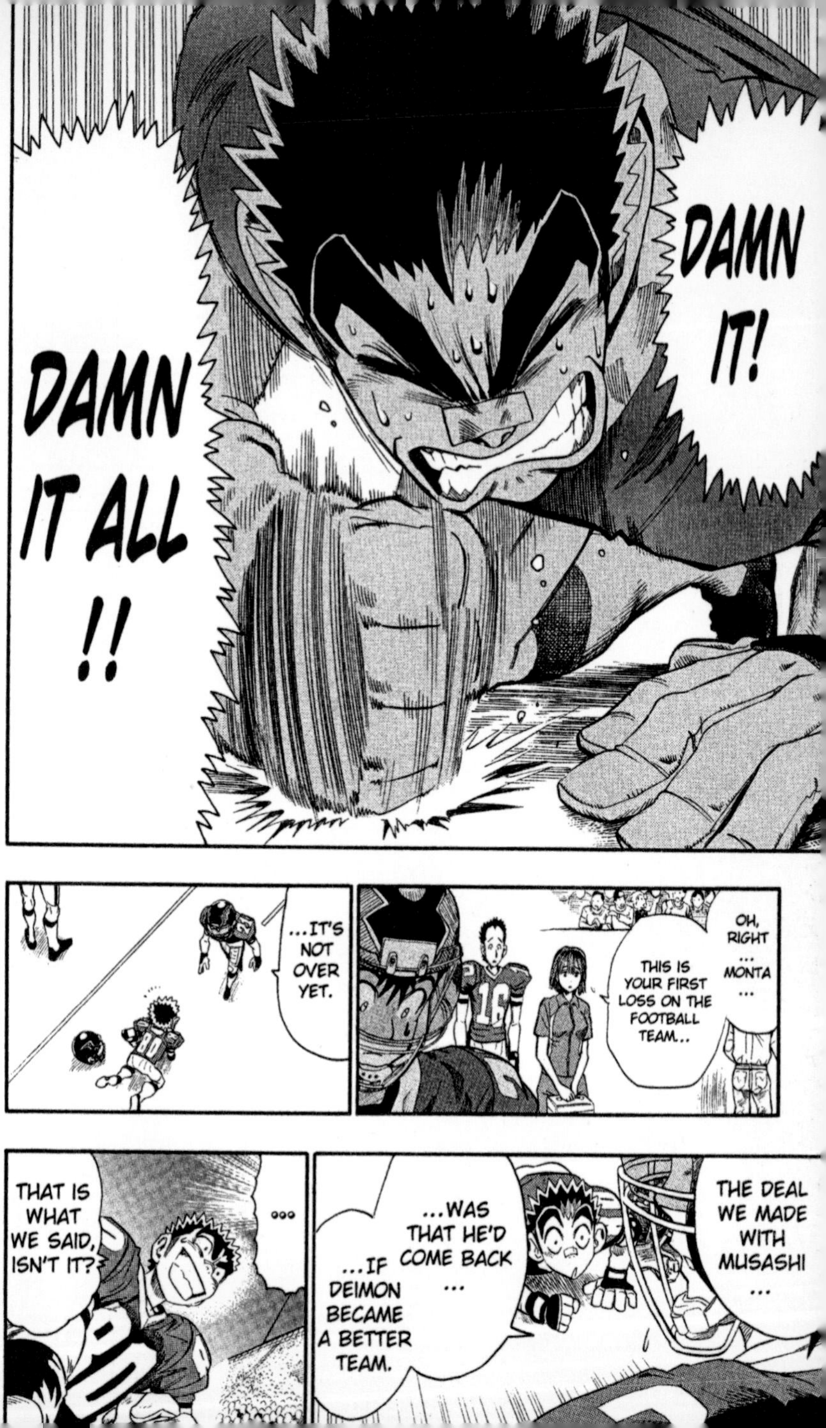
DAMN IT!
DAMN IT ALL !!
OH, RIGHT ... MONTA ...
THIS IS YOUR FIRST LOSS ON THE FOOTBALL TEAM...
...IT'S NOT OVER YET.
THE DEAL WE MADE WITH MUSASHI ...
...WAS THAT HE'D COME BACK ...
...IF DEIMON BECAME A BETTER TEAM.
...
THAT IS WHAT WE SAID, ISN'T IT?

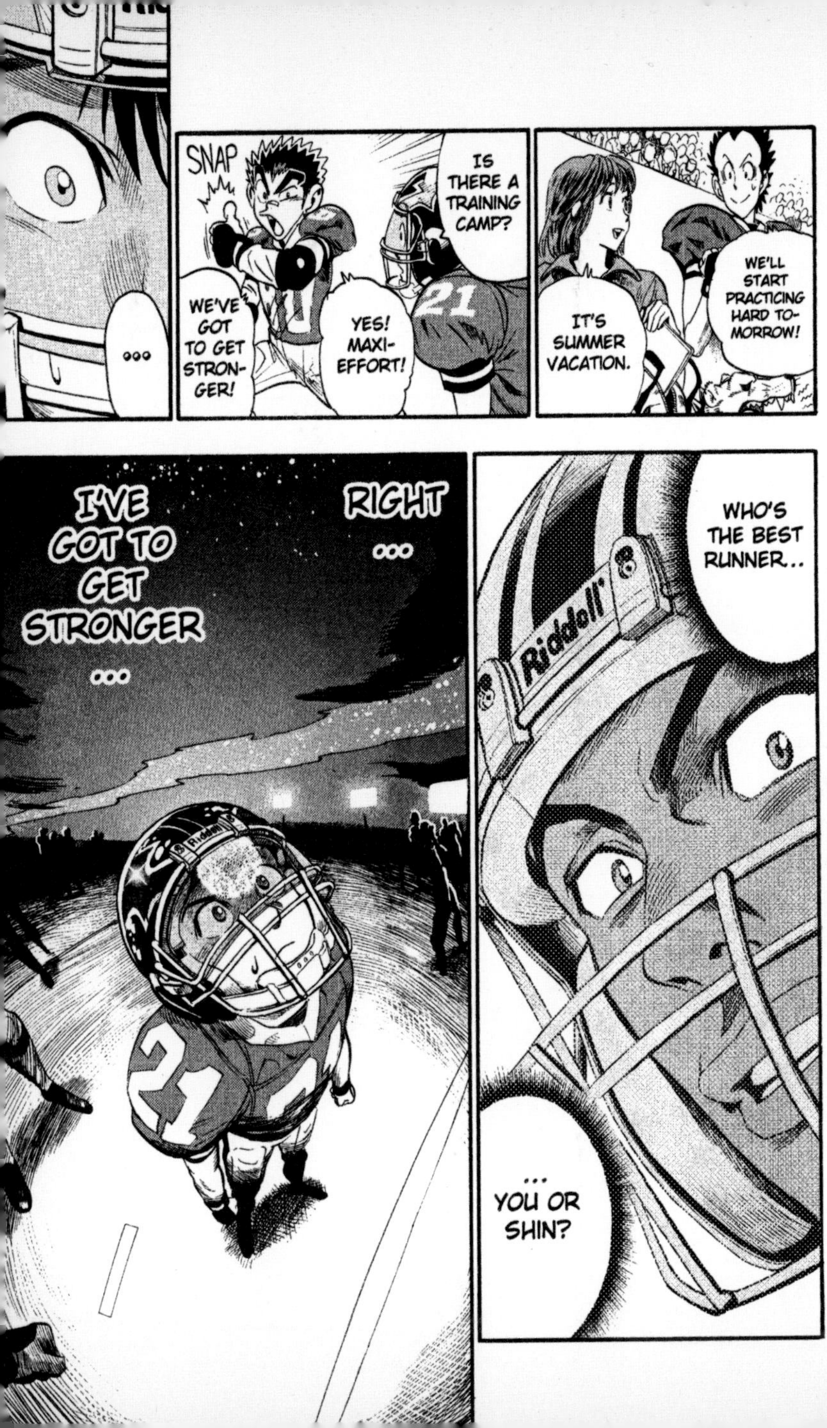
WE'LL START PRACTICING HARD TOMORROW!
IT'S SUMMER VACATION.
IS THERE A TRAINING CAMP?
YES! MAXI-EFFORT!
SNAP
WE'VE GOT TO GET STRONGER!
...
WHO'S THE BEST RUNNER..
... YOU OR SHIN?
RIGHT ...
I'VE GOT TO GET STRONGER ...

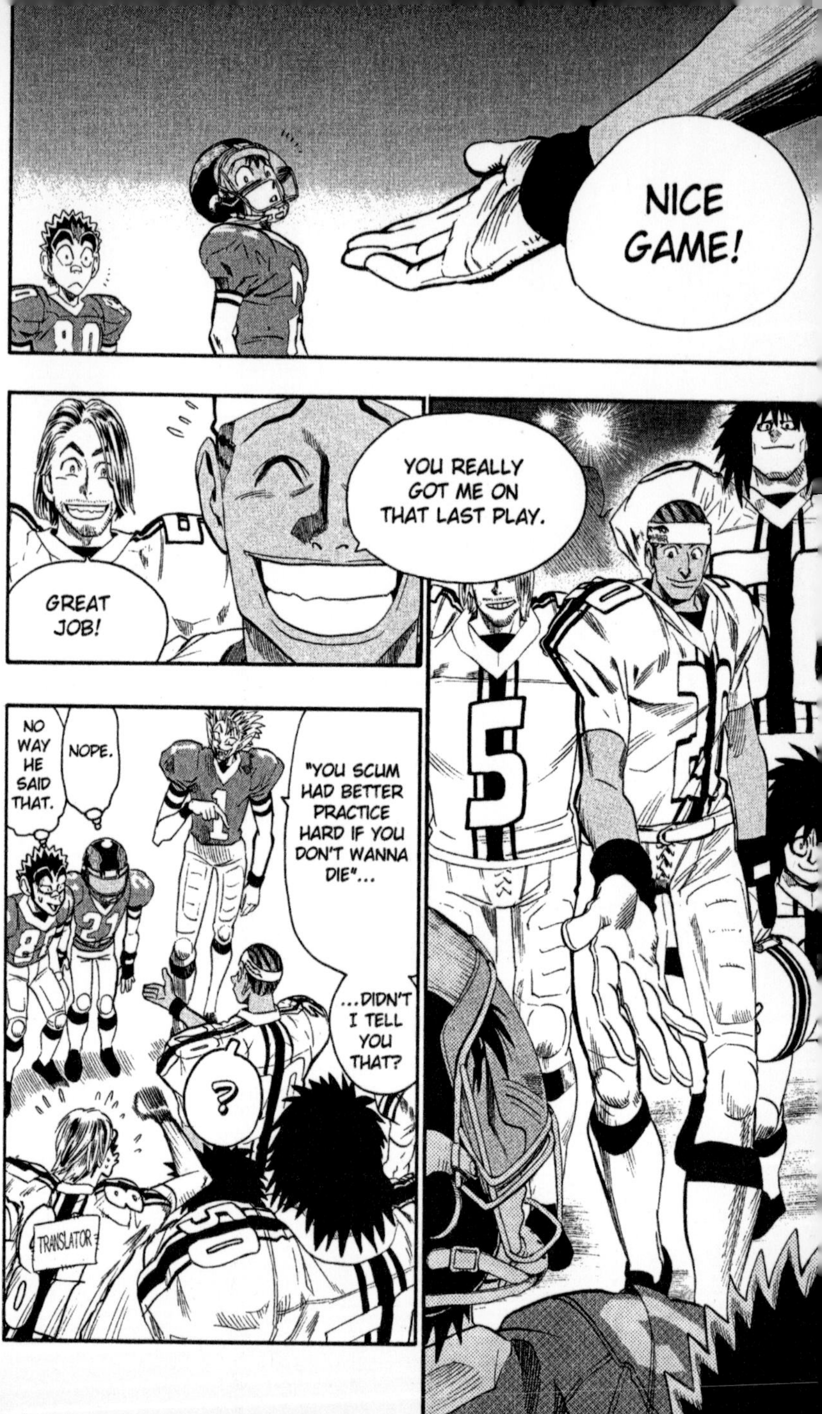
NICE GAME!
YOU REALLY GOT ME ON THAT LAST PLAY.
GREAT JOB!
"YOU SCUM HAD BETTER PRACTICE HARD IF YOU DON'T WANNA DIE"...
...DIDN'T I TELL YOU THAT?
?
NOPE.
NO WAY HE SAID THAT.
TRANSLATOR

READ THIS WAY

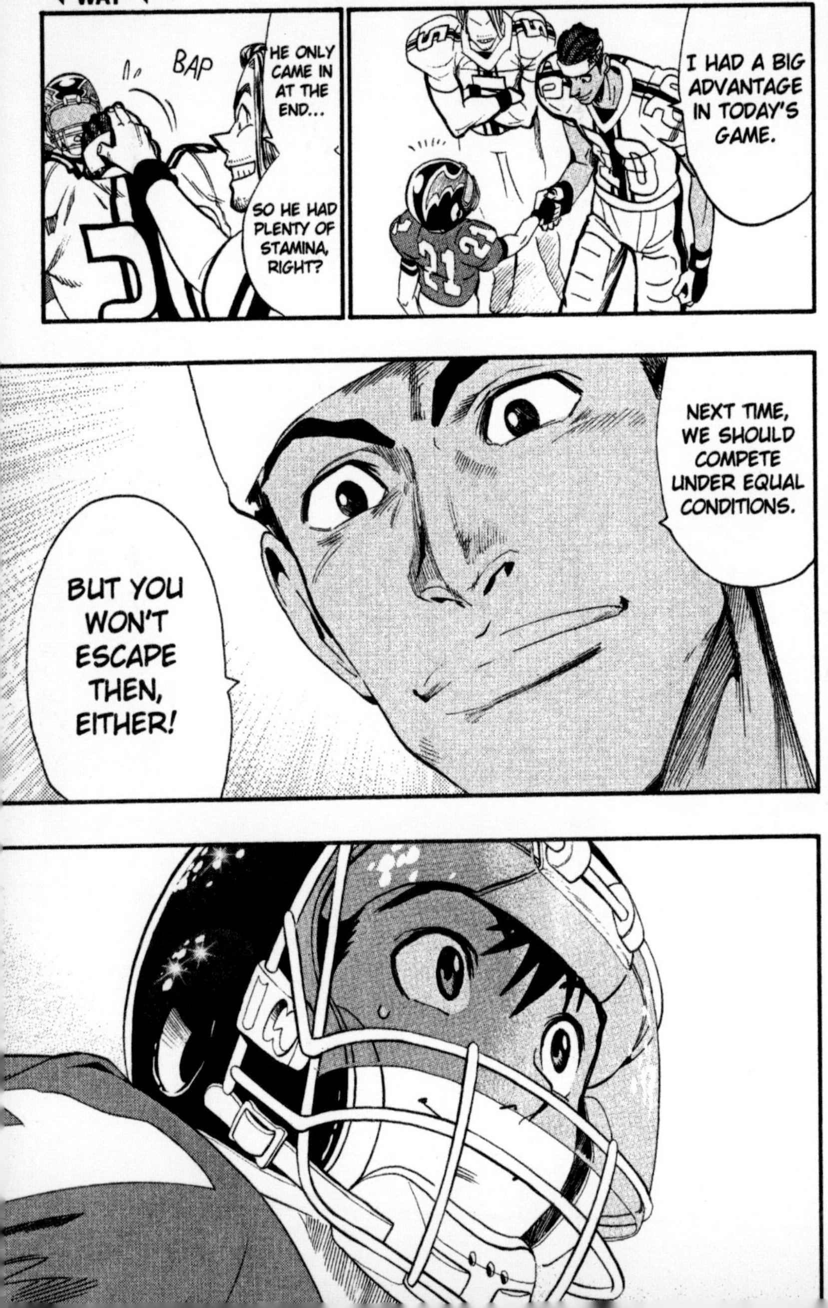
I HAD A BIG ADVANTAGE IN TODAY'S GAME.
HE ONLY CAME IN AT THE END...
BAP
SO HE HAD PLENTY OF STAMINA, RIGHT?
NEXT TIME, WE SHOULD COMPETE UNDER EQUAL CONDITIONS.
BUT YOU WON'T ESCAPE THEN, EITHER!

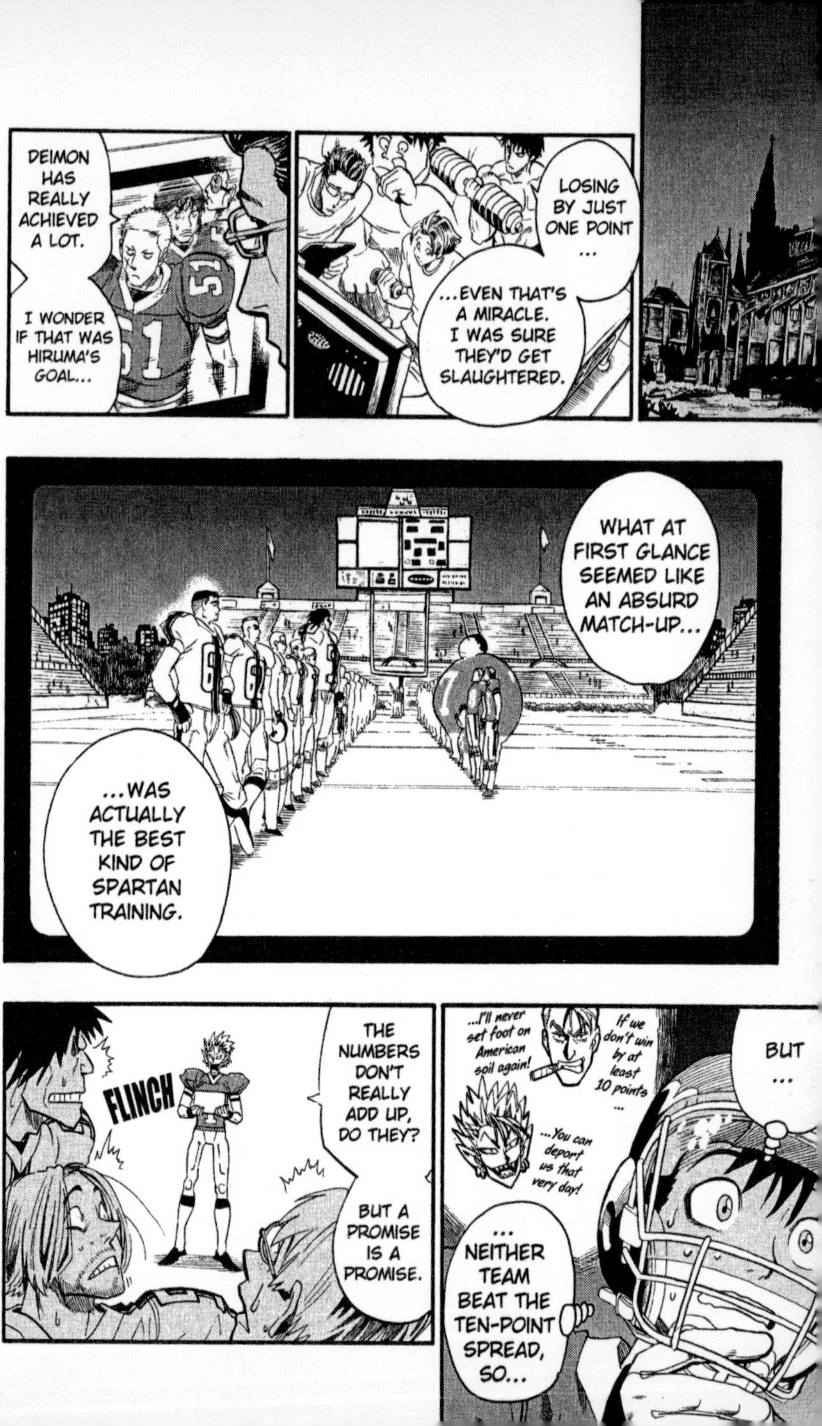

LOSING BY JUST ONE POINT ...
...EVEN THAT'S A MIRACLE. I WAS SURE THEY'D GET SLAUGHTERED.
DEIMON HAS REALLY ACHIEVED A LOT.
I WONDER IF THAT WAS HIRUMA'S GOAL...
WHAT AT FIRST GLANCE SEEMED LIKE AN ABSURD MATCH-UP...
...WAS ACTUALLY THE BEST KIND OF SPARTAN TRAINING.
BUT ...
If we don't win by at least 10 points ...
...I'll never set foot on American soil again!
...You can deport us that very day!
... NEITHER TEAM BEAT THE TEN-POINT SPREAD, SO...
THE NUMBERS DON'T REALLY ADD UP, DO THEY?
BUT A PROMISE IS A PROMISE.
FLINCH

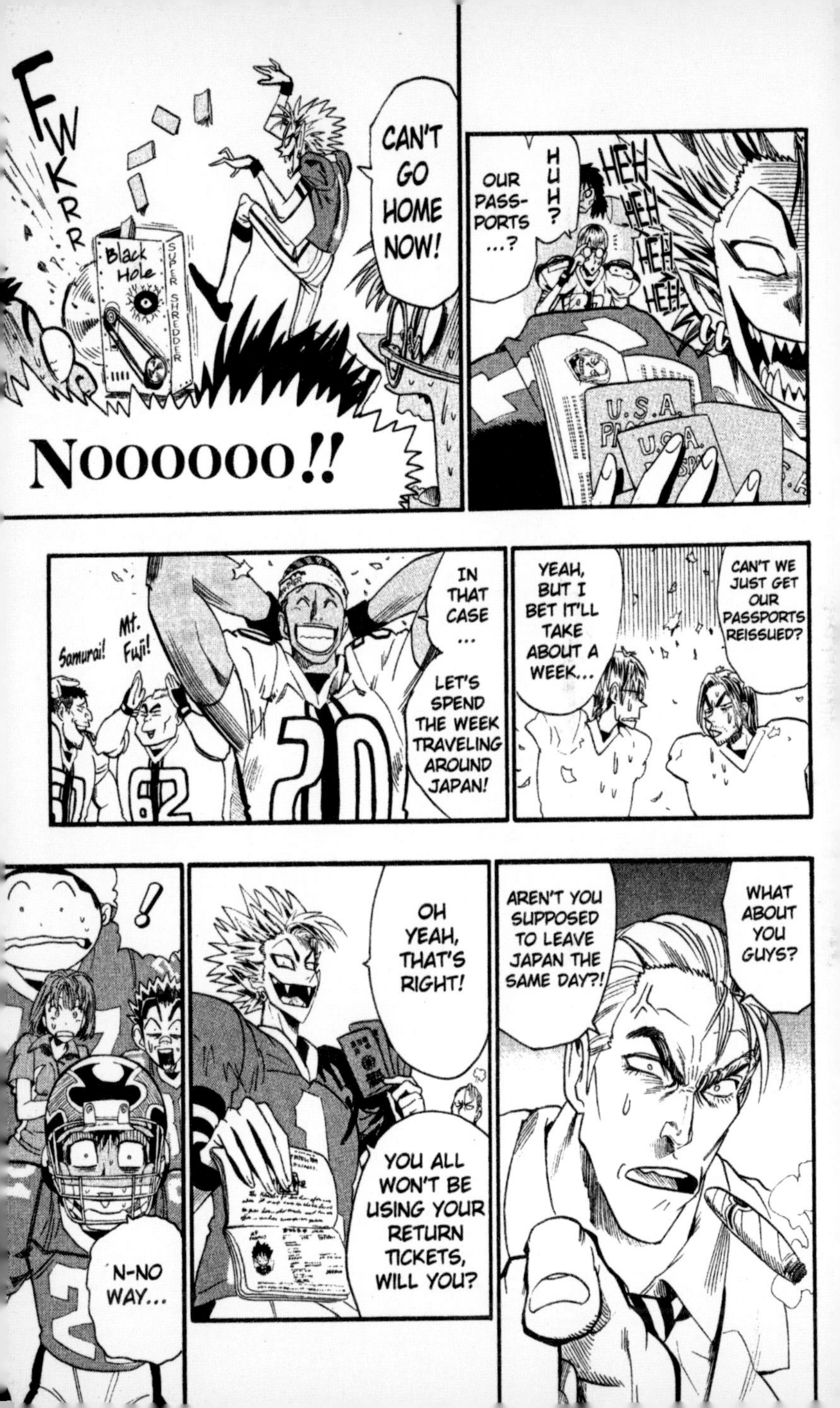
HEH HEH HEH HEH
HUH?
OUR PASSPORTS...?
CAN'T GO HOME NOW!
FWKRR
Black Hole
SUPER SHREDDER
NOOOOOO!!
CAN'T WE JUST GET OUR PASSPORTS REISSUED?
YEAH, BUT I BET IT'LL TAKE ABOUT A WEEK...
IN THAT CASE...
LET'S SPEND THE WEEK TRAVELING AROUND JAPAN!
Mt. Fuji!
Samurai!
WHAT ABOUT YOU GUYS?
AREN'T YOU SUPPOSED TO LEAVE JAPAN THE SAME DAY?!
OH YEAH, THAT'S RIGHT!
YOU ALL WON'T BE USING YOUR RETURN TICKETS, WILL YOU?
!
N-NO WAY...

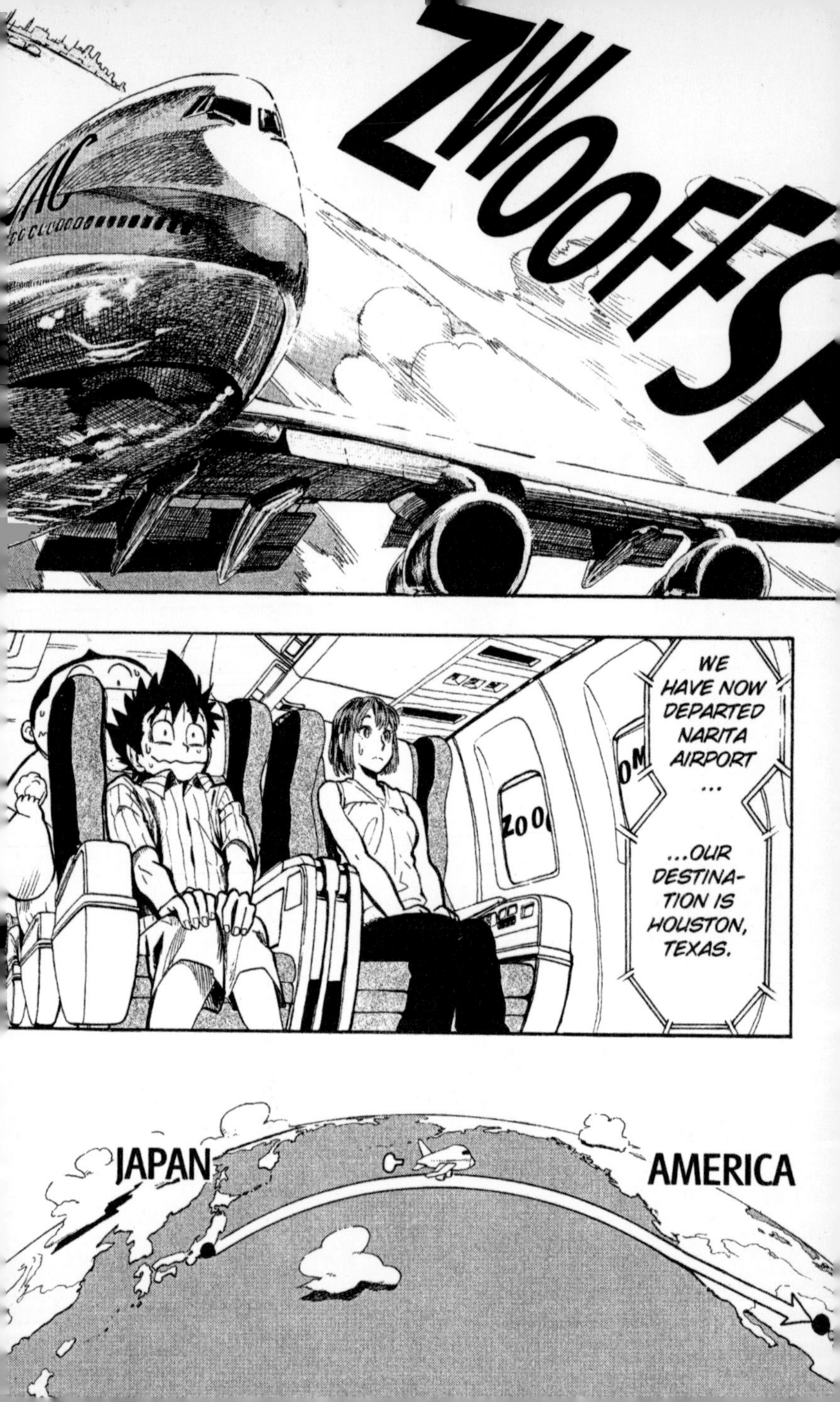
ZWOOFFSH
WE HAVE NOW DEPARTED NARITA AIRPORT ...
...OUR DESTINATION IS HOUSTON, TEXAS.
AMERICA
JAPAN

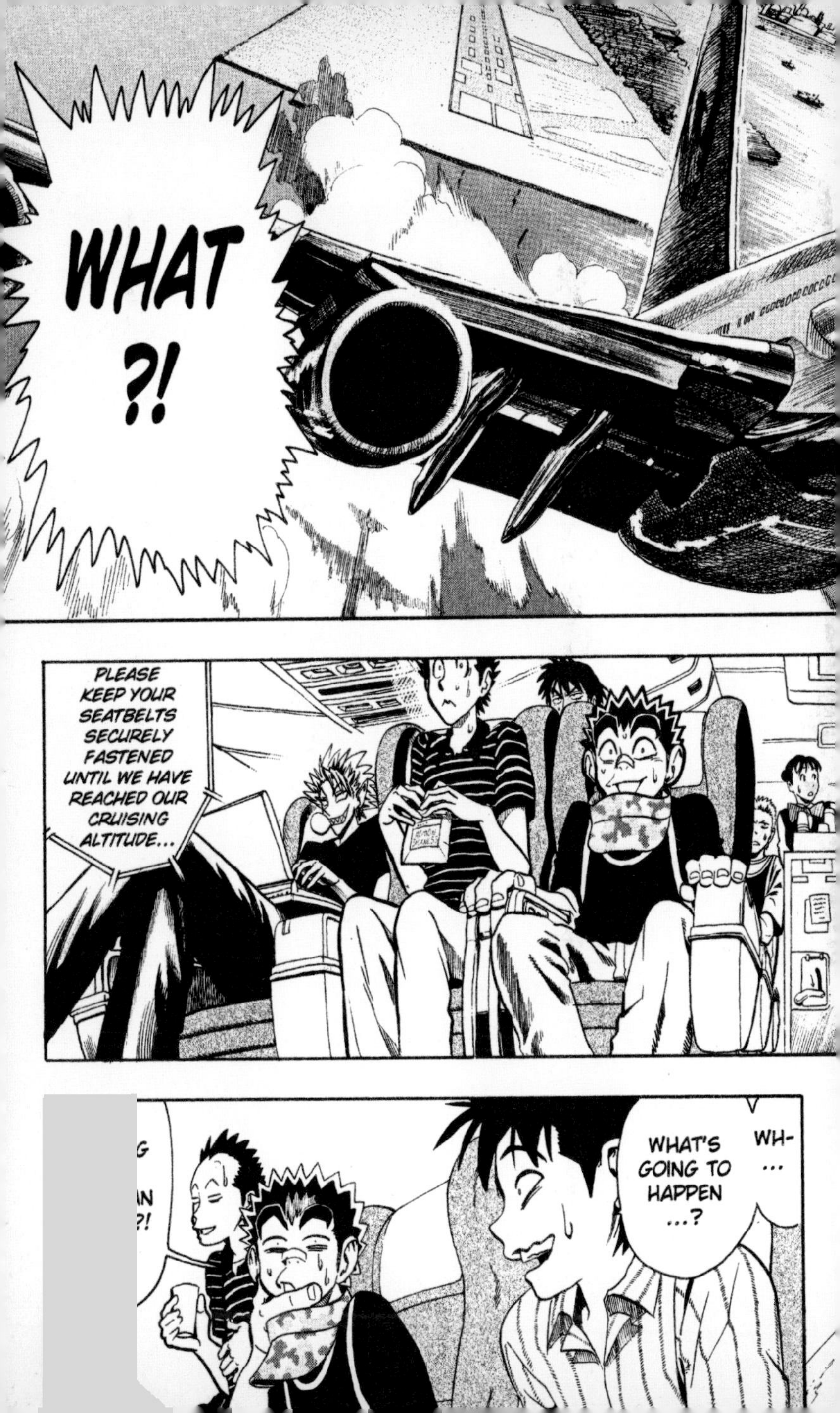
WHAT ?!
PLEASE KEEP YOUR SEATBELTS SECURELY FASTENED UNTIL WE HAVE REACHED OUR CRUISING ALTITUDE...
WH- ...
WHAT'S GOING TO HAPPEN ...?

Eyeshield 21 Survey Corner **Devil Bat 021**

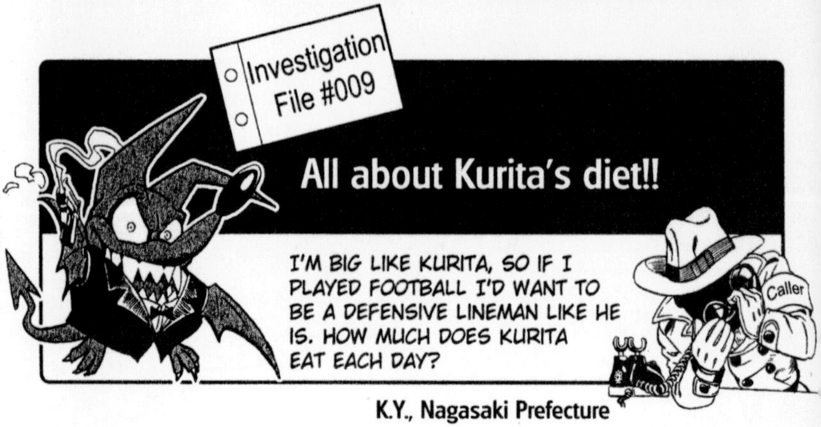
Investigation File #009
All about Kurita's diet!!
I'M BIG LIKE KURITA, SO IF I PLAYED FOOTBALL I'D WANT TO BE A DEFENSIVE LINEMAN LIKE HE IS. HOW MUCH DOES KURITA EAT EACH DAY?
Caller

K.Y., Nagasaki Prefecture

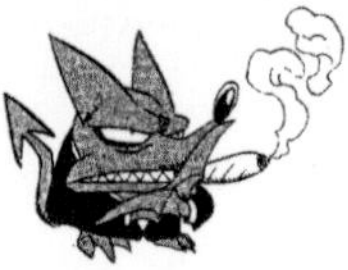

...

NO WONDER HE'S SO HUGE, IF HE EATS THIS MUCH EVERY DAY.

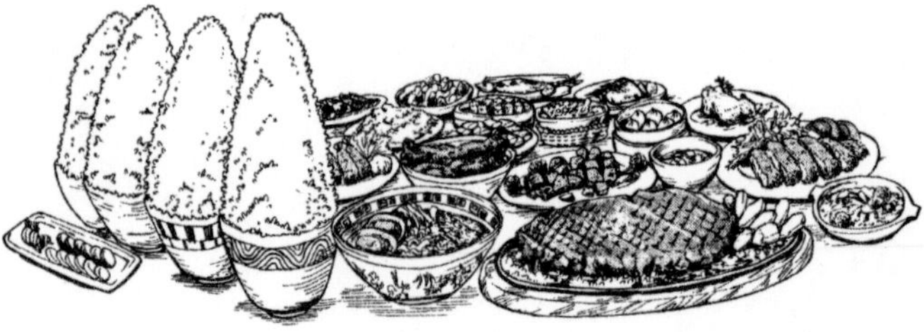

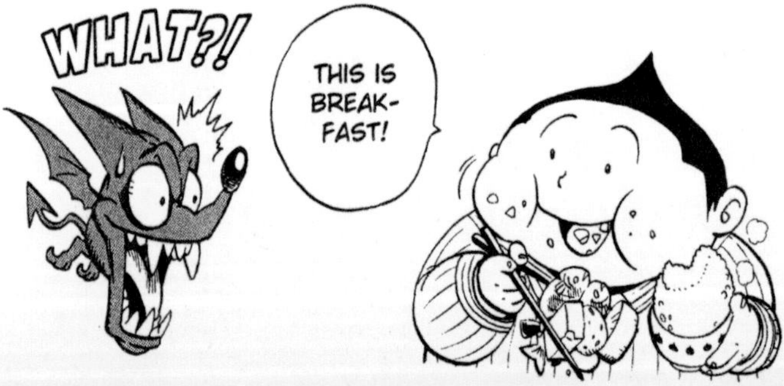
THIS IS BREAK-FAST!
WHAT?!

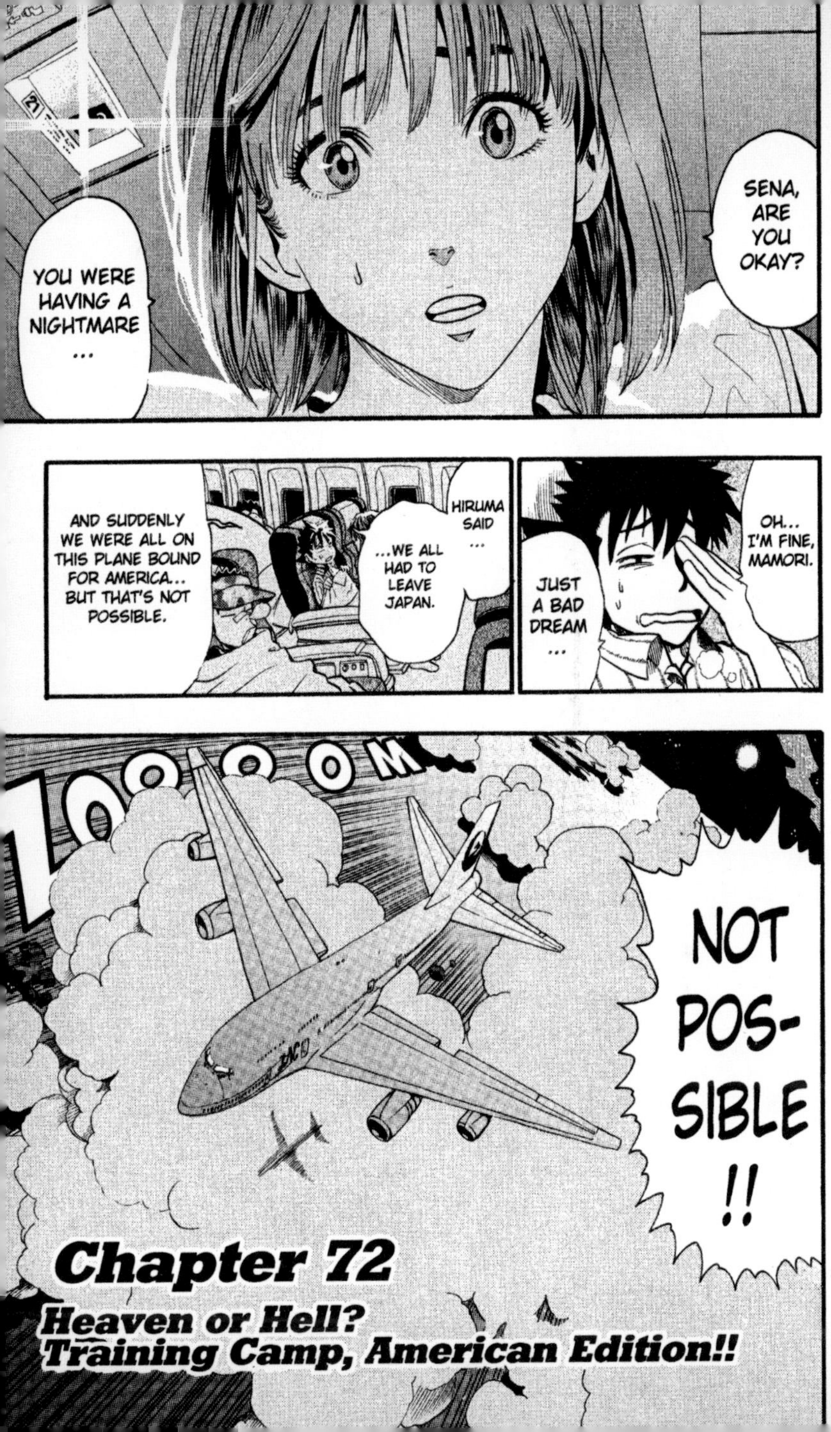
SENA, ARE YOU OKAY?
YOU WERE HAVING A NIGHTMARE ...
OH... I'M FINE, MAMORI.
JUST A BAD DREAM ...
HIRUMA SAID ...
...WE ALL HAD TO LEAVE JAPAN.
AND SUDDENLY WE WERE ALL ON THIS PLANE BOUND FOR AMERICA... BUT THAT'S NOT POSSIBLE.
NOT POS-SIBLE!!

Chapter 72

Heaven or Hell? Training Camp, American Edition!!

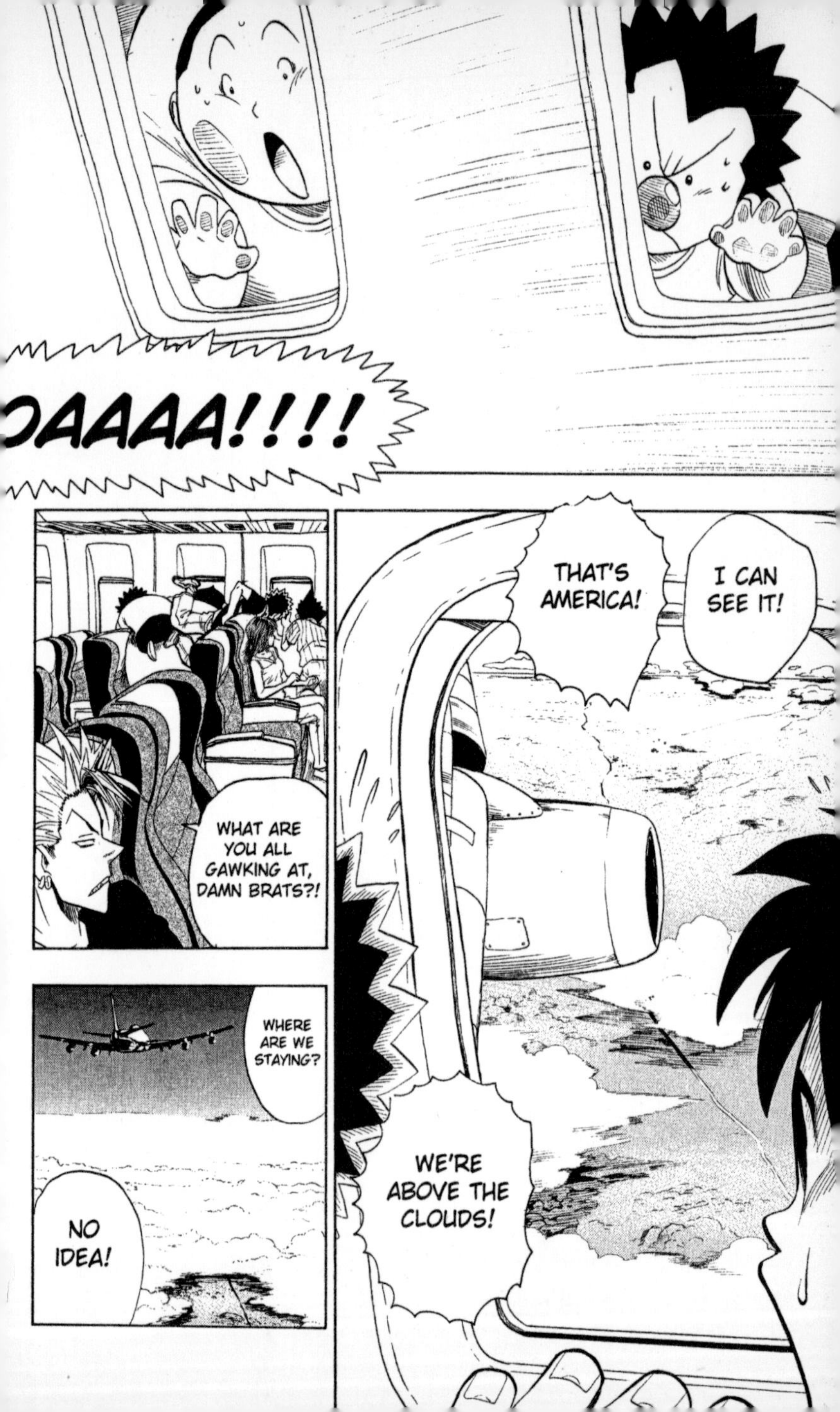
AAAA!!!!
I CAN SEE IT!
THAT'S AMERICA!
WE'RE ABOVE THE CLOUDS!
WHAT ARE YOU ALL GAWKING AT, DAMN BRATS?!
WHERE ARE WE STAYING?
NO IDEA!

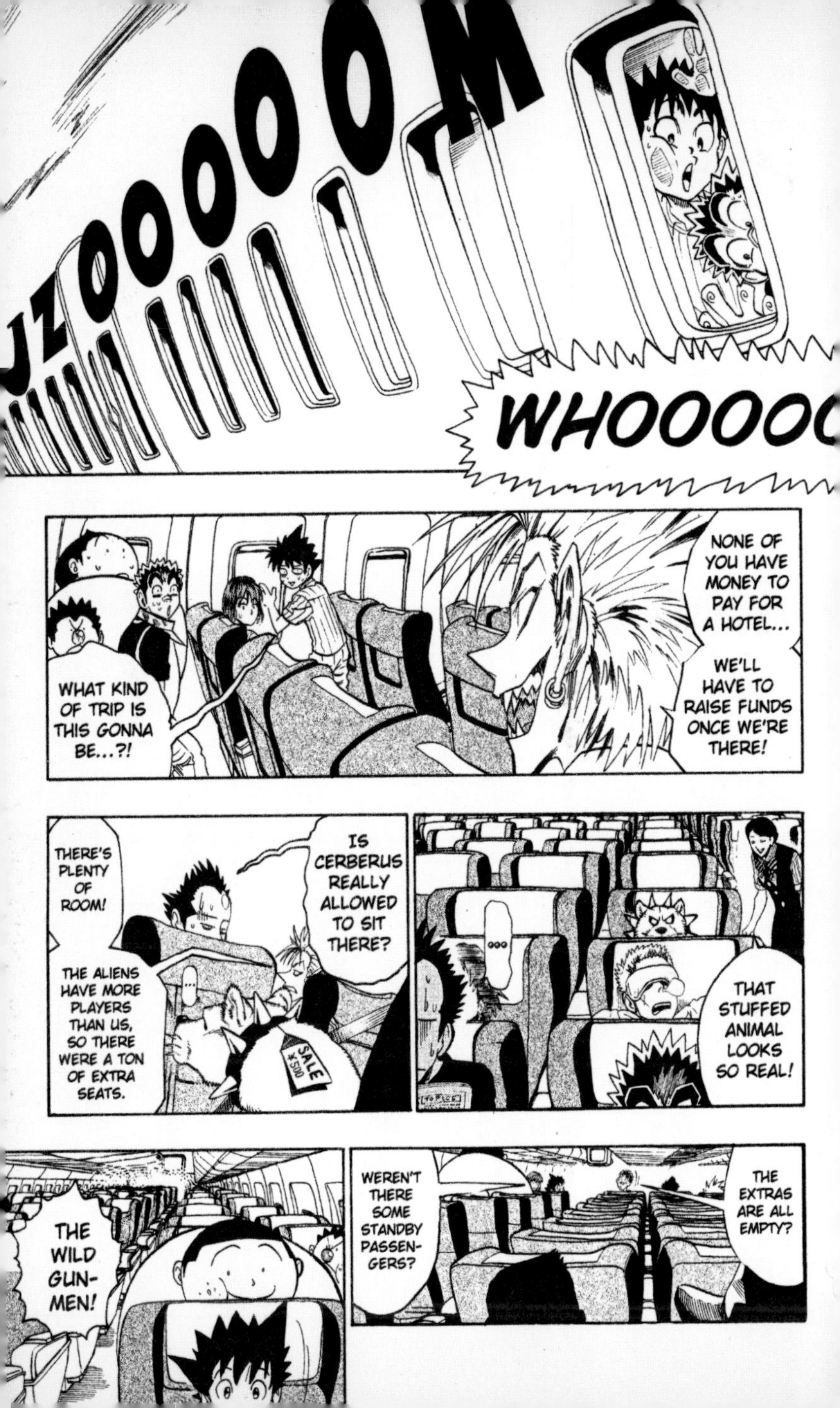
WHOOOOO
ZOOOOOOM
NONE OF YOU HAVE MONEY TO PAY FOR A HOTEL...
WE'LL HAVE TO RAISE FUNDS ONCE WE'RE THERE!
WHAT KIND OF TRIP IS THIS GONNA BE...?!
THAT STUFFED ANIMAL LOOKS SO REAL!
...
IS CERBERUS REALLY ALLOWED TO SIT THERE?
THERE'S PLENTY OF ROOM!
...
THE ALIENS HAVE MORE PLAYERS THAN US, SO THERE WERE A TON OF EXTRA SEATS.
SALE ¥500
THE EXTRAS ARE ALL EMPTY?
WEREN'T THERE SOME STANDBY PASSEN-GERS?
THE WILD GUN-MEN!

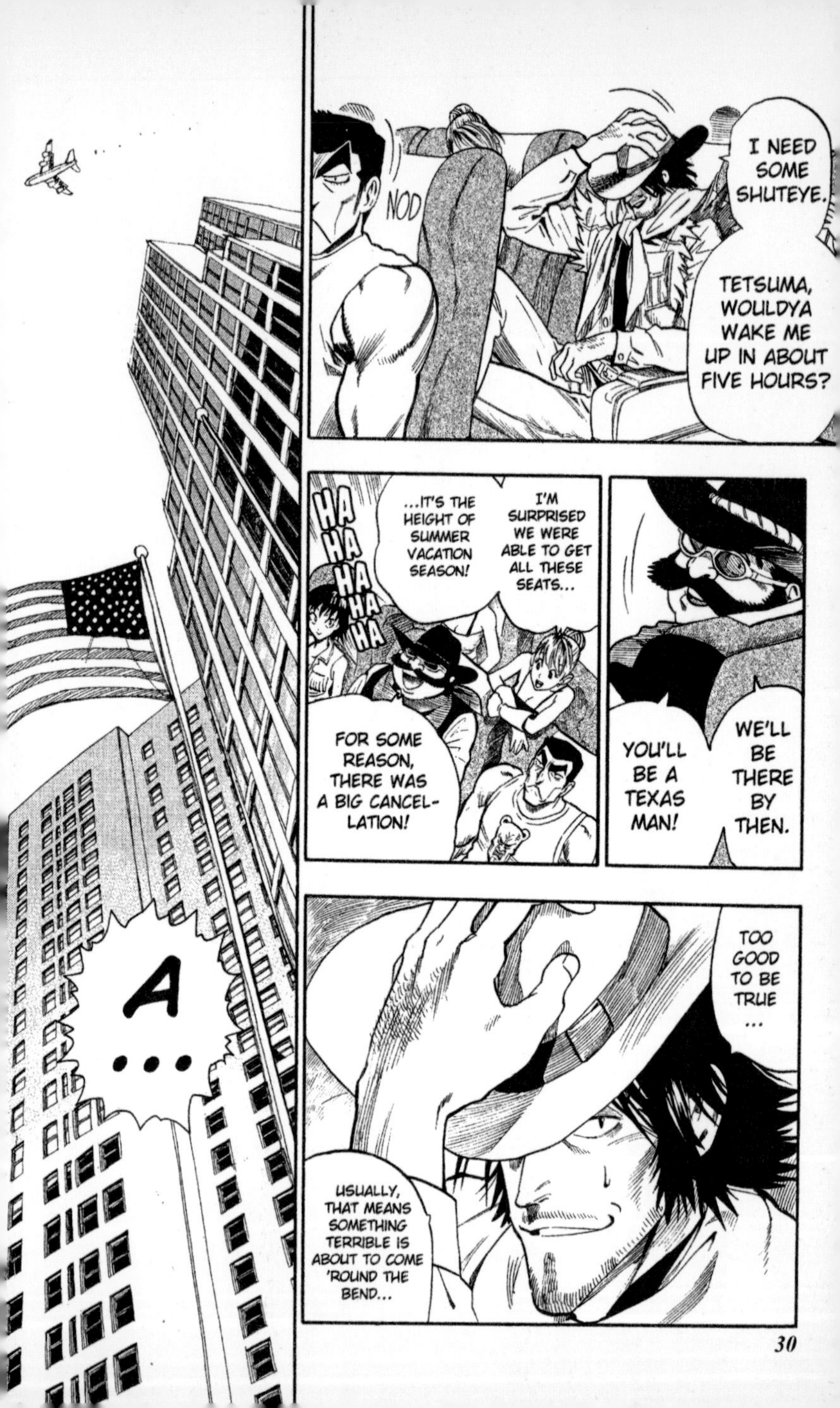
I NEED SOME SHUTEYE.
TETSUMA, WOULDYA WAKE ME UP IN ABOUT FIVE HOURS?
NOD
WE'LL BE THERE BY THEN.
YOU'LL BE A TEXAS MAN!
I'M SURPRISED WE WERE ABLE TO GET ALL THESE SEATS...
...IT'S THE HEIGHT OF SUMMER VACATION SEASON!
HA HA HA HA HA
FOR SOME REASON, THERE WAS A BIG CANCEL-LATION!
TOO GOOD TO BE TRUE ...
USUALLY, THAT MEANS SOMETHING TERRIBLE IS ABOUT TO COME 'ROUND THE BEND...
A ...

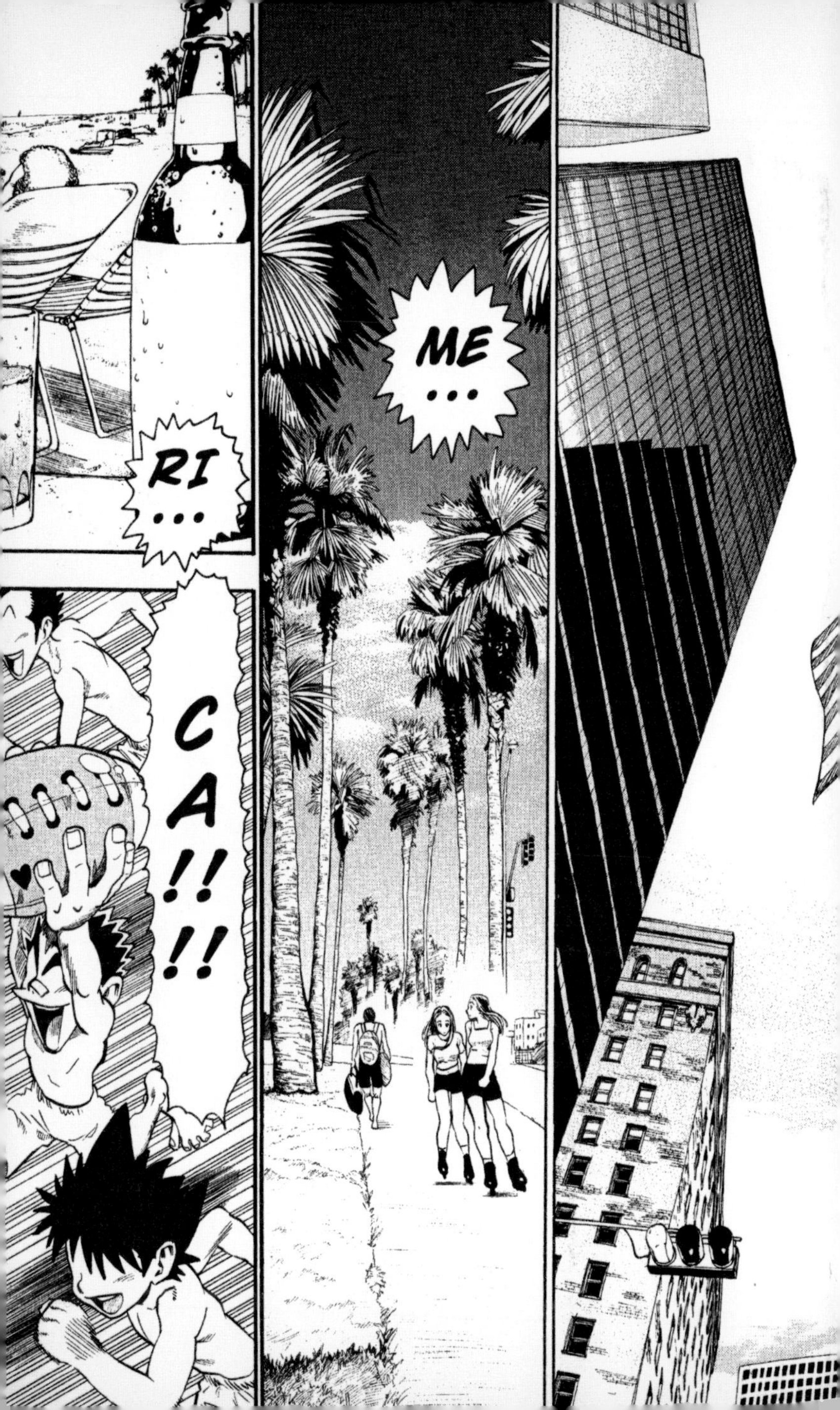
ME...
RI...
CA!!!!

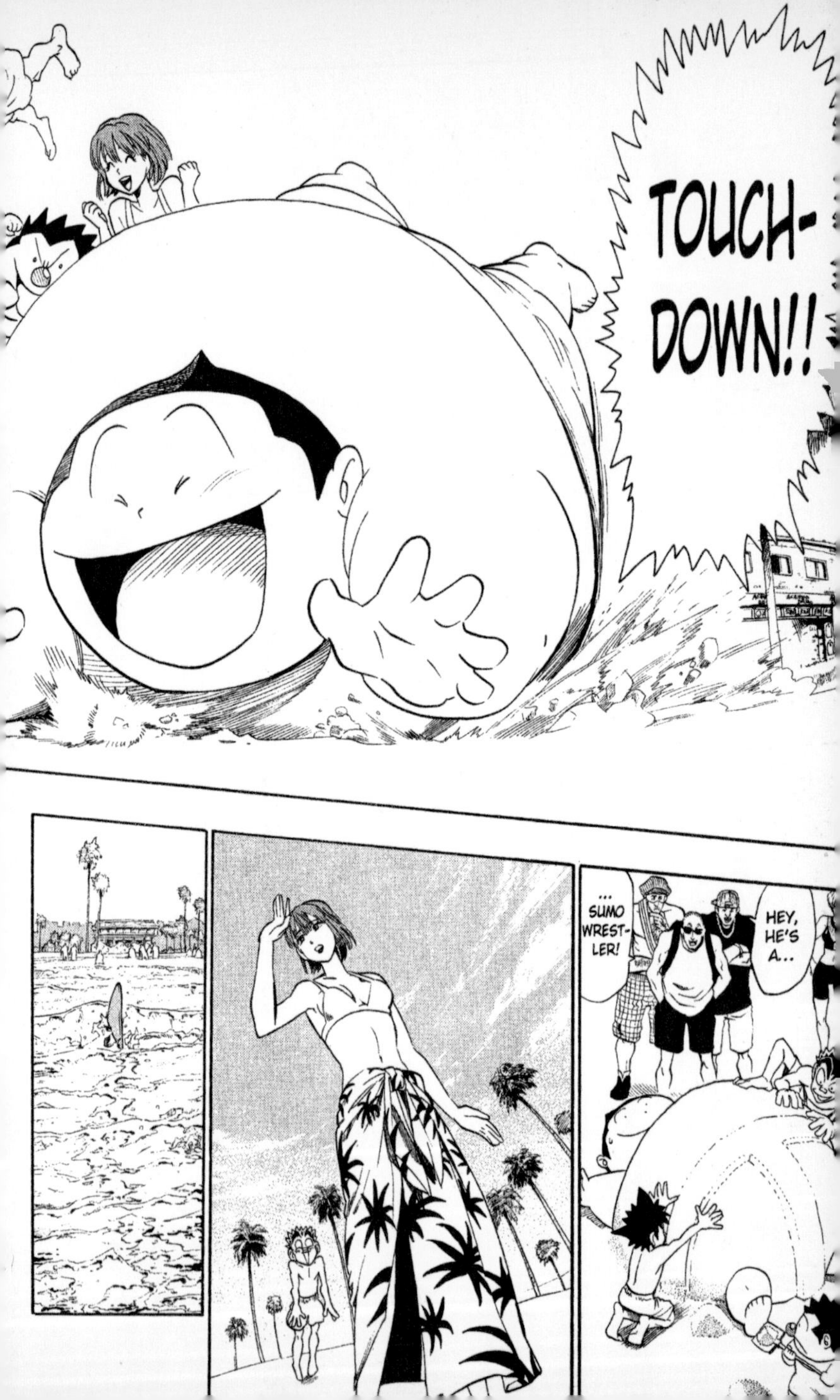

TOUCH-DOWN!!
HEY, HE'S A...
... SUMO WREST-LER!

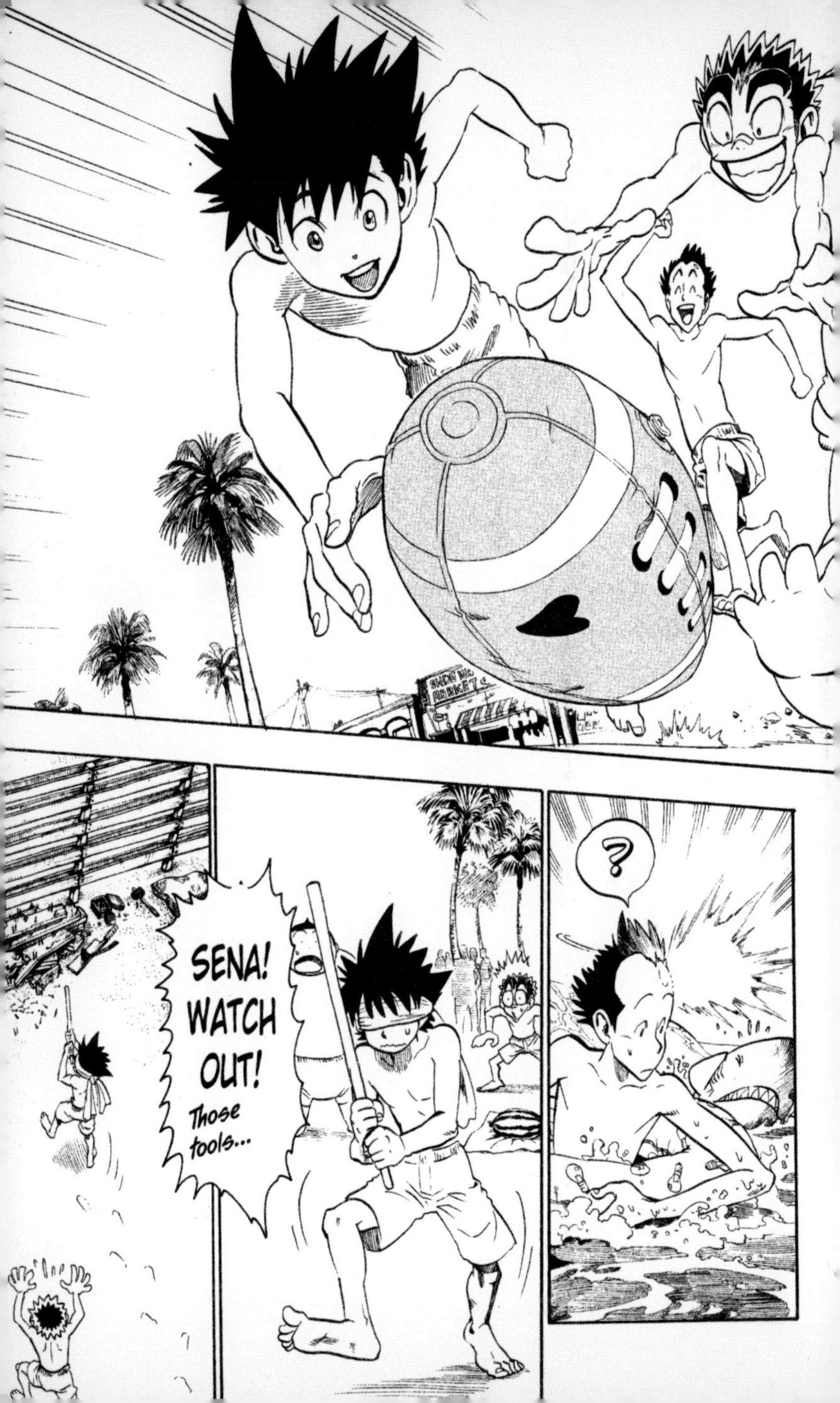
?
SENA! WATCH OUT! Those tools...

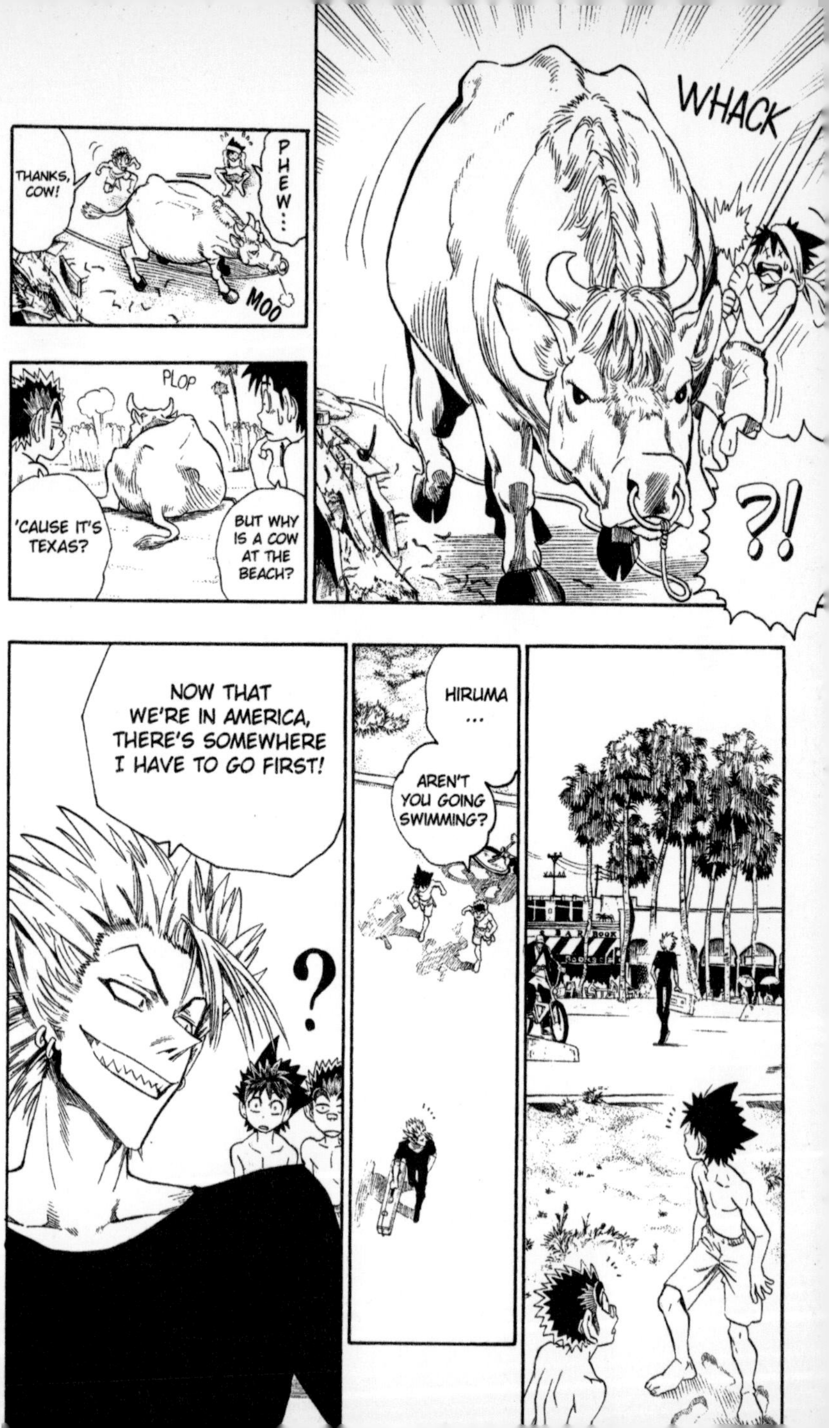
WHACK
?!
PHEW...
THANKS, COW!
MOO
PLOP
BUT WHY IS A COW AT THE BEACH?
'CAUSE IT'S TEXAS?
HIRUMA ...
AREN'T YOU GOING SWIMMING?
NOW THAT WE'RE IN AMERICA, THERE'S SOMEWHERE I HAVE TO GO FIRST!
?

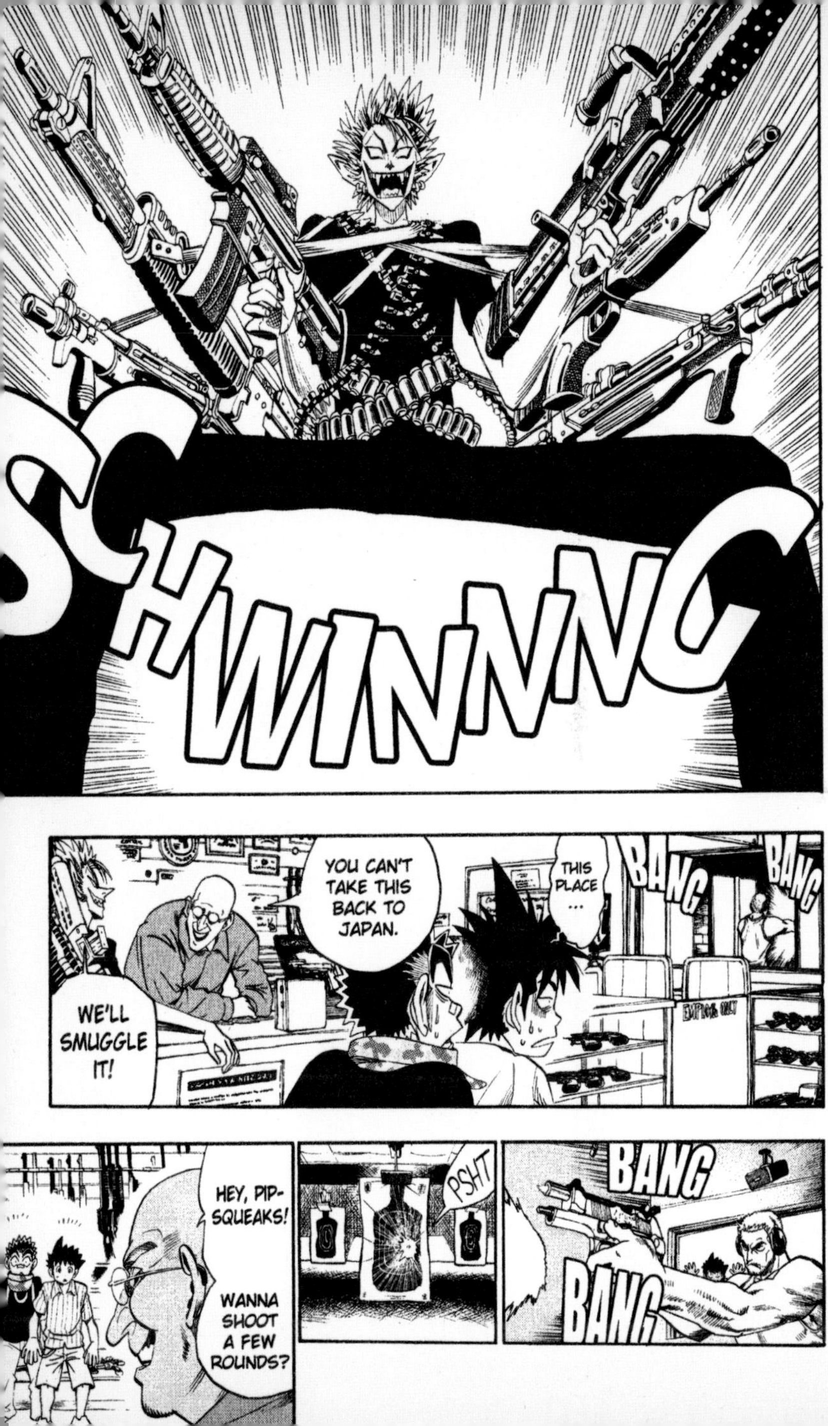
SCHWINNNG
BANG
BANG
THIS PLACE...
YOU CAN'T TAKE THIS BACK TO JAPAN.
WE'LL SMUGGLE IT!
BANG
BANG
PSHT
HEY, PIP-SQUEAKS!
WANNA SHOOT A FEW ROUNDS?

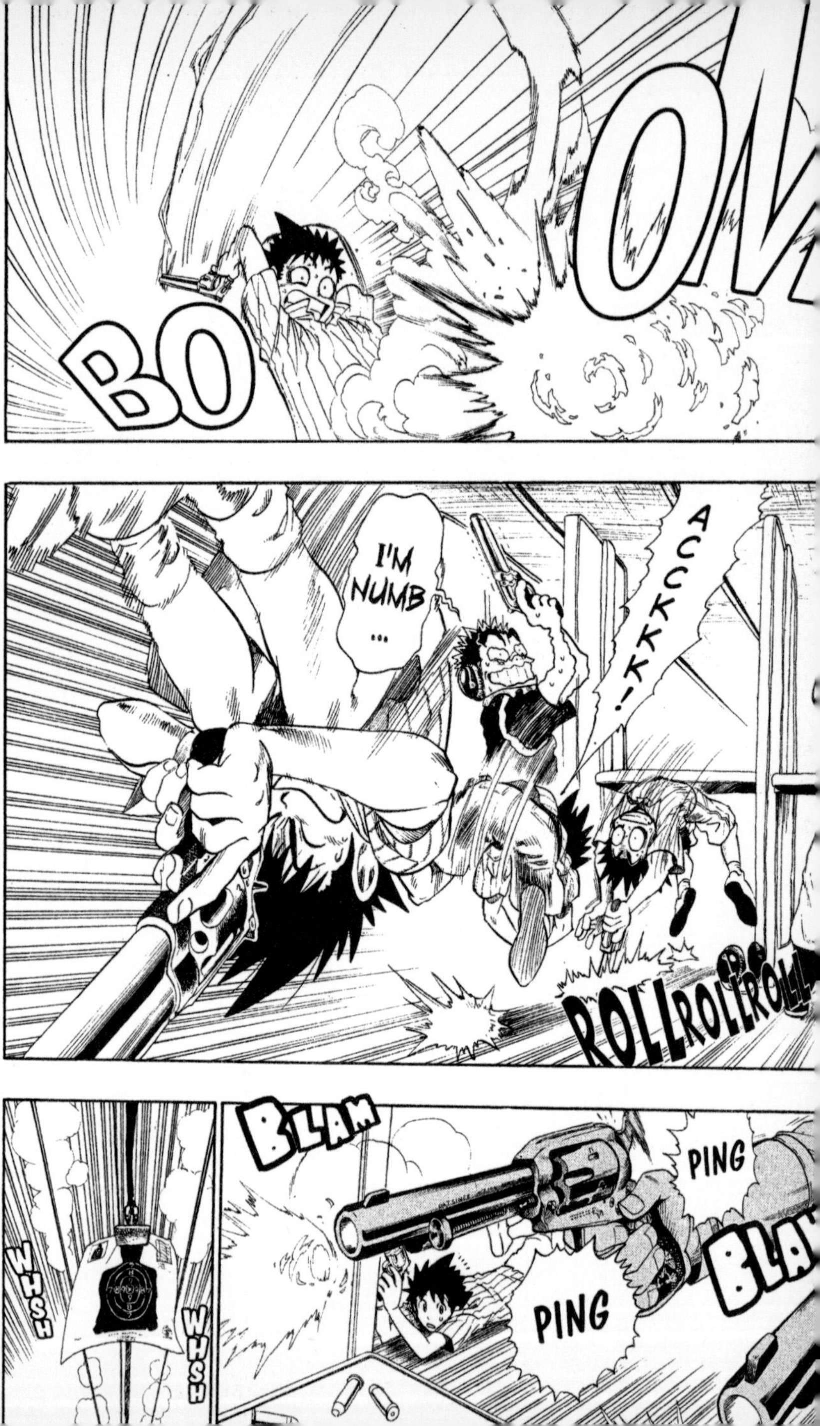
BO
OM
ACCKKKK!
I'M NUMB ...
ROLLROLLROLL
BLAM
PING
BLA
PING
WHSH
WHSH

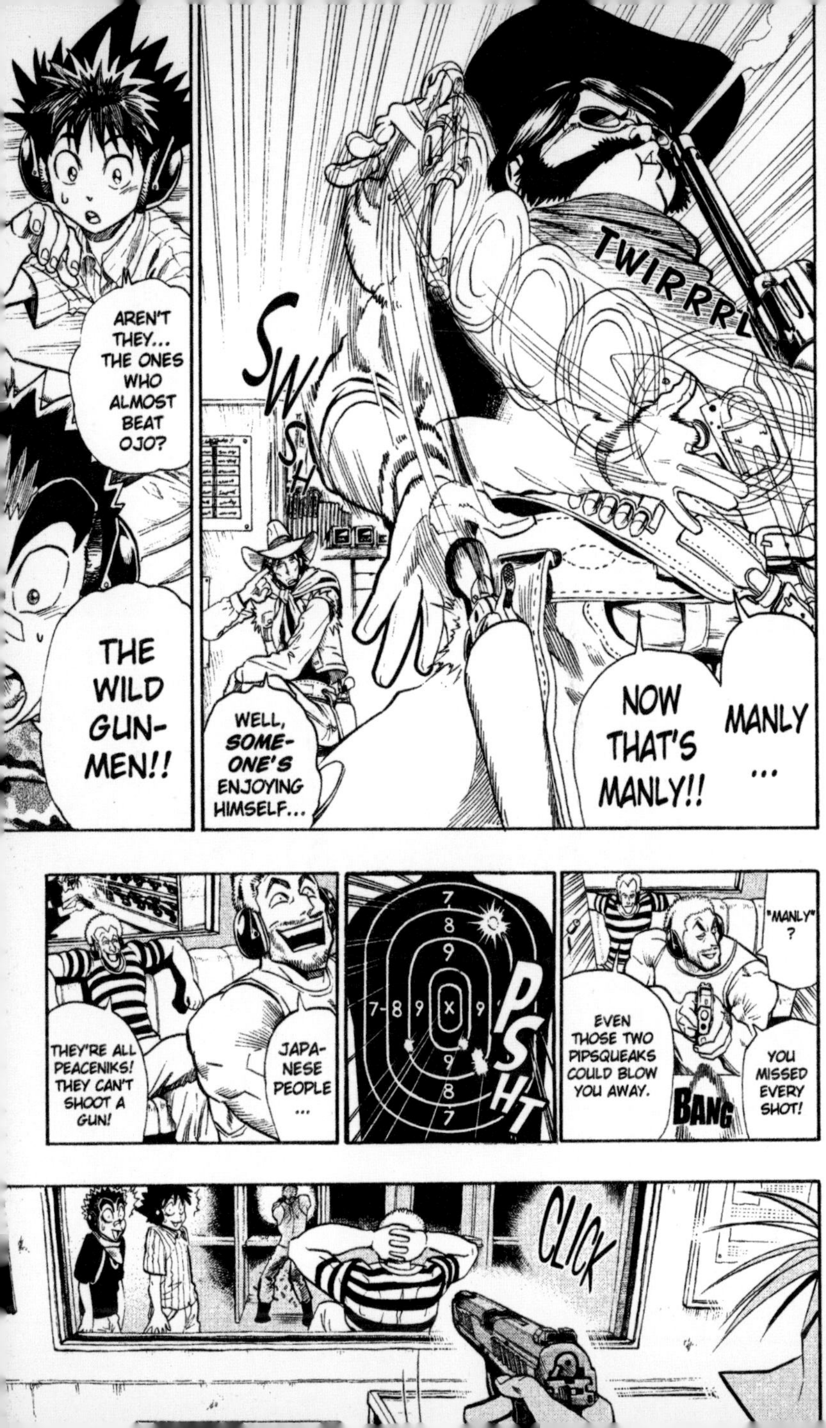
TWIRRRL
SWSH
MANLY ...
NOW THAT'S MANLY!!
WELL, SOME-ONE'S ENJOYING HIMSELF...
AREN'T THEY... THE ONES WHO ALMOST BEAT OJO?
THE WILD GUN-MEN!!
"MANLY" ?
YOU MISSED EVERY SHOT!
EVEN THOSE TWO PIPSQUEAKS COULD BLOW YOU AWAY.
BANG
PSHT
JAPA-NESE PEOPLE ...
THEY'RE ALL PEACENIKS! THEY CAN'T SHOOT A GUN!
CLICK

NOT BAD...

I'LL BUY THIS ONE TOO.

WHZ

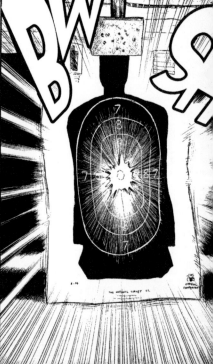

BW

BW

OH...

THEY WERE ON TV... THE AMERICAN GAME...

...DEI-MON?

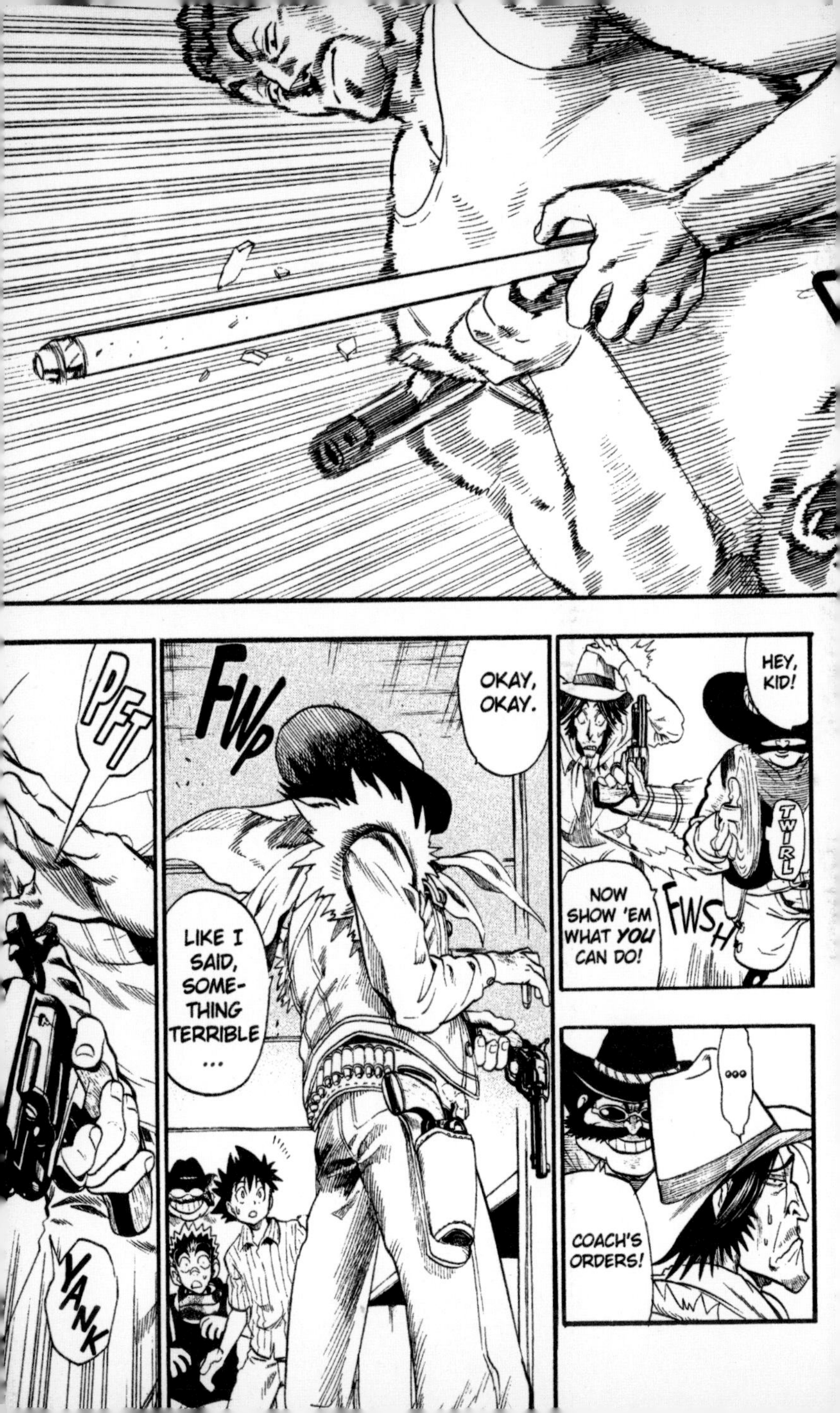
HEY, KID!
TWIRL
NOW SHOW 'EM WHAT YOU CAN DO!
FWSH
...
COACH'S ORDERS!
OKAY, OKAY.
FWP
LIKE I SAID, SOME-THING TERRIBLE ...
PFT
YANK

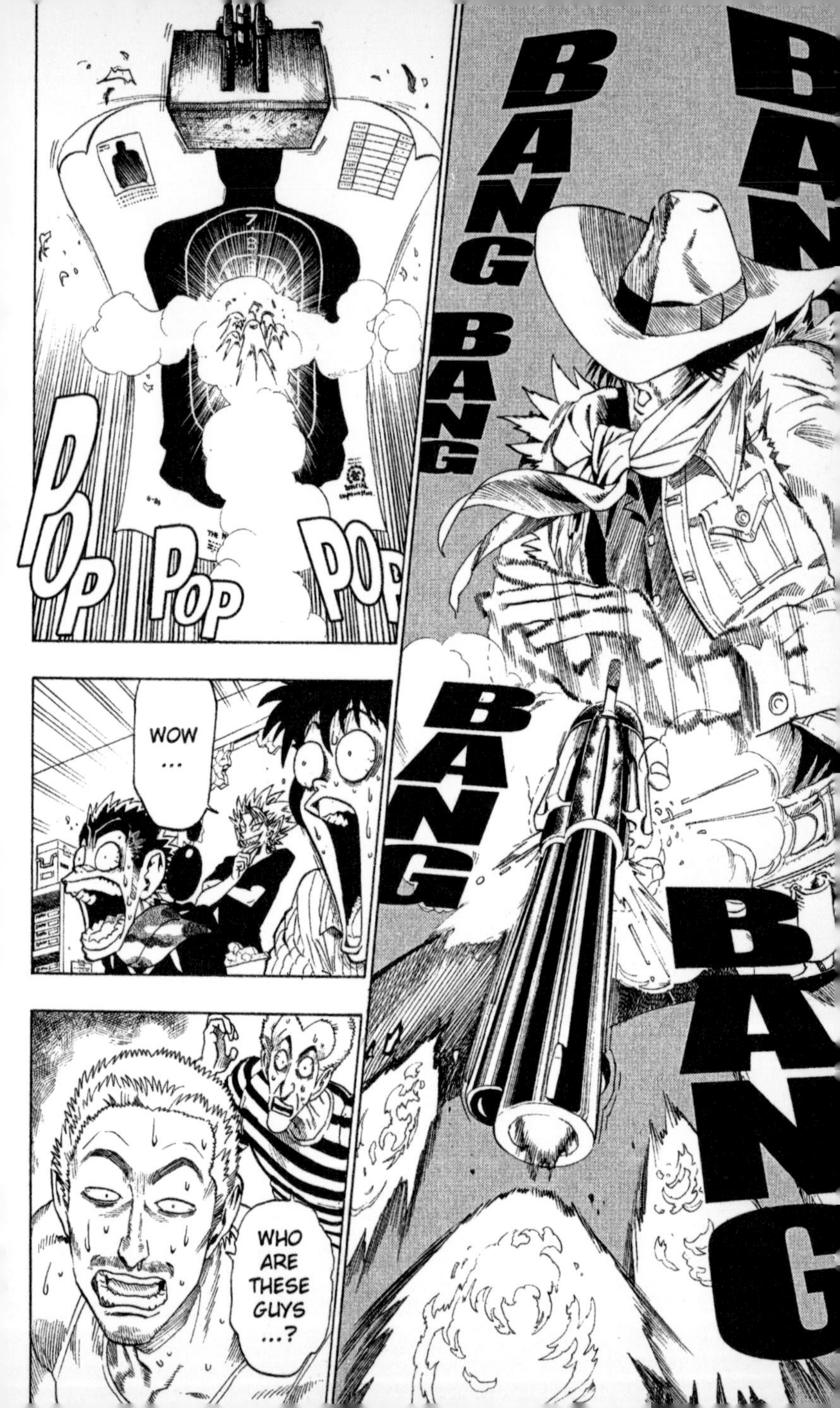

BANG
BANG
BANG
BANG
POP
POP
POP
WOW...
WHO ARE THESE GUYS...?

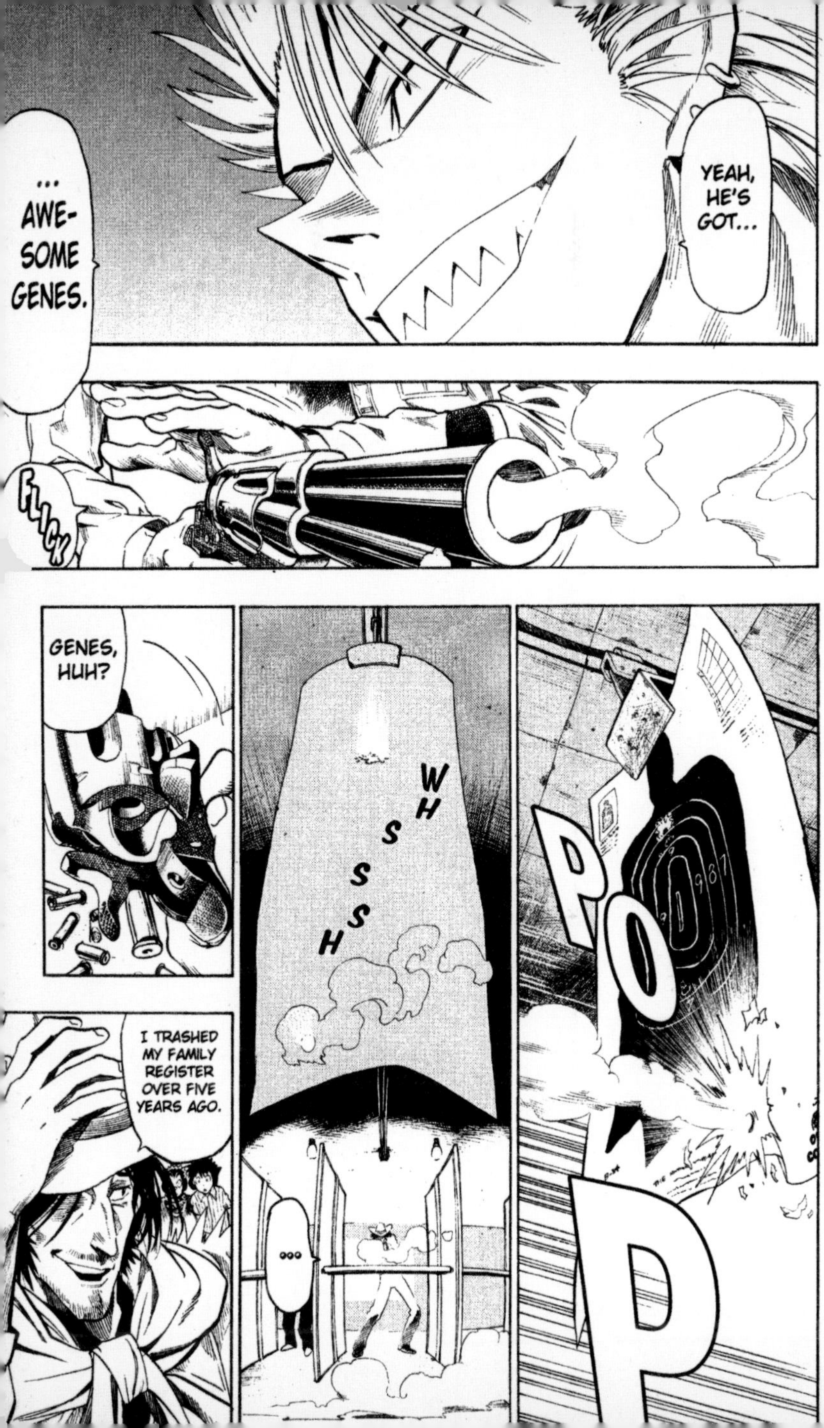
YEAH, HE'S GOT...
... AWE-SOME GENES.
FLICK
POP
WHSSSH
...
GENES, HUH?
I TRASHED MY FAMILY REGISTER OVER FIVE YEARS AGO.

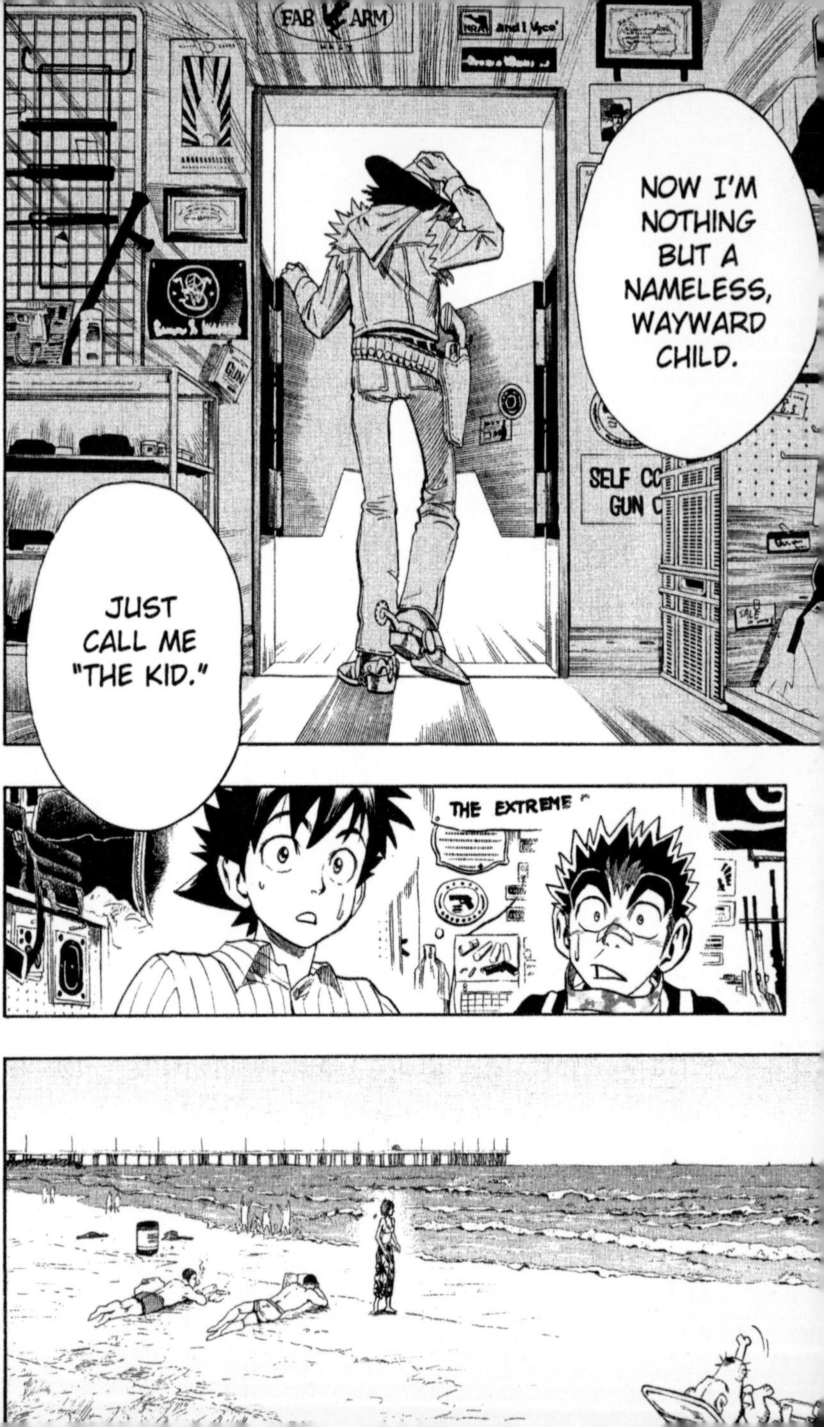
FAB ARM
NOW I'M NOTHING BUT A NAMELESS, WAYWARD CHILD.
GUN
JUST CALL ME "THE KID."
THE EXTREME

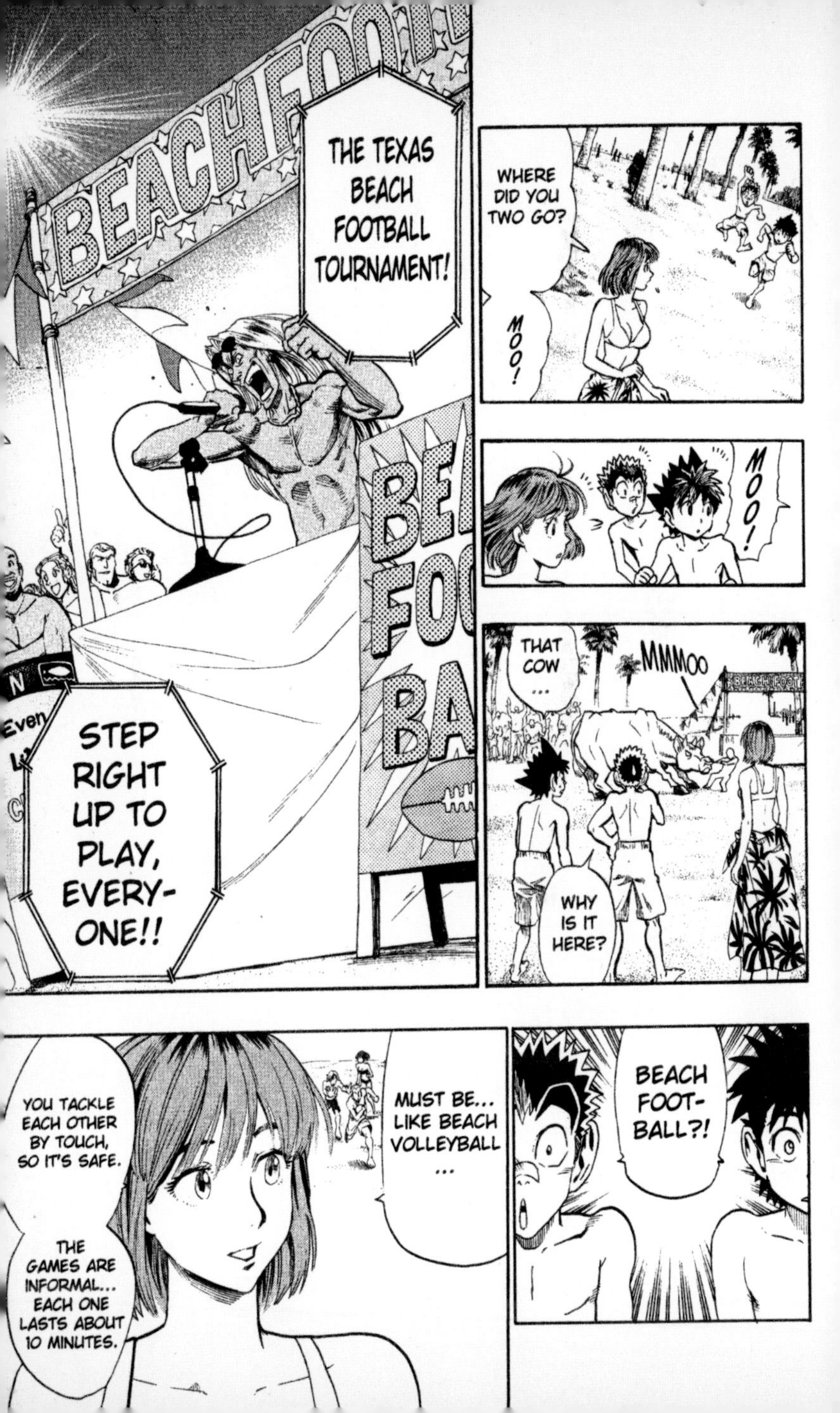
WHERE DID YOU TWO GO?
MOO!
MOO!
THAT COW...
MMMOO
WHY IS IT HERE?
THE TEXAS BEACH FOOTBALL TOURNAMENT!
STEP RIGHT UP TO PLAY, EVERY-ONE!!
BEACH FOOT-BALL?!
MUST BE... LIKE BEACH VOLLEYBALL...
YOU TACKLE EACH OTHER BY TOUCH, SO IT'S SAFE.
THE GAMES ARE INFORMAL... EACH ONE LASTS ABOUT 10 MINUTES.

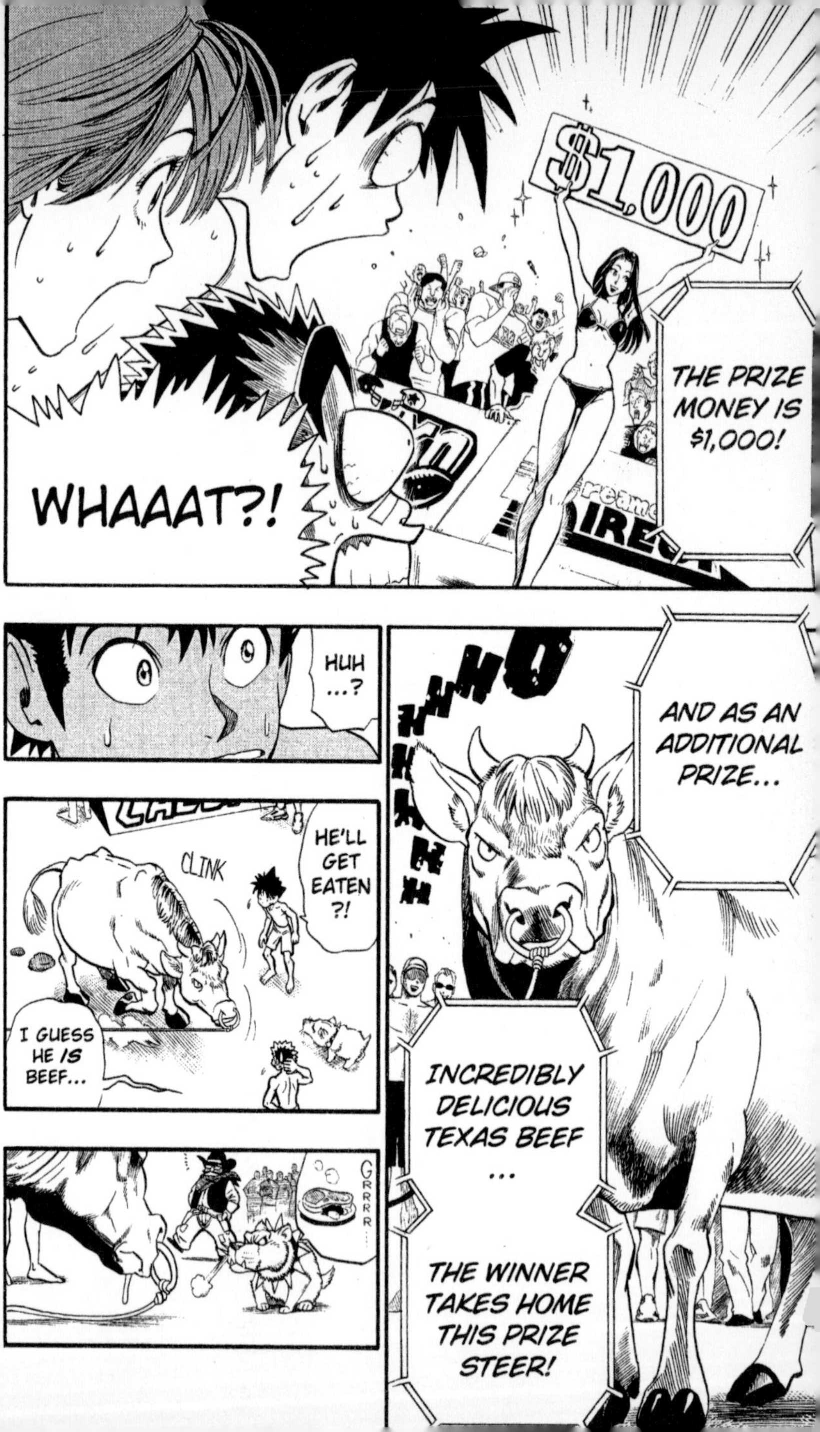

$1,000
THE PRIZE MONEY IS $1,000!
WHAAAT?!
AND AS AN ADDITIONAL PRIZE...
INCREDIBLY DELICIOUS TEXAS BEEF ...
THE WINNER TAKES HOME THIS PRIZE STEER!
HUH ...?
HE'LL GET EATEN ?!
CLINK
I GUESS HE *IS* BEEF...
GRRRR...

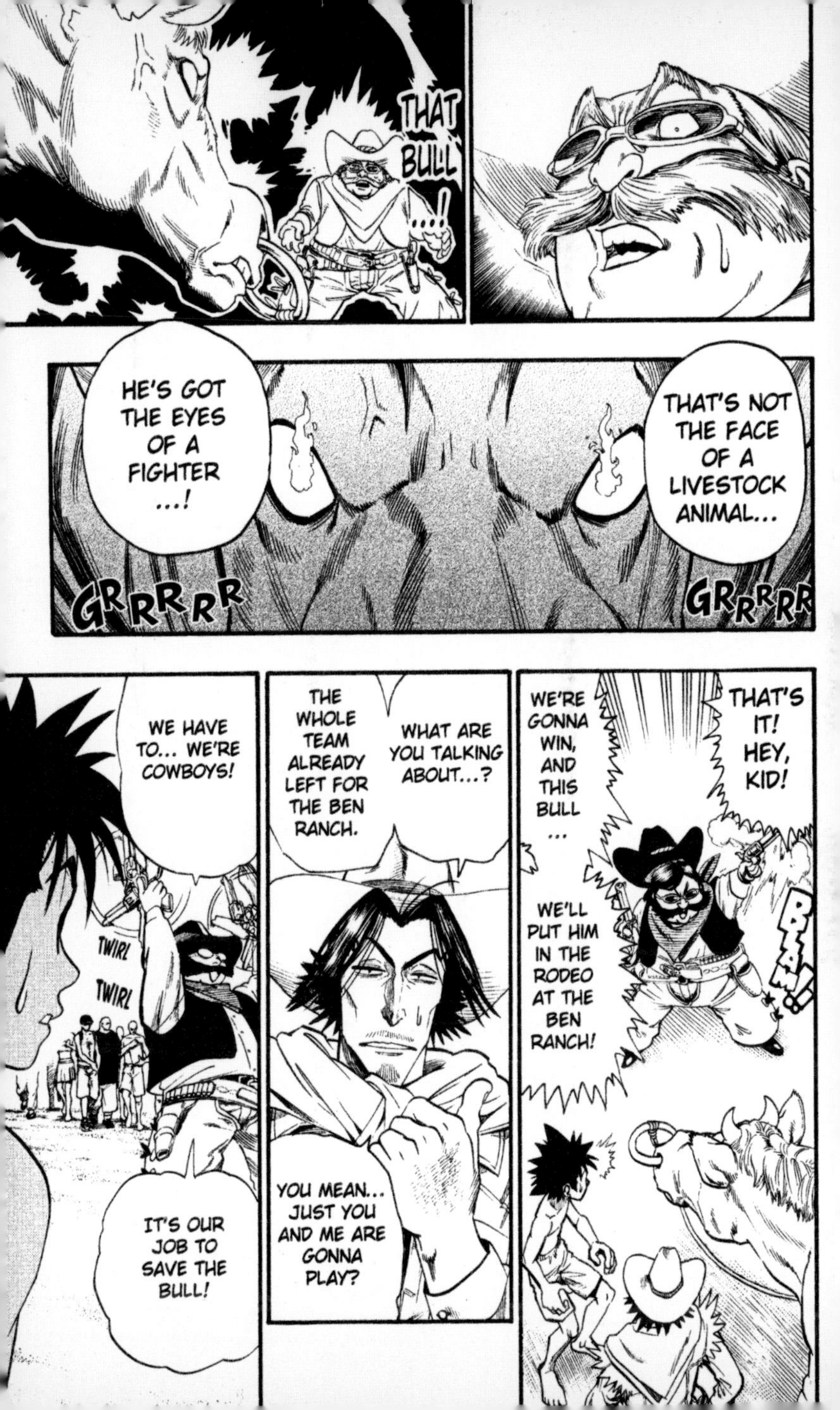
THAT BULL .....!
GRRRRR
THAT'S NOT THE FACE OF A LIVESTOCK ANIMAL...
GRRRRR
HE'S GOT THE EYES OF A FIGHTER ...!
THAT'S IT! HEY, KID!
WE'RE GONNA WIN, AND THIS BULL ...
WE'LL PUT HIM IN THE RODEO AT THE BEN RANCH!
BLAM!!
WHAT ARE YOU TALKING ABOUT...?
THE WHOLE TEAM ALREADY LEFT FOR THE BEN RANCH.
YOU MEAN... JUST YOU AND ME ARE GONNA PLAY?
WE HAVE TO... WE'RE COWBOYS!
TWIRL
TWIRL
IT'S OUR JOB TO SAVE THE BULL!

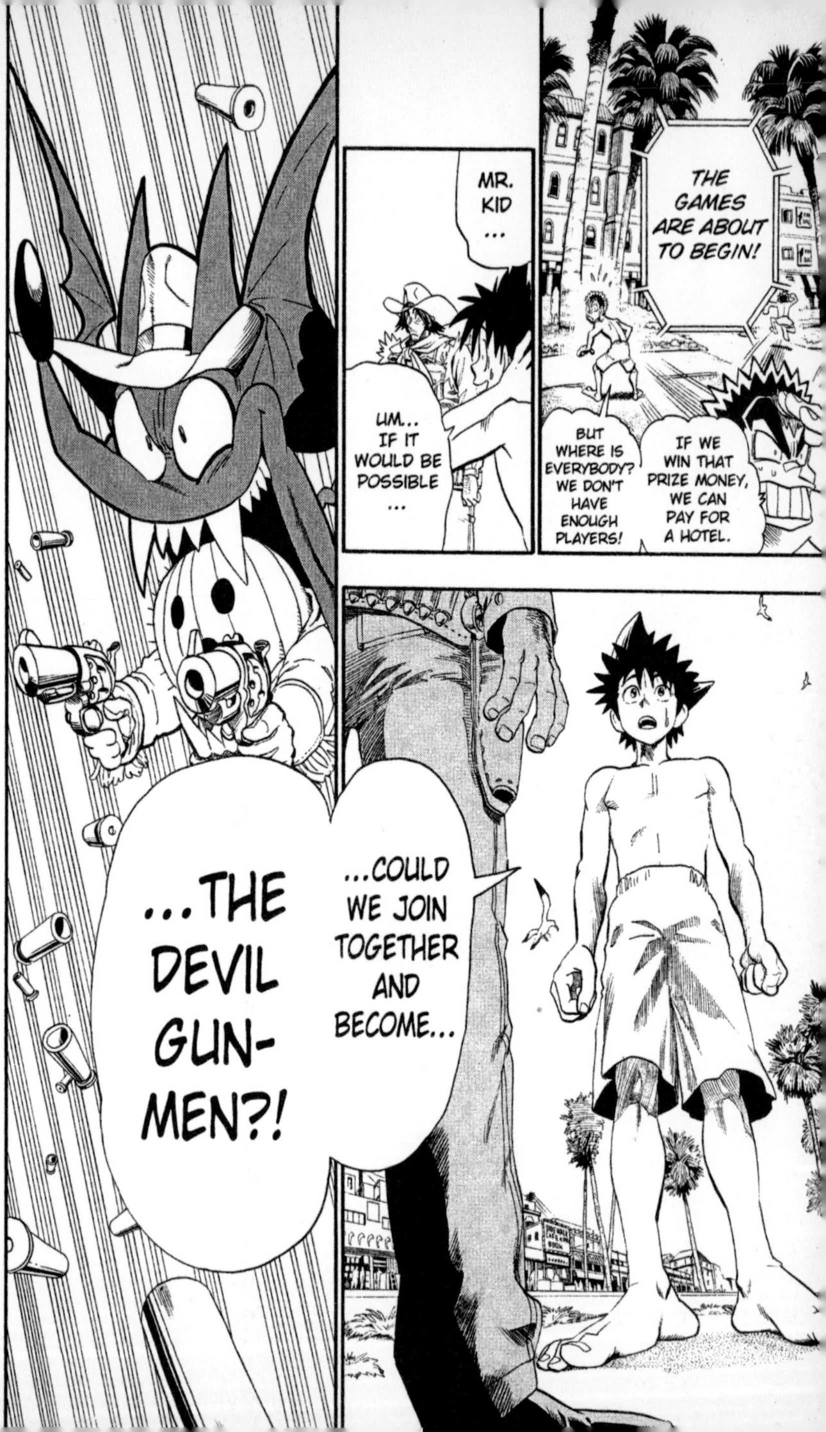
THE GAMES ARE ABOUT TO BEGIN!
IF WE WIN THAT PRIZE MONEY, WE CAN PAY FOR A HOTEL.
BUT WHERE IS EVERYBODY? WE DON'T HAVE ENOUGH PLAYERS!
MR. KID ...
UM... IF IT WOULD BE POSSIBLE ...
...COULD WE JOIN TOGETHER AND BECOME...
...THE DEVIL GUN-MEN?!

Chapter 73
The All-Star Devil Gunmen

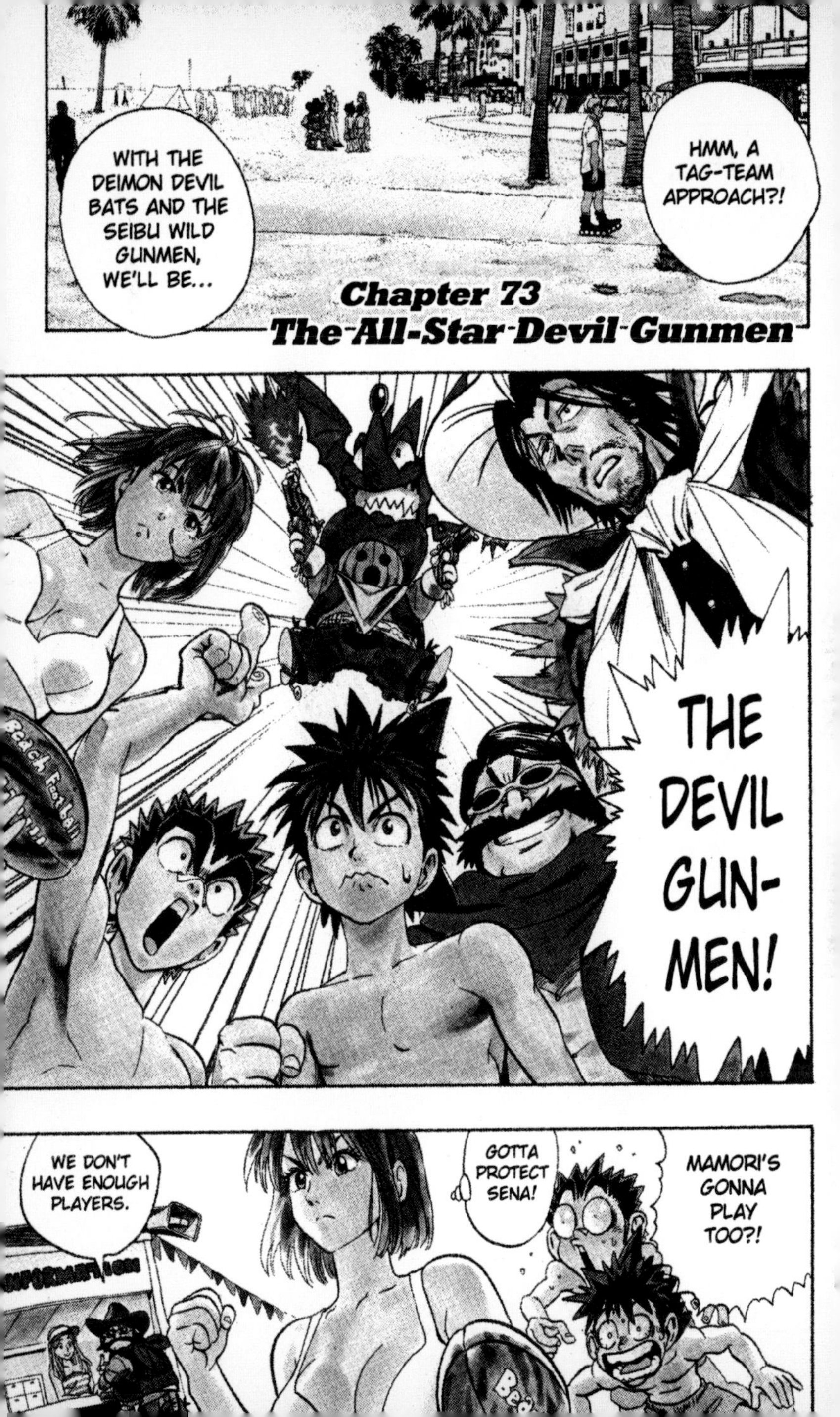
HMM, A TAG-TEAM APPROACH?!
WITH THE DEIMON DEVIL BATS AND THE SEIBU WILD GUNMEN, WE'LL BE...
THE DEVIL GUN-MEN!
MAMORI'S GONNA PLAY TOO?!
GOTTA PROTECT SENA!
WE DON'T HAVE ENOUGH PLAYERS.

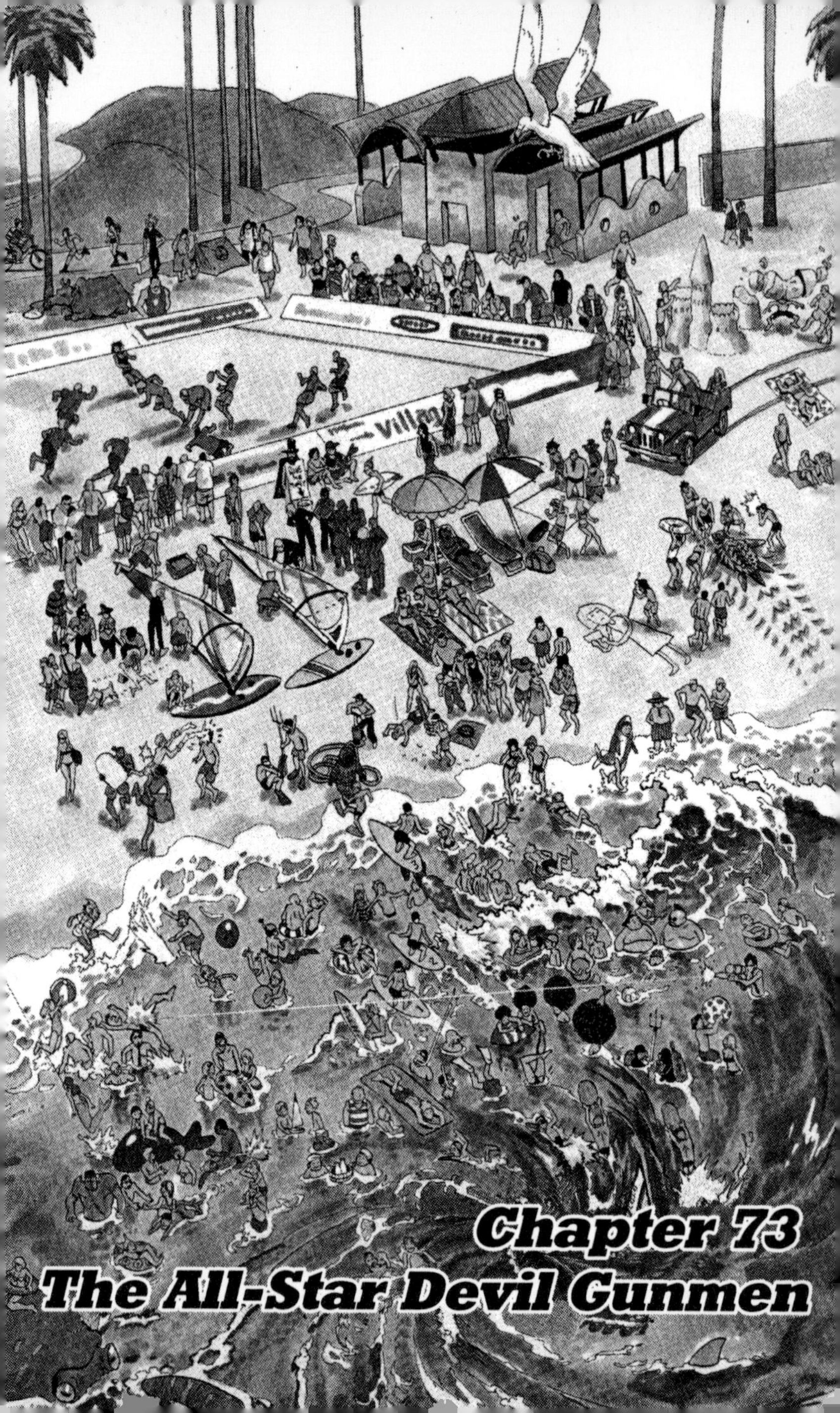

Chapter 73
The All-Star Devil Gunmen

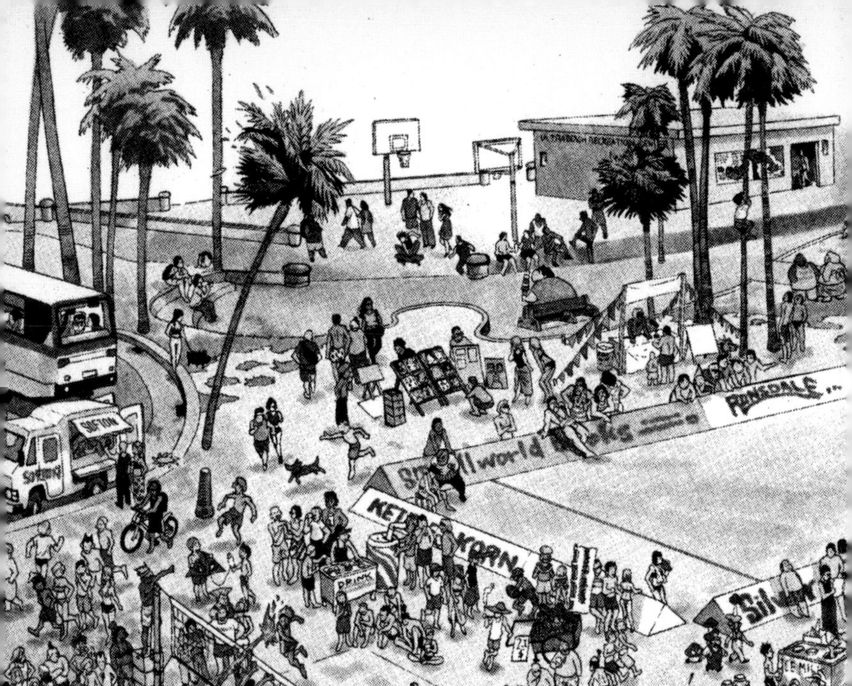

Find the Devil Bats players!!

Beach football is about to start, but where did all the Devil Bats players go?! Help find them!

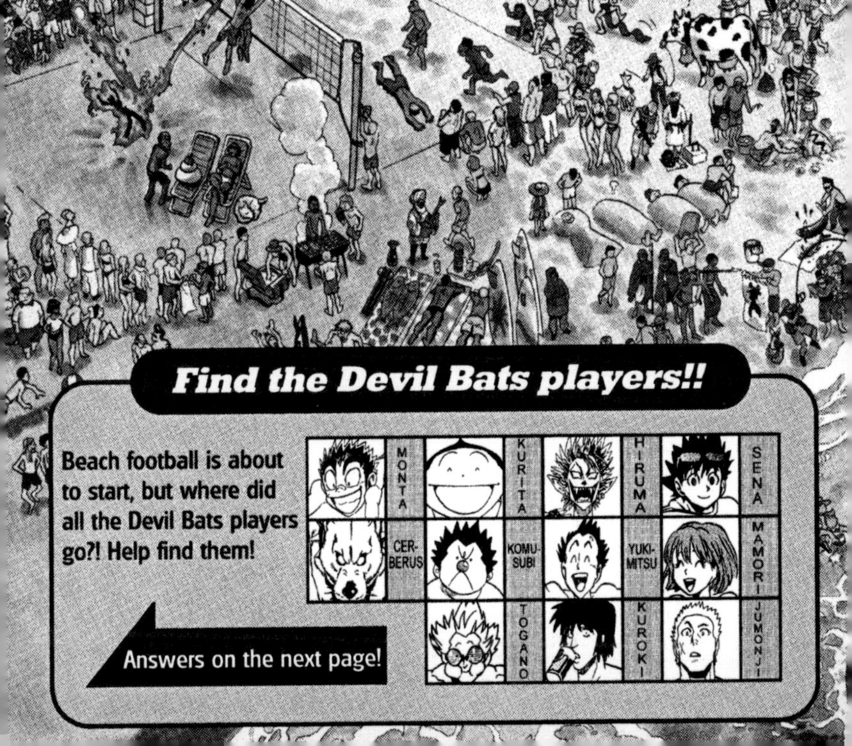
MONTA
KURITA
HIRUMA
SENA
CER-BERUS
KOMU-SUBI
YUKI-MITSU
MAMORI
TOGANO
KUROKI
JUMONJI

Answers on the next page!

Find the Devil Bats players!! Answers

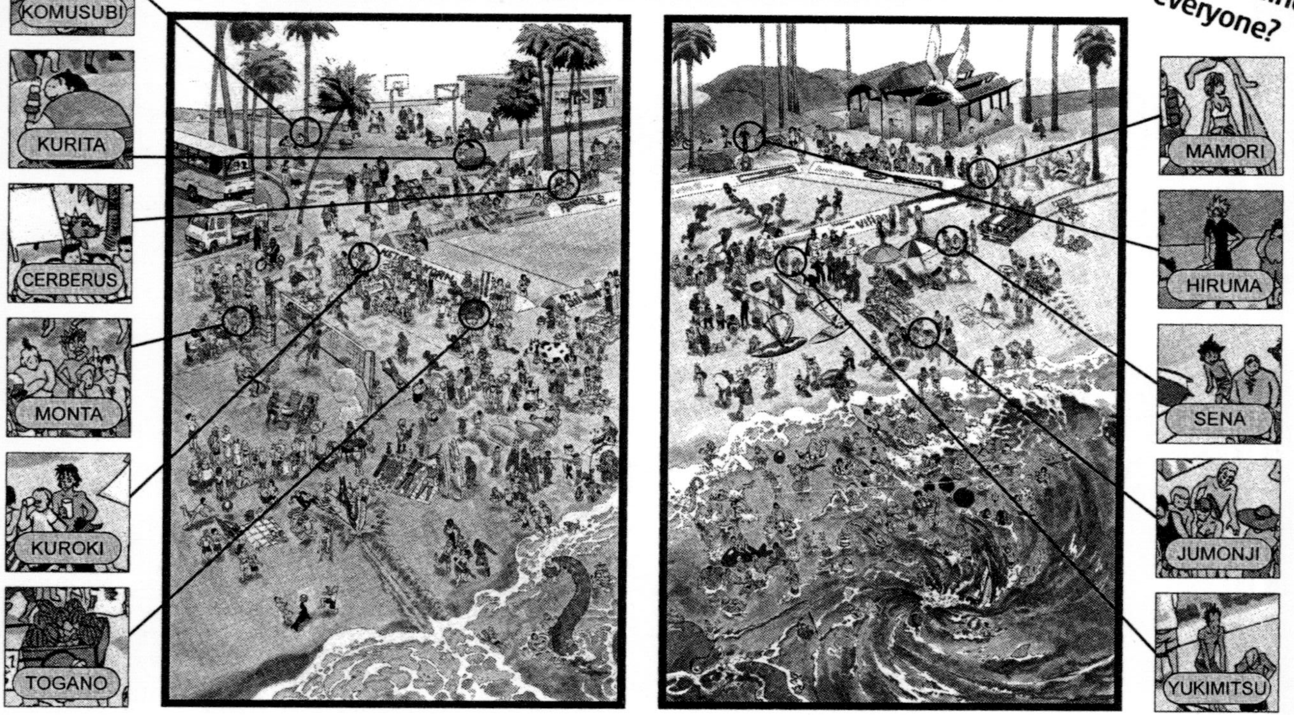
MAMORI
HIRUMA
SENA
JUMONJI
YUKIMITSU
KOMUSUBI
KURITA
CERBERUS
MONTA
KUROKI
TOGANO

Were you able to find everyone?

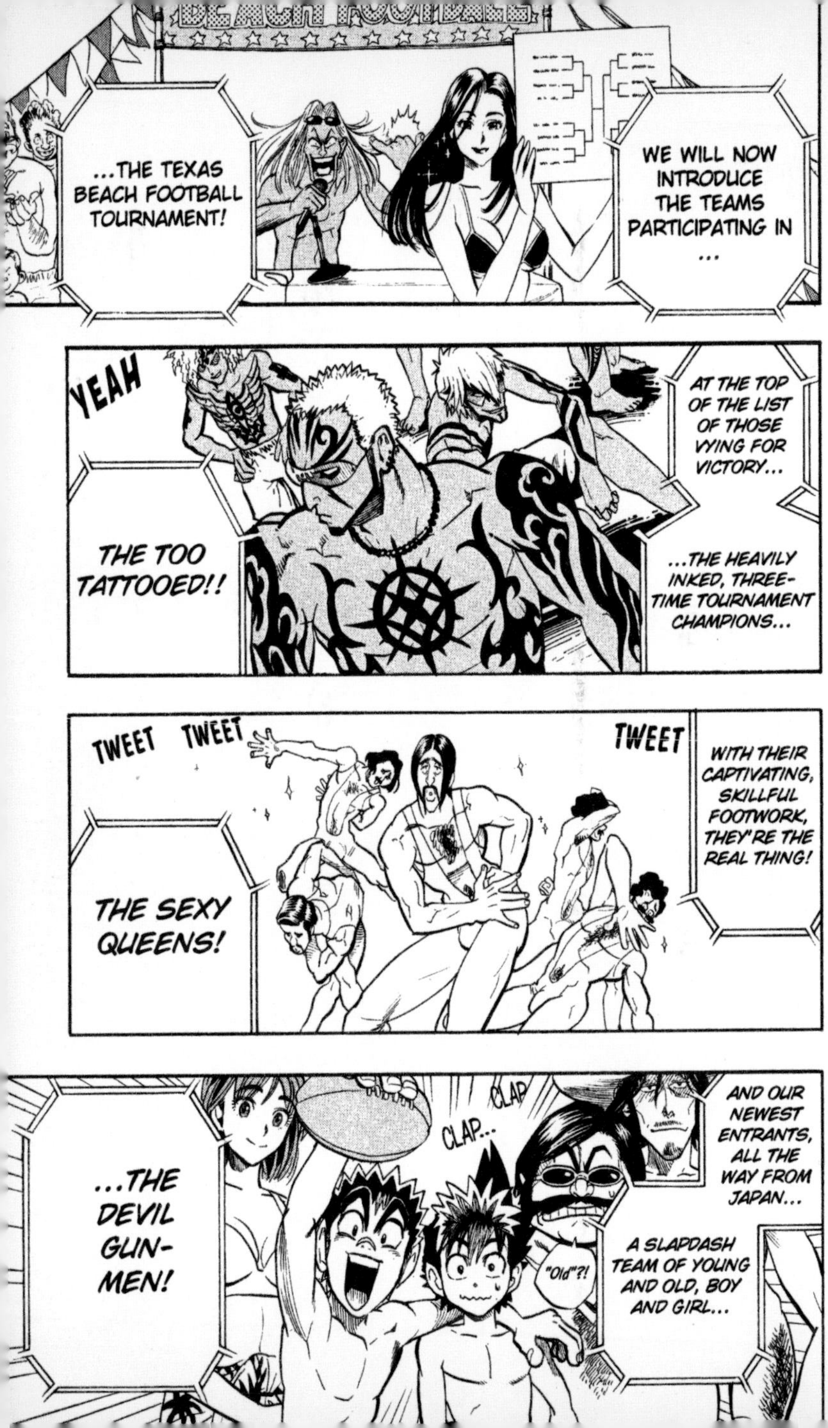
WE WILL NOW INTRODUCE THE TEAMS PARTICIPATING IN ...
...THE TEXAS BEACH FOOTBALL TOURNAMENT!
AT THE TOP OF THE LIST OF THOSE VYING FOR VICTORY...
YEAH
...THE HEAVILY INKED, THREE-TIME TOURNAMENT CHAMPIONS...
THE TOO TATTOOED!!
TWEET
WITH THEIR CAPTIVATING, SKILLFUL FOOTWORK, THEY'RE THE REAL THING!
TWEET TWEET
THE SEXY QUEENS!
AND OUR NEWEST ENTRANTS, ALL THE WAY FROM JAPAN...
CLAP
CLAP...
A SLAPDASH TEAM OF YOUNG AND OLD, BOY AND GIRL...
"Old"?!
...THE DEVIL GUN-MEN!

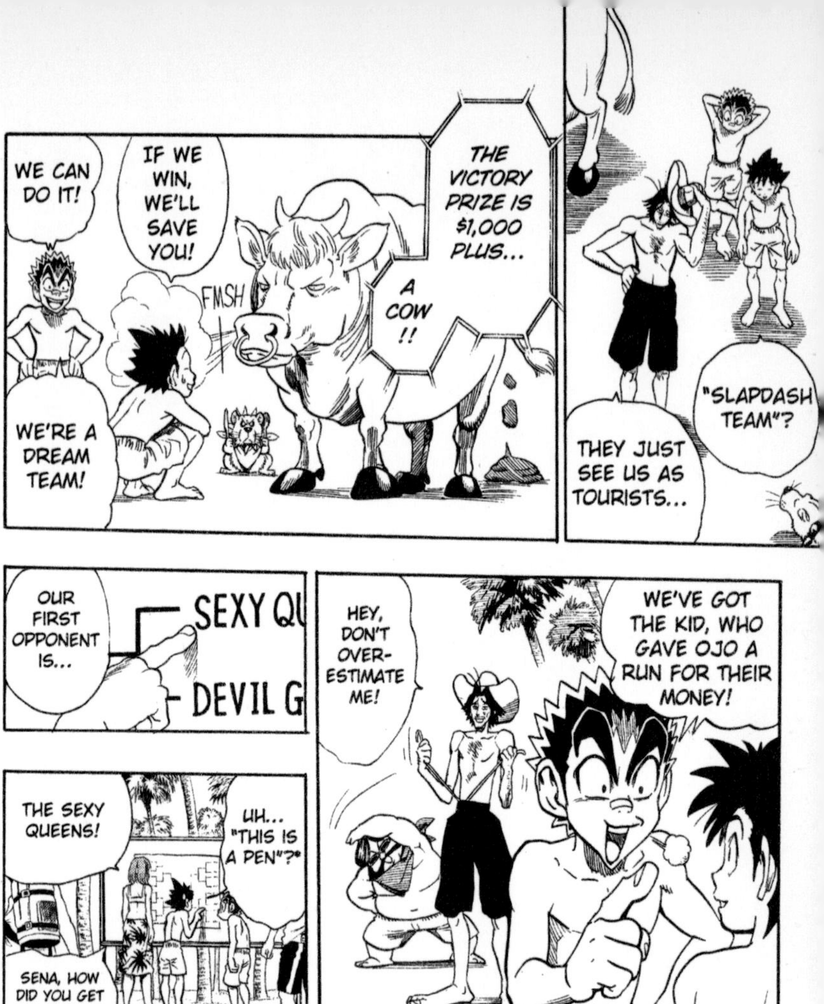
"SLAPDASH TEAM"?
THEY JUST SEE US AS TOURISTS...
THE VICTORY PRIZE IS $1,000 PLUS...
A COW!!
IF WE WIN, WE'LL SAVE YOU!
FMSH
WE CAN DO IT!
WE'RE A DREAM TEAM!
WE'VE GOT THE KID, WHO GAVE OJO A RUN FOR THEIR MONEY!
HEY, DON'T OVER-ESTIMATE ME!
OUR FIRST OPPONENT IS...
SEXY QU
DEVIL G
UH... "THIS IS A PEN"?*
THE SEXY QUEENS!
SENA, HOW DID YOU GET INTO HIGH SCHOOL?!

*"THIS IS A PEN" IS THE CLASSIC FIRST SENTENCE TAUGHT IN INTRO ENGLISH CLASSES IN JAPAN.

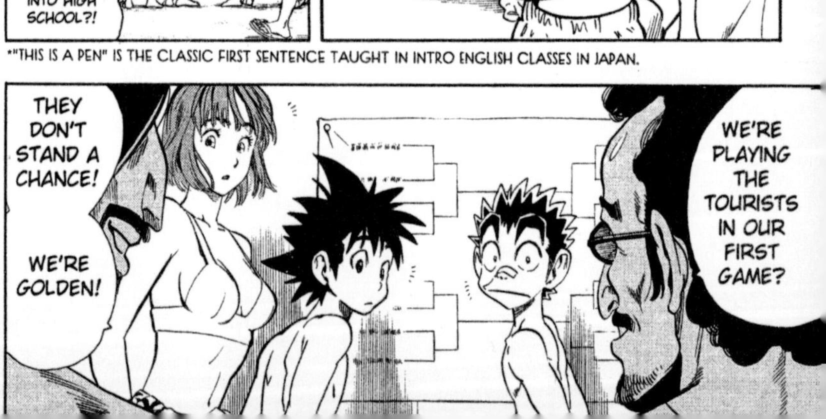
WE'RE PLAYING THE TOURISTS IN OUR FIRST GAME?
THEY DON'T STAND A CHANCE!
WE'RE GOLDEN!

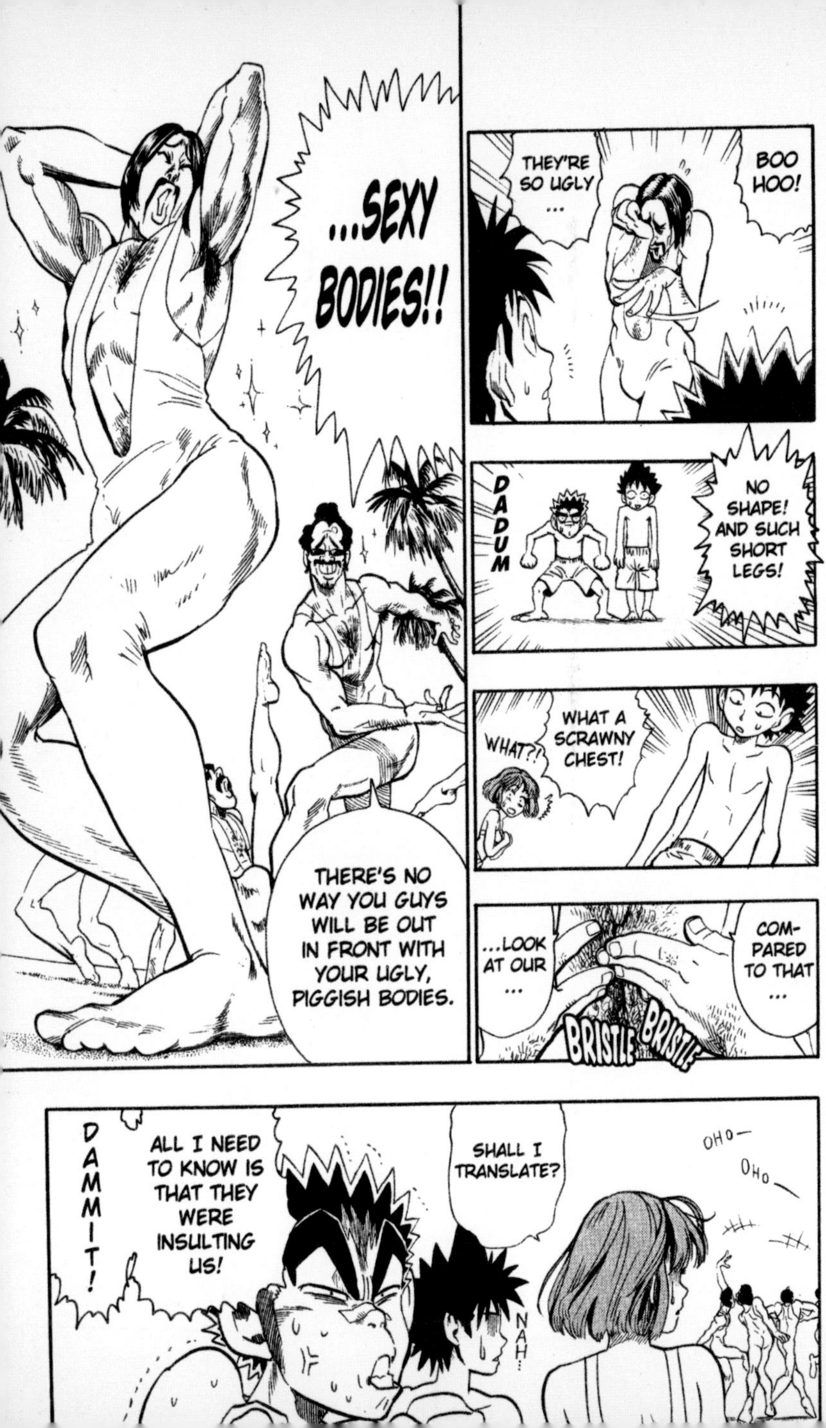
BOO HOO!
THEY'RE SO UGLY ...
NO SHAPE! AND SUCH SHORT LEGS!
DADUM
WHAT A SCRAWNY CHEST!
WHAT?!
COM-PARED TO THAT ...
...LOOK AT OUR ...
BRISTLE BRISTLE
...SEXY BODIES!!
THERE'S NO WAY YOU GUYS WILL BE OUT IN FRONT WITH YOUR UGLY, PIGGISH BODIES.
OHO— OHO
SHALL I TRANSLATE?
NAH...
ALL I NEED TO KNOW IS THAT THEY WERE INSULTING US!
DAMMIT!

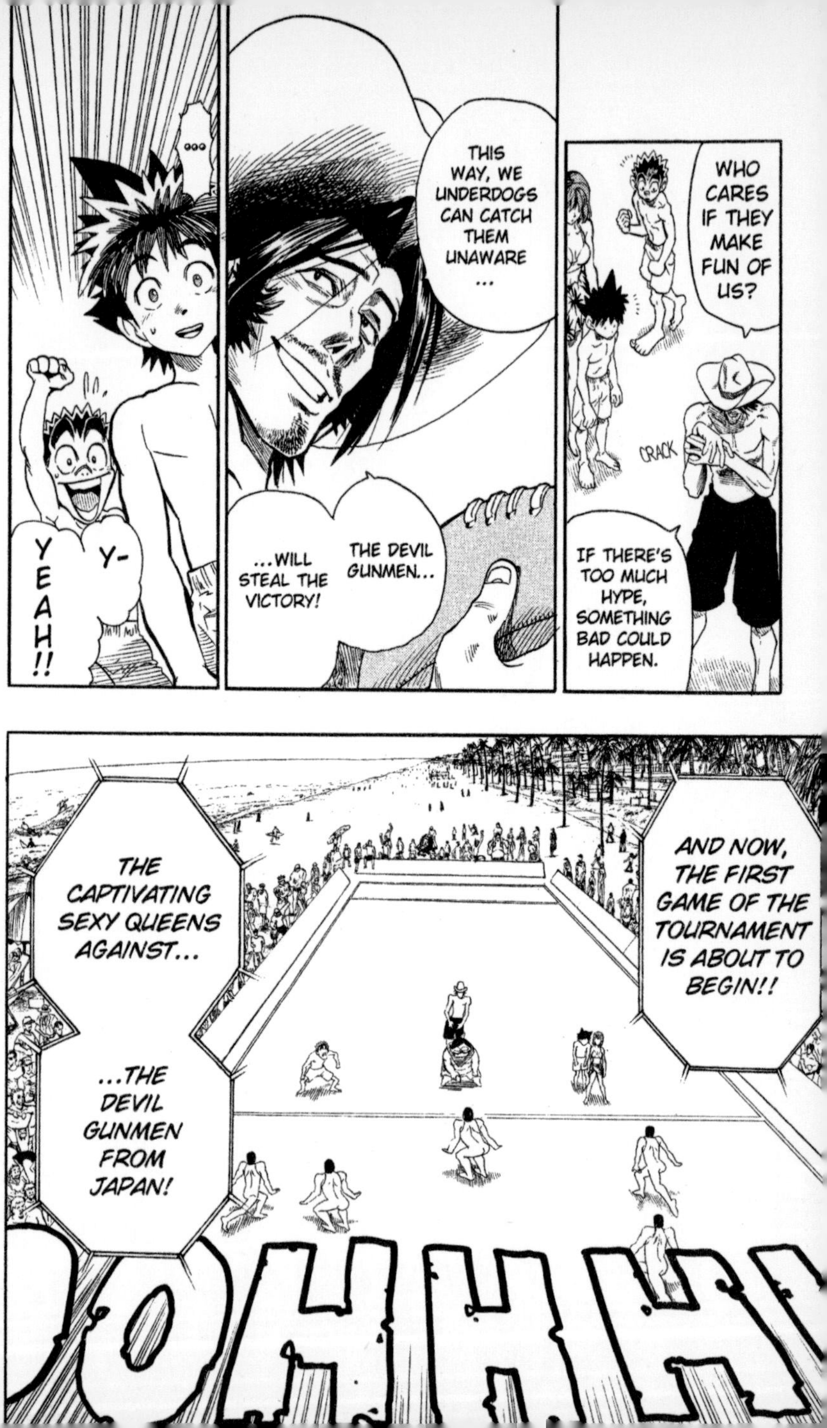
WHO CARES IF THEY MAKE FUN OF US?
CRACK
IF THERE'S TOO MUCH HYPE, SOMETHING BAD COULD HAPPEN.
THIS WAY, WE UNDERDOGS CAN CATCH THEM UNAWARE ...
THE DEVIL GUNMEN...
...WILL STEAL THE VICTORY!
...
Y-
YEAH!!
AND NOW, THE FIRST GAME OF THE TOURNAMENT IS ABOUT TO BEGIN!!
THE CAPTIVATING SEXY QUEENS AGAINST...
...THE DEVIL GUNMEN FROM JAPAN!
OHHH

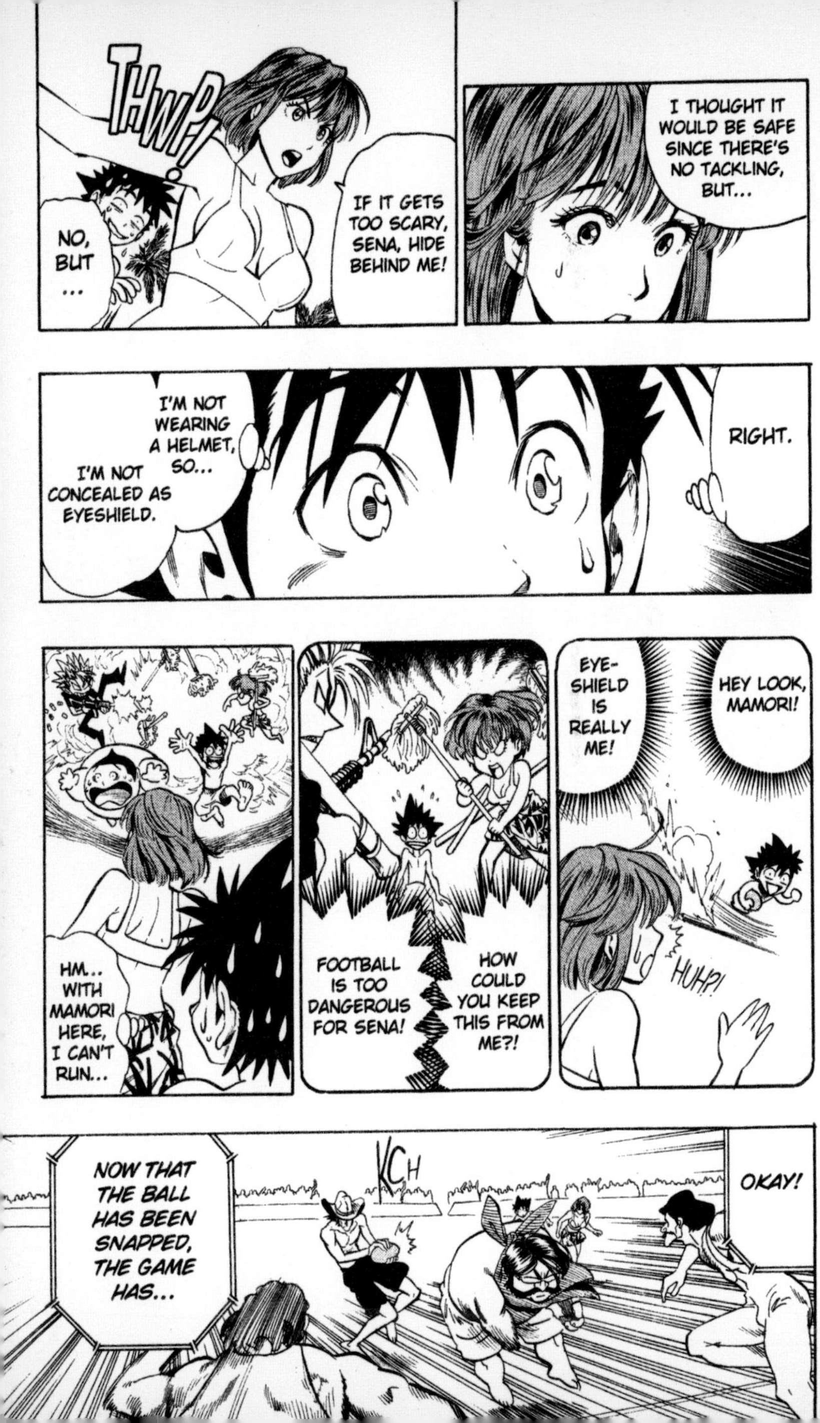
I THOUGHT IT WOULD BE SAFE SINCE THERE'S NO TACKLING, BUT...
IF IT GETS TOO SCARY, SENA, HIDE BEHIND ME!
THWIP!
NO, BUT ...
RIGHT.
I'M NOT WEARING A HELMET, SO...
I'M NOT CONCEALED AS EYESHIELD.
HEY LOOK, MAMORI!
EYE-SHIELD IS REALLY ME!
HUH?!
HOW COULD YOU KEEP THIS FROM ME?!
FOOTBALL IS TOO DANGEROUS FOR SENA!
HM.. WITH MAMORI HERE, I CAN'T RUN...
OKAY!
KCH
NOW THAT THE BALL HAS BEEN SNAPPED, THE GAME HAS...

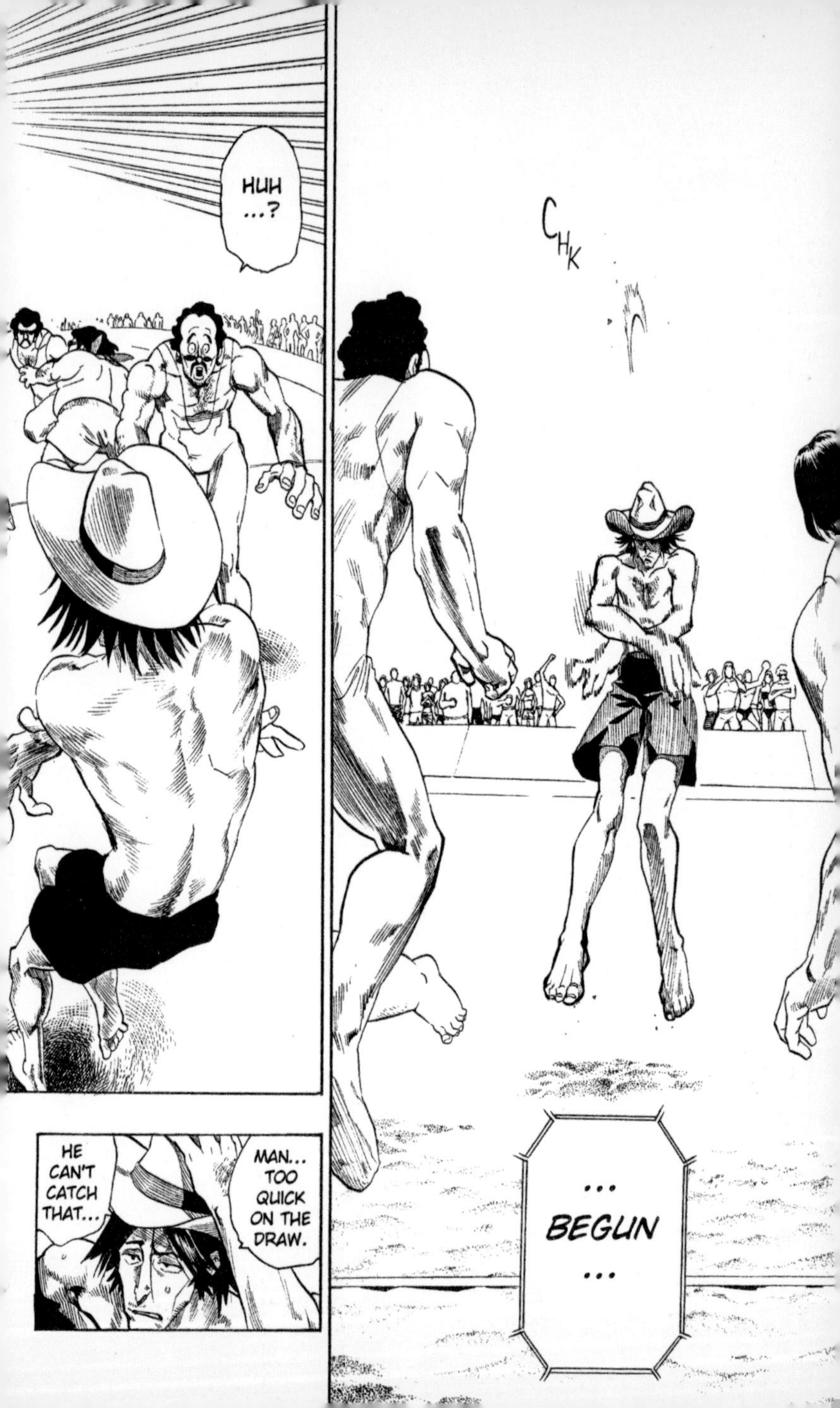
CHK
... BEGUN ...
HUH ...?
MAN... TOO QUICK ON THE DRAW.
HE CAN'T CATCH THAT...

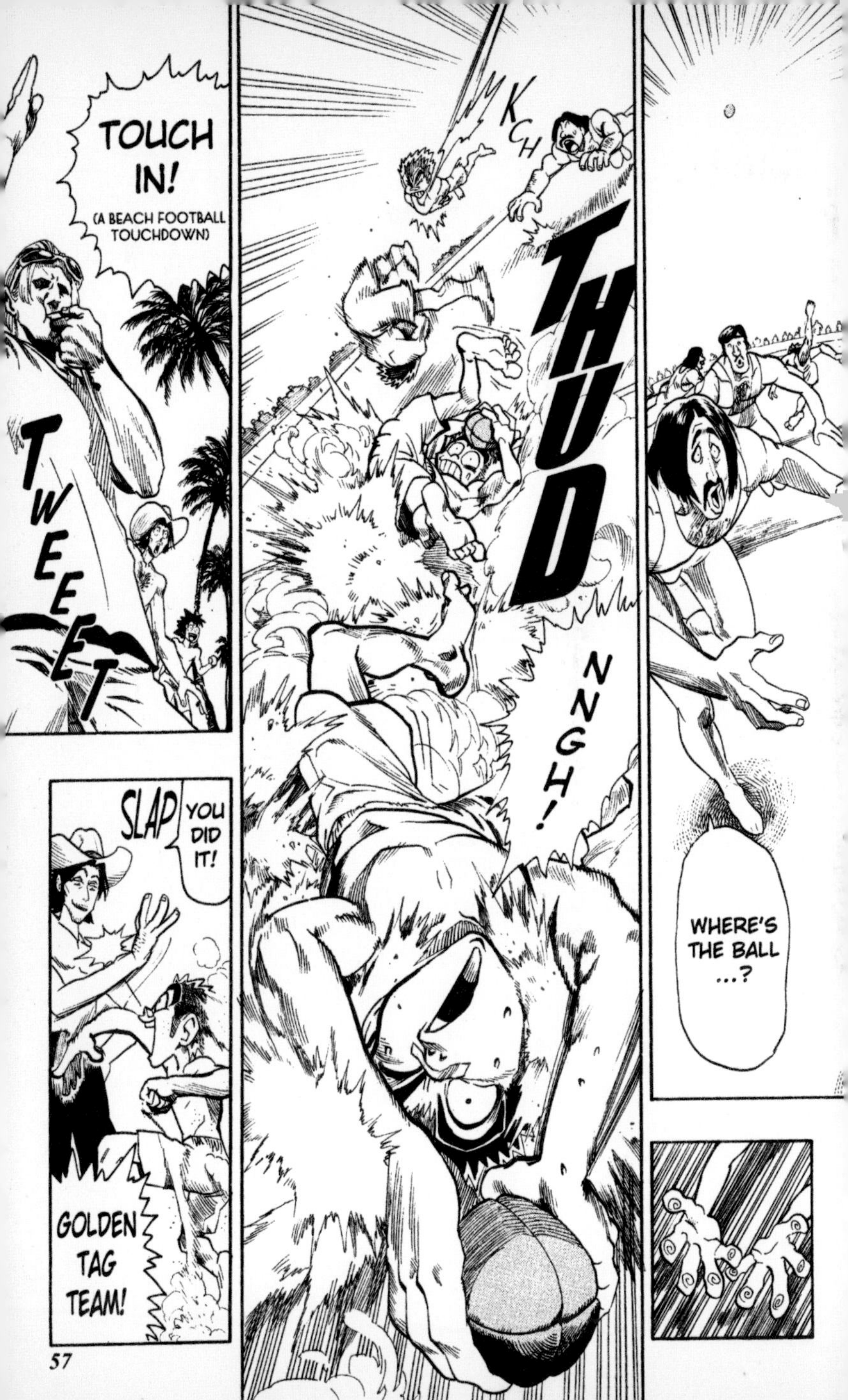

WHERE'S THE BALL ...?
KCH
THUD
NNGH!
TOUCH IN!
(A BEACH FOOTBALL TOUCHDOWN)
TWEEEET
SLAP
YOU DID IT!
GOLDEN TAG TEAM!

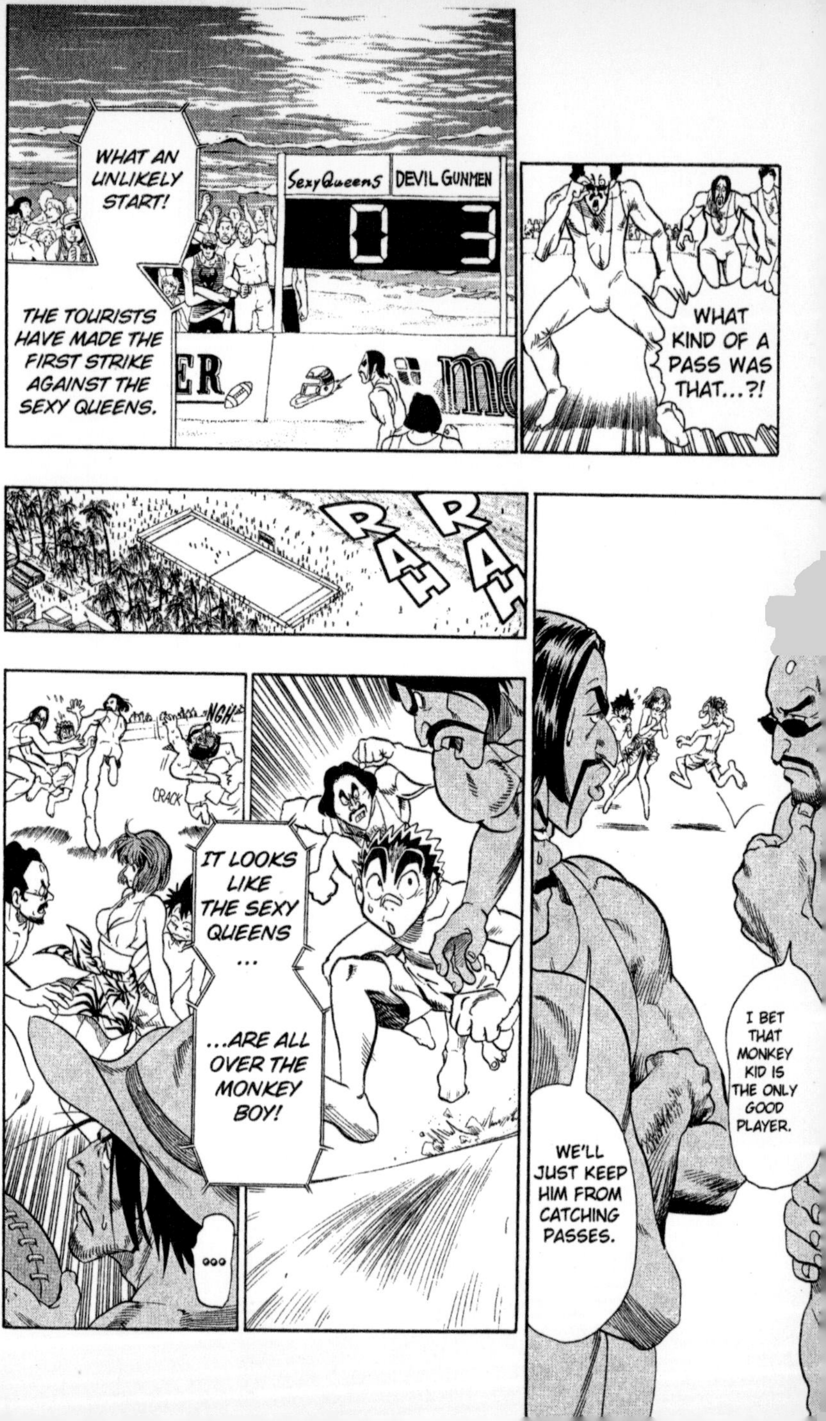
WHAT KIND OF A PASS WAS THAT...?!
SexyQueenS
DEVIL GUNMEN
0
3
WHAT AN UNLIKELY START!
THE TOURISTS HAVE MADE THE FIRST STRIKE AGAINST THE SEXY QUEENS.
I BET THAT MONKEY KID IS THE ONLY GOOD PLAYER.
WE'LL JUST KEEP HIM FROM CATCHING PASSES.
RAH
RAH
IT LOOKS LIKE THE SEXY QUEENS...
...ARE ALL OVER THE MONKEY BOY!
NGH
CRACK
...

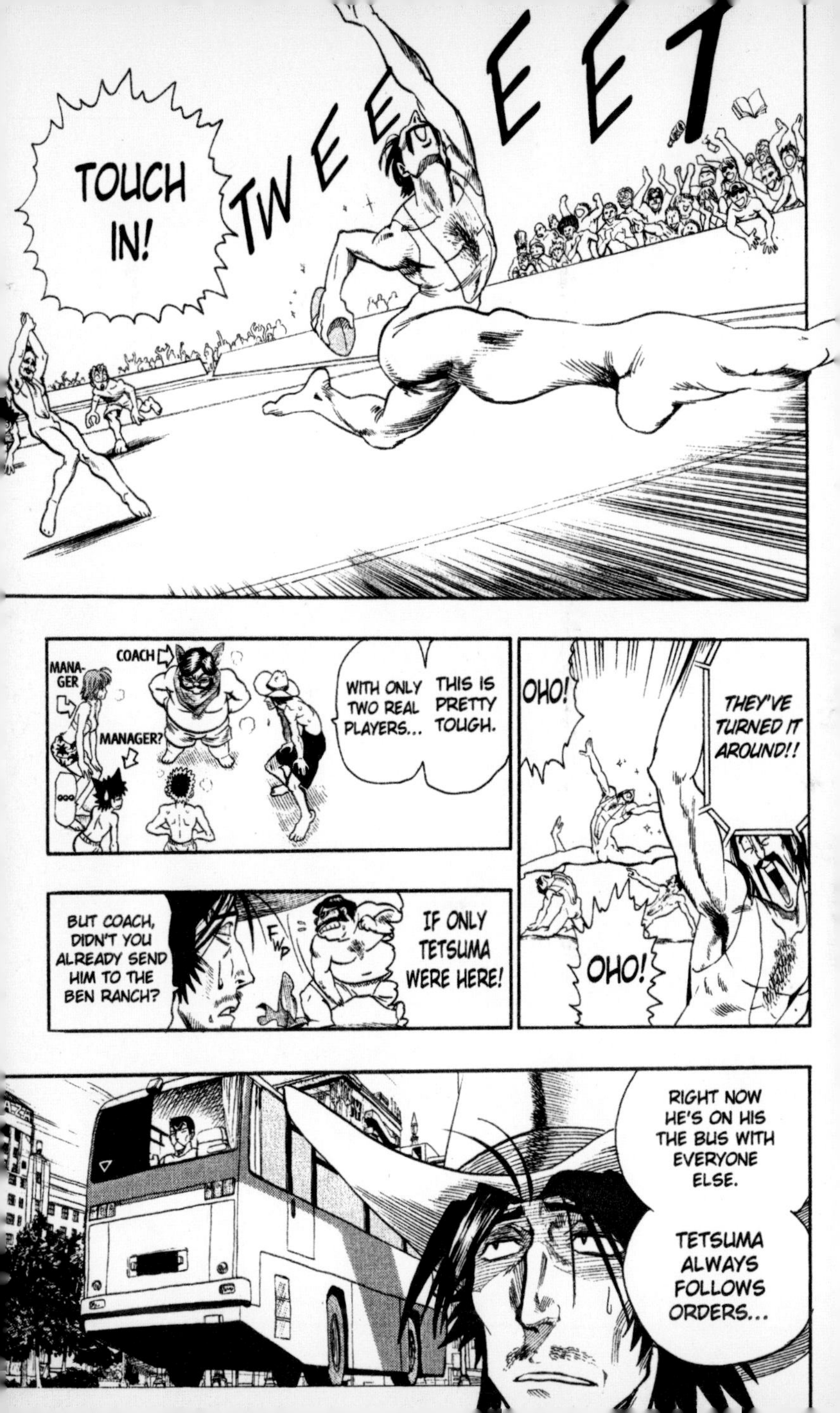
TWEEEET
TOUCH IN!
OHO!
THEY'VE TURNED IT AROUND!!
OHO!
WITH ONLY TWO REAL PLAYERS... THIS IS PRETTY TOUGH.
COACH
MANA-GER
MANAGER?
IF ONLY TETSUMA WERE HERE!
FWP
BUT COACH, DIDN'T YOU ALREADY SEND HIM TO THE BEN RANCH?
RIGHT NOW HE'S ON HIS THE BUS WITH EVERYONE ELSE.
TETSUMA ALWAYS FOLLOWS ORDERS...

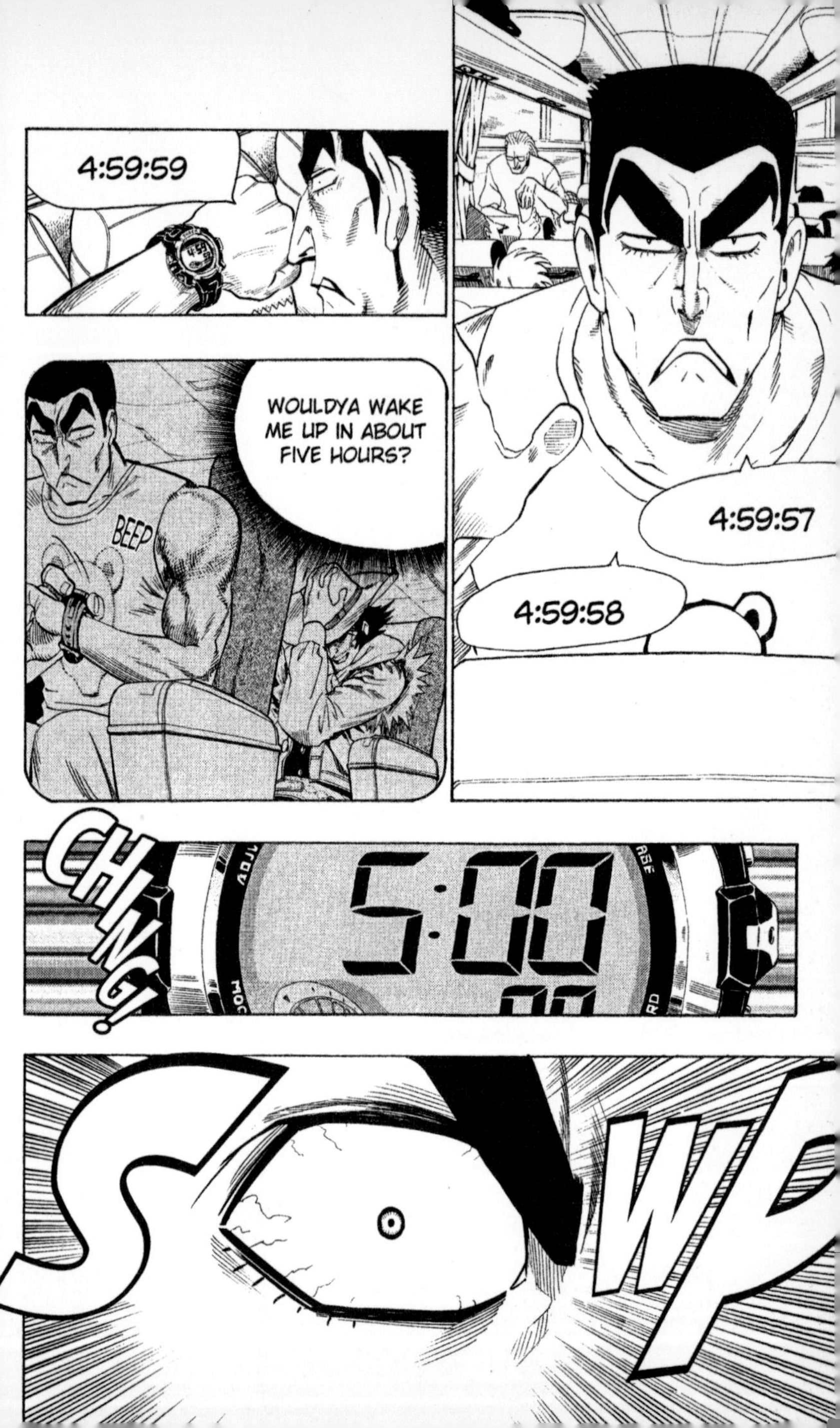
4:59:57
4:59:58
4:59:59
WOULDYA WAKE ME UP IN ABOUT FIVE HOURS?
BEEP
CHING!
5:00

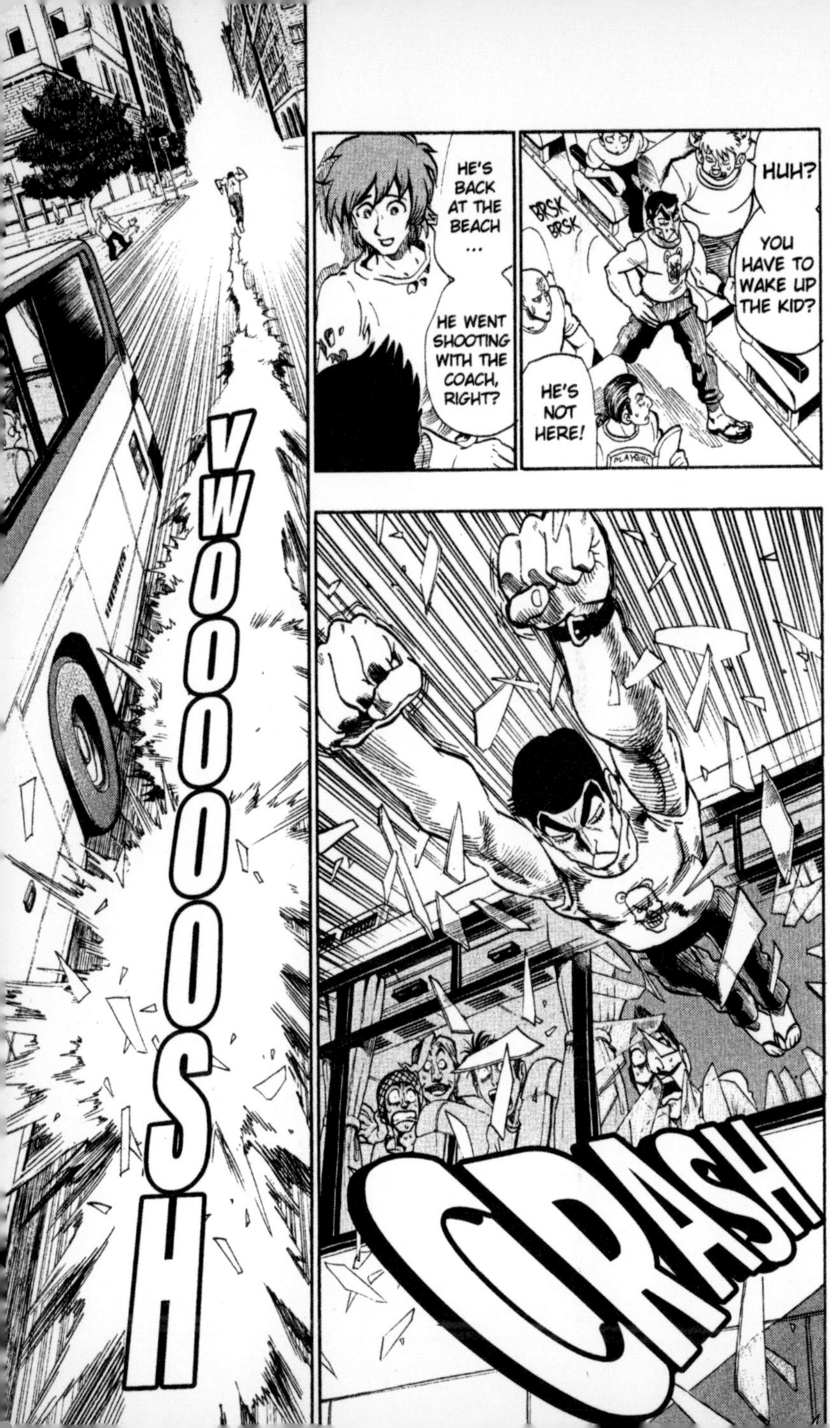
HUH?
YOU HAVE TO WAKE UP THE KID?
BRSK BRSK
HE'S NOT HERE!
PLAYGIRL
HE'S BACK AT THE BEACH ...
HE WENT SHOOTING WITH THE COACH, RIGHT?
CRASH
VWOOOOOOOSH

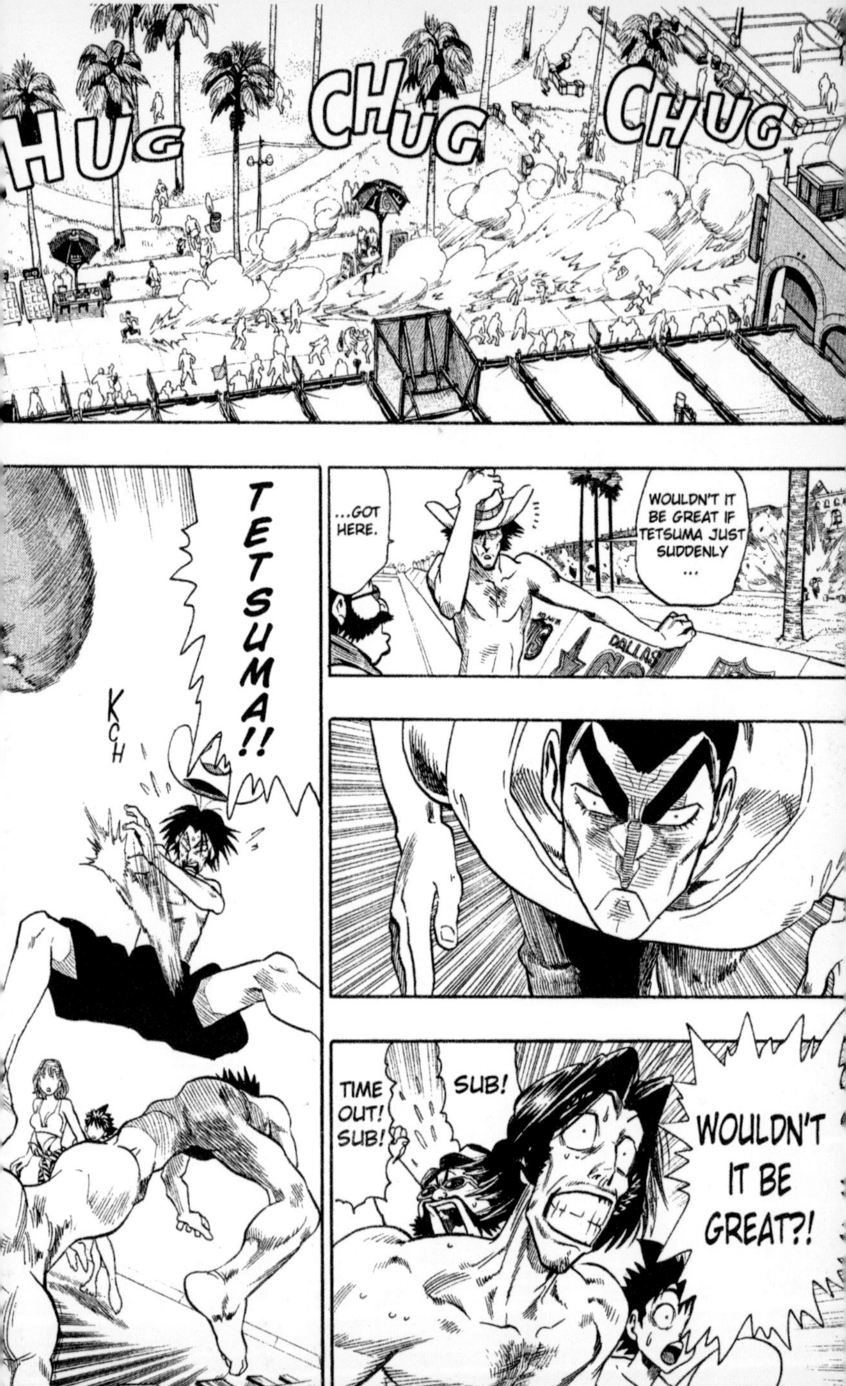
CHUG
CHUG
HUG
WOULDN'T IT BE GREAT IF TETSUMA JUST SUDDENLY ...
...GOT HERE.
WOULDN'T IT BE GREAT?!
SUB!
TIME OUT! SUB!
TETSUMA!!
KCH

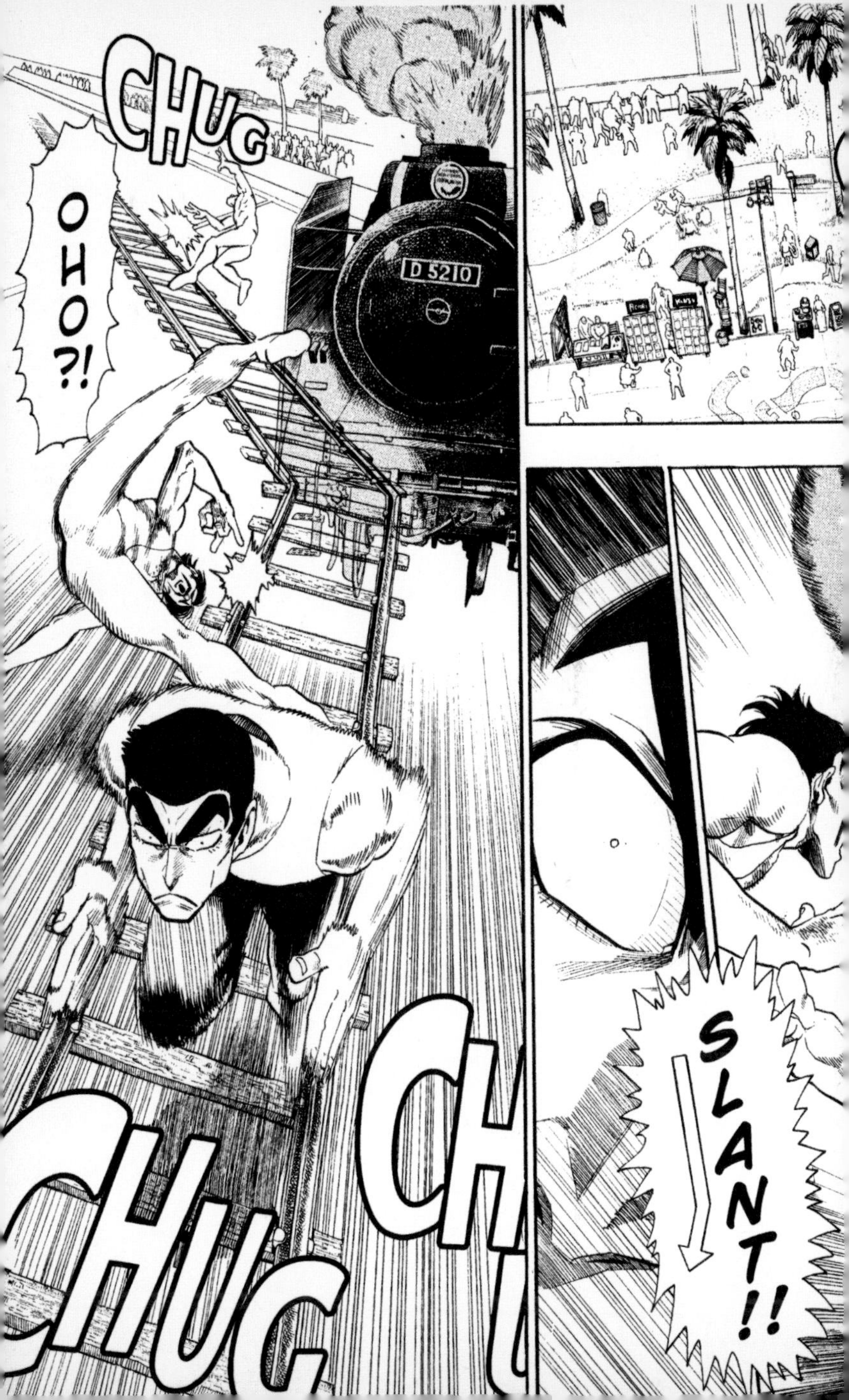
SLANT!!
CHUG
OHO?!
D 5210
CH
CHUG

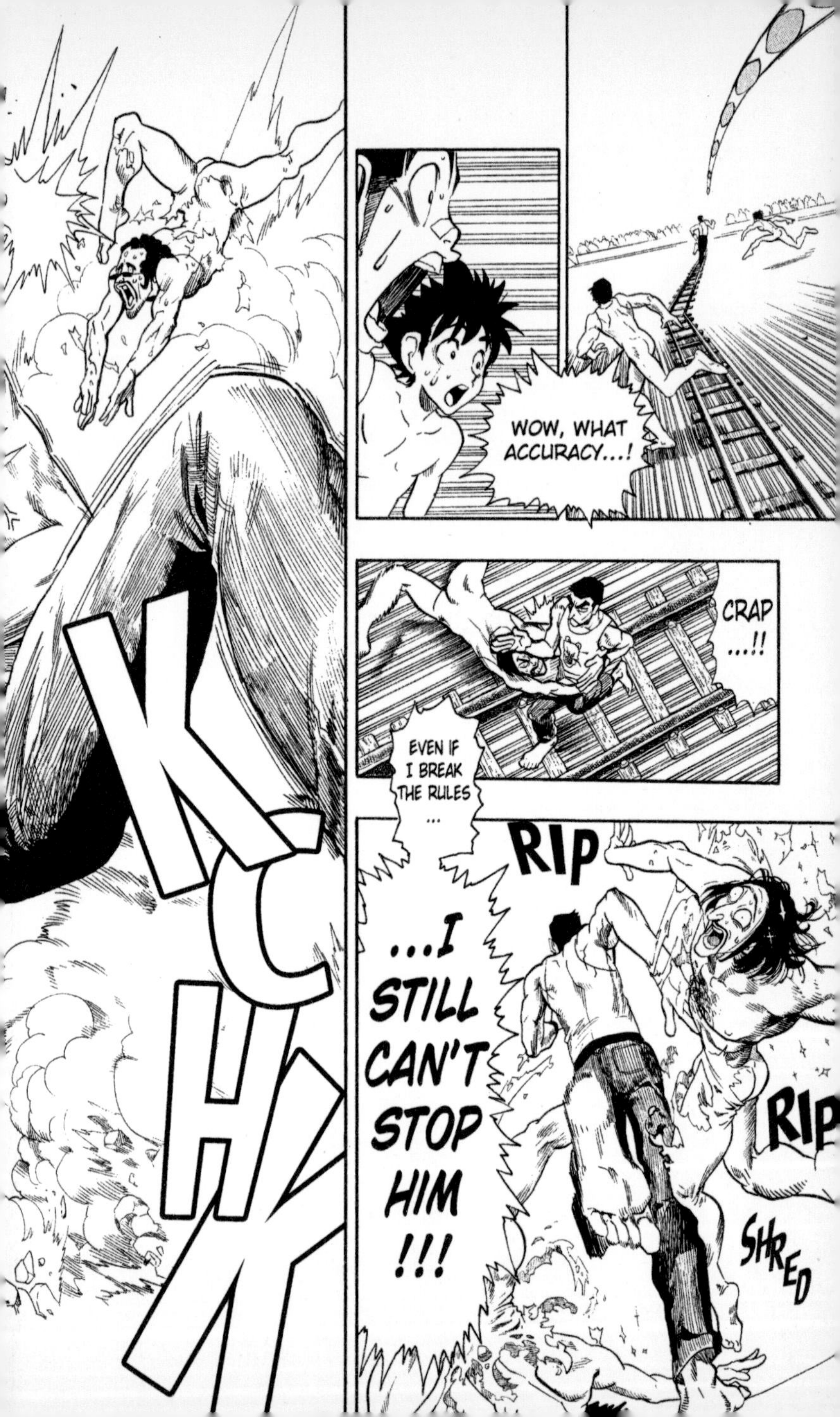
WOW, WHAT ACCURACY...!
CRAP ...!!
EVEN IF I BREAK THE RULES ...
...I STILL CAN'T STOP HIM !!!
RIP
RIP
SHRED
KCHK

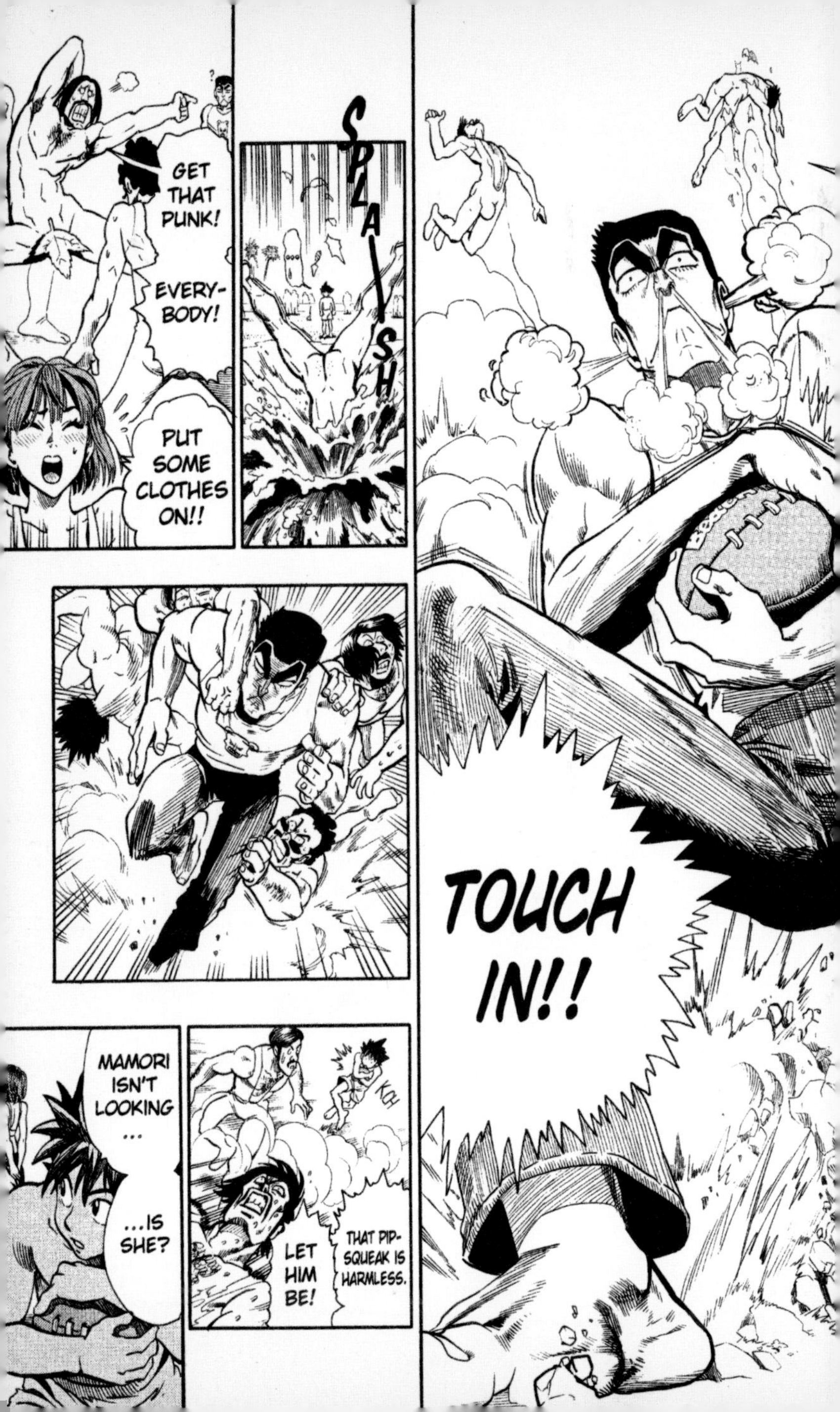
TOUCH IN!!
SPLASH
GET THAT PUNK!
EVERY-BODY!
PUT SOME CLOTHES ON!!
THAT PIP-SQUEAK IS HARMLESS.
KCH
LET HIM BE!
MAMORI ISN'T LOOKING...
...IS SHE?

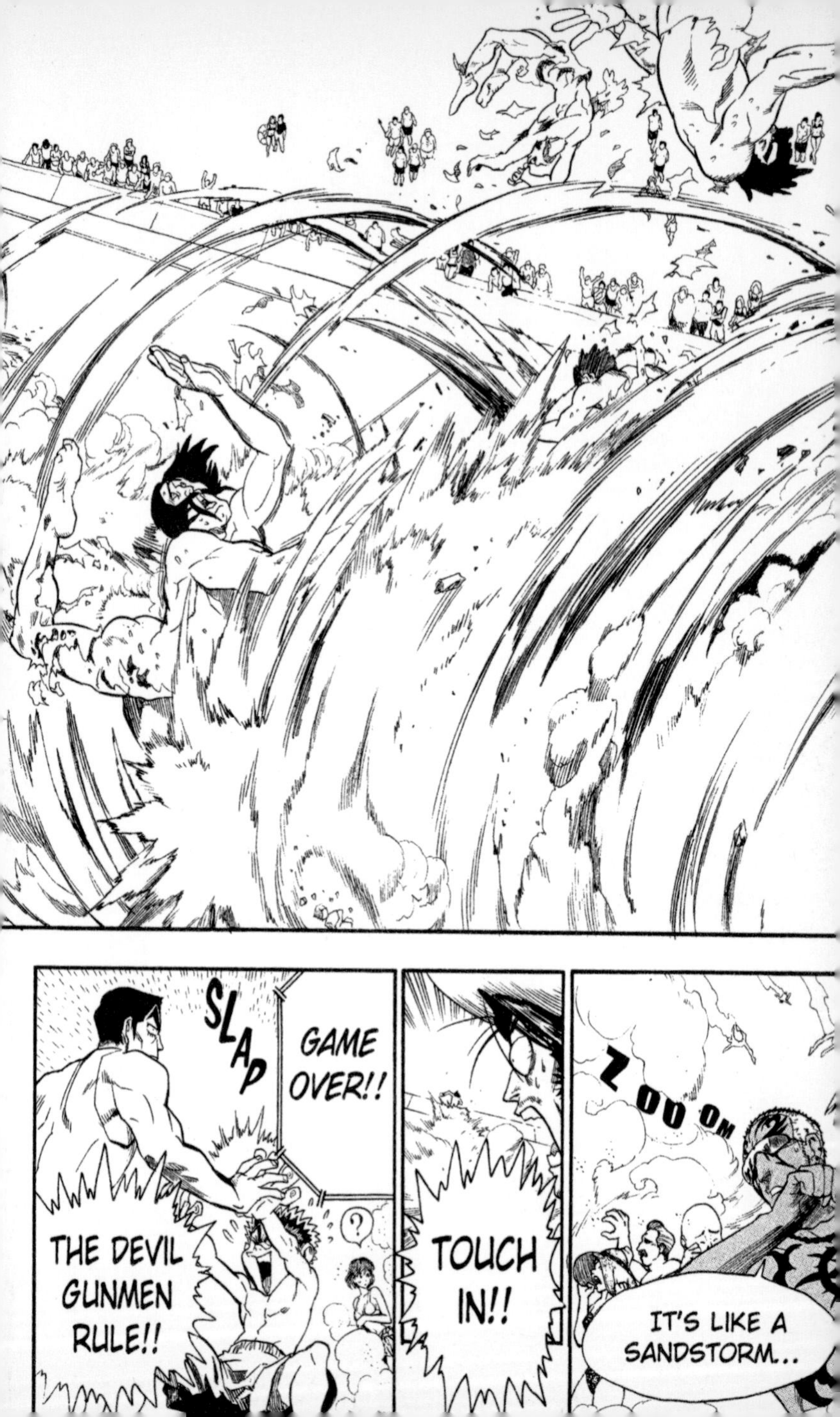
ZOOOM
IT'S LIKE A SANDSTORM...
TOUCH IN!!
GAME OVER!!
SLAP
?
THE DEVIL GUNMEN RULE!!

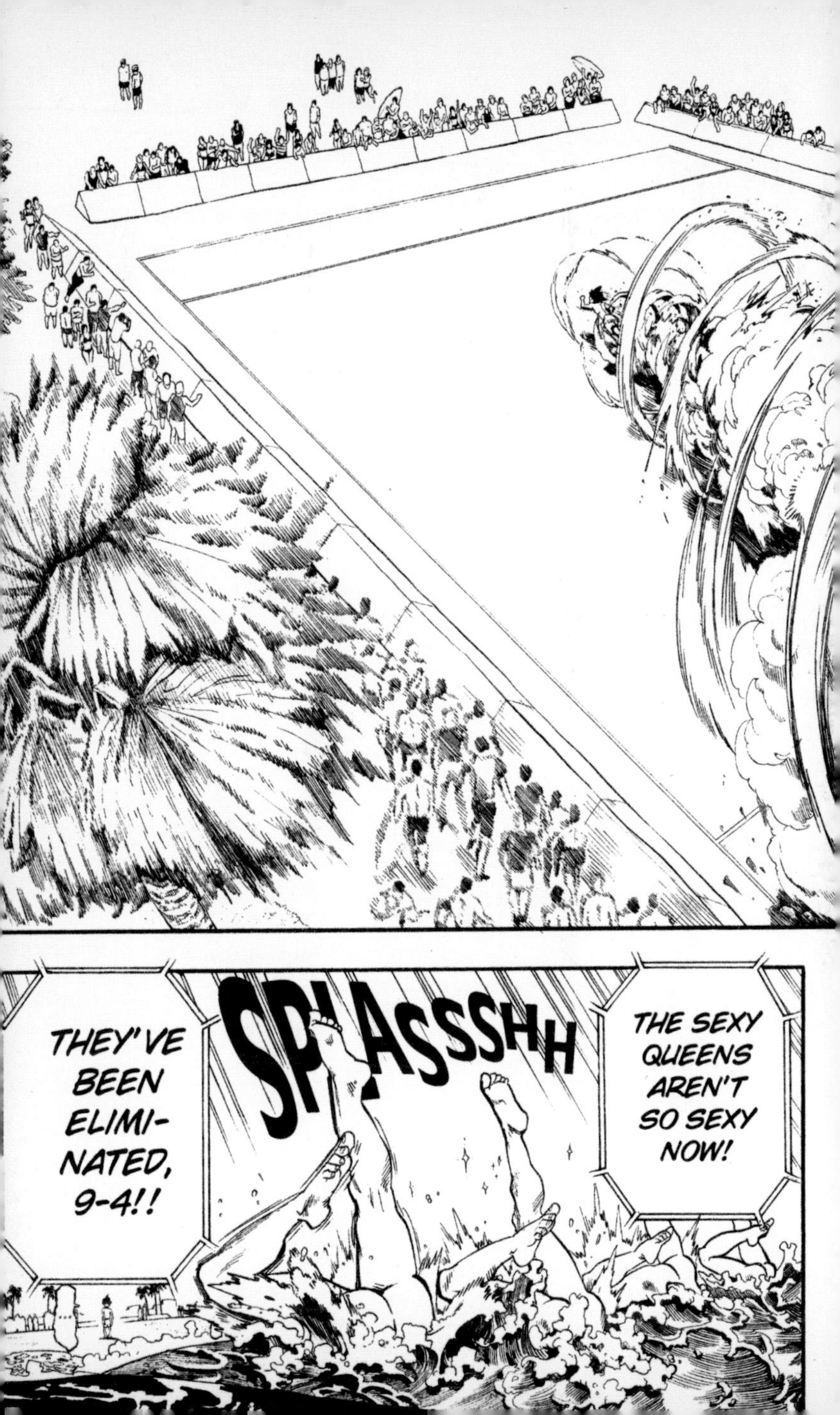
THE SEXY QUEENS AREN'T SO SEXY NOW!
SPLASSSHH
THEY'VE BEEN ELIMI-NATED, 9-4!!

Eyeshield 21 Survey Corner **Devil Bat 021**

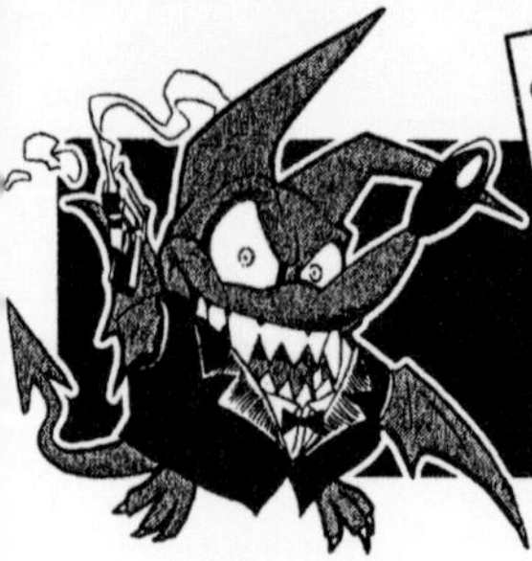

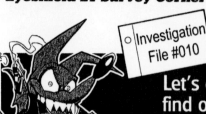

Investigation File #010

Let's do a survey to find out everyone's birthday!!

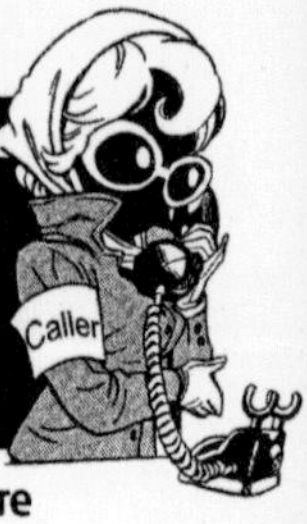
Caller

S.H., Yamagata Prefecture

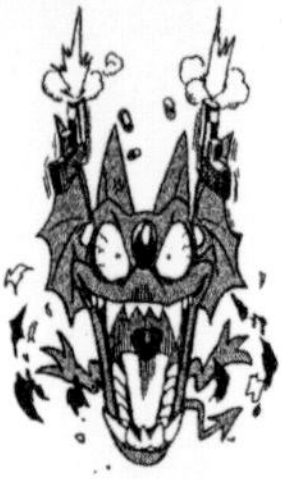

AAAH, WHAT AN ANNOYING SURVEY, DAMMIT!! WELL, I GUESS I WAS ABLE TO FIND EVERYTHING OUT ALL AT ONCE! YOU CAN SECRETLY ROOT FOR THE PLAYER WHOSE BIRTHDAY IS CLOSEST TO YOURS!

Sena Kobayakawa	12/21	Taro Raimon	8/31	Ryokan Kurita	7/7
Daikichi Komusubi	1/1	Manabu Yukimitsu	2/29	Tetsuo Ishimaru	5/26
Kazuki Jumonji	10/1	Koji Kuroki	9/2	Shozo Togano	10/13
Hiruma		Gen Takekura	4/2	Mamori Anezaki	11/24
The Kid		Jo Tetsuma	5/15	Kotaro Sasaki	7/19
Seijuro Shin	7/9	Haruto Sakuraba	3/12	Makoto Otawara	6/15
Ichiro Takami	9/14	Koharu Wakana	3/1	Yusuke Murata	7/4
Unsui Kongo	5/31	Agon Kongo	5/31	Ikkyu Hosokawa	1/9
Gondayu Yamabushi	8/14	Riichiro Inagaki	6/20	Rui Habashira	1/25
Mamoru Bamba	6/25	Kiminari Harao	8/22	Ken Kamaguruma	12/8
Homer	11/3	Panther	2/20	Watt	8/10
Little Gonzales	4/4	Big Gonzales	10/28	Kaoru Hatsujo	4/26

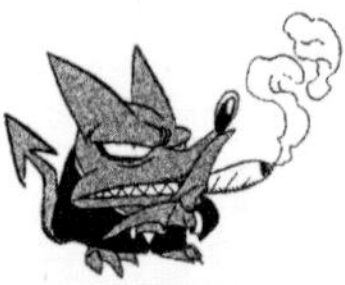

SHUT UP! I KNOW WHAT YOU'RE GONNA SAY. THAT MY JOB NOW IS TO DO SURVEYS... WELL, I GUESS THAT'S HOW IT IS.

BY THE WAY, THERE ARE TWO NAMES MIXED IN HERE THAT DON'T BELONG. DID YOU NOTICE?

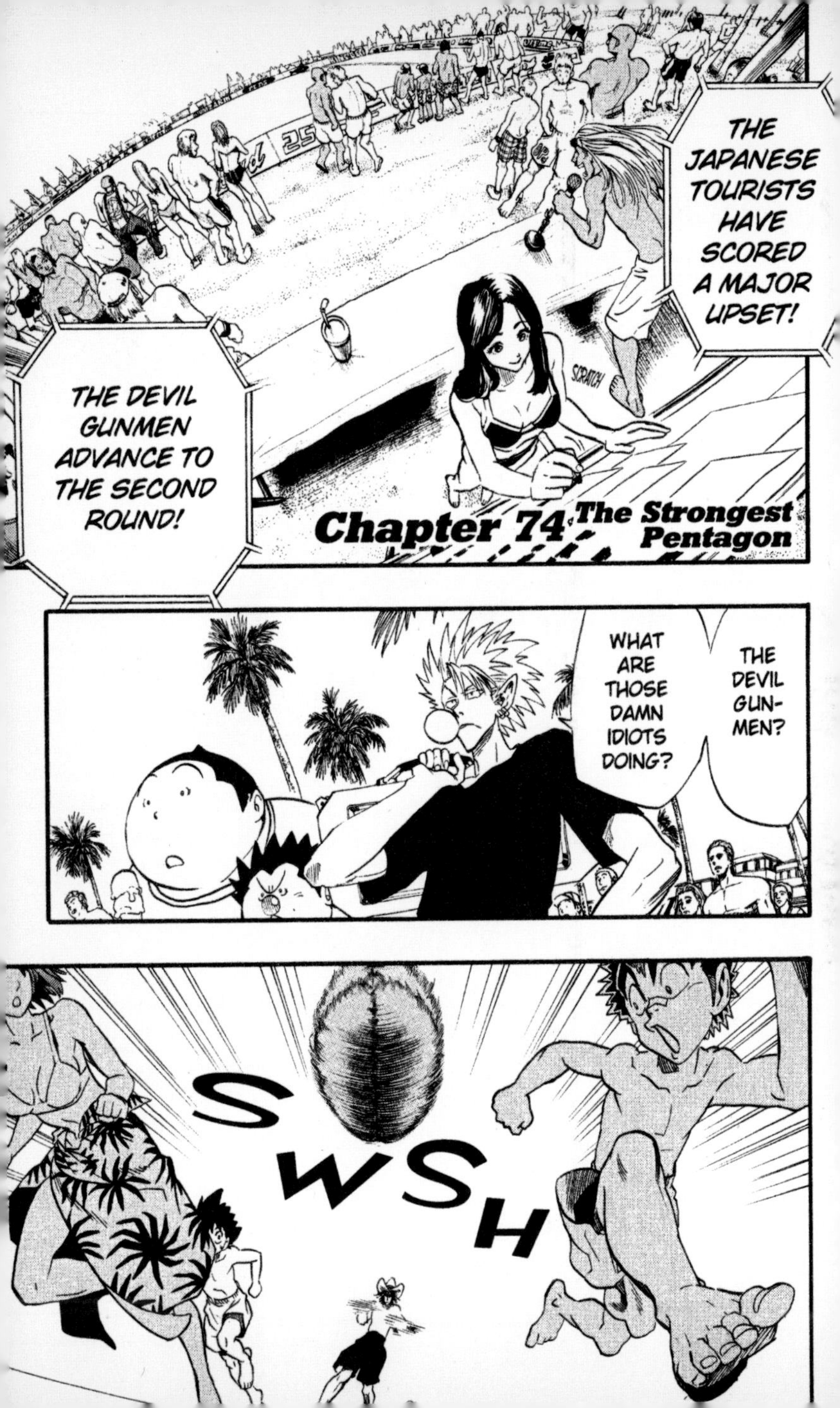
THE JAPANESE TOURISTS HAVE SCORED A MAJOR UPSET!
SCRATCH
THE DEVIL GUNMEN ADVANCE TO THE SECOND ROUND!
Chapter 74: The Strongest Pentagon
THE DEVIL GUN-MEN?
WHAT ARE THOSE DAMN IDIOTS DOING?
SWSH

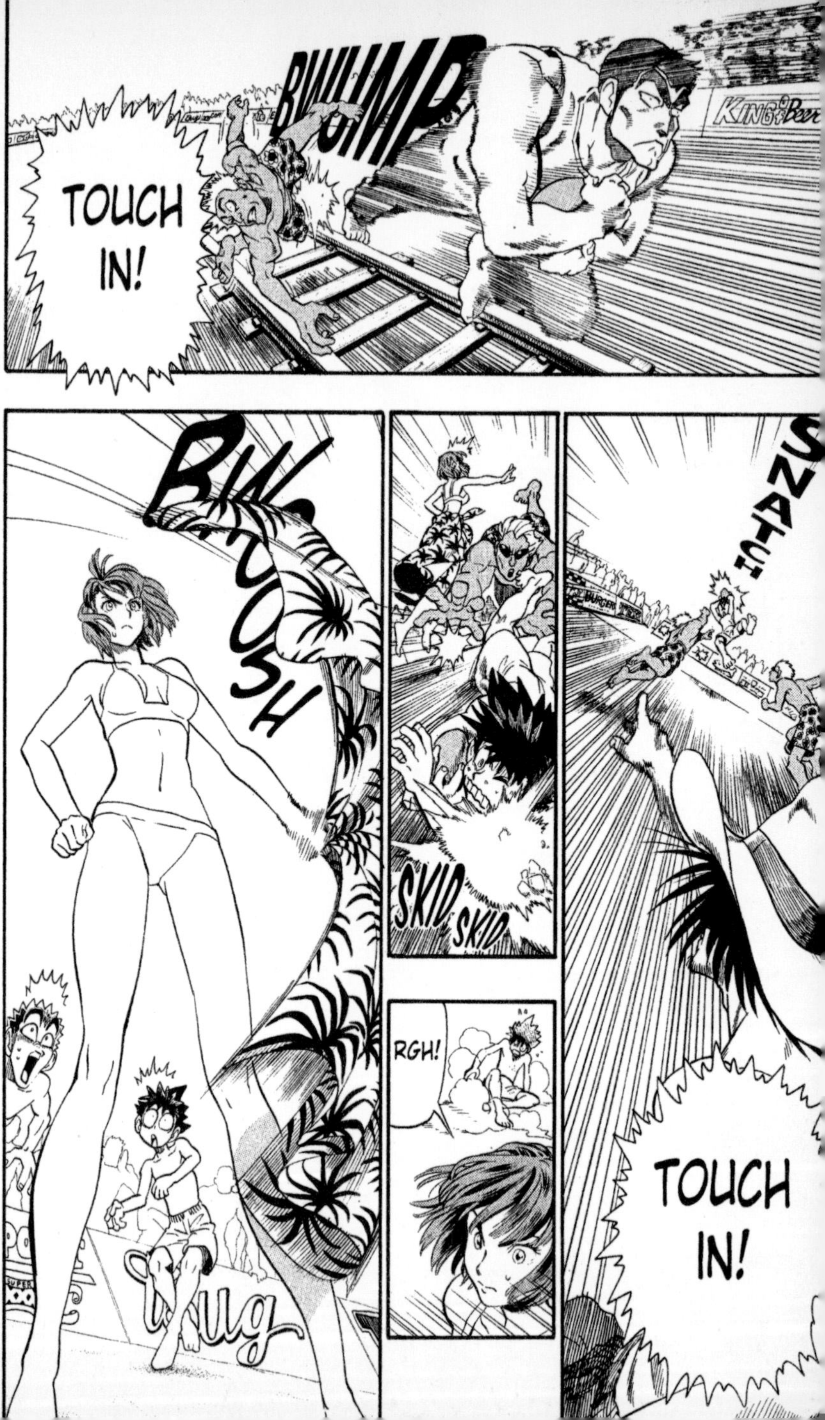

KING Beer
BUMP
TOUCH IN!
SNATCH
TOUCH IN!
SKID SKID
RGH!
BWOOSH

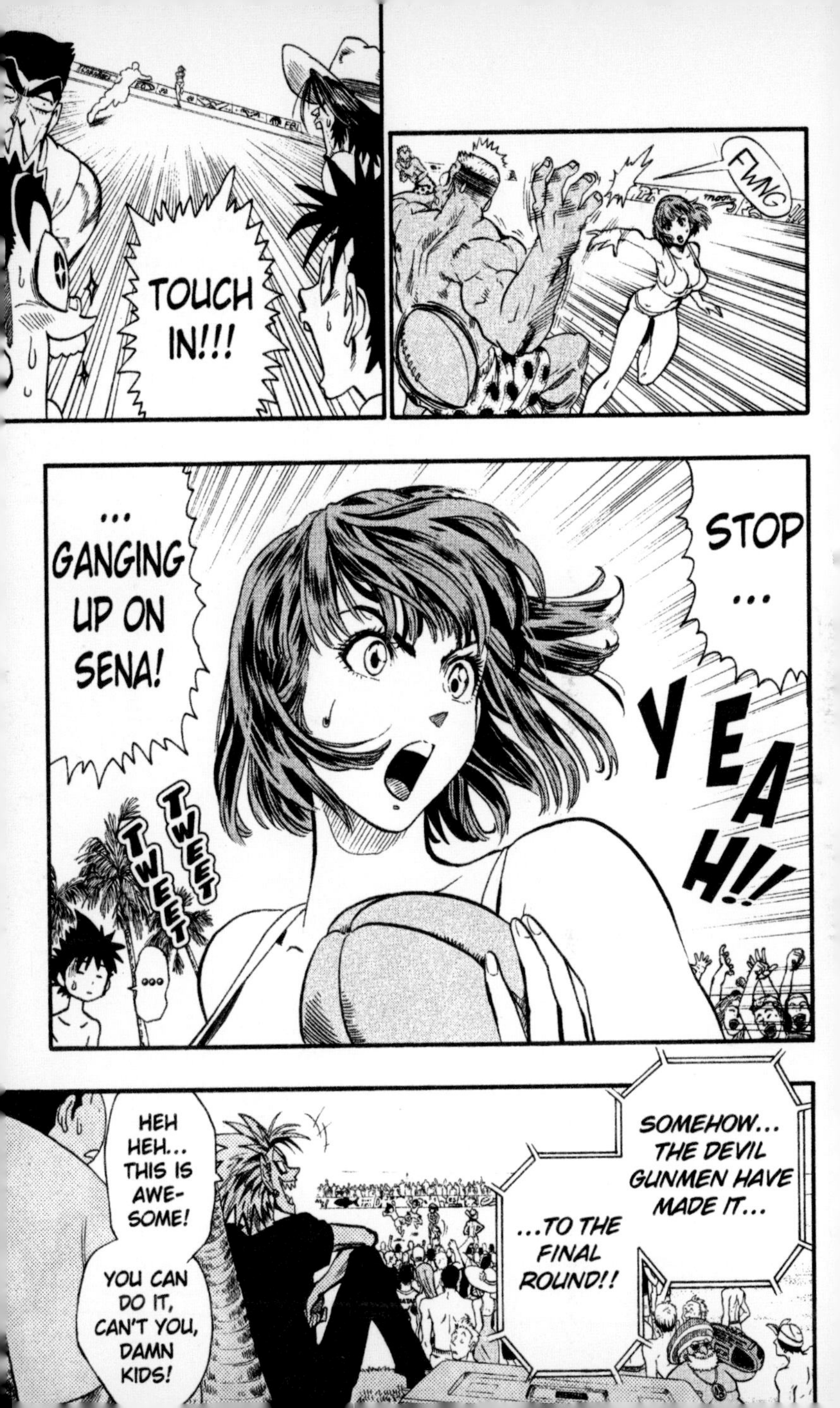
FWNG
TOUCH IN!!!
STOP ...
YEAH!!
... GANGING UP ON SENA!
TWEET TWEET
...
SOMEHOW... THE DEVIL GUNMEN HAVE MADE IT...
...TO THE FINAL ROUND!!
HEH HEH... THIS IS AWESOME!
YOU CAN DO IT, CAN'T YOU, DAMN KIDS!

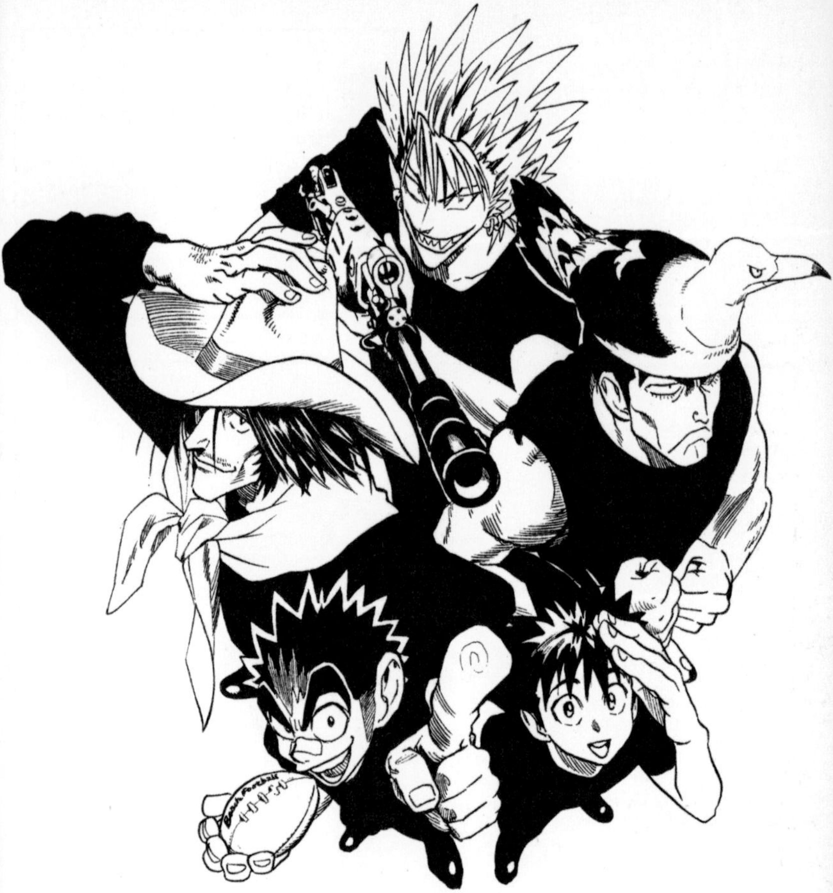

Chapter 74
The Strongest Pentagon

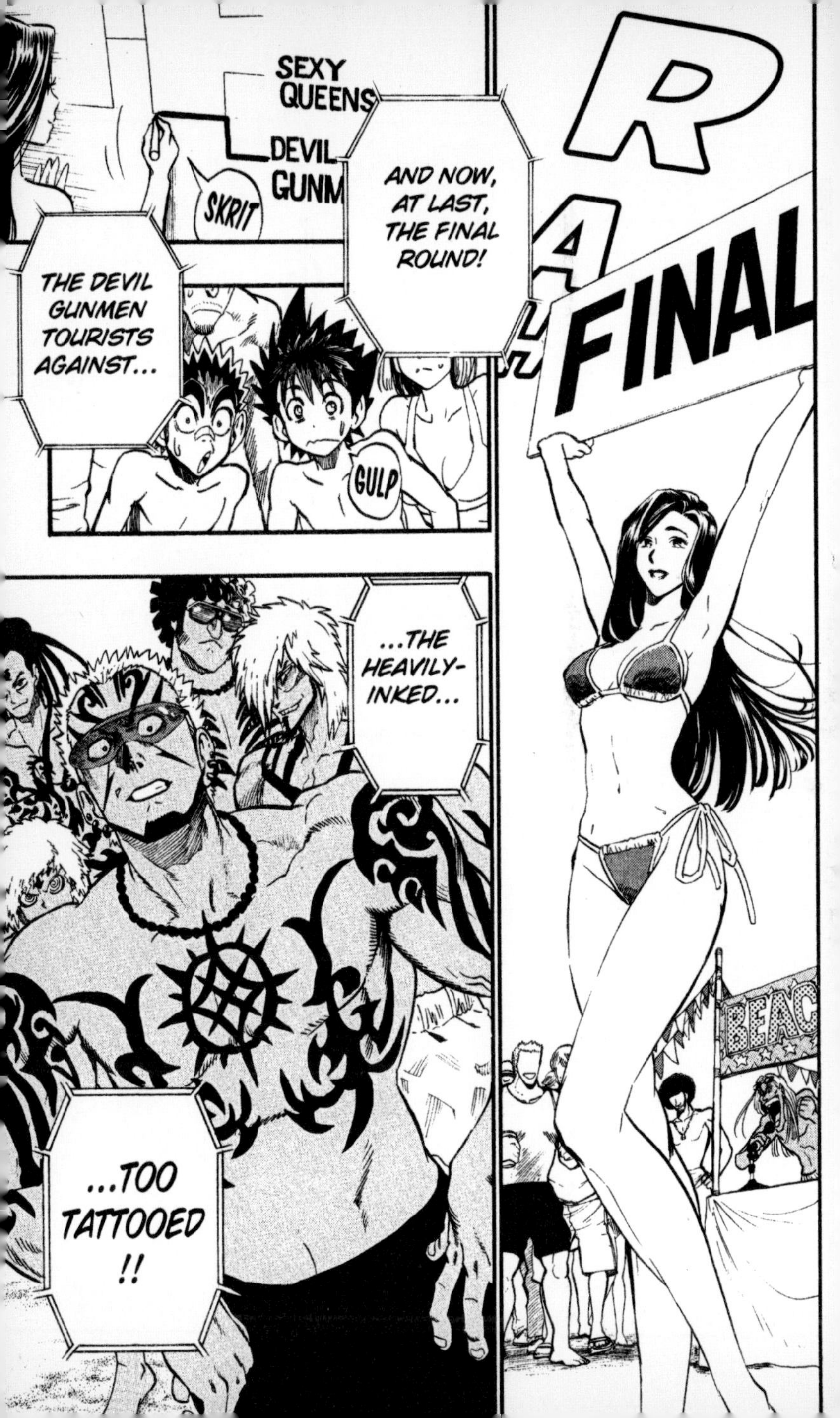
AND NOW, AT LAST, THE FINAL ROUND!
SEXY QUEENS
DEVIL GUNM
SKRIT
THE DEVIL GUNMEN TOURISTS AGAINST...
GULP
...THE HEAVILY-INKED...
...TOO TATTOOED !!
FINAL

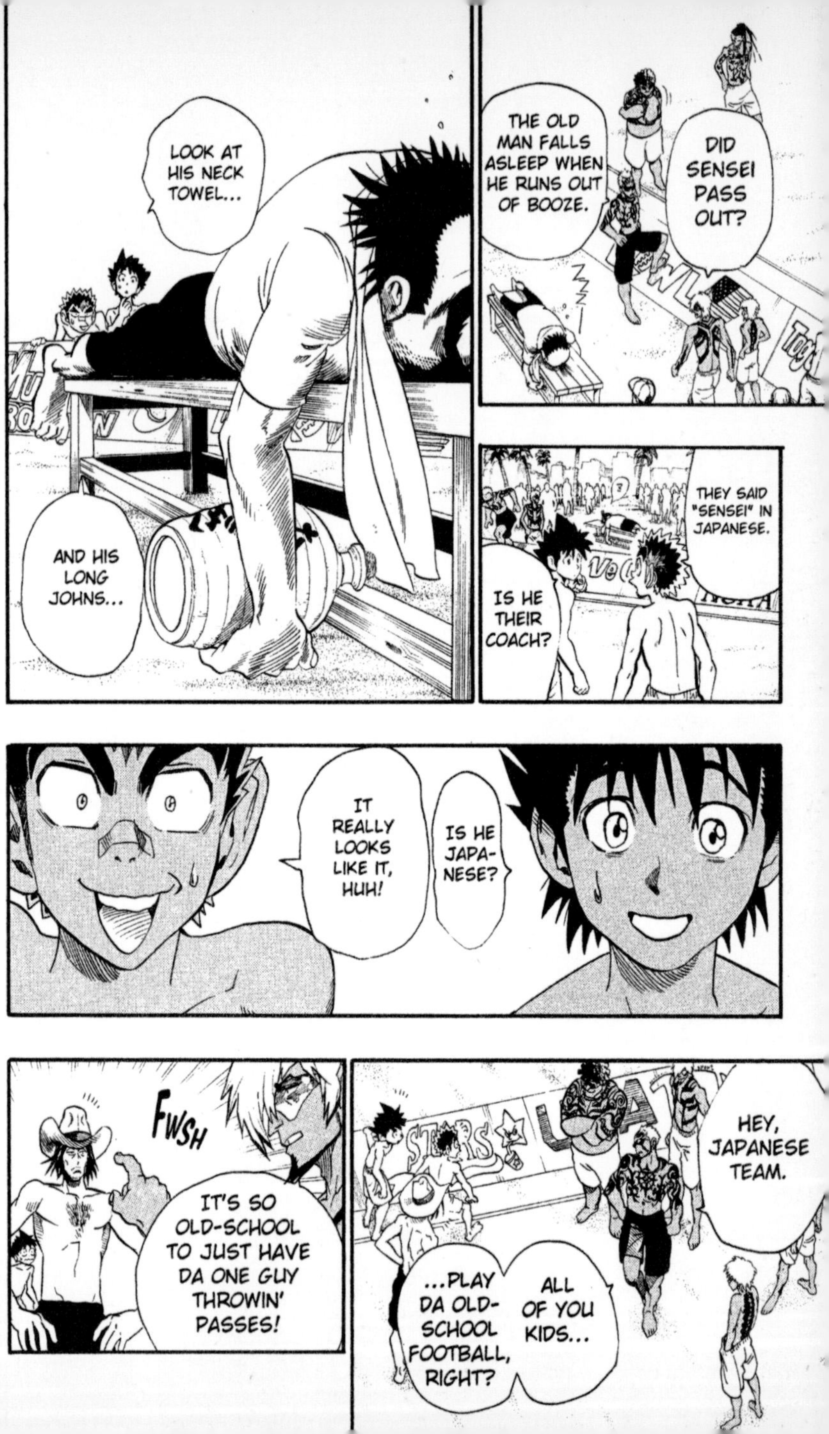
DID SENSEI PASS OUT?
THE OLD MAN FALLS ASLEEP WHEN HE RUNS OUT OF BOOZE.
THEY SAID "SENSEI" IN JAPANESE.
IS HE THEIR COACH?
LOOK AT HIS NECK TOWEL...
AND HIS LONG JOHNS...
IS HE JAPA-NESE?
IT REALLY LOOKS LIKE IT, HUH!
HEY, JAPANESE TEAM.
ALL OF YOU KIDS...
...PLAY DA OLD-SCHOOL FOOTBALL, RIGHT?
FWSH
IT'S SO OLD-SCHOOL TO JUST HAVE DA ONE GUY THROWIN' PASSES!

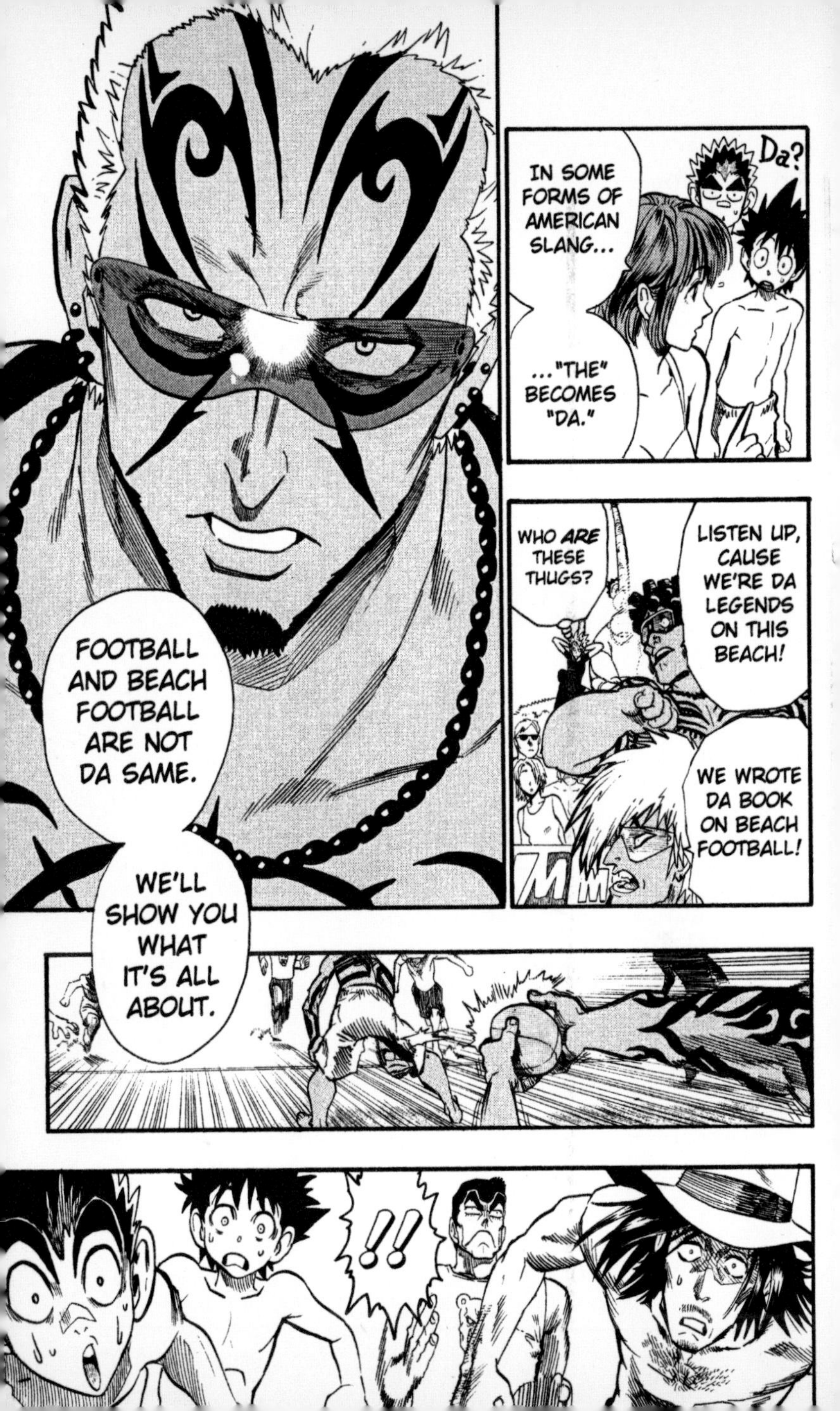
Da?
IN SOME FORMS OF AMERICAN SLANG...
..."THE" BECOMES "DA."
LISTEN UP, CAUSE WE'RE DA LEGENDS ON THIS BEACH!
WHO *ARE* THESE THUGS?
WE WROTE DA BOOK ON BEACH FOOTBALL!
FOOTBALL AND BEACH FOOTBALL ARE NOT DA SAME.
WE'LL SHOW YOU WHAT IT'S ALL ABOUT.
!!

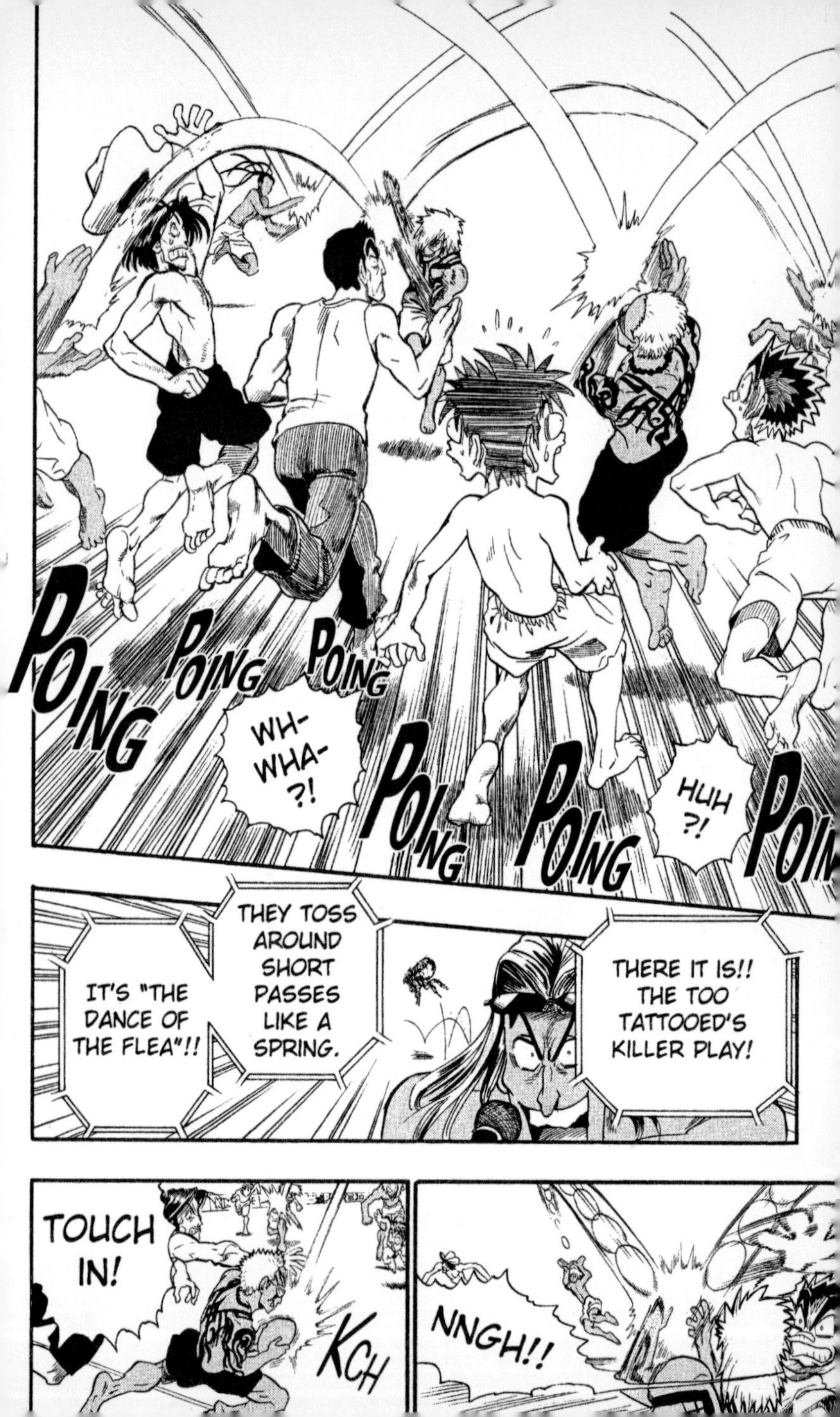
POIN
HUH ?!
POING
POING
WH- WHA- ?!
POING
POING
POING
THERE IT IS!! THE TOO TATTOOED'S KILLER PLAY!
THEY TOSS AROUND SHORT PASSES LIKE A SPRING.
IT'S "THE DANCE OF THE FLEA"!!
NNGH!!
KCH
TOUCH IN!

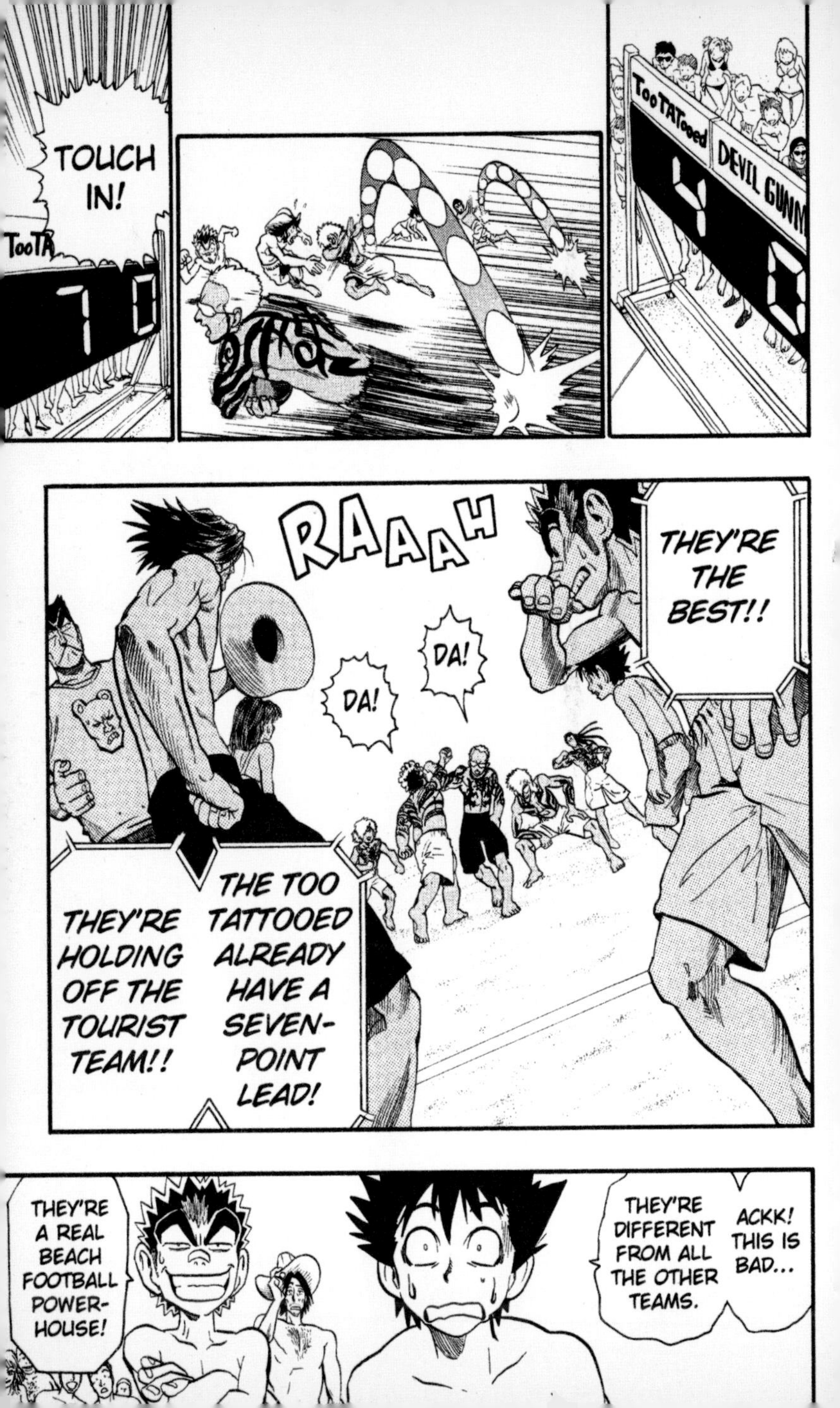
TooTATooed
DEVIL GUNM
TOUCH IN!
TooTA
7 0
RAAAH
THEY'RE THE BEST!!
DA!
DA!
THE TOO TATTOOED ALREADY HAVE A SEVEN-POINT LEAD!
THEY'RE HOLDING OFF THE TOURIST TEAM!!
ACKK! THIS IS BAD...
THEY'RE DIFFERENT FROM ALL THE OTHER TEAMS.
THEY'RE A REAL BEACH FOOTBALL POWER-HOUSE!

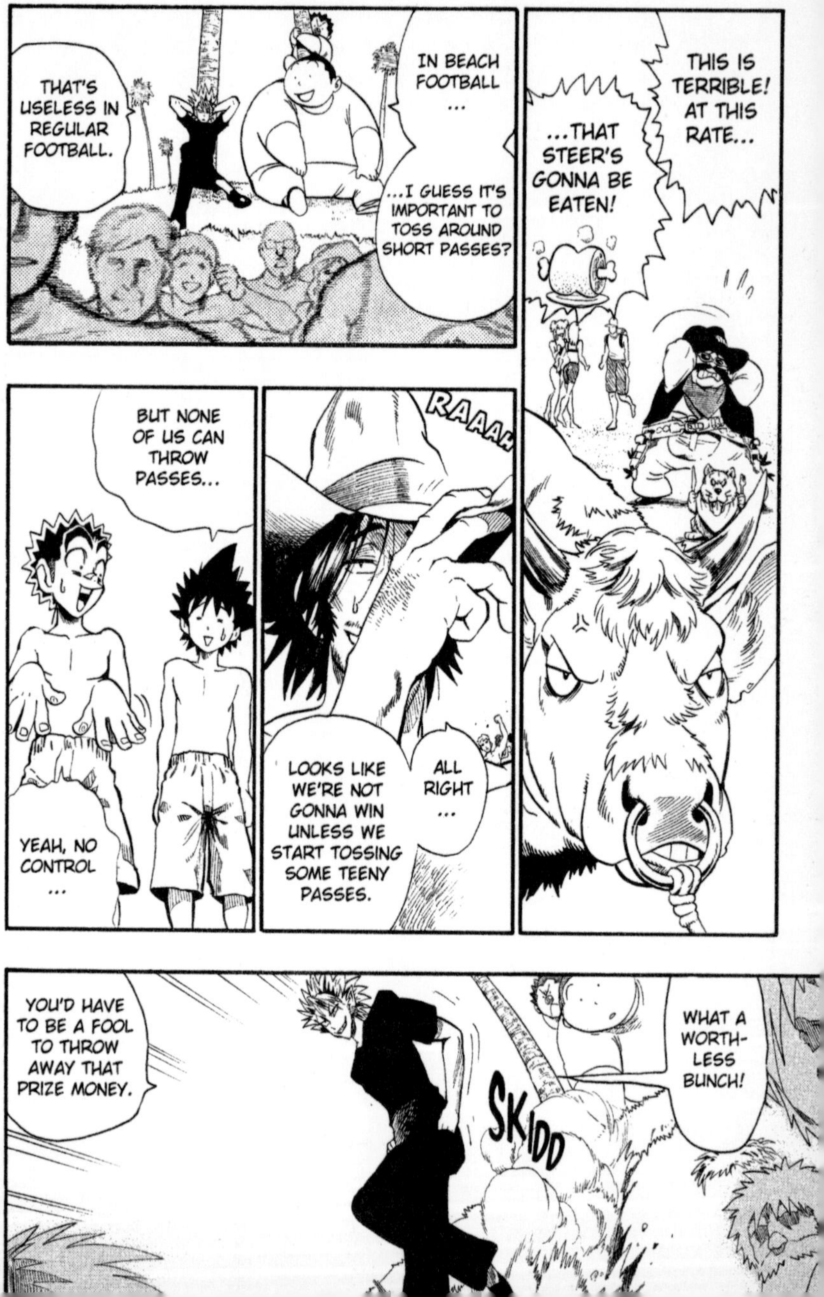
THIS IS TERRIBLE! AT THIS RATE...
...THAT STEER'S GONNA BE EATEN!
IN BEACH FOOTBALL ...
...I GUESS IT'S IMPORTANT TO TOSS AROUND SHORT PASSES?
THAT'S USELESS IN REGULAR FOOTBALL.
RAAAAH
ALL RIGHT ...
LOOKS LIKE WE'RE NOT GONNA WIN UNLESS WE START TOSSING SOME TEENY PASSES.
BUT NONE OF US CAN THROW PASSES...
YEAH, NO CONTROL ...
WHAT A WORTH-LESS BUNCH!
SKIDD
YOU'D HAVE TO BE A FOOL TO THROW AWAY THAT PRIZE MONEY.

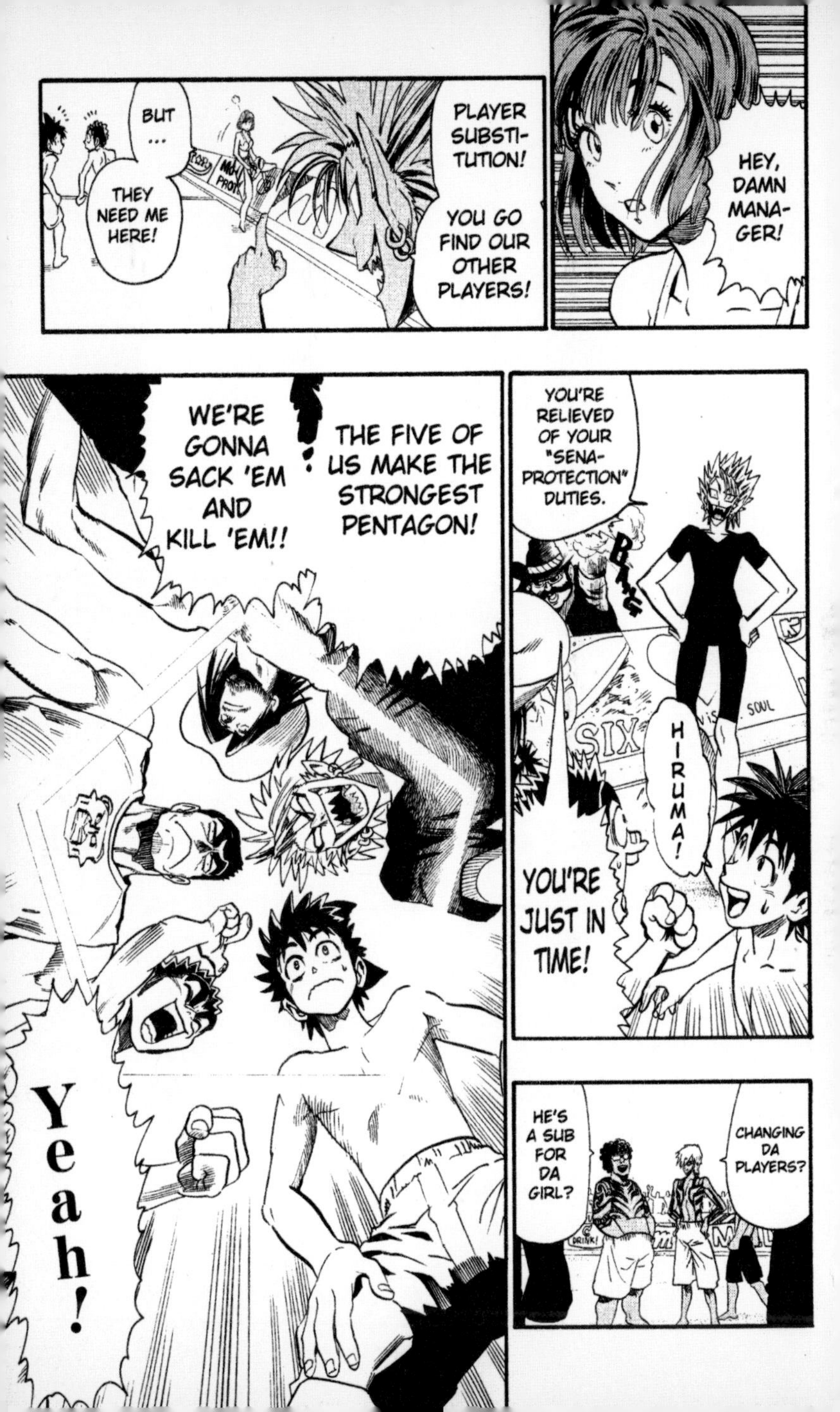
HEY, DAMN MANA-GER!
PLAYER SUBSTI-TUTION!
YOU GO FIND OUR OTHER PLAYERS!
BUT ...
THEY NEED ME HERE!
YOU'RE RELIEVED OF YOUR "SENA-PROTECTION" DUTIES.
BANG
SIX
SOUL
HIRUMA!
YOU'RE JUST IN TIME!
CHANGING DA PLAYERS?
HE'S A SUB FOR DA GIRL?
THE FIVE OF US MAKE THE STRONGEST PENTAGON!
WE'RE GONNA SACK 'EM AND KILL 'EM!!
Yeah!

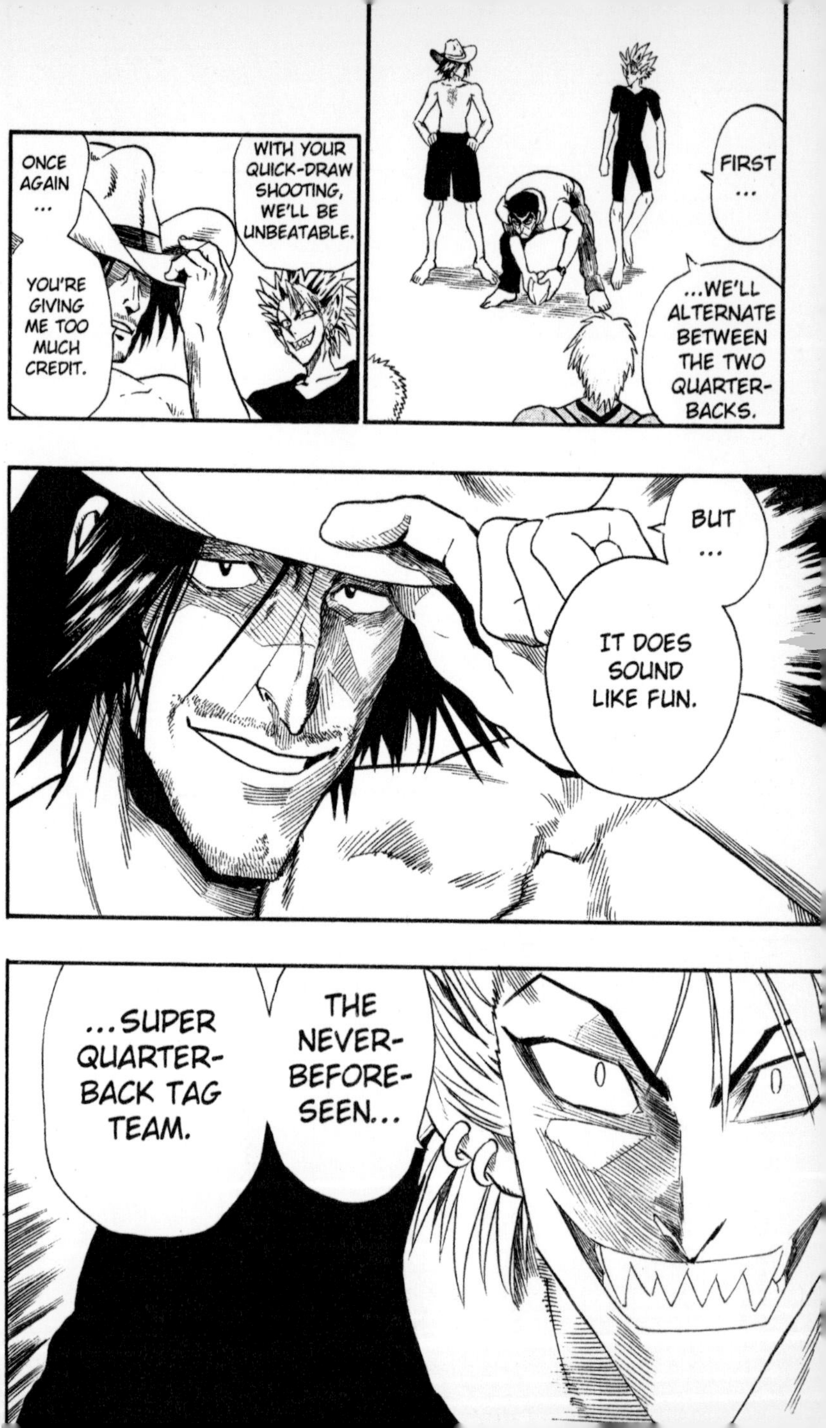
FIRST...
...WE'LL ALTERNATE BETWEEN THE TWO QUARTER-BACKS.
WITH YOUR QUICK-DRAW SHOOTING, WE'LL BE UNBEATABLE.
ONCE AGAIN...
YOU'RE GIVING ME TOO MUCH CREDIT.
BUT...
IT DOES SOUND LIKE FUN.
THE NEVER-BEFORE-SEEN...
...SUPER QUARTER-BACK TAG TEAM.

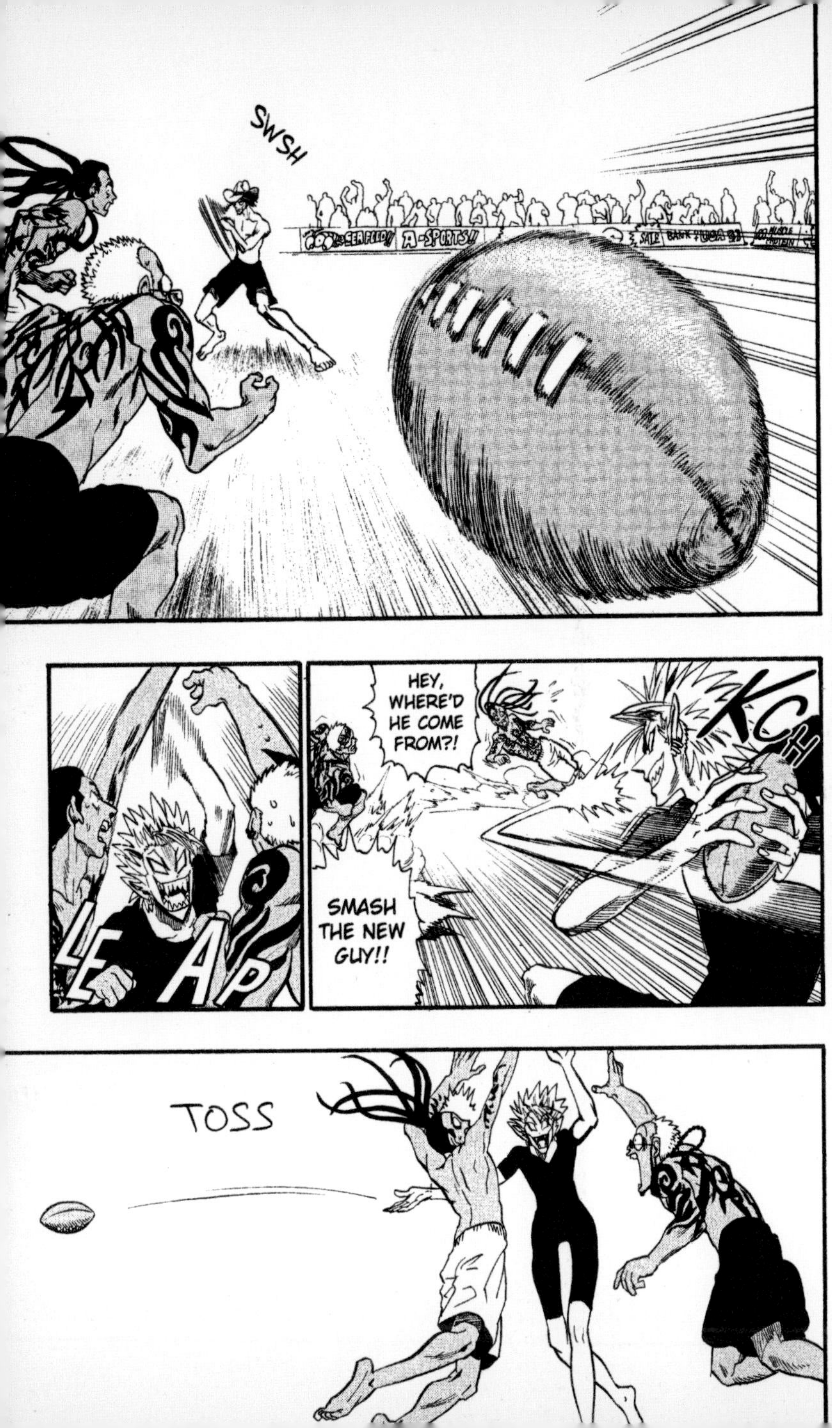
SWSH
A-SPORTS!!
HEY, WHERE'D HE COME FROM?!
KCH
SMASH THE NEW GUY!!
LEAP
TOSS

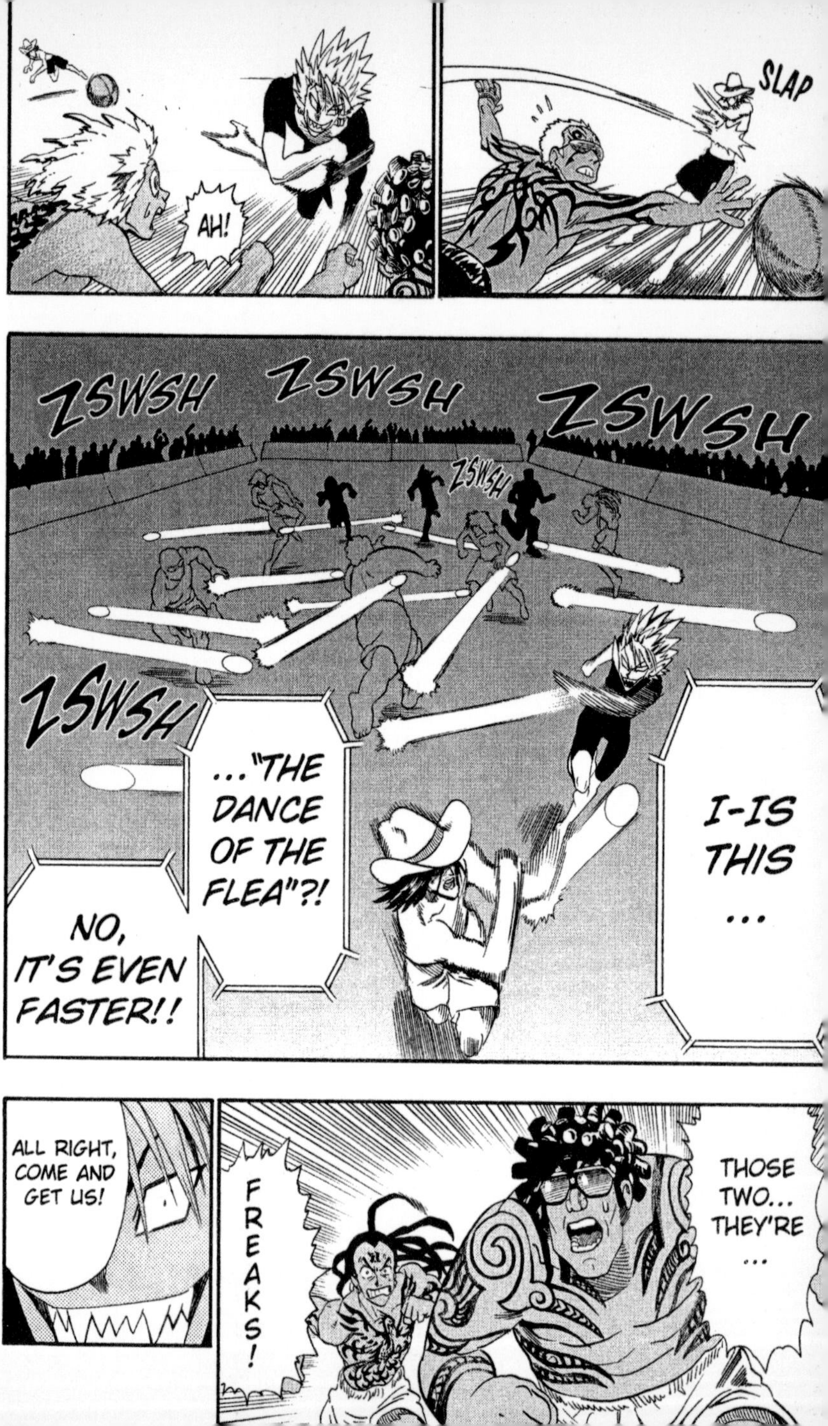
SLAP
AH!
ZSWSH
ZSWSH
ZSWSH
ZSWSH
ZSWSH
I-IS THIS ...
..."THE DANCE OF THE FLEA"?!
NO, IT'S EVEN FASTER!!
THOSE TWO... THEY'RE ...
FREAKS!
ALL RIGHT, COME AND GET US!

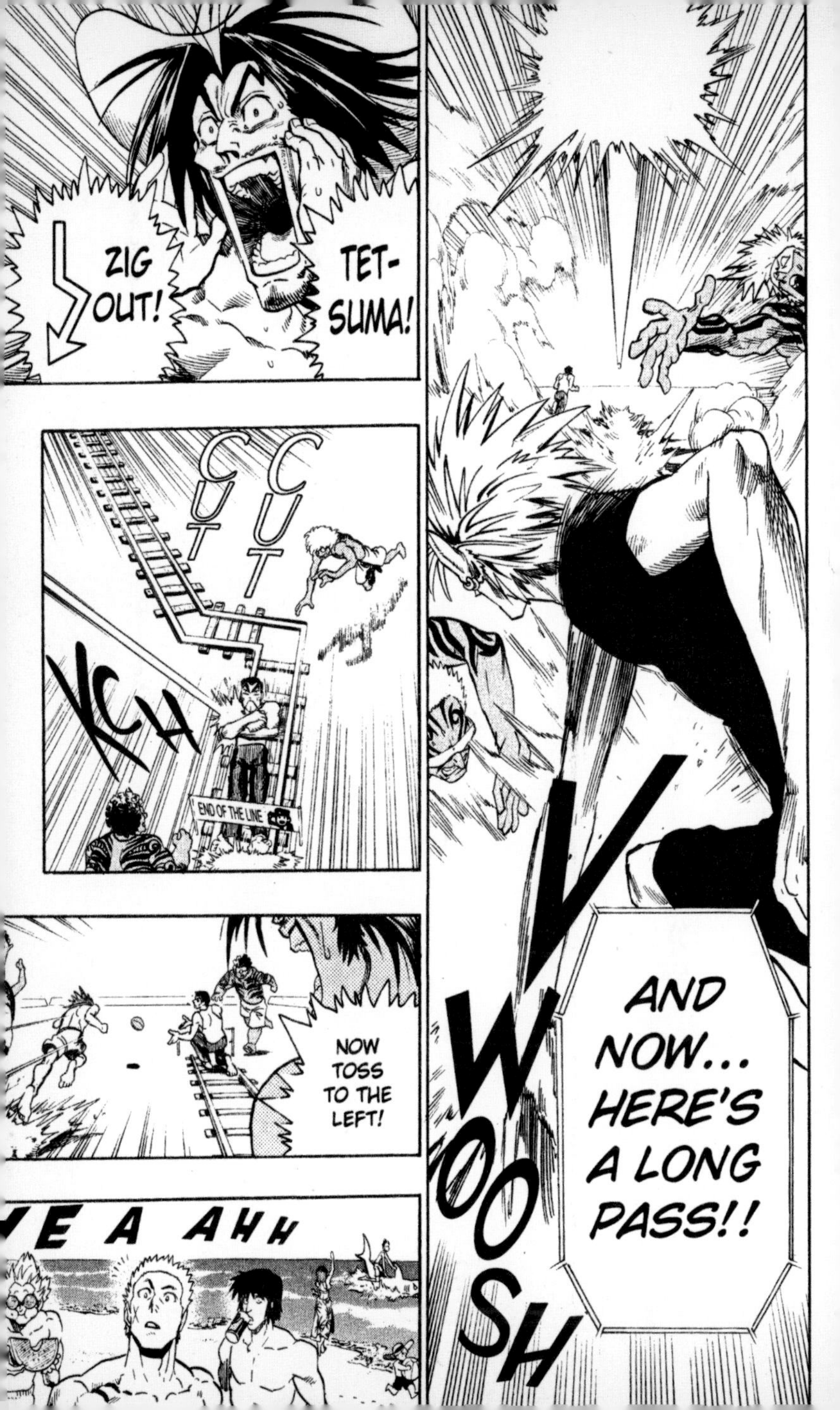
TET-SUMA!
ZIG OUT!
CUT
CUT
KCH
END OF THE LINE
NOW TOSS TO THE LEFT!
EEAAHH
AND NOW... HERE'S A LONG PASS!!
WHOOOOSH

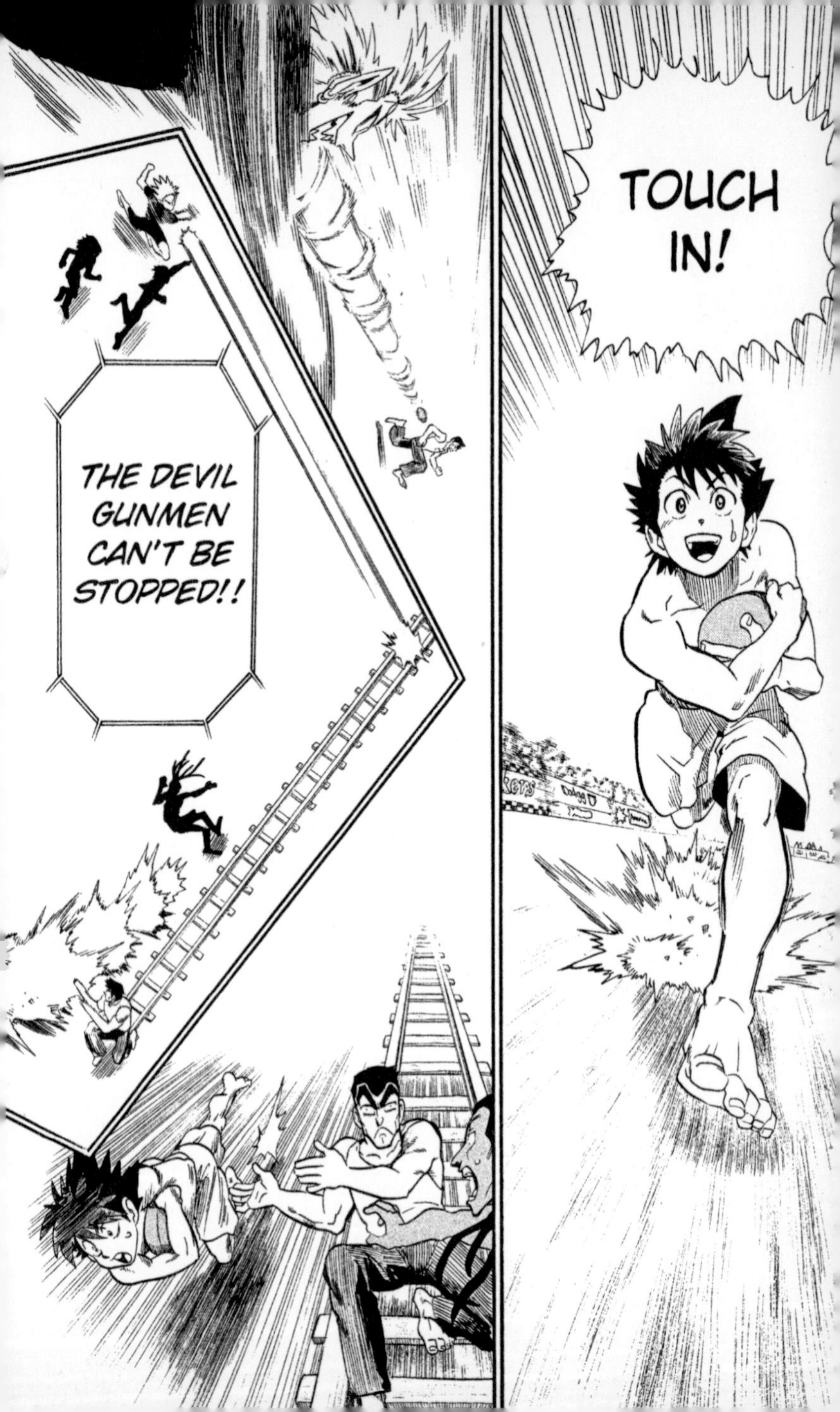
TOUCH IN!
THE DEVIL GUNMEN CAN'T BE STOPPED!!

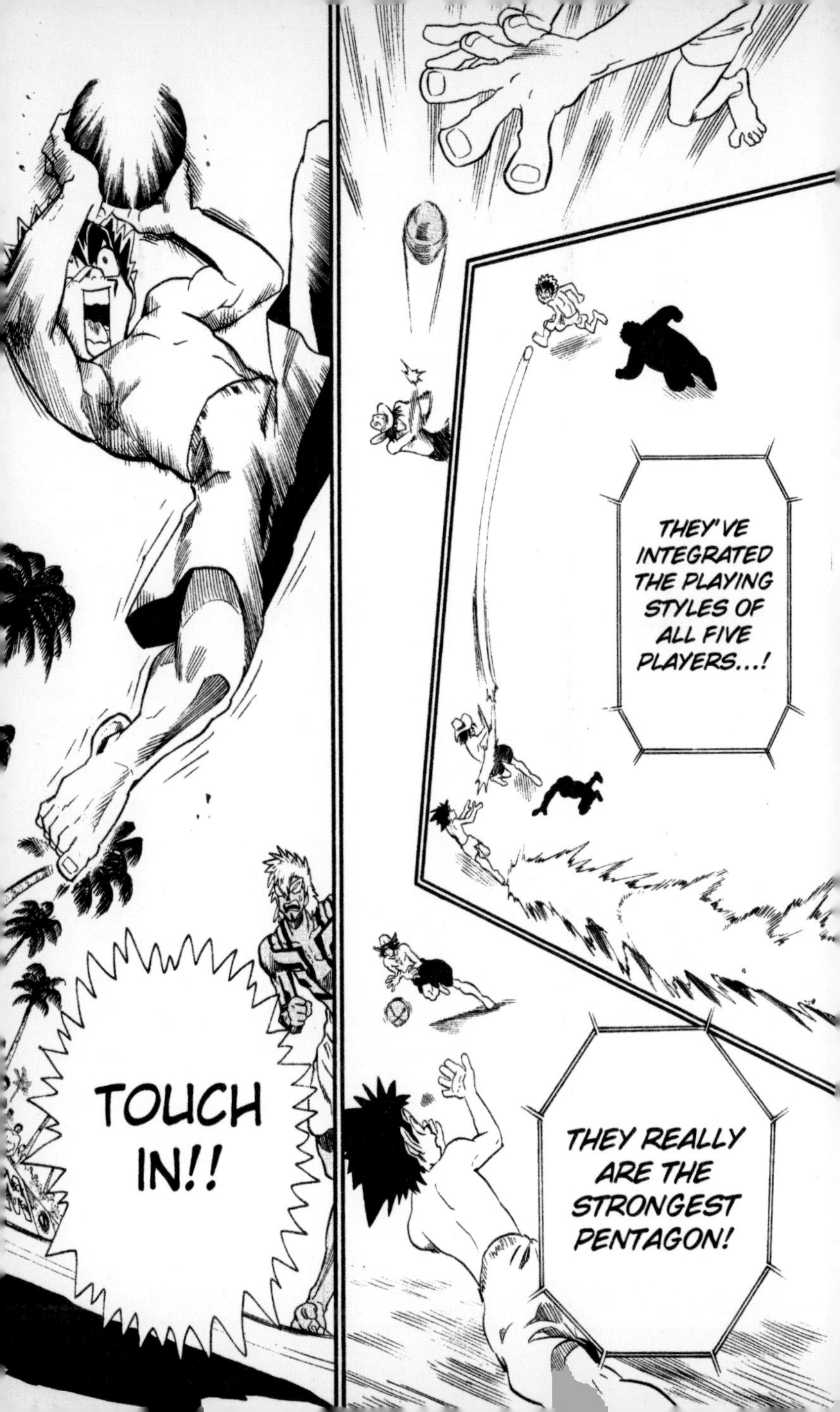
THEY'VE INTEGRATED THE PLAYING STYLES OF ALL FIVE PLAYERS...!
THEY REALLY ARE THE STRONGEST PENTAGON!
TOUCH IN!!

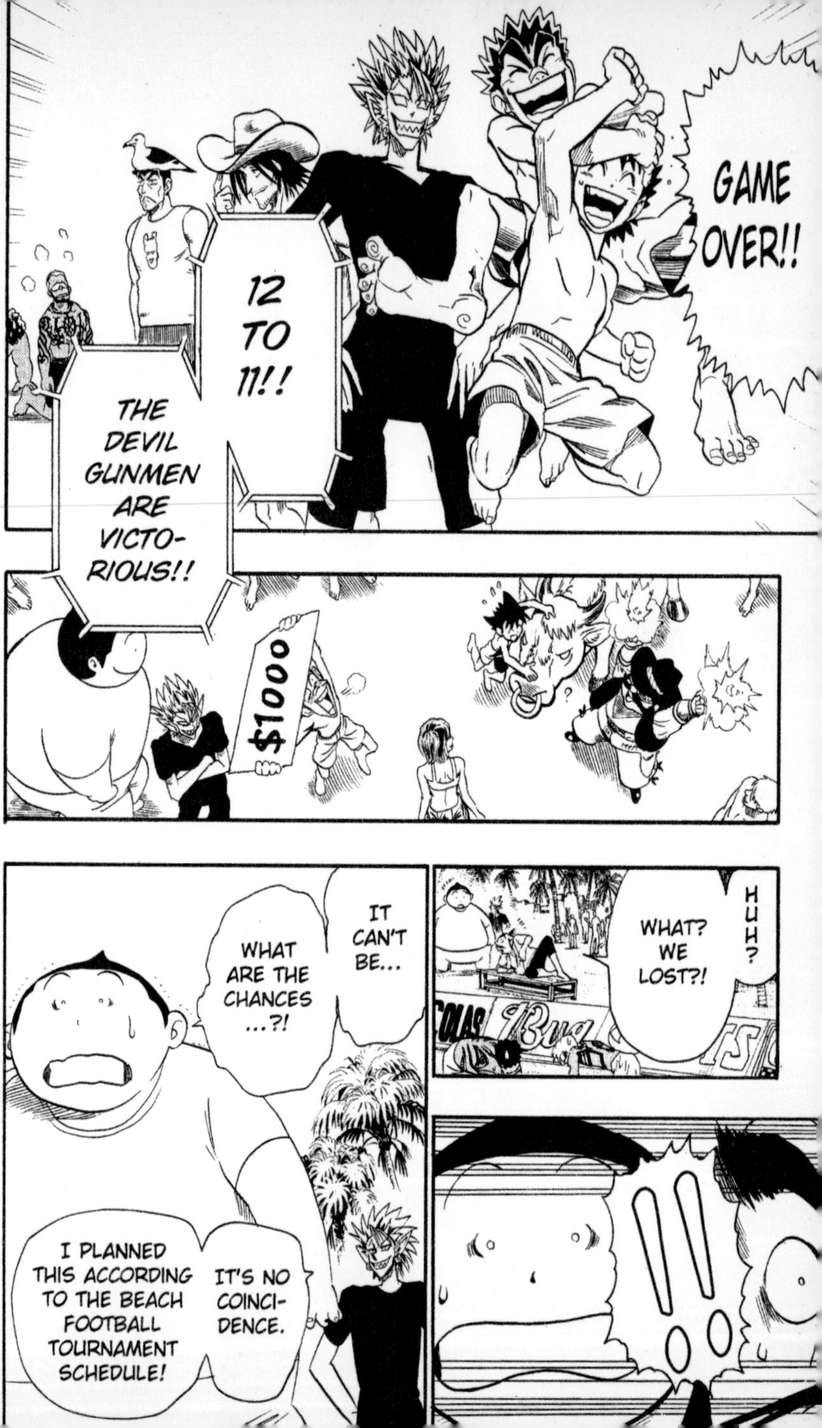
GAME OVER!!
12 TO 11!!
THE DEVIL GUNMEN ARE VICTORIOUS!!
$1000
HUH?
WHAT? WE LOST?!
!!
IT CAN'T BE...
WHAT ARE THE CHANCES ...?!
IT'S NO COINCIDENCE.
I PLANNED THIS ACCORDING TO THE BEACH FOOTBALL TOURNAMENT SCHEDULE!

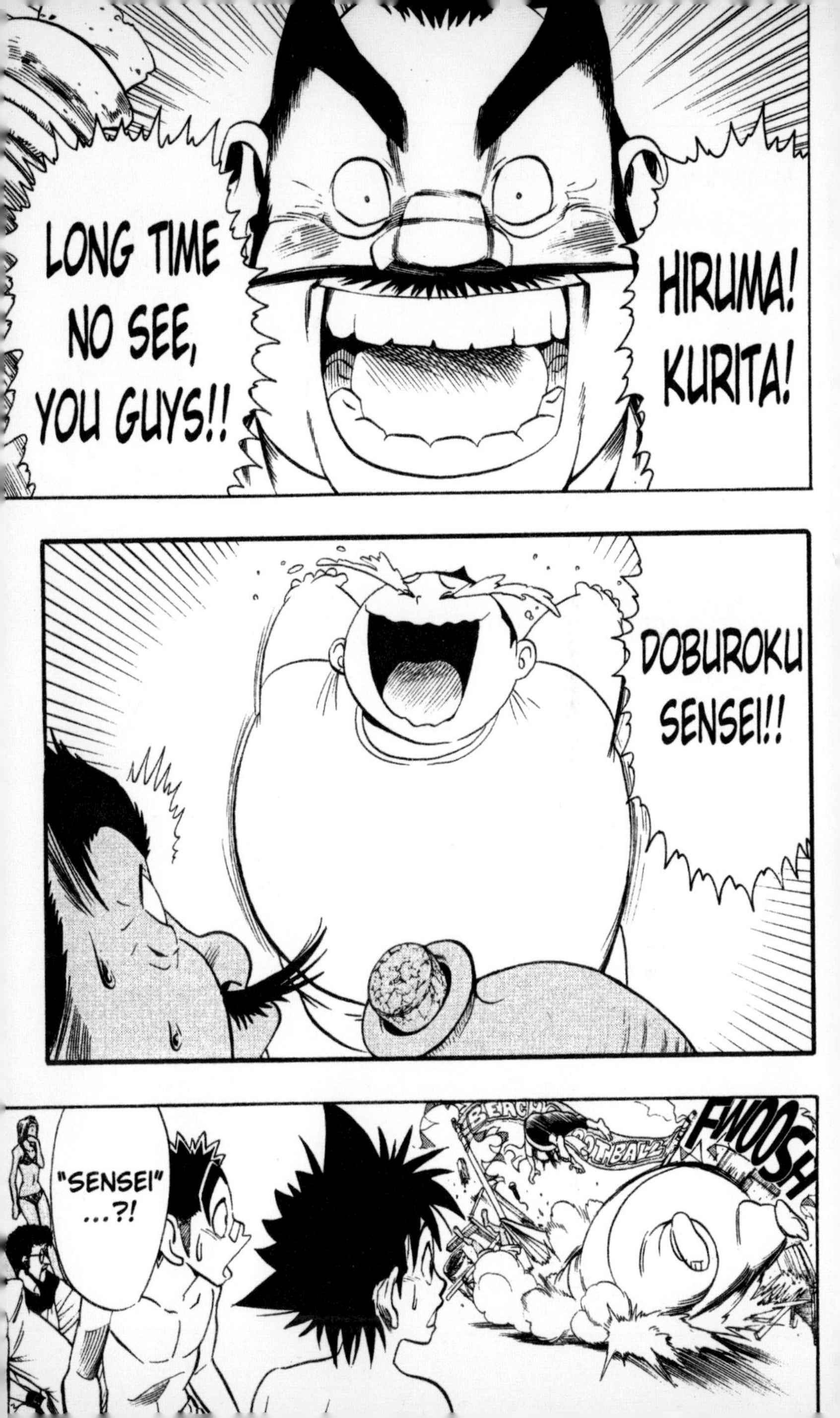
HIRUMA! KURITA!
LONG TIME NO SEE, YOU GUYS!!
DOBUROKU SENSEI!!
FWOOSH
"SENSEI" ...?!

Eyeshield 21 Survey Corner **Devil Bat 021**

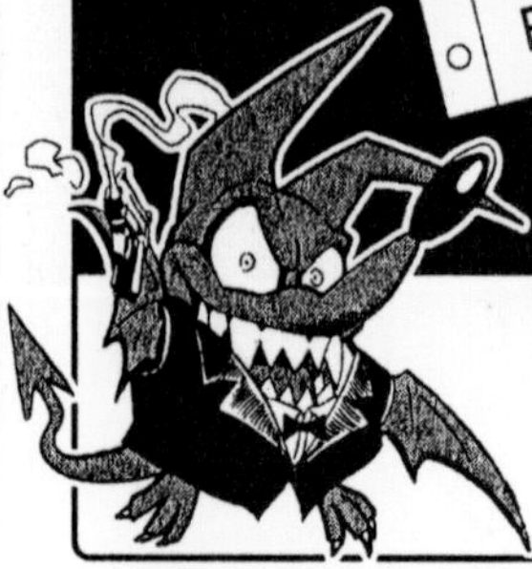

Investigation File #011

Find out how Komusubi got into Deimon High School!!

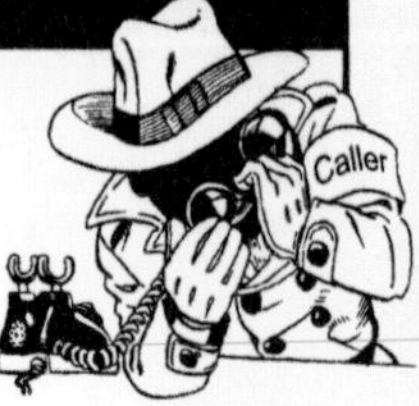
Caller

DAIKICHI KOMUSUBI NEVER SPEAKS AT ALL. HOW DID HE EVER MAKE IT THROUGH THE ADMISSIONS INTERVIEW AT DEIMON?

Y.G., Hokkaido

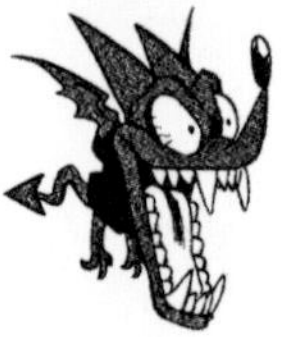

HIS NAME, DAIKICHI, MEANS "GOOD FORTUNE," DOESN'T IT?!
THE GYM TEACHER, WHO UNDERSTANDS THE "LANGUAGE OF STRONG MEN," WAS ON THE INTERVIEW COMMITTEE!

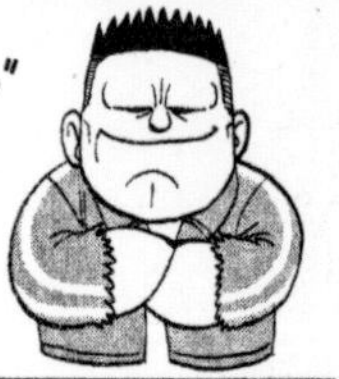

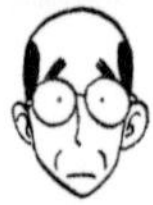

WELL THEN, PLEASE TELL US WHY YOU WOULD LIKE TO GO TO DEIMON HIGH SCHOOL.

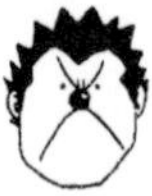

UMFF!!

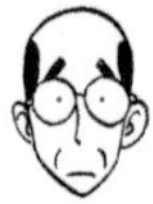

...??

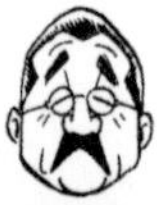

(THIS KID WILL NEVER MAKE IT...)

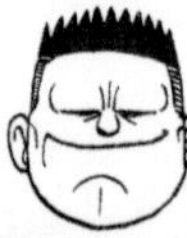

WHAT? DID YOU SAY, "I WANT TO STRIVE FOR THE BEST IN MY STUDIES AS WELL AS IN SPORTS, SO MY IDEAL SCHOOL WOULD HAVE AN ACTIVE ATHLETIC PROGRAM. DEIMON VALUES ITS STUDENTS' AUTONOMY, WHICH ENCOURAGES VIGOROUS INDEPENDENT EXTRACURRICULAR ACTIVITIES. THAT'S THE KIND OF ACADEMIC ENVIRONMENT TO WHICH I ASPIRE"?

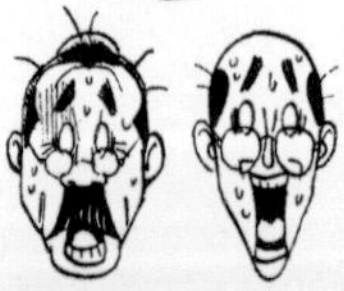

WHA--?! HE DIDN'T SAY THAT!!!

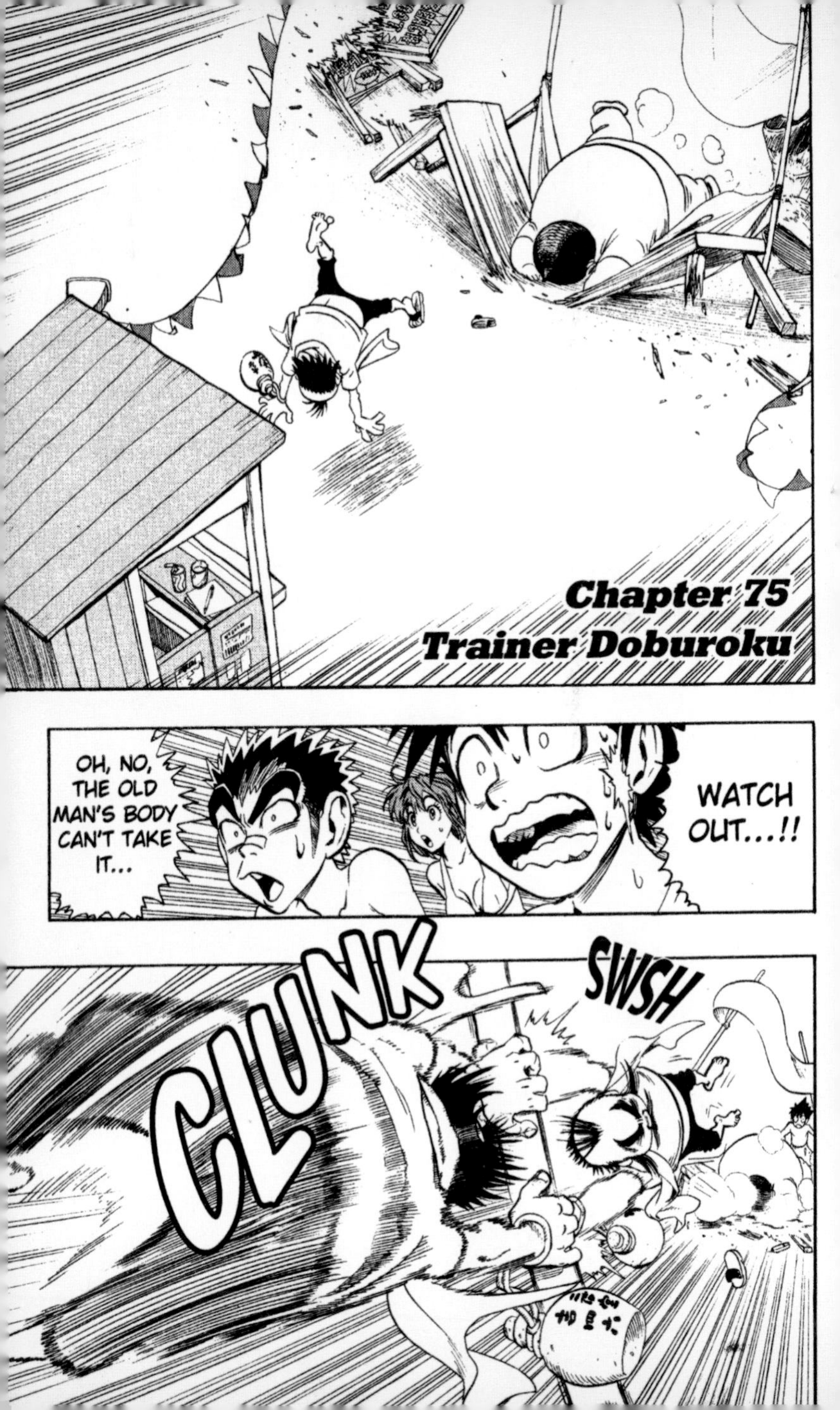
Chapter 75
Trainer Doburoku
WATCH OUT...!!
OH, NO, THE OLD MAN'S BODY CAN'T TAKE IT...
SWSH
CLUNK

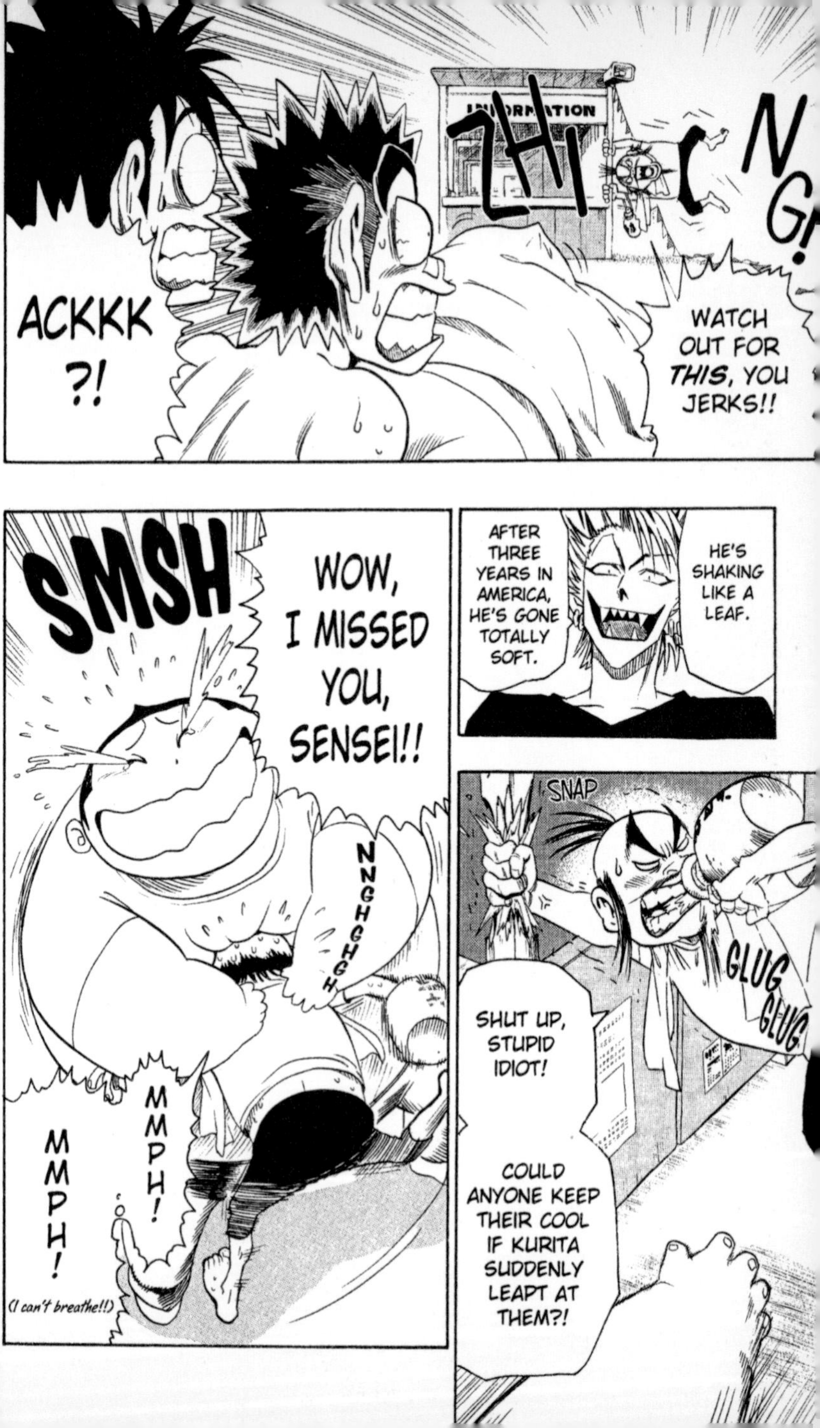
WATCH OUT FOR THIS, YOU JERKS!!
ZHING!
ACKKK ?!
HE'S SHAKING LIKE A LEAF.
AFTER THREE YEARS IN AMERICA, HE'S GONE TOTALLY SOFT.
SNAP
GLUG GLUG
SHUT UP, STUPID IDIOT!
COULD ANYONE KEEP THEIR COOL IF KURITA SUDDENLY LEAPT AT THEM?!
WOW, I MISSED YOU, SENSEI!!
SMSH
NNGHGHGHGH
MMPH!
MMPH!
(I can't breathe!!)

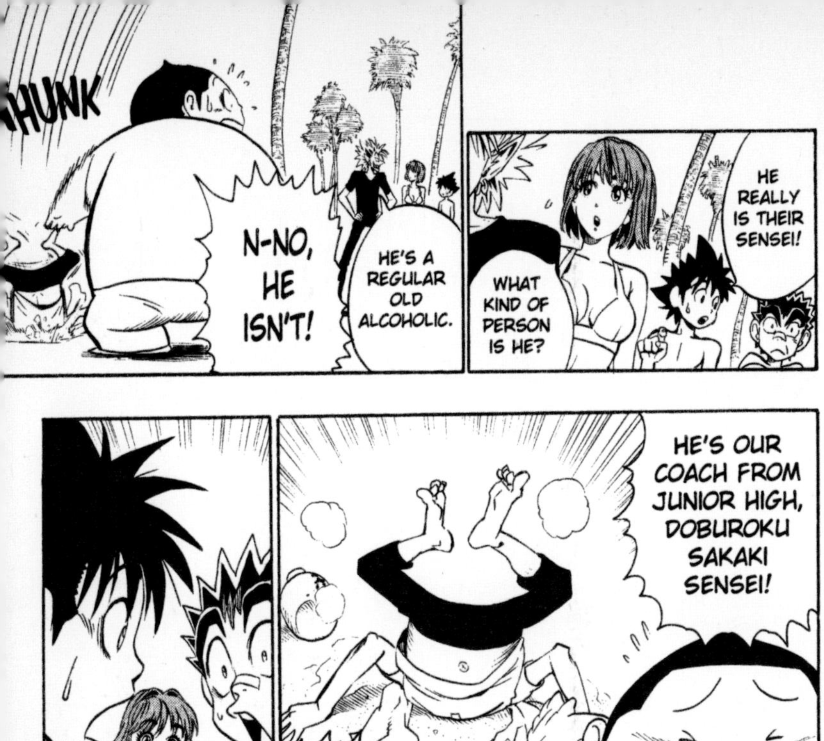
HE REALLY IS THEIR SENSEI!
WHAT KIND OF PERSON IS HE?
HE'S A REGULAR OLD ALCOHOLIC.
N-NO, HE ISN'T!
THUNK
HE'S OUR COACH FROM JUNIOR HIGH, DOBUROKU SAKAKI SENSEI!
HE'S THE ONE WHO TAUGHT ME AND HIRUMA AND MUSASHI ...
...HOW TO PLAY FOOT-BALL!

*DOBUROKU'S NAME IS A PLAY ON DIFFERENT WORDS FOR SAKÉ.

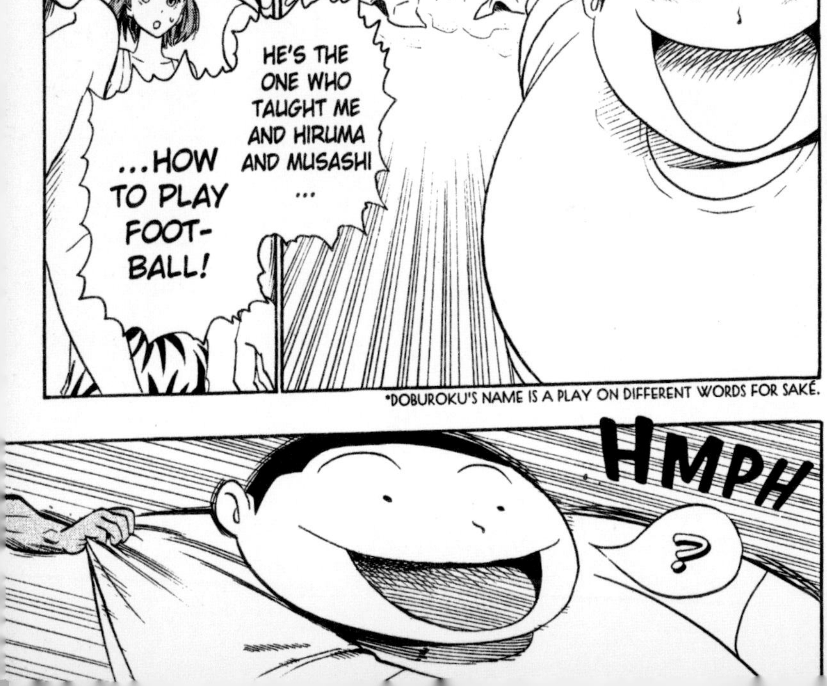
HMPH
?

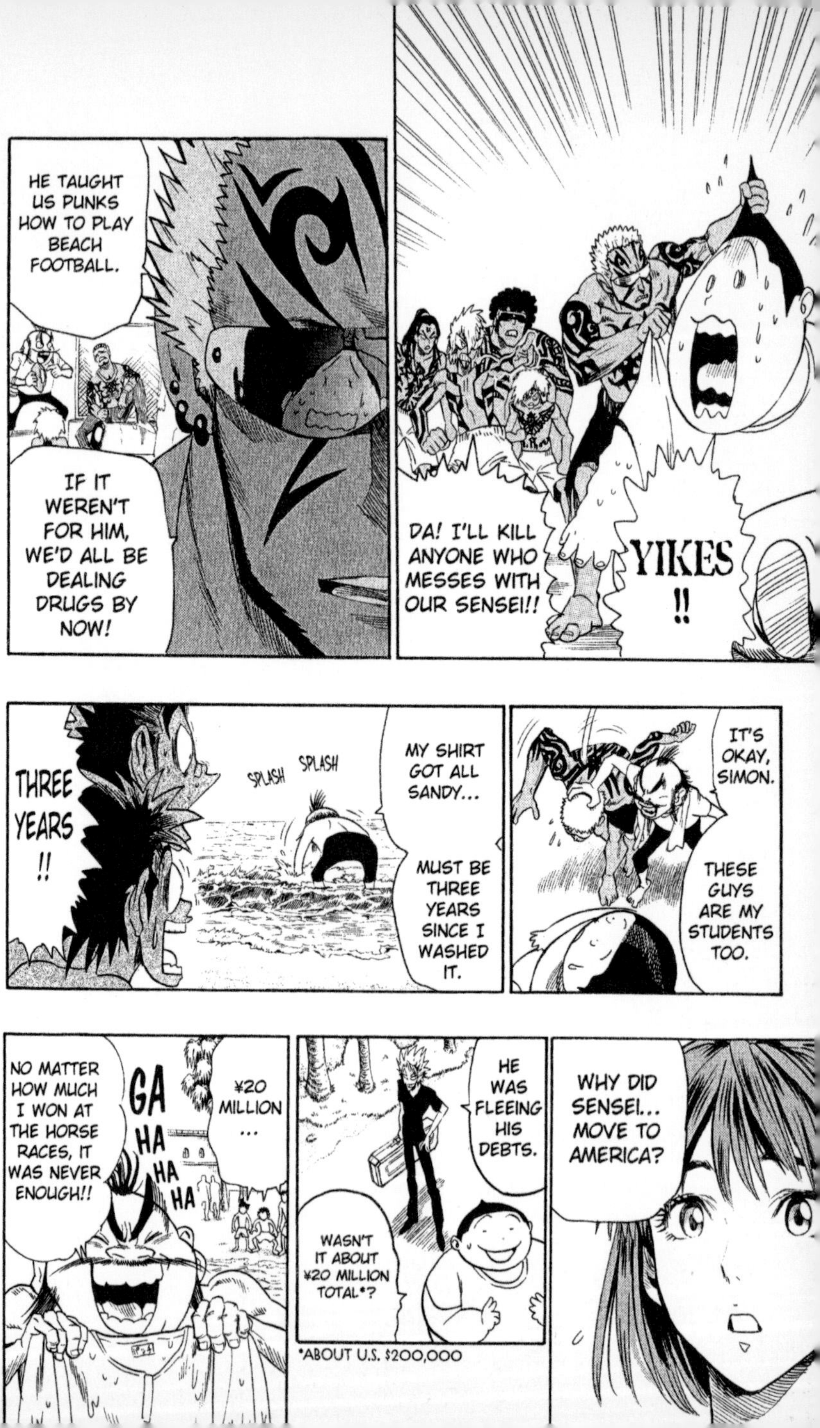
DA! I'LL KILL ANYONE WHO MESSES WITH OUR SENSEI!!
YIKES!!
HE TAUGHT US PUNKS HOW TO PLAY BEACH FOOTBALL.
IF IT WEREN'T FOR HIM, WE'D ALL BE DEALING DRUGS BY NOW!
IT'S OKAY, SIMON.
THESE GUYS ARE MY STUDENTS TOO.
MY SHIRT GOT ALL SANDY...
SPLASH
SPLASH
MUST BE THREE YEARS SINCE I WASHED IT.
THREE YEARS!!
WHY DID SENSEI... MOVE TO AMERICA?
HE WAS FLEEING HIS DEBTS.
WASN'T IT ABOUT ¥20 MILLION TOTAL*?
¥20 MILLION...
GA HA HA HA
NO MATTER HOW MUCH I WON AT THE HORSE RACES, IT WAS NEVER ENOUGH!!

*ABOUT U.S. $200,000

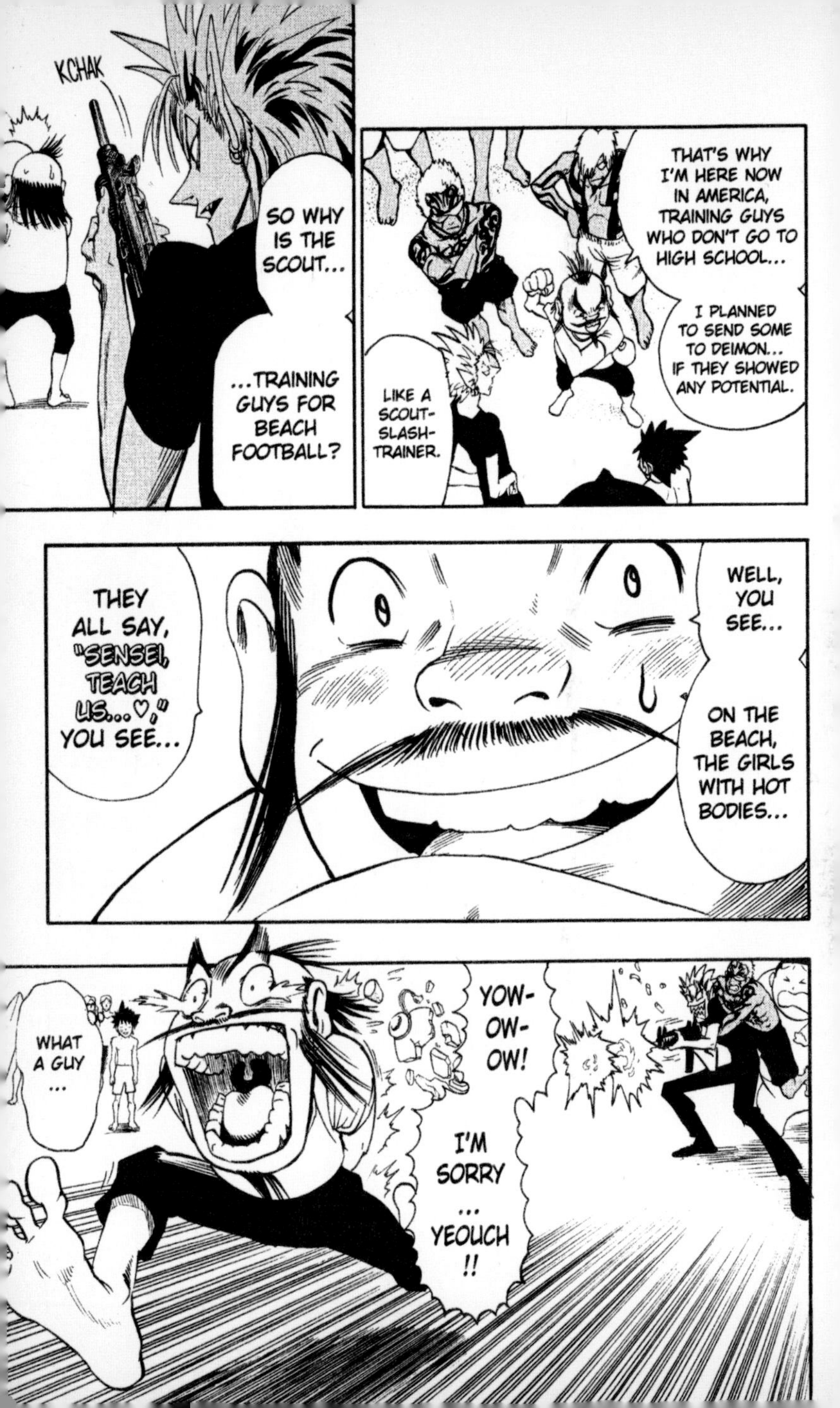
THAT'S WHY I'M HERE NOW IN AMERICA, TRAINING GUYS WHO DON'T GO TO HIGH SCHOOL...
I PLANNED TO SEND SOME TO DEIMON... IF THEY SHOWED ANY POTENTIAL.
LIKE A SCOUT-SLASH-TRAINER.
KCHAK
SO WHY IS THE SCOUT...
...TRAINING GUYS FOR BEACH FOOTBALL?
WELL, YOU SEE...
ON THE BEACH, THE GIRLS WITH HOT BODIES...
THEY ALL SAY, "SENSEI, TEACH US...♡," YOU SEE...
YOW-OW-OW!
I'M SORRY ... YEOUCH !!
WHAT A GUY ...

Chapter 75
Trainer Doburoku

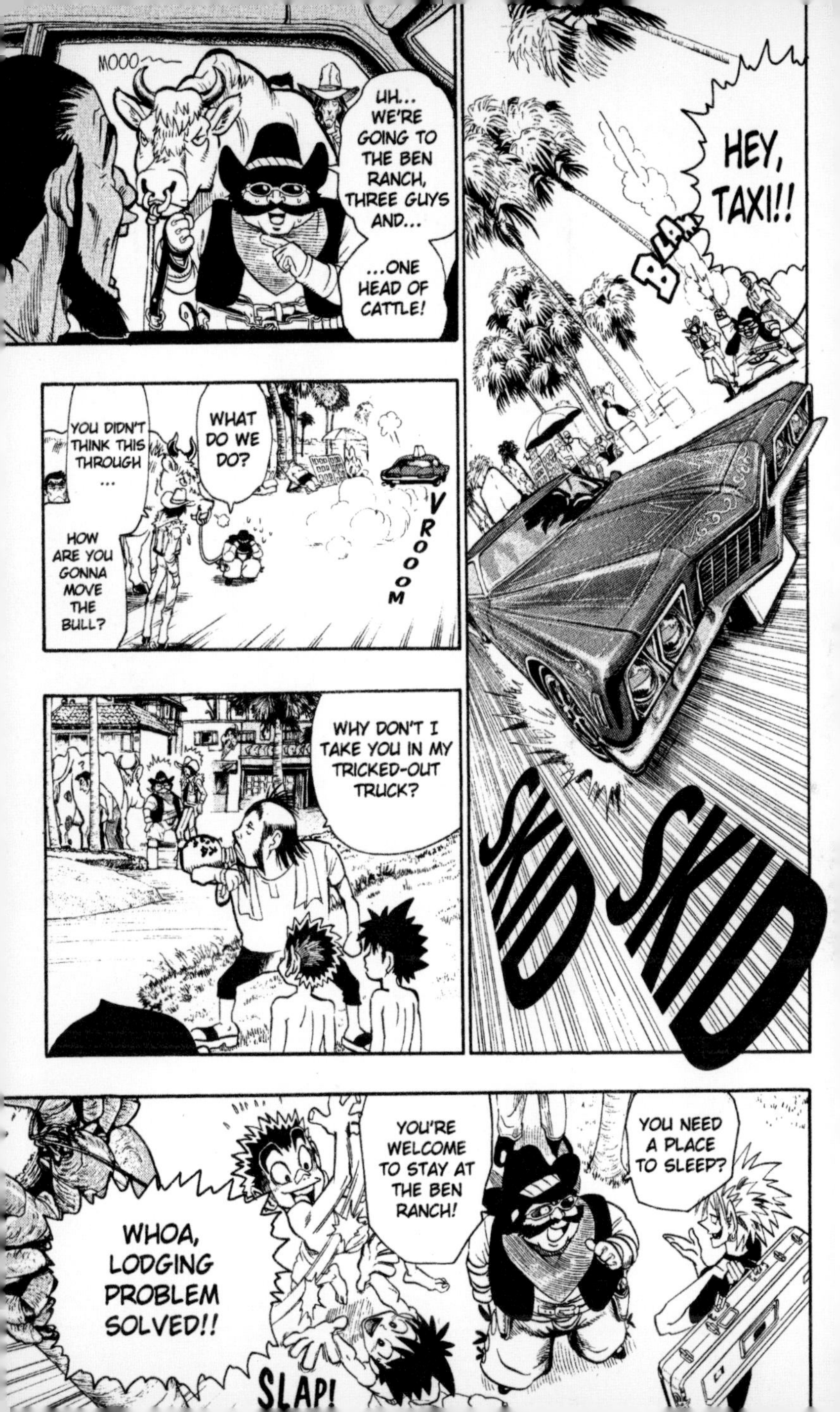
HEY, TAXI!!
BLAM
SKID SKID
UH... WE'RE GOING TO THE BEN RANCH, THREE GUYS AND...
...ONE HEAD OF CATTLE!
MOOO
VROOOOM
WHAT DO WE DO?
YOU DIDN'T THINK THIS THROUGH ...
HOW ARE YOU GONNA MOVE THE BULL?
WHY DON'T I TAKE YOU IN MY TRICKED-OUT TRUCK?
YOU NEED A PLACE TO SLEEP?
YOU'RE WELCOME TO STAY AT THE BEN RANCH!
WHOA, LODGING PROBLEM SOLVED!!
SLAP!

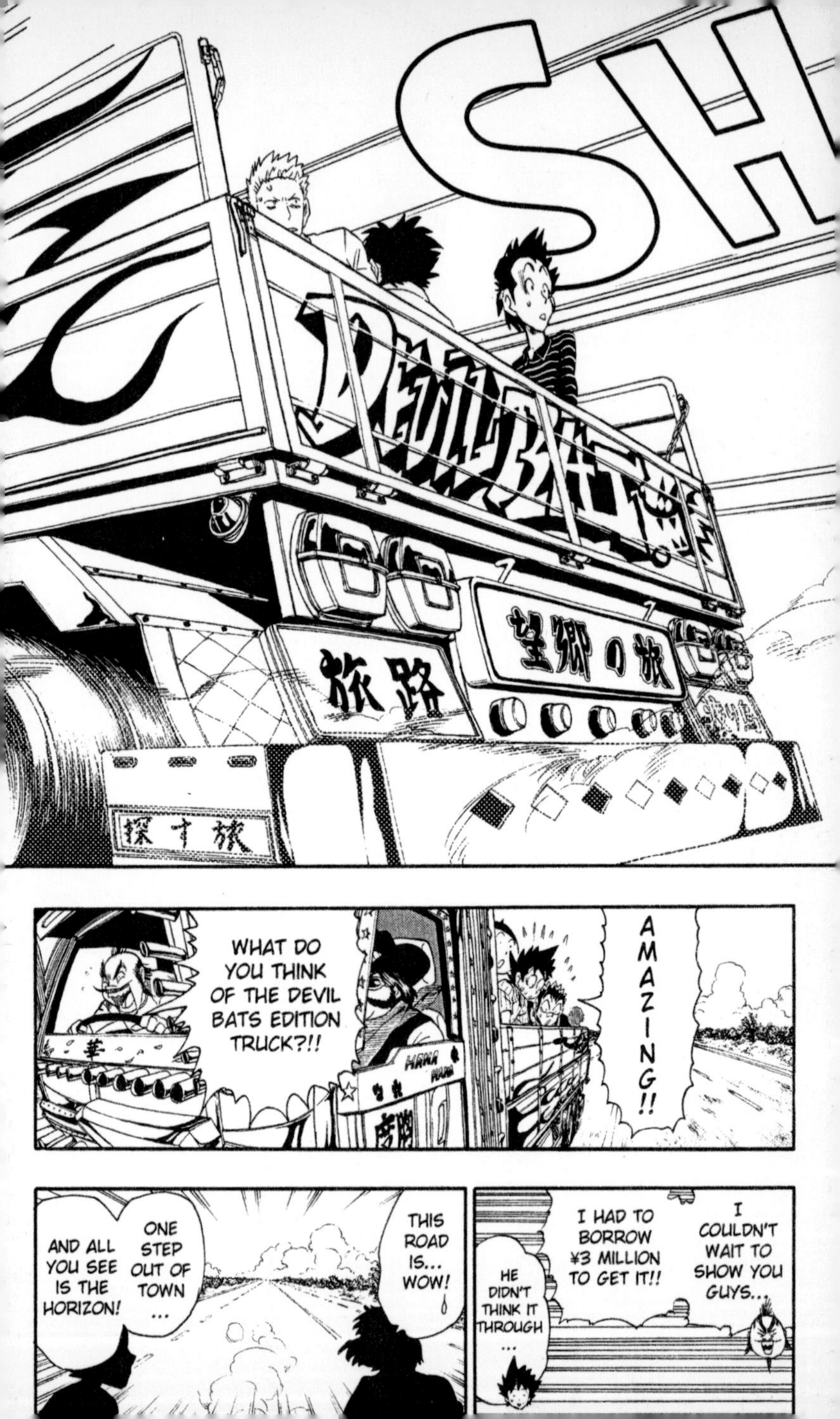
SH
望郷の旅
旅路
探す旅
AMAZING!!
WHAT DO YOU THINK OF THE DEVIL BATS EDITION TRUCK?!!
I COULDN'T WAIT TO SHOW YOU GUYS...
I HAD TO BORROW ¥3 MILLION TO GET IT!!
HE DIDN'T THINK IT THROUGH...
THIS ROAD IS... WOW!
ONE STEP OUT OF TOWN...
AND ALL YOU SEE IS THE HORIZON!

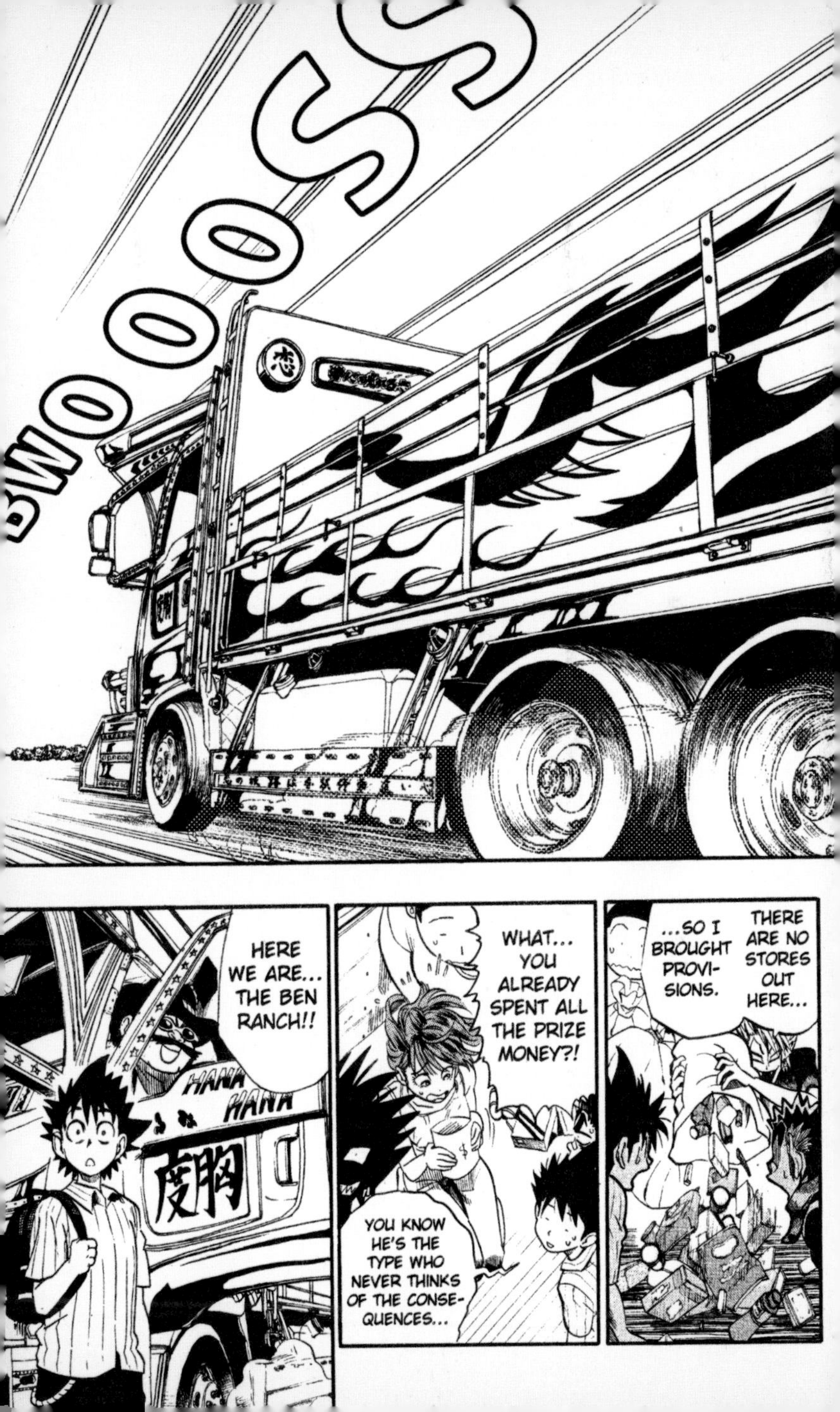
BWOOOOSS
THERE ARE NO STORES OUT HERE...
...SO I BROUGHT PROVI-SIONS.
WHAT... YOU ALREADY SPENT ALL THE PRIZE MONEY?!
YOU KNOW HE'S THE TYPE WHO NEVER THINKS OF THE CONSE-QUENCES...
HERE WE ARE... THE BEN RANCH!!
HANA HANA
度胸

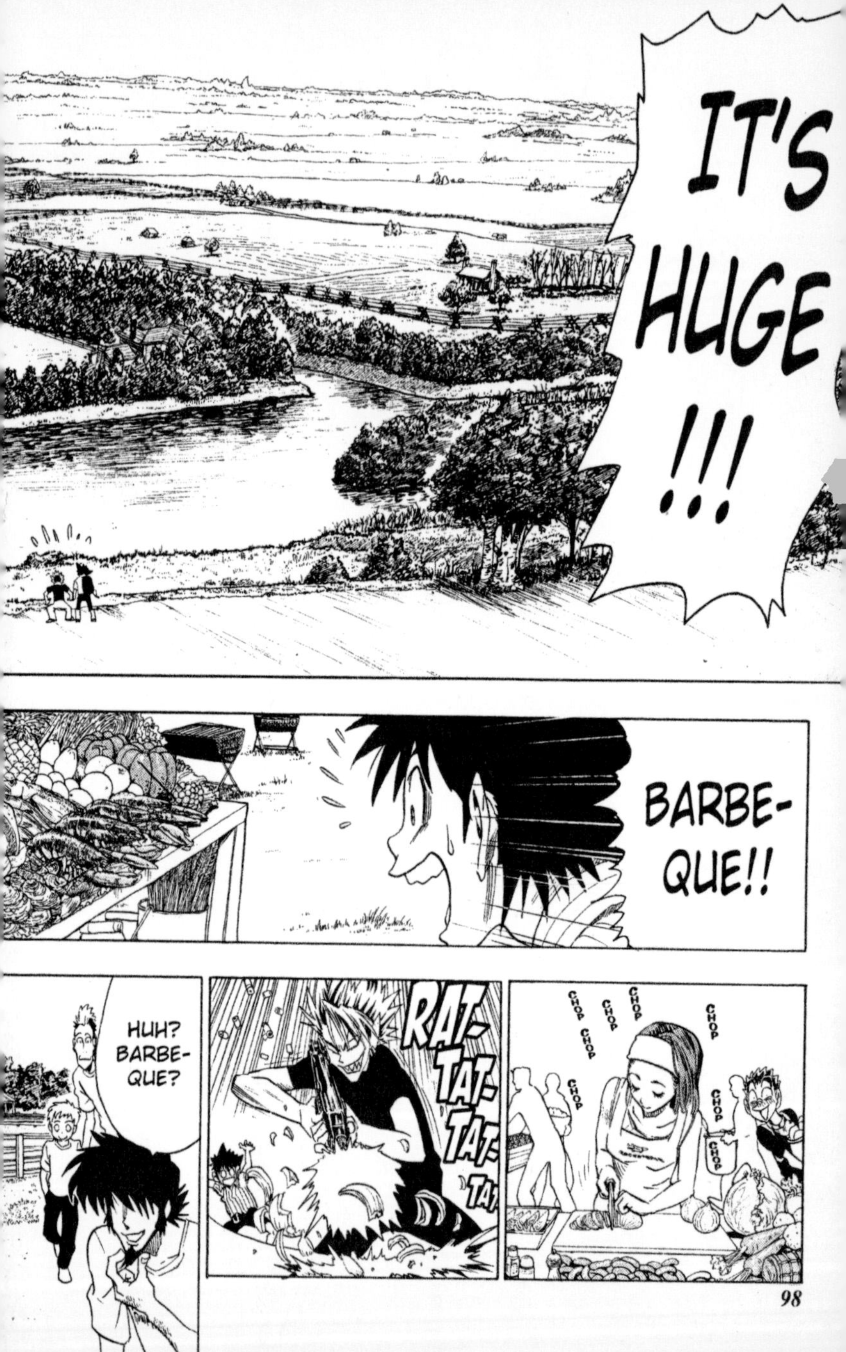
IT'S HUGE!!!
BARBE-QUE!!
CHOP
CHOP
CHOP
CHOP
CHOP
CHOP
CHOP
CHOP
RAT-TAT-TAT-TAT
HUH? BARBE-QUE?

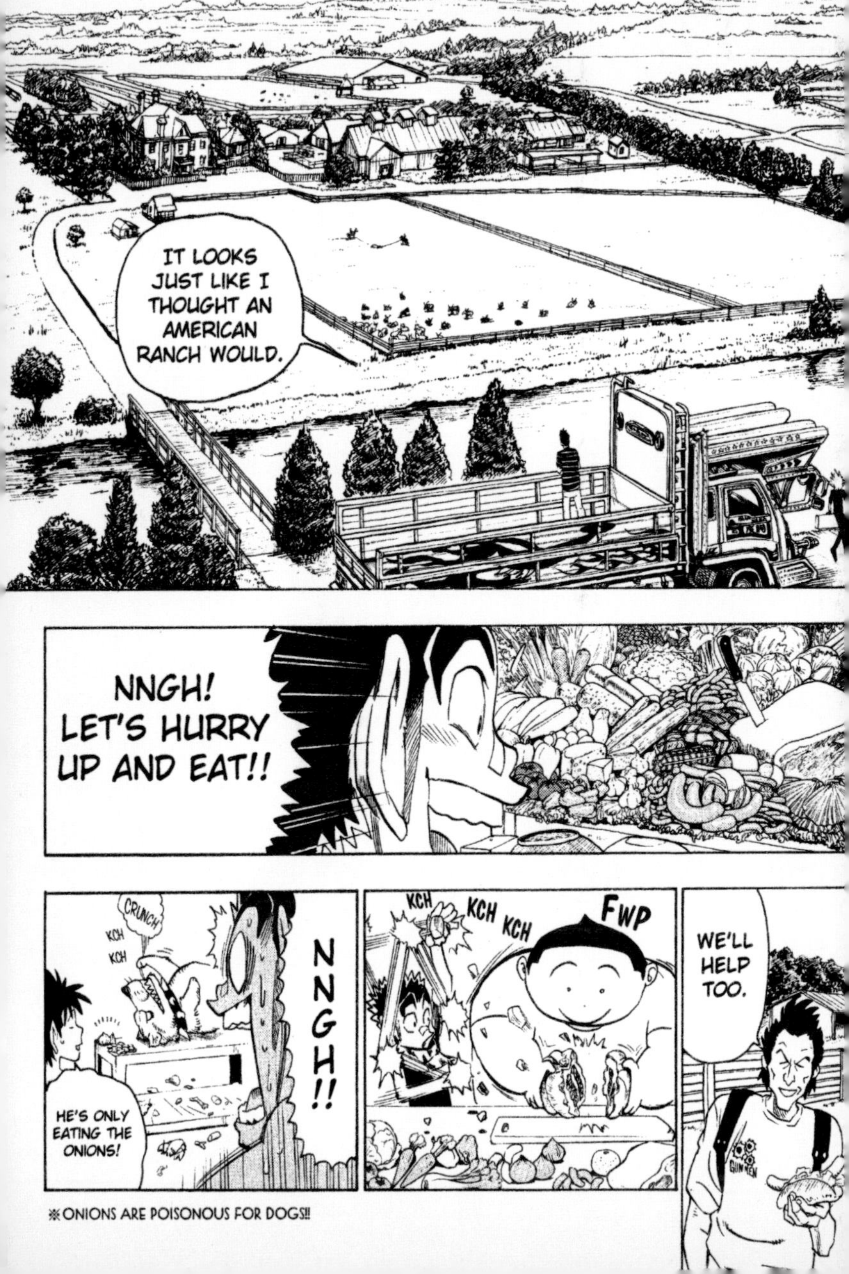
IT LOOKS JUST LIKE I THOUGHT AN AMERICAN RANCH WOULD.
NNGH! LET'S HURRY UP AND EAT!!
WE'LL HELP TOO.
FWP
KCH
KCH
KCH
NNGH!!
CRUNCH
KCH
KCH
HE'S ONLY EATING THE ONIONS!

※ONIONS ARE POISONOUS FOR DOGS!!

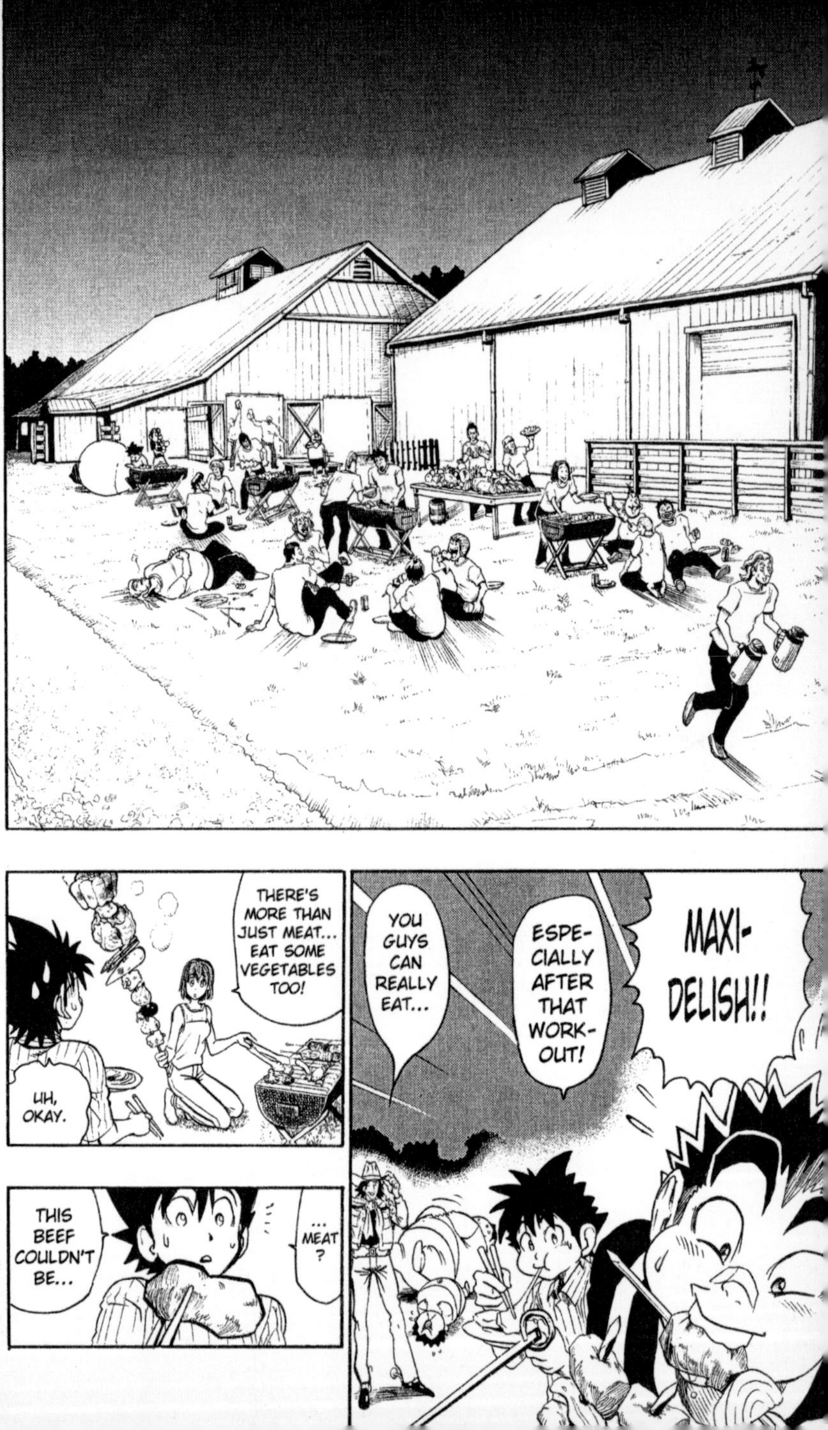
MAXI-DELISH!!
ESPECIALLY AFTER THAT WORKOUT!
YOU GUYS CAN REALLY EAT...
THERE'S MORE THAN JUST MEAT... EAT SOME VEGETABLES TOO!
UH, OKAY.
...MEAT?
THIS BEEF COULDN'T BE...

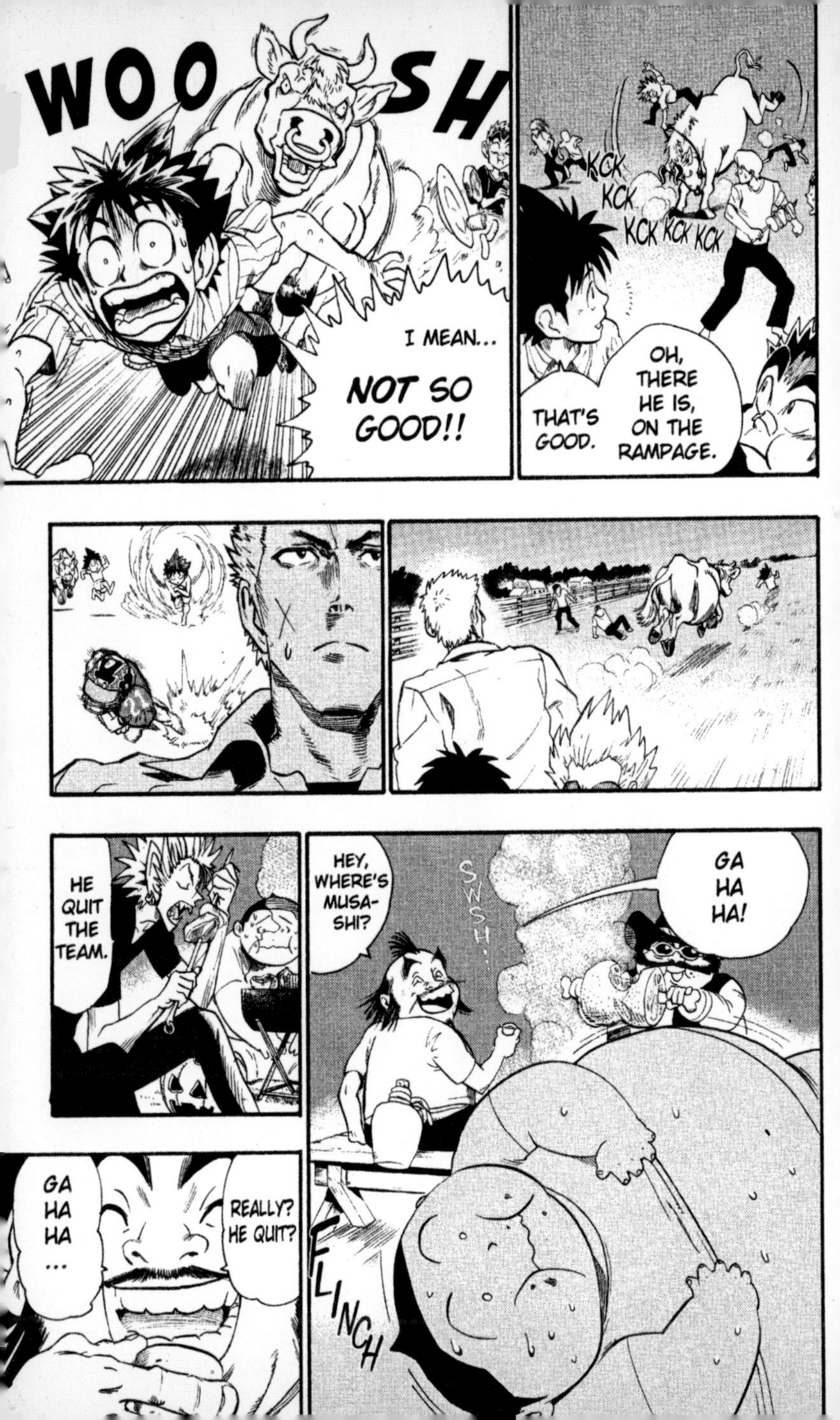
KCK
KCK
KCK KCK KCK
OH, THERE HE IS, ON THE RAMPAGE.
THAT'S GOOD.
WOOSH
I MEAN...
NOT SO GOOD!!
GA HA HA!
SWSH..
HEY, WHERE'S MUSA-SHI?
FLINCH
HE QUIT THE TEAM.
REALLY? HE QUIT?
GA HA HA ...

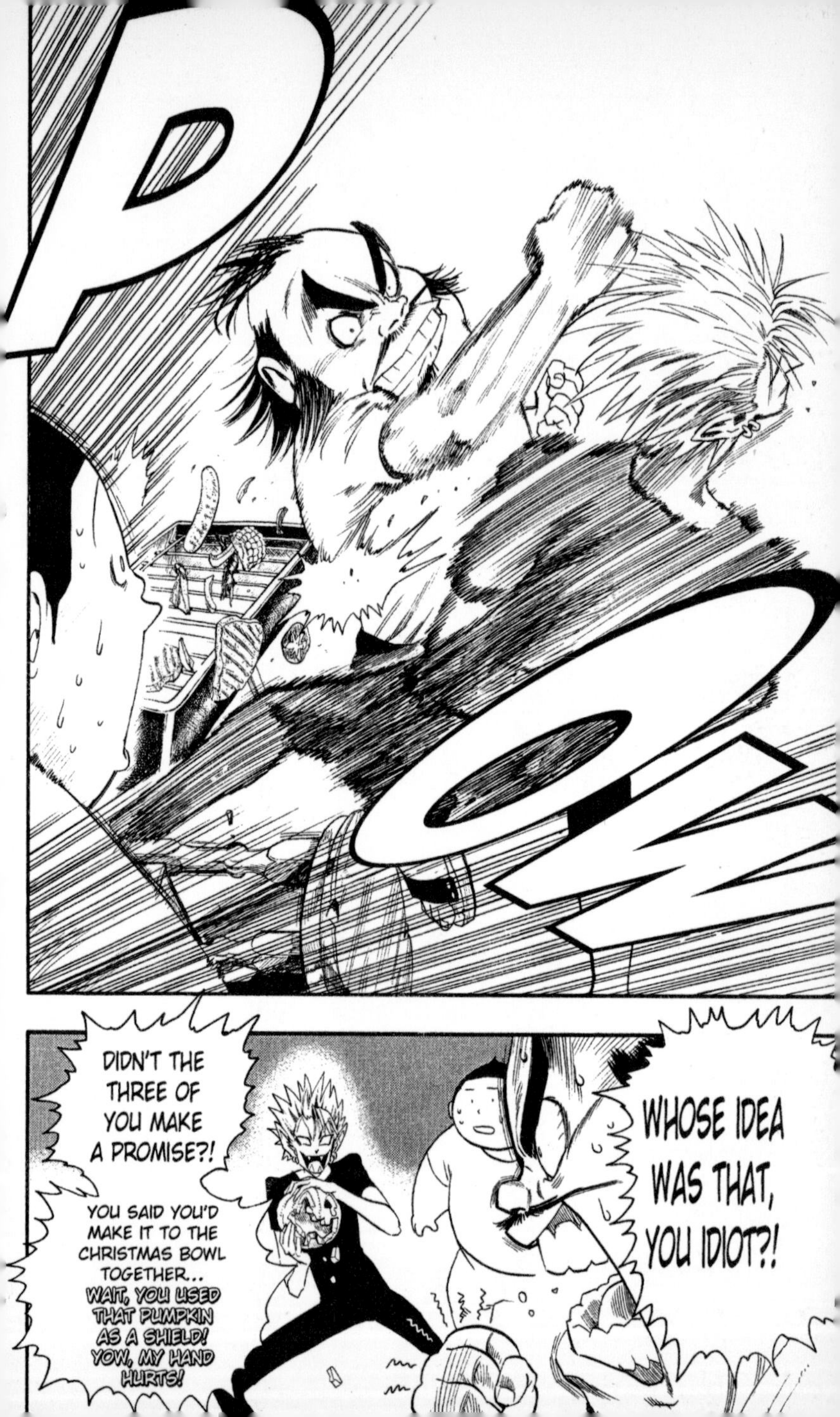
POW
WHOSE IDEA WAS THAT, YOU IDIOT?!
DIDN'T THE THREE OF YOU MAKE A PROMISE?!
YOU SAID YOU'D MAKE IT TO THE CHRISTMAS BOWL TOGETHER...
WAIT, YOU USED THAT PUMPKIN AS A SHIELD! YOW, MY HAND HURTS!

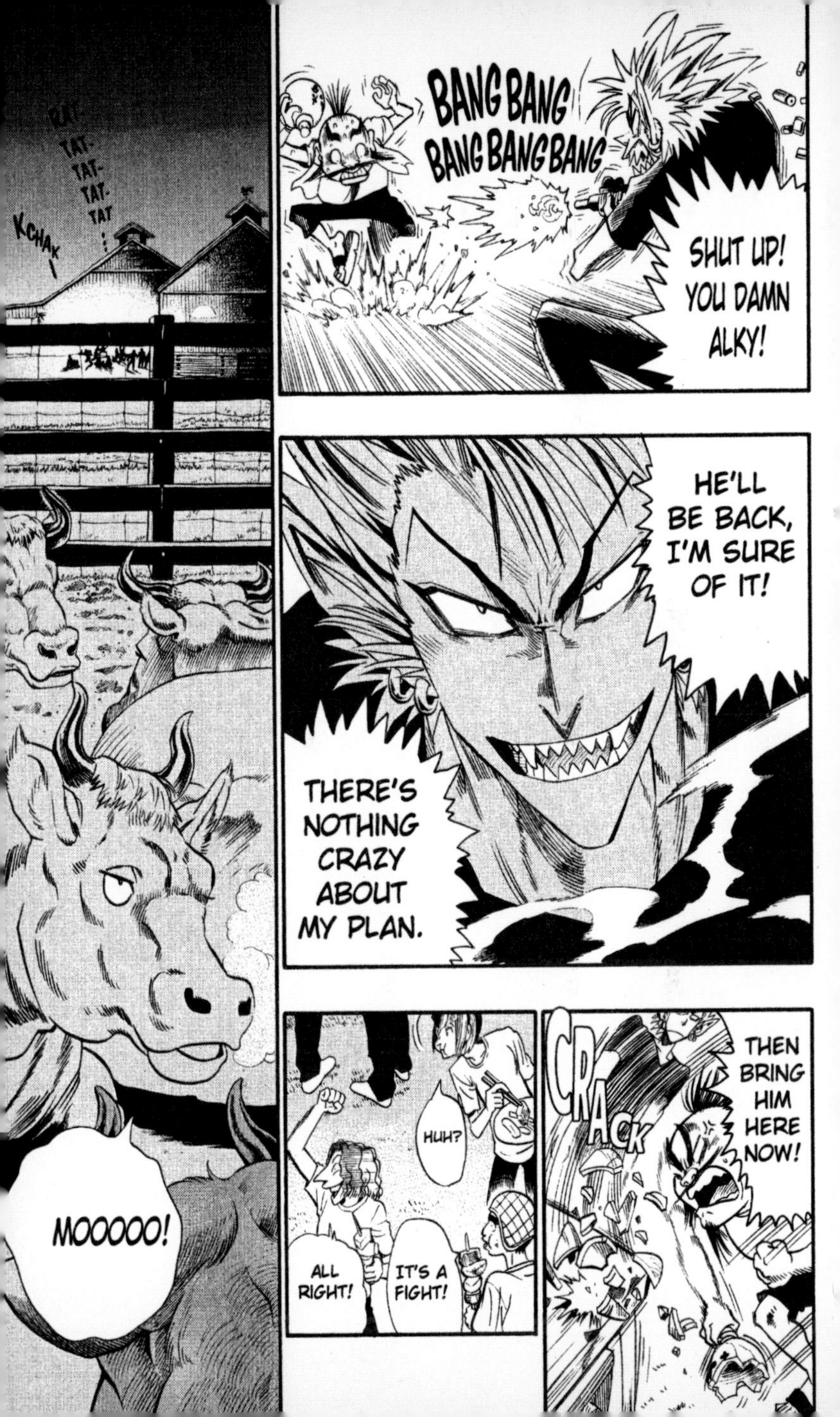
BANG BANG
BANG BANG BANG
SHUT UP! YOU DAMN ALKY!
HE'LL BE BACK, I'M SURE OF IT!
THERE'S NOTHING CRAZY ABOUT MY PLAN.
CRACK
THEN BRING HIM HERE NOW!
HUH?
IT'S A FIGHT!
ALL RIGHT!
RAT-TAT-TAT-TAT-TAT
KCHAK
MOOOOO!

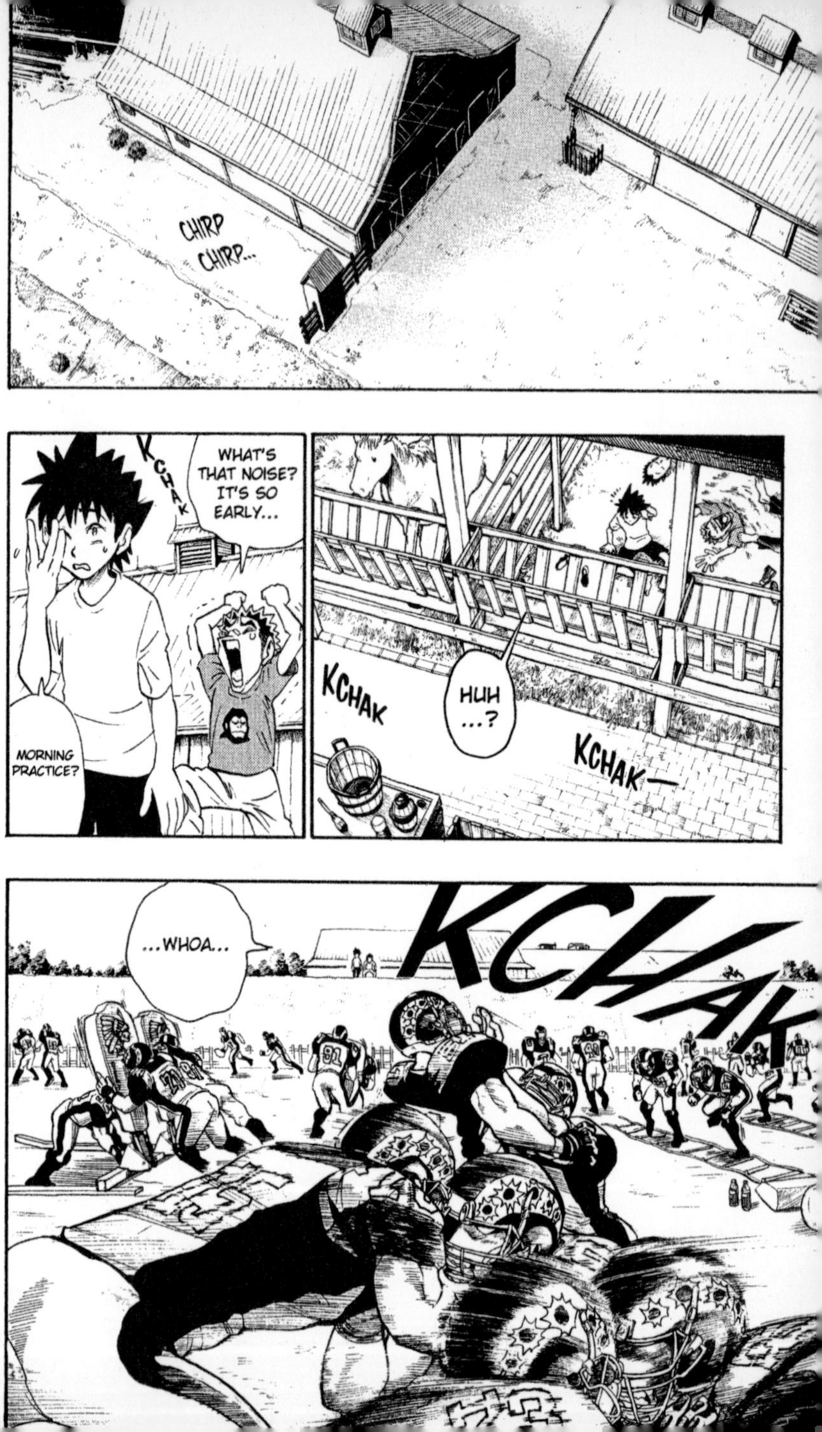
CHIRP CHIRP...
HUH ...?
KCHAK
KCHAK—
KCHAK
WHAT'S THAT NOISE? IT'S SO EARLY...
MORNING PRACTICE?
...WHOA...
KCHAK

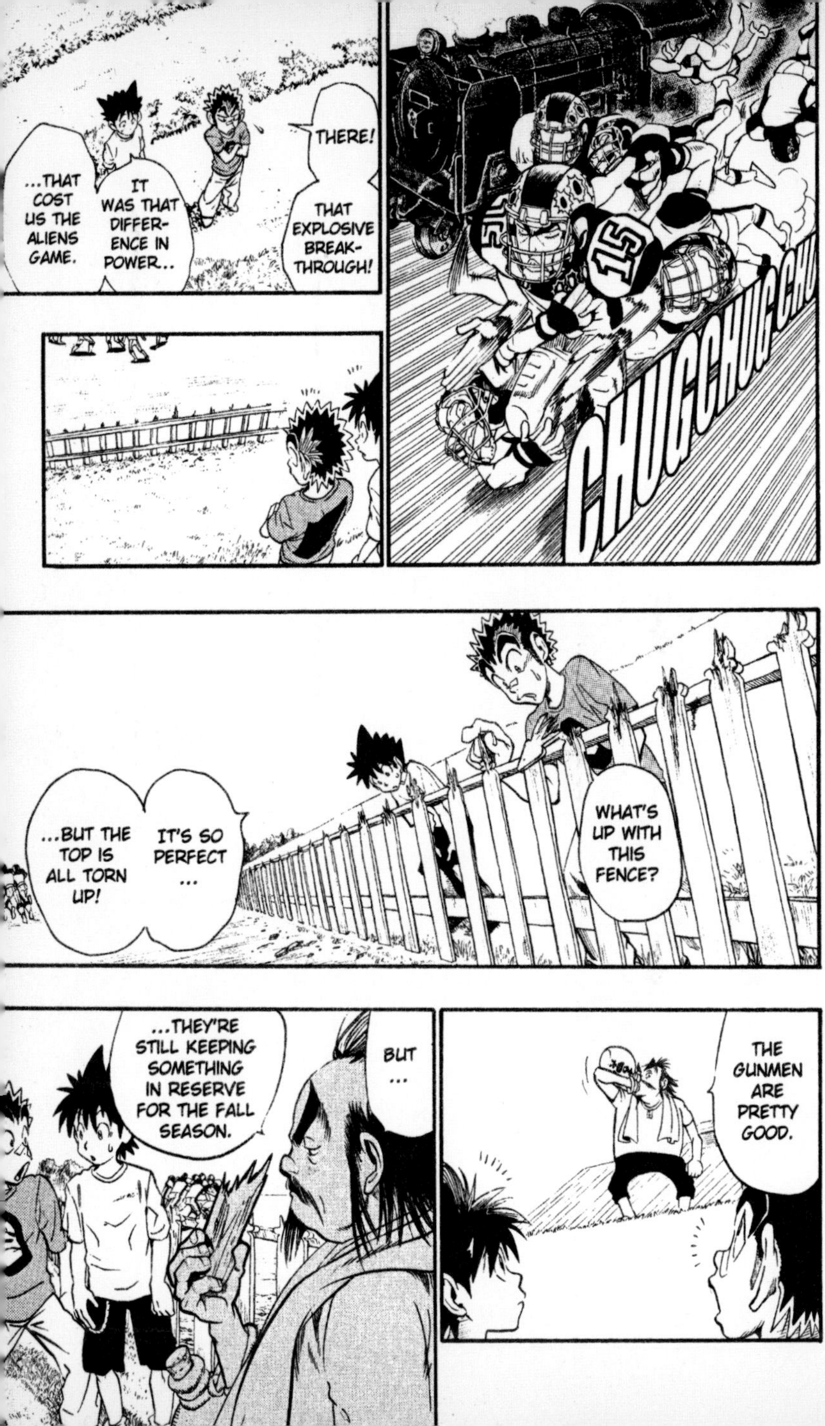
CHUGCHUGCHU
THERE!
THAT EXPLOSIVE BREAKTHROUGH!
IT WAS THAT DIFFERENCE IN POWER...
...THAT COST US THE ALIENS GAME.
WHAT'S UP WITH THIS FENCE?
IT'S SO PERFECT...
...BUT THE TOP IS ALL TORN UP!
THE GUNMEN ARE PRETTY GOOD.
BUT...
...THEY'RE STILL KEEPING SOMETHING IN RESERVE FOR THE FALL SEASON.

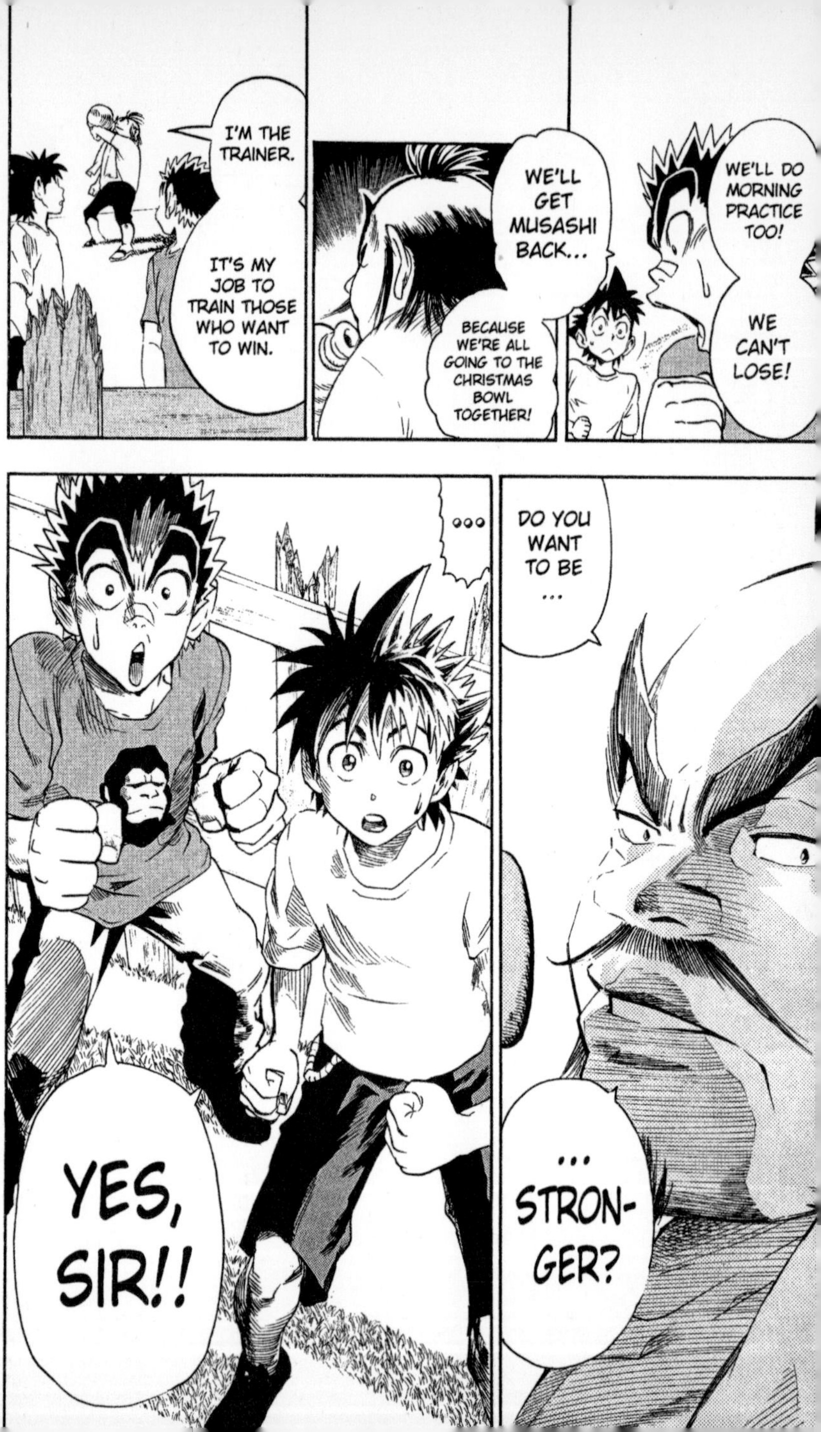
WE'LL DO MORNING PRACTICE TOO!
WE CAN'T LOSE!
WE'LL GET MUSASHI BACK...
BECAUSE WE'RE ALL GOING TO THE CHRISTMAS BOWL TOGETHER!
I'M THE TRAINER.
IT'S MY JOB TO TRAIN THOSE WHO WANT TO WIN.
DO YOU WANT TO BE ...
... STRON-GER?
...
YES, SIR!!

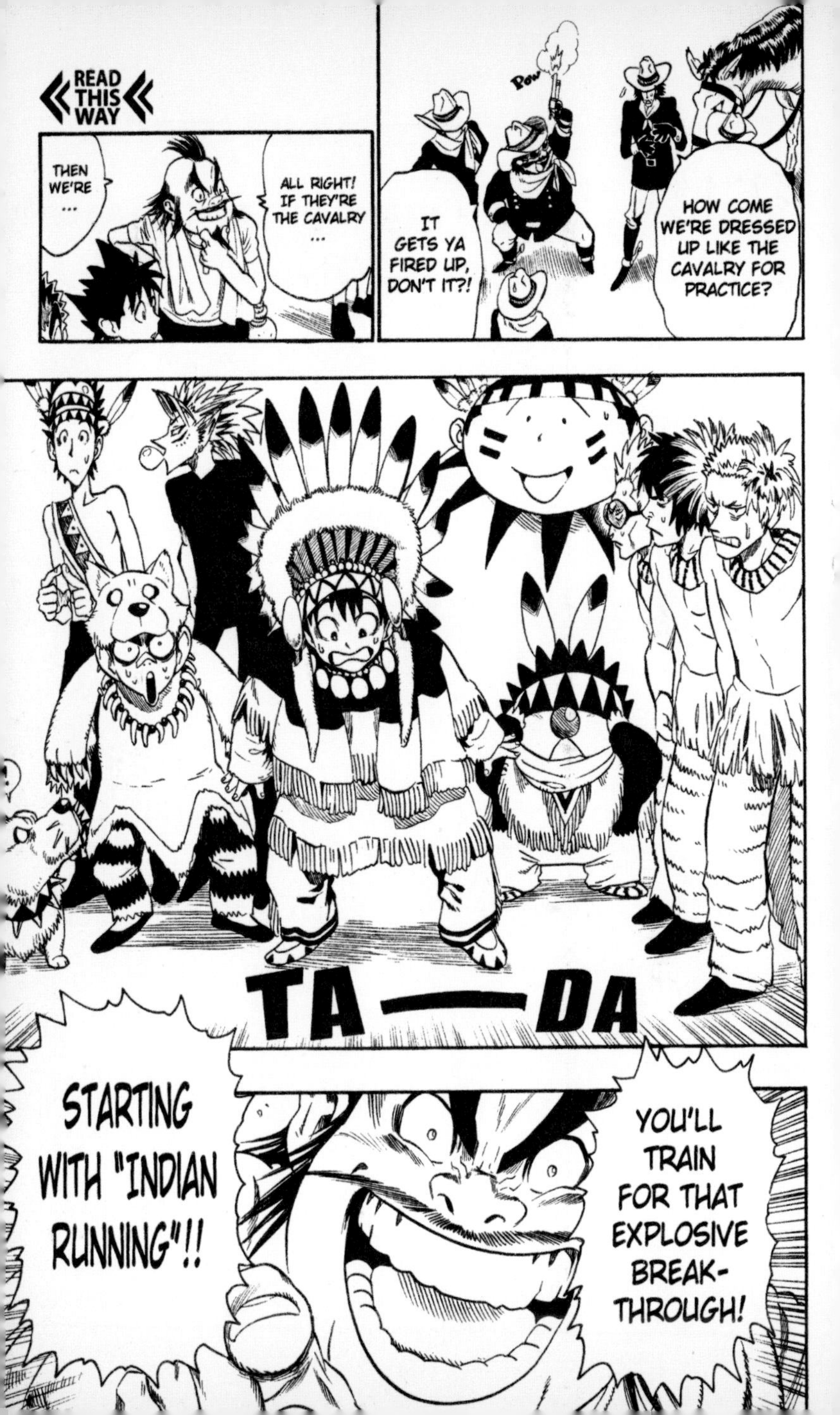
READ THIS WAY
HOW COME WE'RE DRESSED UP LIKE THE CAVALRY FOR PRACTICE?
POW
IT GETS YA FIRED UP, DON'T IT?!
ALL RIGHT! IF THEY'RE THE CAVALRY ...
THEN WE'RE ...
TA—DA
YOU'LL TRAIN FOR THAT EXPLOSIVE BREAK-THROUGH!
STARTING WITH "INDIAN RUNNING"!!

Eyeshield 21 Survey Corner **Devil Bat 021**

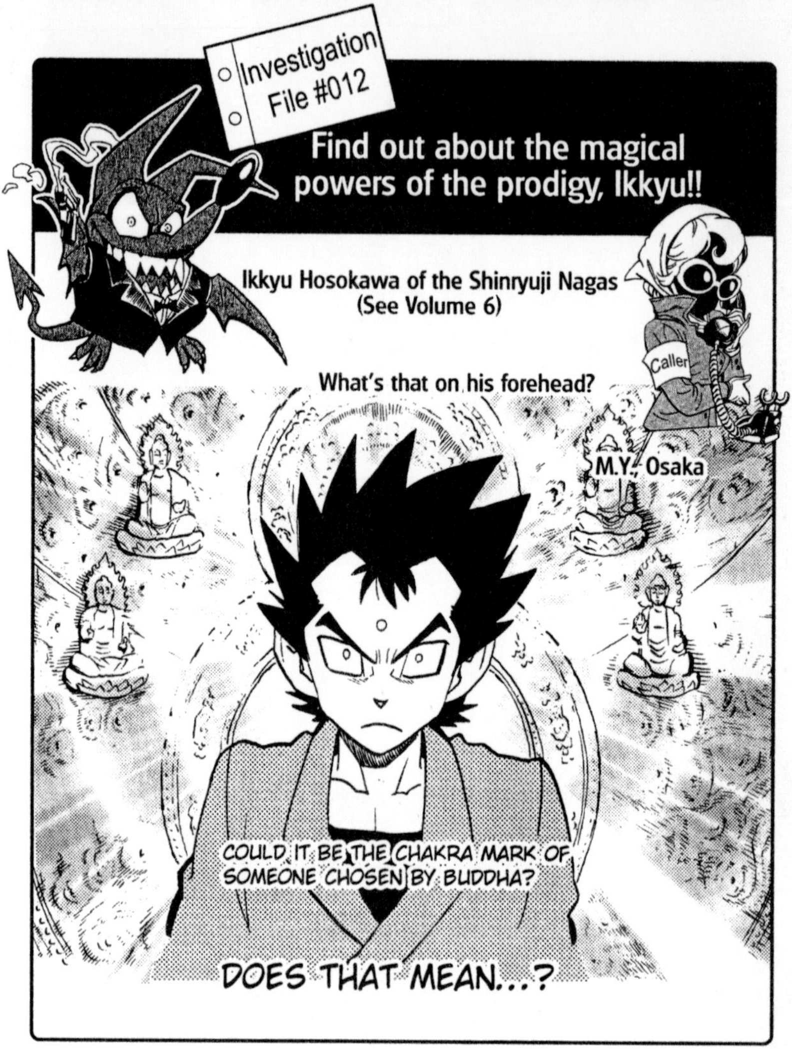
Investigation File #012
Find out about the magical powers of the prodigy, Ikkyu!!
Ikkyu Hosokawa of the Shinryuji Nagas (See Volume 6)
Caller
What's that on his forehead?
M.Y., Osaka
COULD IT BE THE CHAKRA MARK OF SOMEONE CHOSEN BY BUDDHA?
DOES THAT MEAN...?

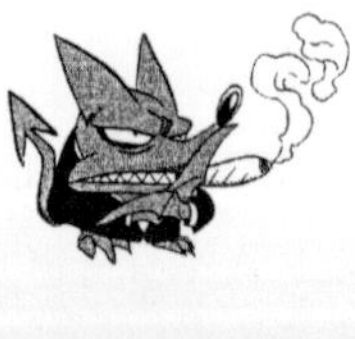

IT'S A MOLE.

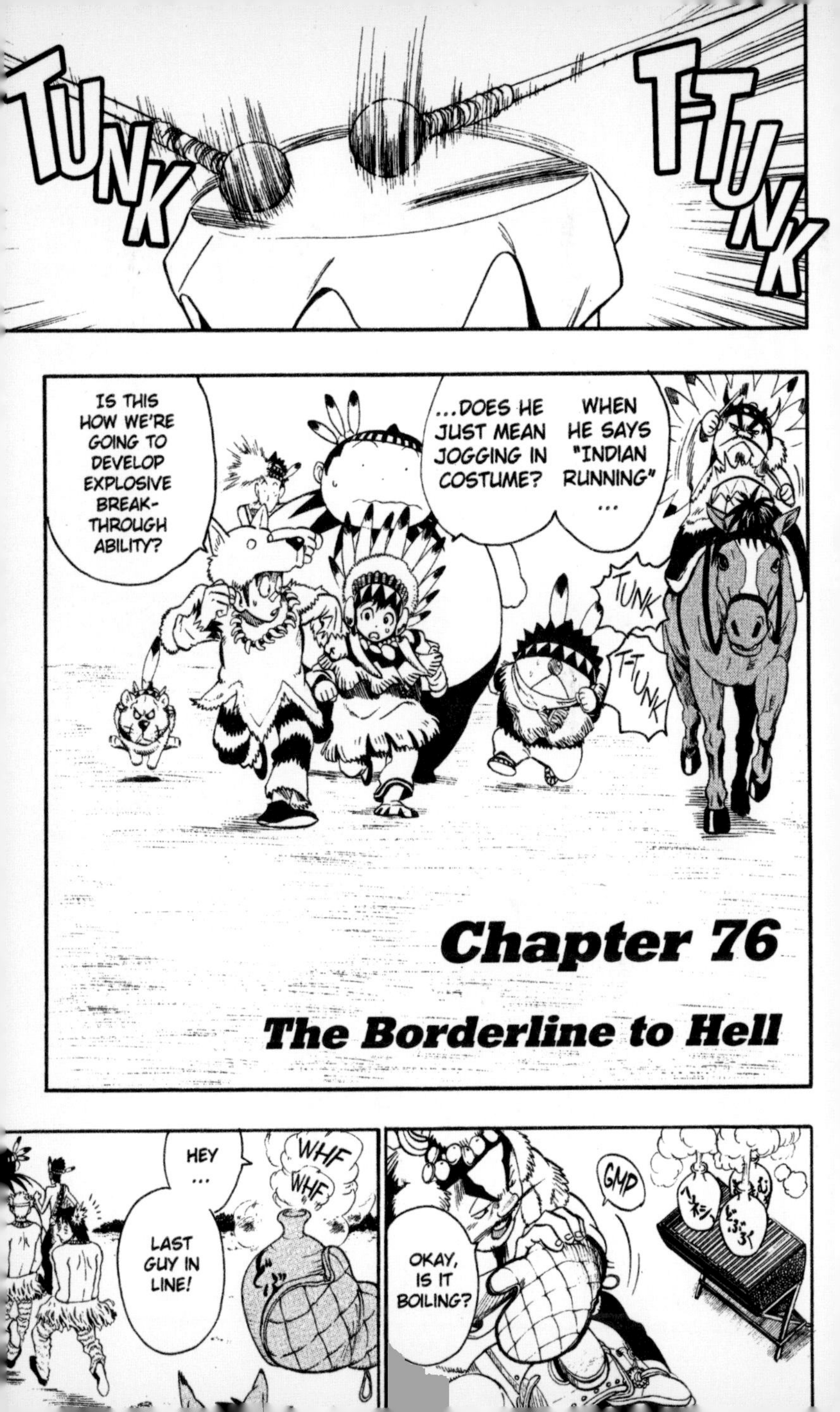

TUNK
T-TUNK
WHEN HE SAYS "INDIAN RUNNING" ...
...DOES HE JUST MEAN JOGGING IN COSTUME?
IS THIS HOW WE'RE GOING TO DEVELOP EXPLOSIVE BREAK-THROUGH ABILITY?
TUNK
T-TUNK
Chapter 76
The Borderline to Hell
GMP
OKAY, IS IT BOILING?
WHF
WHF
HEY ...
LAST GUY IN LINE!

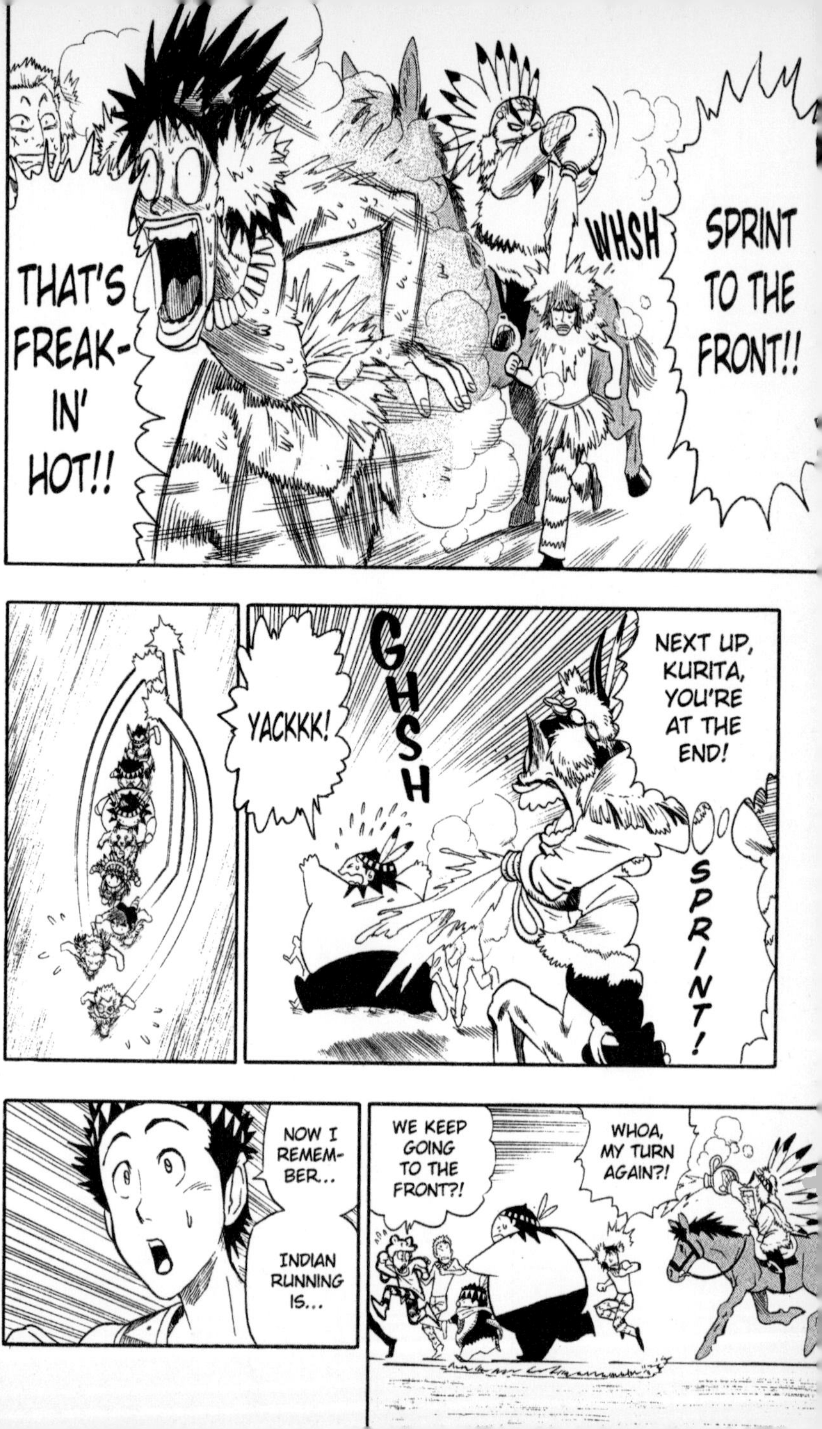
SPRINT TO THE FRONT!!
WHSH
THAT'S FREAK-IN' HOT!!
NEXT UP, KURITA, YOU'RE AT THE END!
SPRINT!
GHSH
YACKKK!
WHOA, MY TURN AGAIN?!
WE KEEP GOING TO THE FRONT?!
NOW I REMEM-BER...
INDIAN RUNNING IS...

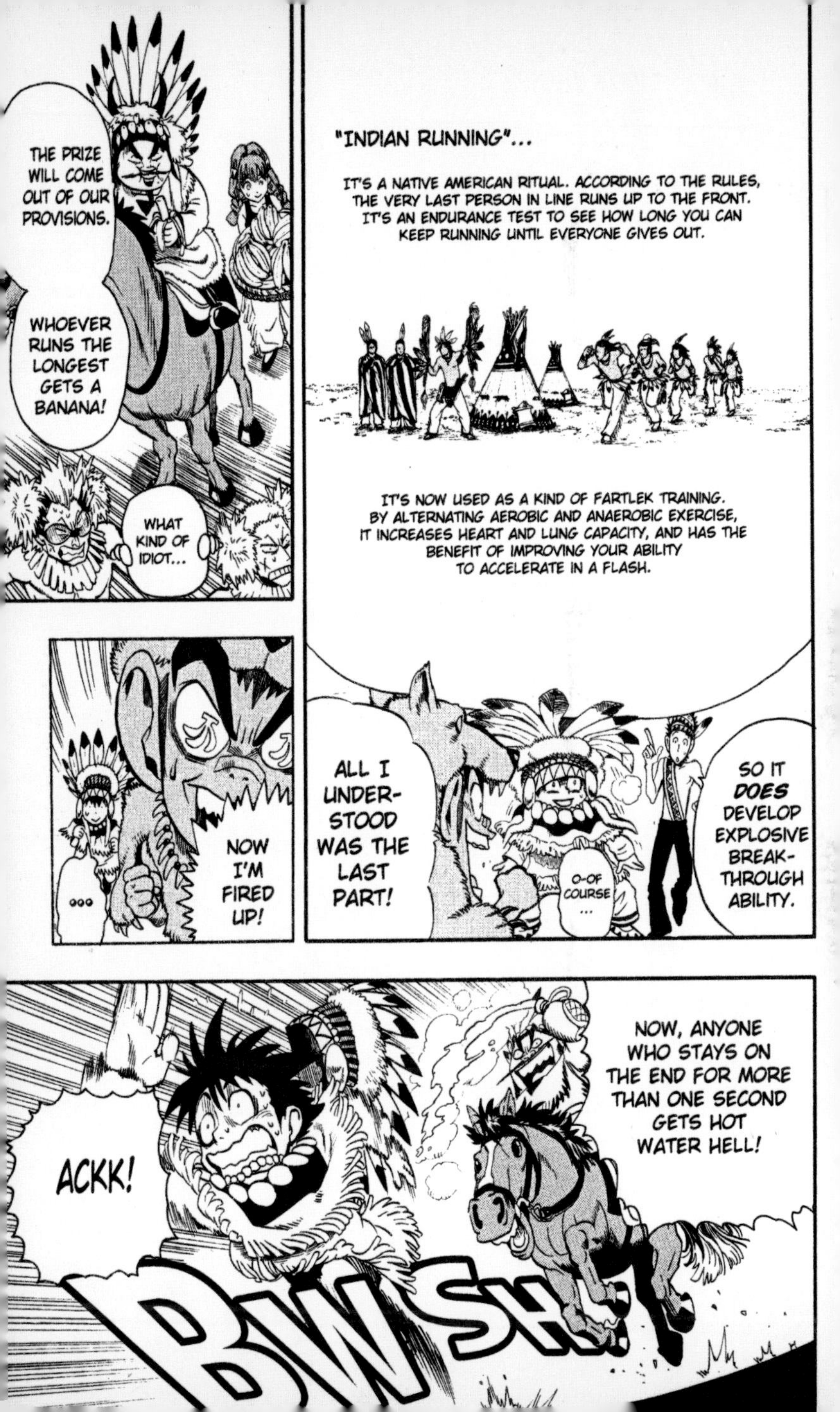
"INDIAN RUNNING"...
IT'S A NATIVE AMERICAN RITUAL. ACCORDING TO THE RULES, THE VERY LAST PERSON IN LINE RUNS UP TO THE FRONT. IT'S AN ENDURANCE TEST TO SEE HOW LONG YOU CAN KEEP RUNNING UNTIL EVERYONE GIVES OUT.
IT'S NOW USED AS A KIND OF FARTLEK TRAINING. BY ALTERNATING AEROBIC AND ANAEROBIC EXERCISE, IT INCREASES HEART AND LUNG CAPACITY, AND HAS THE BENEFIT OF IMPROVING YOUR ABILITY TO ACCELERATE IN A FLASH.
SO IT *DOES* DEVELOP EXPLOSIVE BREAK-THROUGH ABILITY.
ALL I UNDER-STOOD WAS THE LAST PART!
O-OF COURSE...
THE PRIZE WILL COME OUT OF OUR PROVISIONS.
WHOEVER RUNS THE LONGEST GETS A BANANA!
WHAT KIND OF IDIOT...
NOW I'M FIRED UP!
NOW, ANYONE WHO STAYS ON THE END FOR MORE THAN ONE SECOND GETS HOT WATER HELL!
ACKK!
BWSH!!

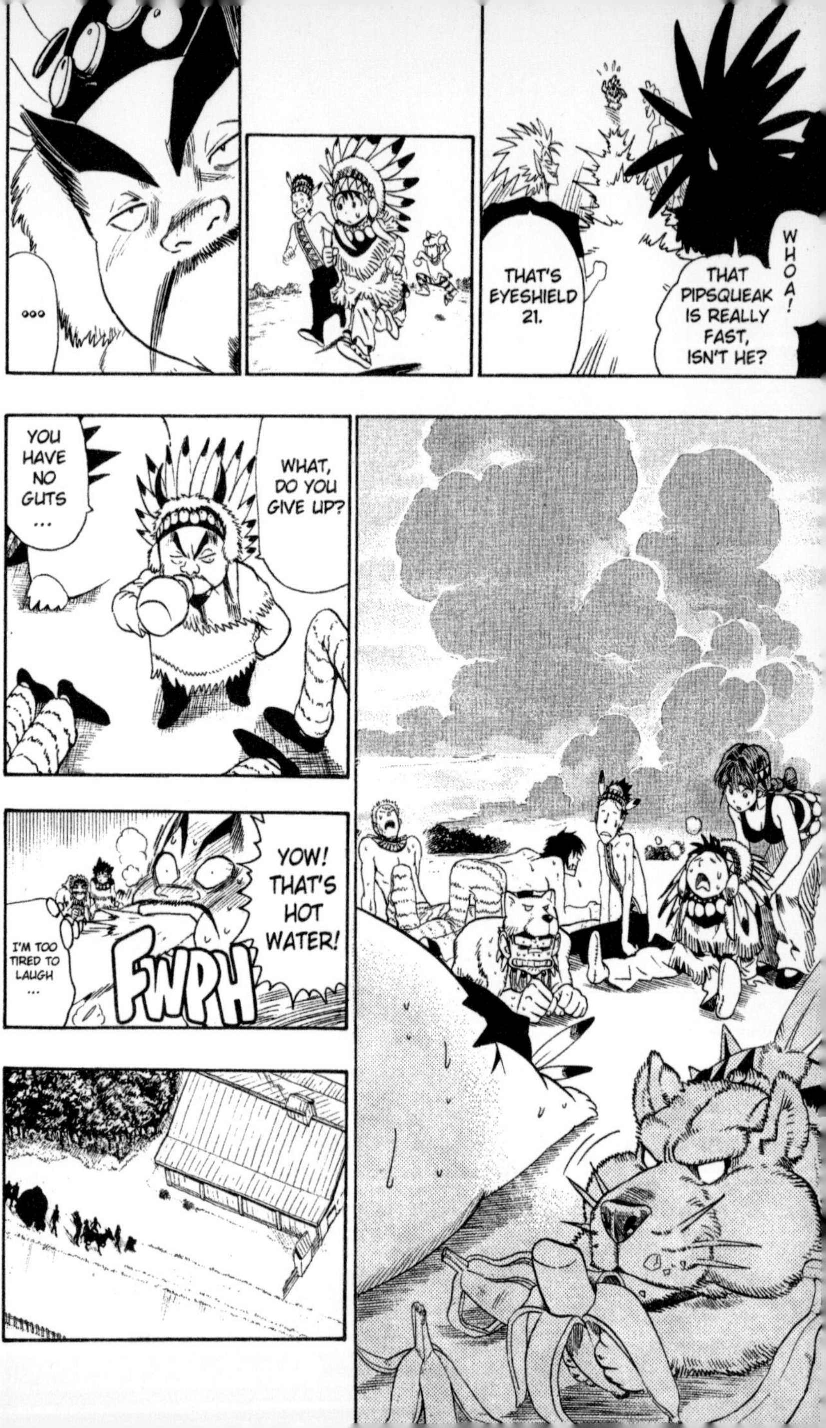
WHOA!
THAT PIPSQUEAK IS REALLY FAST, ISN'T HE?
THAT'S EYESHIELD 21.
...
WHAT, DO YOU GIVE UP?
YOU HAVE NO GUTS ...
YOW! THAT'S HOT WATER!
FWPH
I'M TOO TIRED TO LAUGH ...

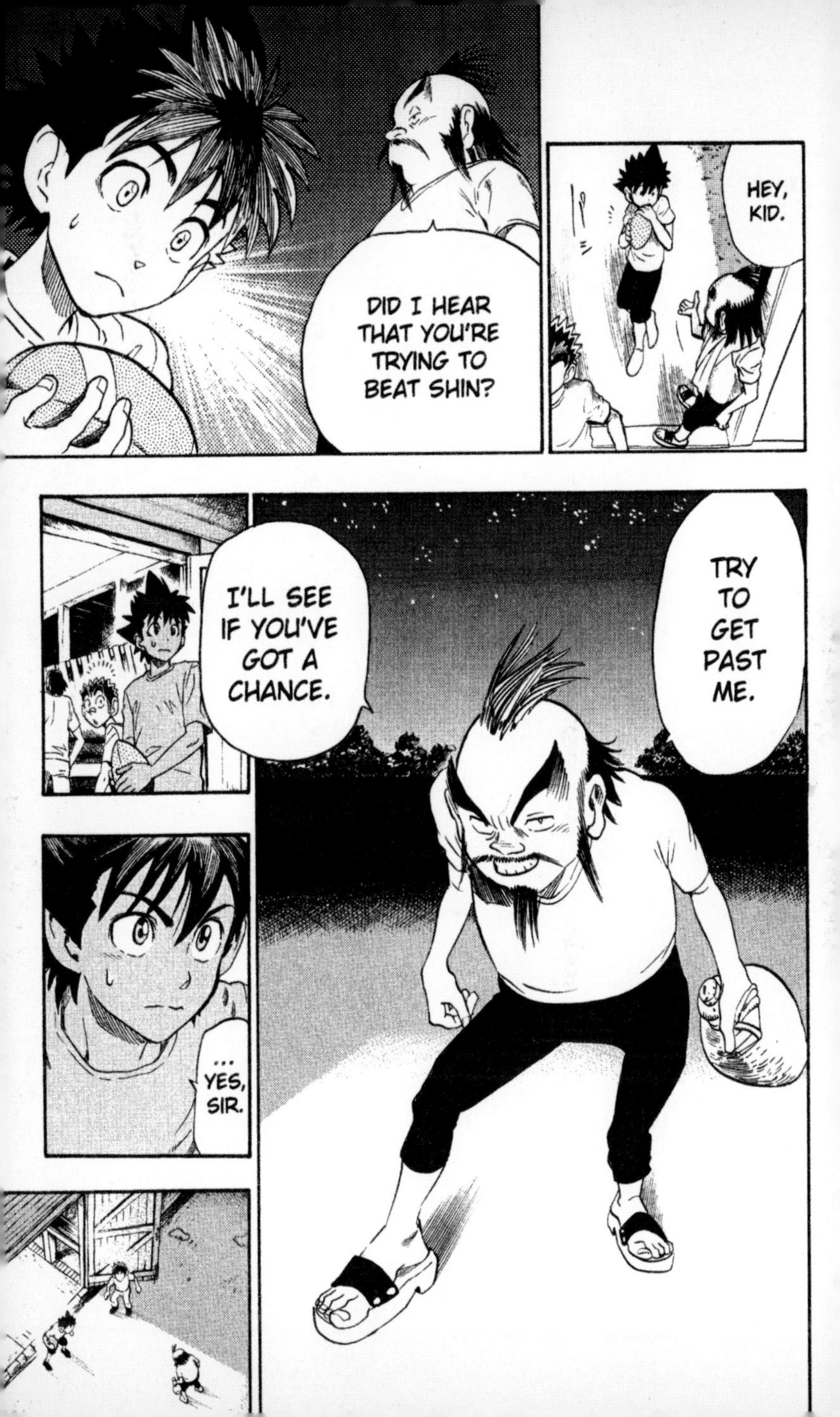
HEY, KID.
DID I HEAR THAT YOU'RE TRYING TO BEAT SHIN?
TRY TO GET PAST ME.
I'LL SEE IF YOU'VE GOT A CHANCE.
...YES, SIR.

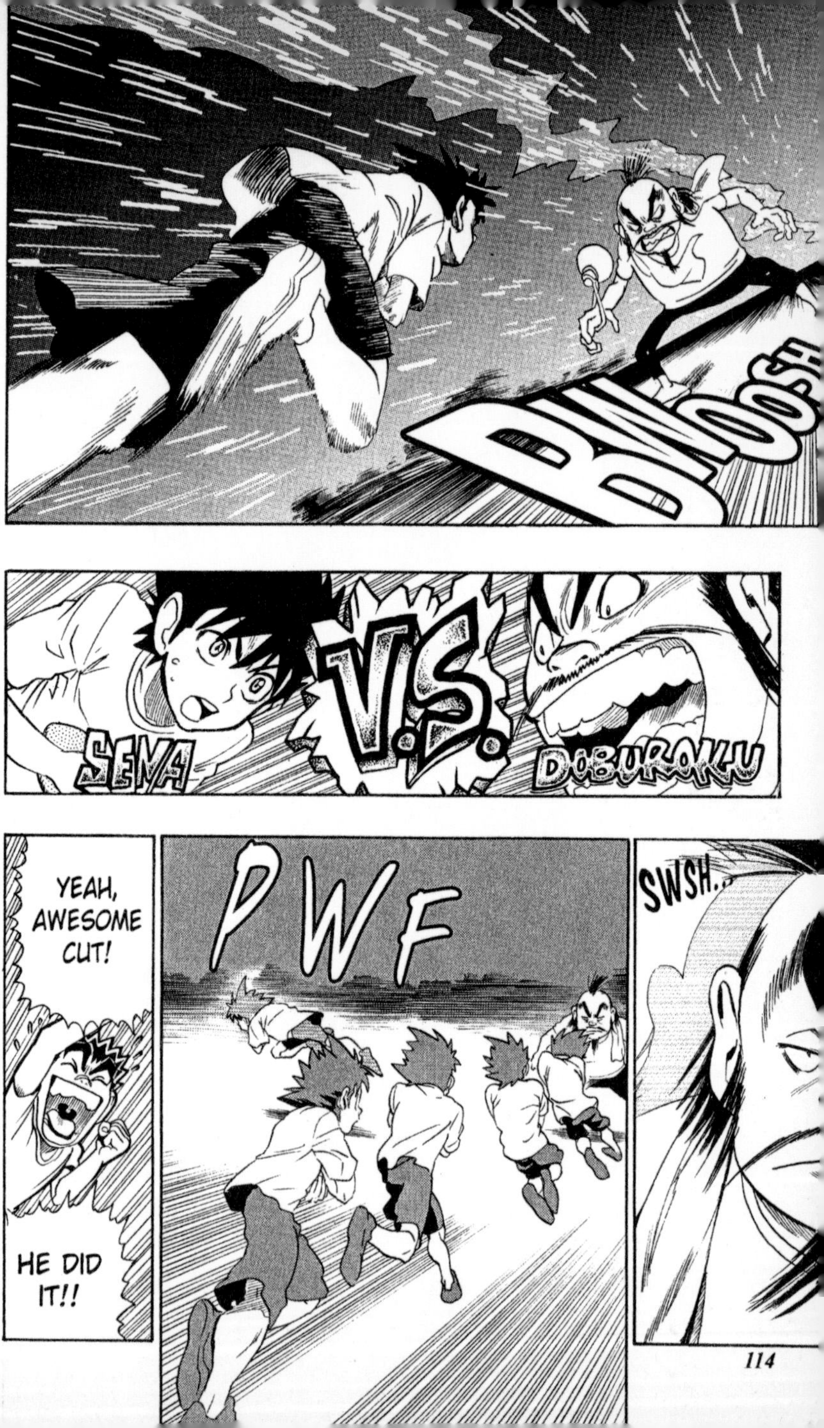
BWOOSH
SENA
V.S.
DOBUROKU
SWSH...
PWF
YEAH, AWESOME CUT!
HE DID IT!!

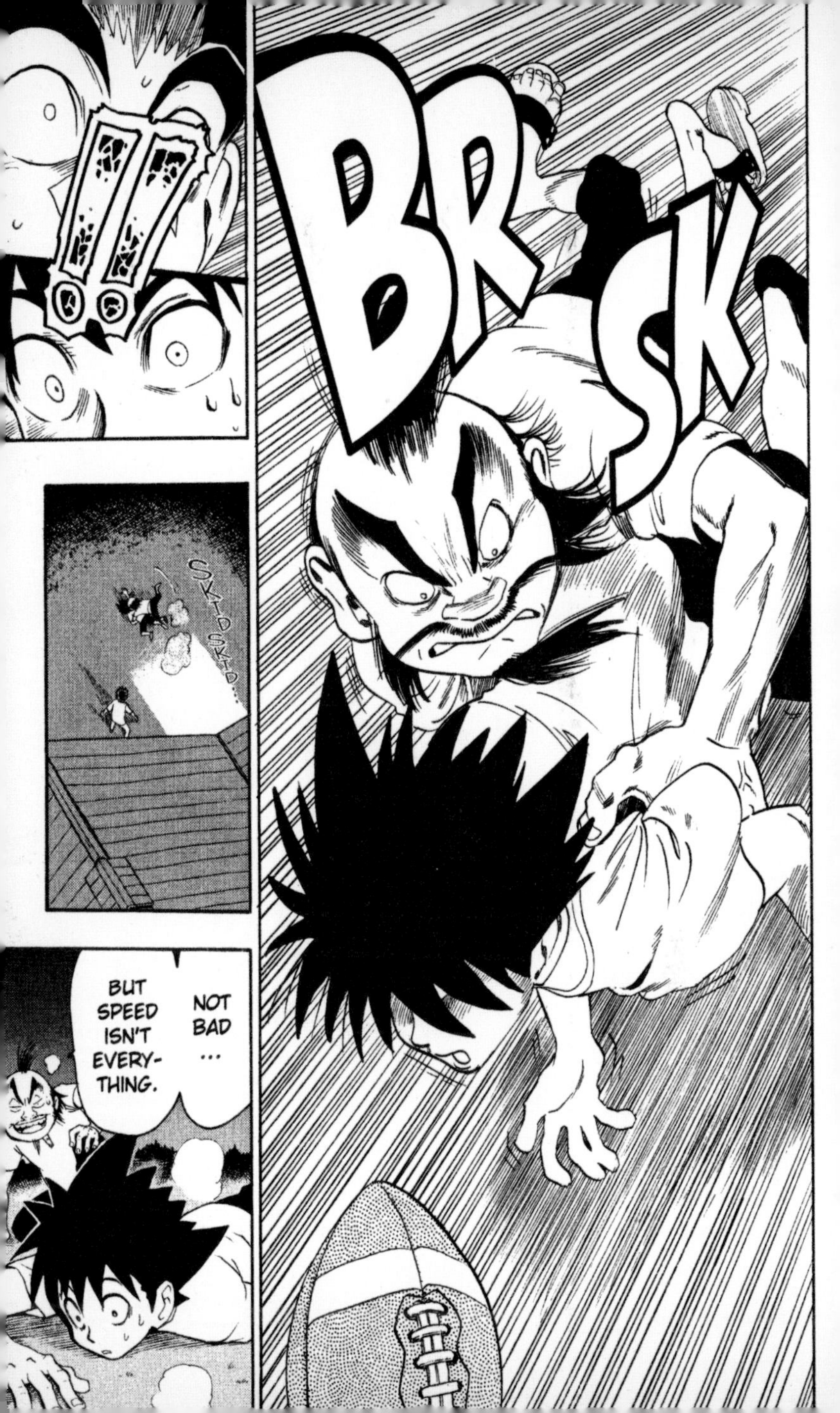
BRSK
!!
SKID SKID...
NOT BAD...
BUT SPEED ISN'T EVERYTHING.

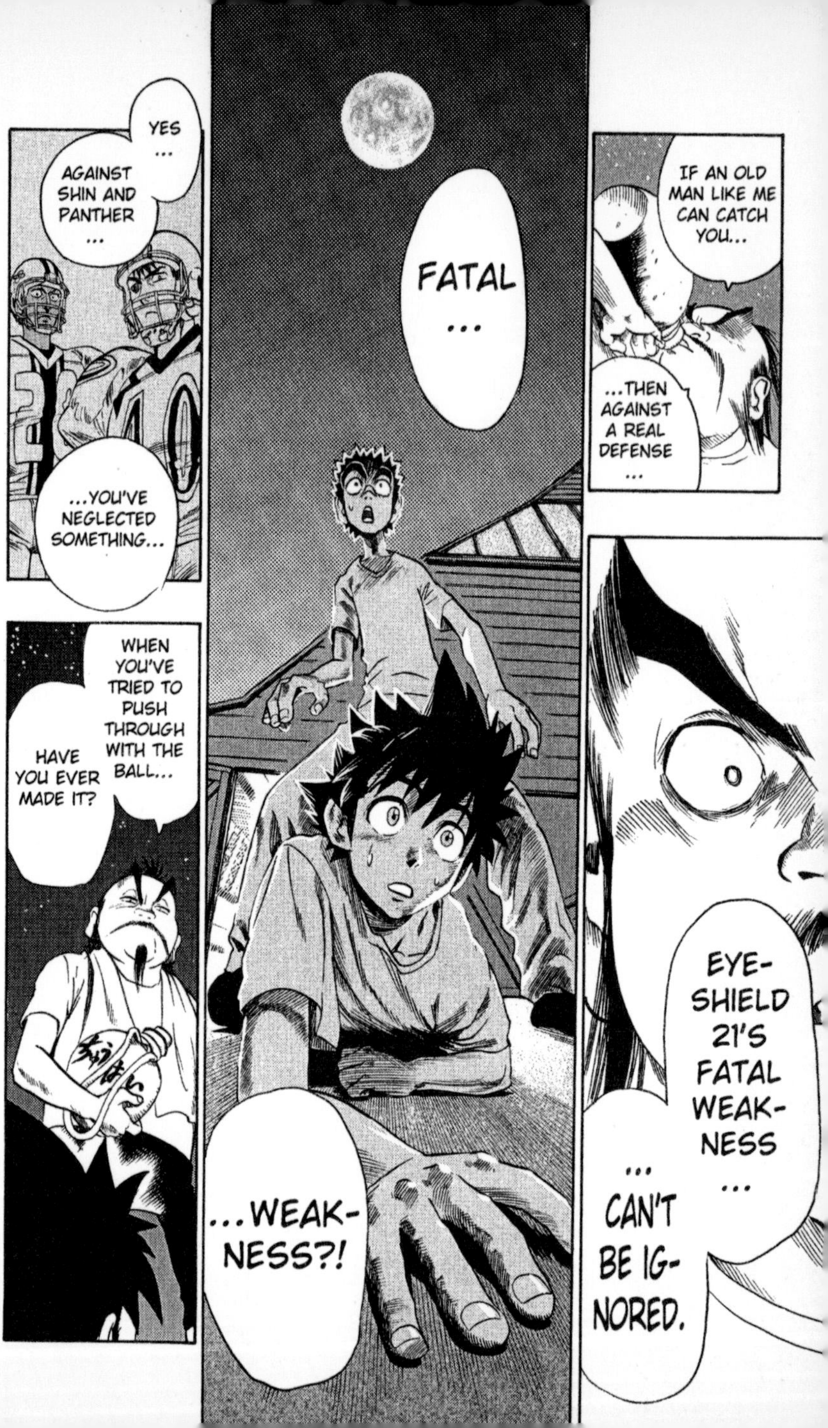
IF AN OLD MAN LIKE ME CAN CATCH YOU...
...THEN AGAINST A REAL DEFENSE ...
EYE-SHIELD 21'S FATAL WEAK-NESS ...
... CAN'T BE IG-NORED.
FATAL ...
...WEAK-NESS?!
YES ...
AGAINST SHIN AND PANTHER ...
...YOU'VE NEGLECTED SOMETHING...
WHEN YOU'VE TRIED TO PUSH THROUGH WITH THE BALL...
HAVE YOU EVER MADE IT?

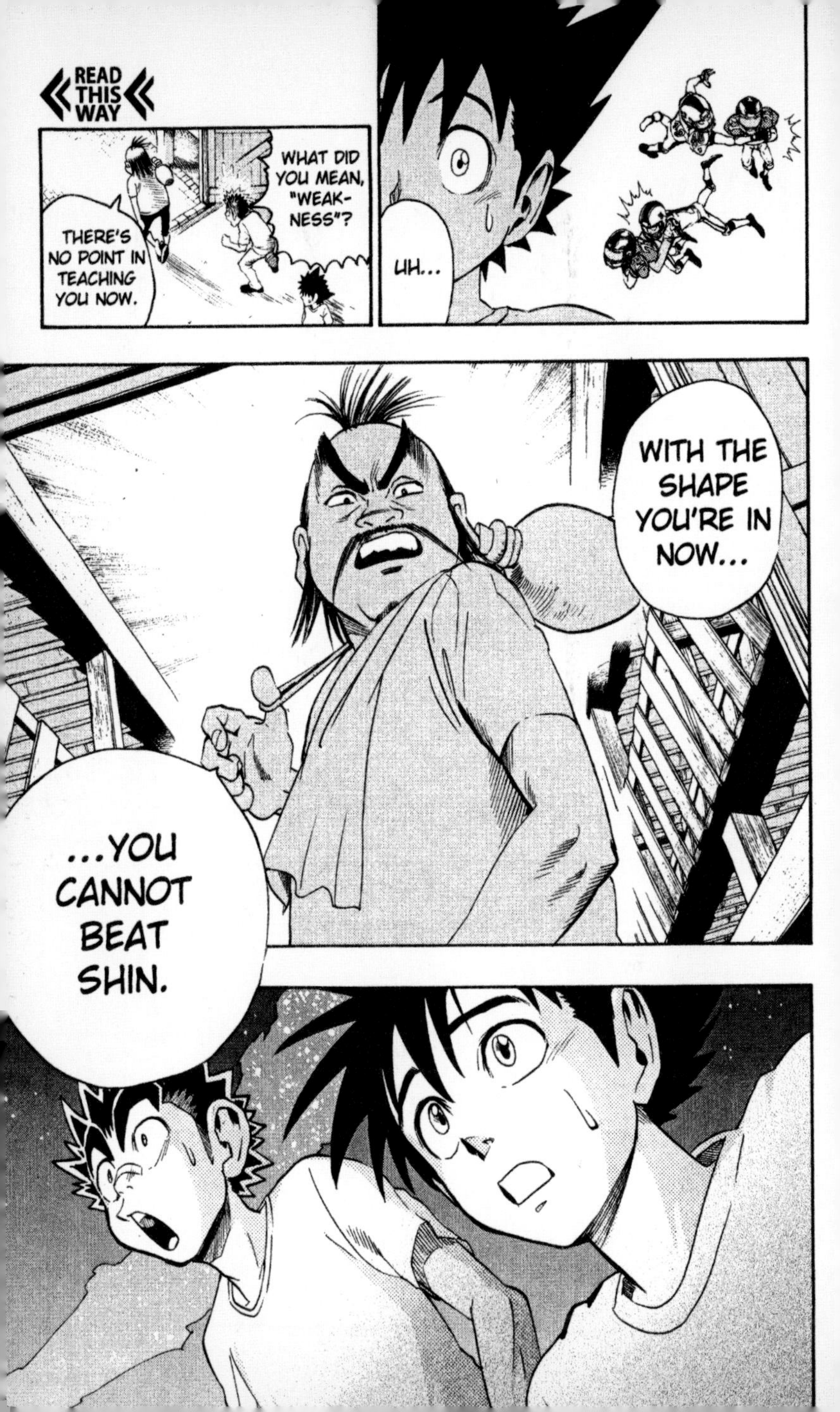
READ THIS WAY
UH...
WHAT DID YOU MEAN, "WEAK-NESS"?
THERE'S NO POINT IN TEACHING YOU NOW.
WITH THE SHAPE YOU'RE IN NOW...
...YOU CANNOT BEAT SHIN.

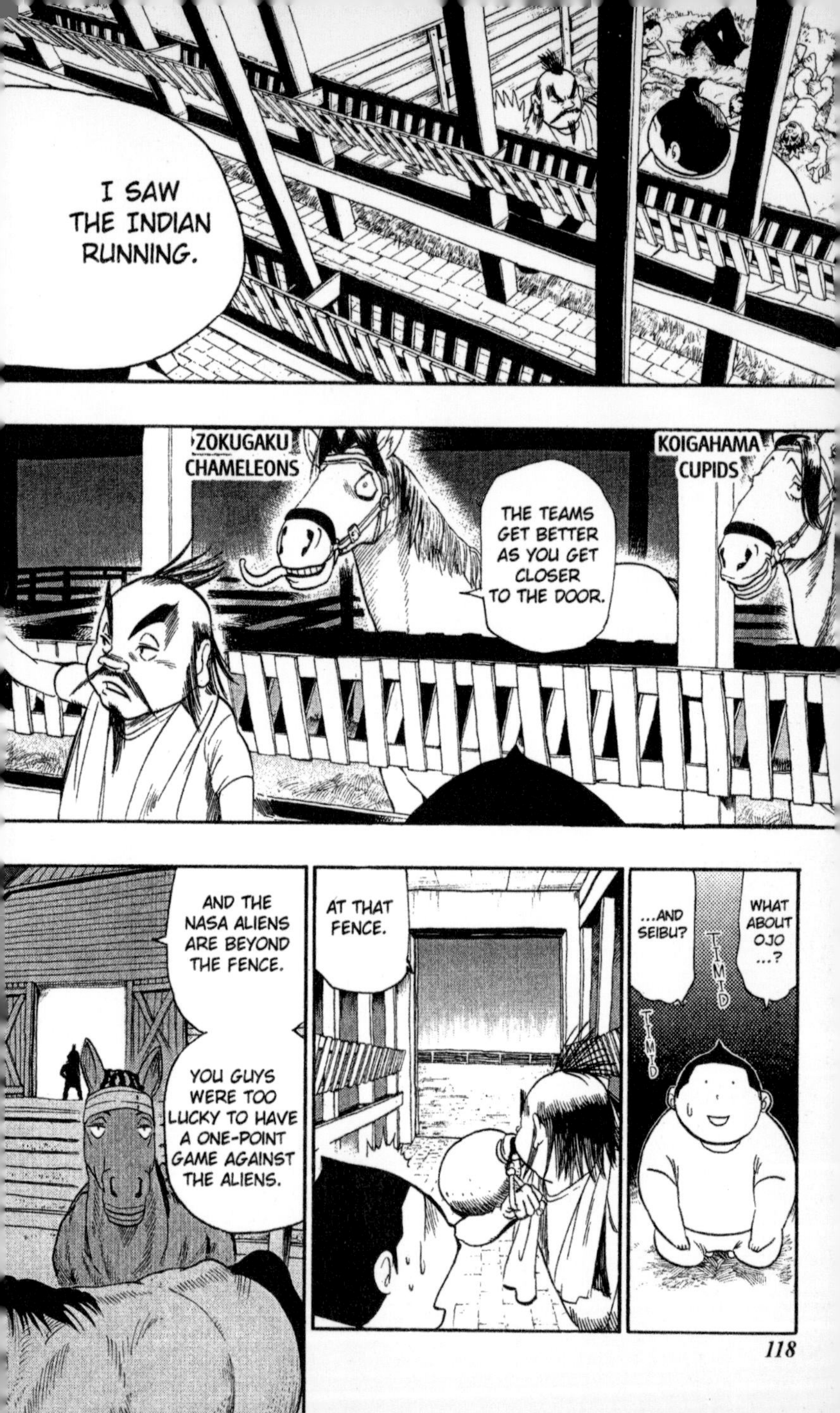
I SAW THE INDIAN RUNNING.
KOIGAHAMA CUPIDS
THE TEAMS GET BETTER AS YOU GET CLOSER TO THE DOOR.
ZOKUGAKU CHAMELEONS
WHAT ABOUT OJO ...?
...AND SEIBU?
TIMID
TIMID
AT THAT FENCE.
AND THE NASA ALIENS ARE BEYOND THE FENCE.
YOU GUYS WERE TOO LUCKY TO HAVE A ONE-POINT GAME AGAINST THE ALIENS.

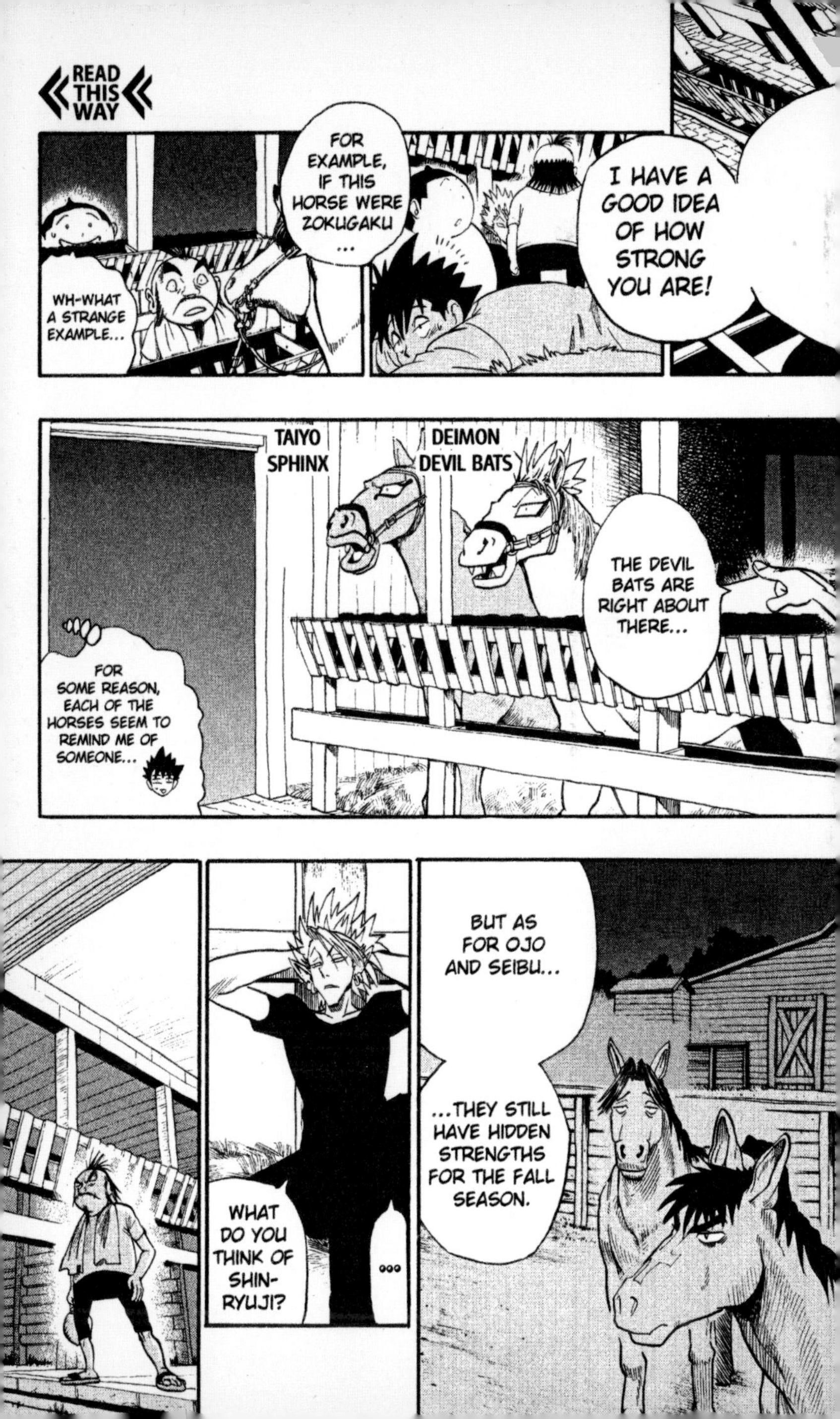
READ THIS WAY
I HAVE A GOOD IDEA OF HOW STRONG YOU ARE!
FOR EXAMPLE, IF THIS HORSE WERE ZOKUGAKU...
WH-WHAT A STRANGE EXAMPLE...
DEIMON DEVIL BATS
TAIYO SPHINX
THE DEVIL BATS ARE RIGHT ABOUT THERE...
FOR SOME REASON, EACH OF THE HORSES SEEM TO REMIND ME OF SOMEONE...
BUT AS FOR OJO AND SEIBU...
...THEY STILL HAVE HIDDEN STRENGTHS FOR THE FALL SEASON.
...
WHAT DO YOU THINK OF SHIN-RYUJI?

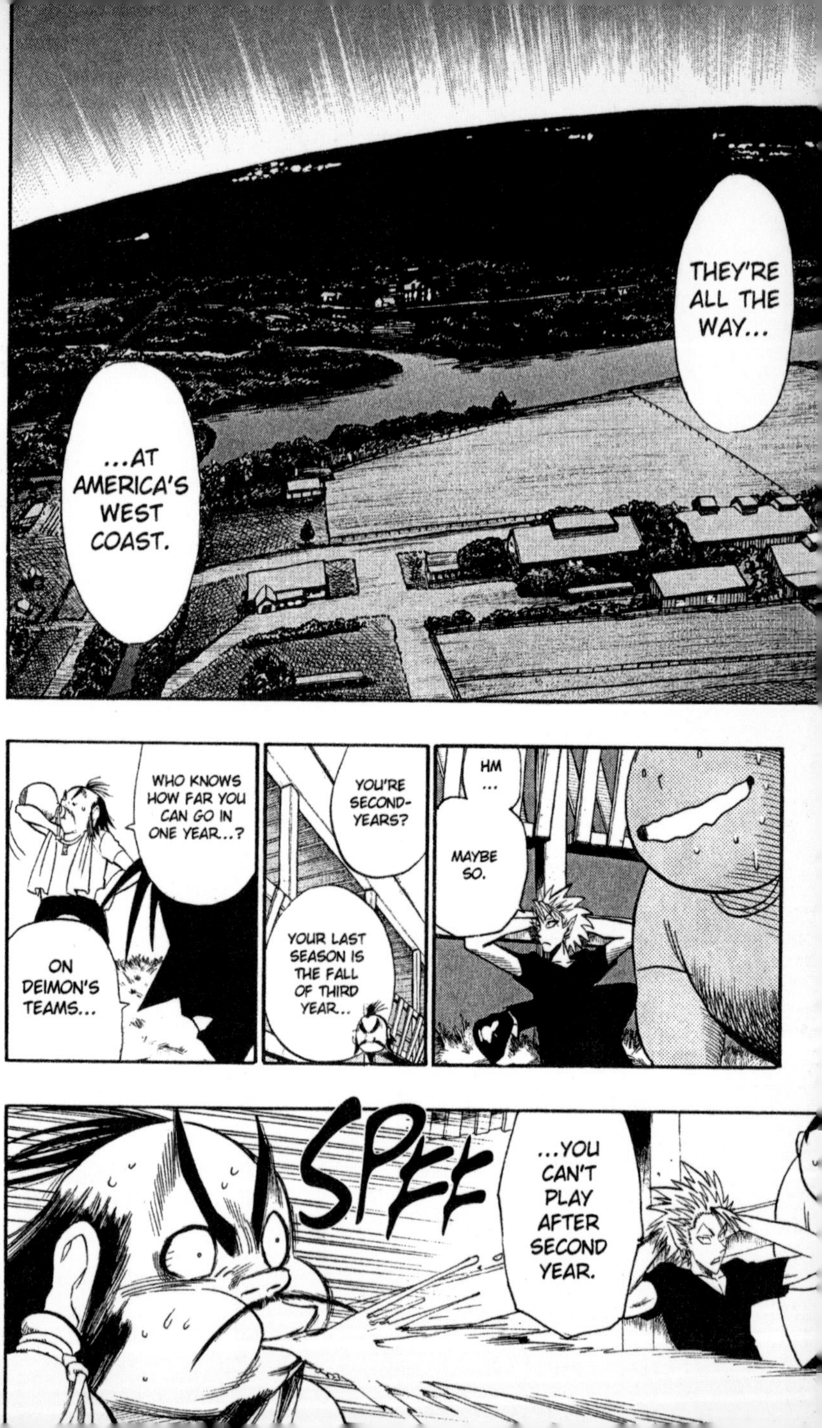
THEY'RE ALL THE WAY...
...AT AMERICA'S WEST COAST.
HM ...
MAYBE SO.
YOU'RE SECOND-YEARS?
YOUR LAST SEASON IS THE FALL OF THIRD YEAR...
WHO KNOWS HOW FAR YOU CAN GO IN ONE YEAR...?
ON DEIMON'S TEAMS...
SPFF
...YOU CAN'T PLAY AFTER SECOND YEAR.

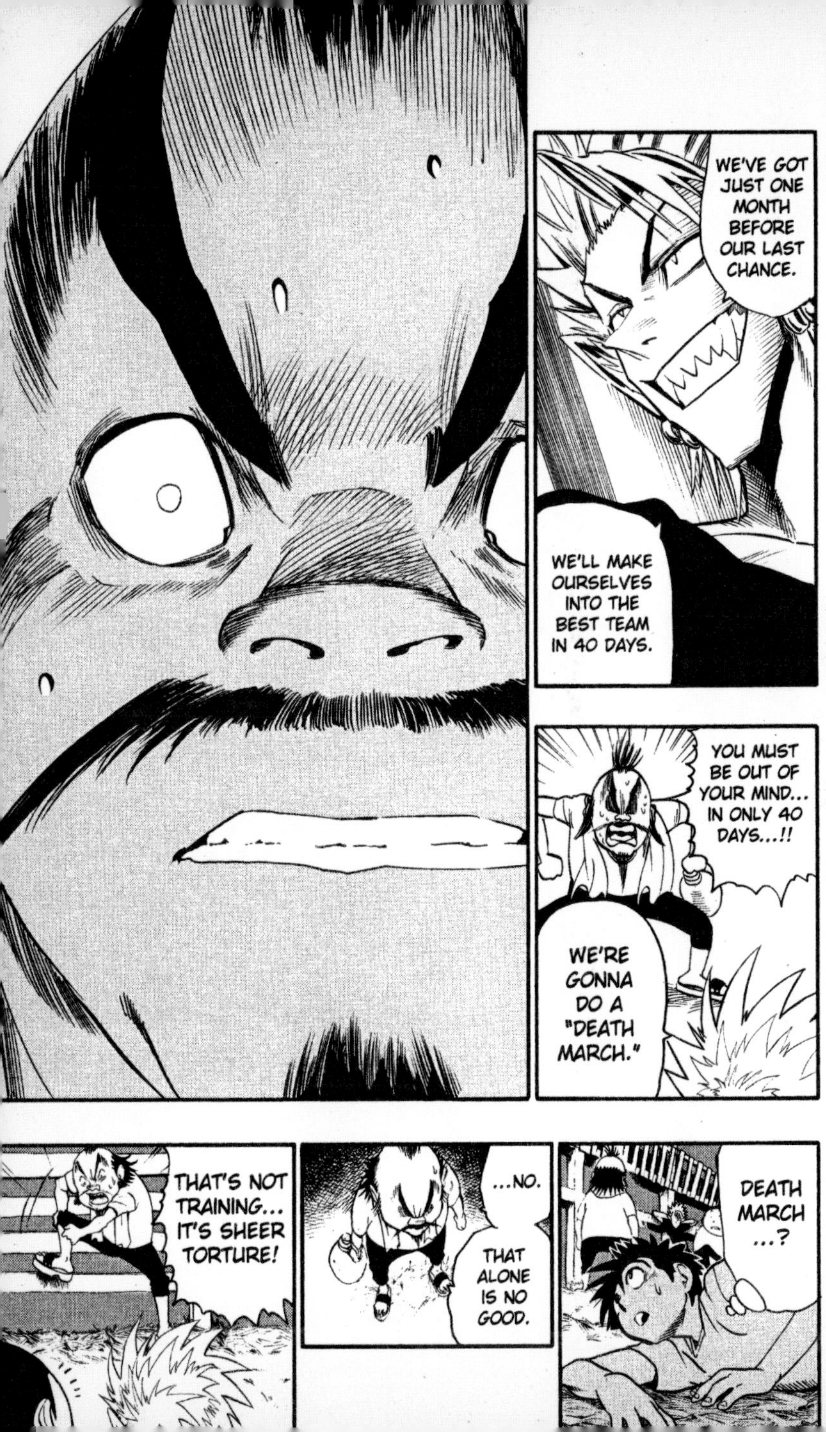
WE'VE GOT JUST ONE MONTH BEFORE OUR LAST CHANCE.
WE'LL MAKE OURSELVES INTO THE BEST TEAM IN 40 DAYS.
YOU MUST BE OUT OF YOUR MIND... IN ONLY 40 DAYS...!!
WE'RE GONNA DO A "DEATH MARCH."
DEATH MARCH ...?
...NO.
THAT ALONE IS NO GOOD.
THAT'S NOT TRAINING... IT'S SHEER TORTURE!

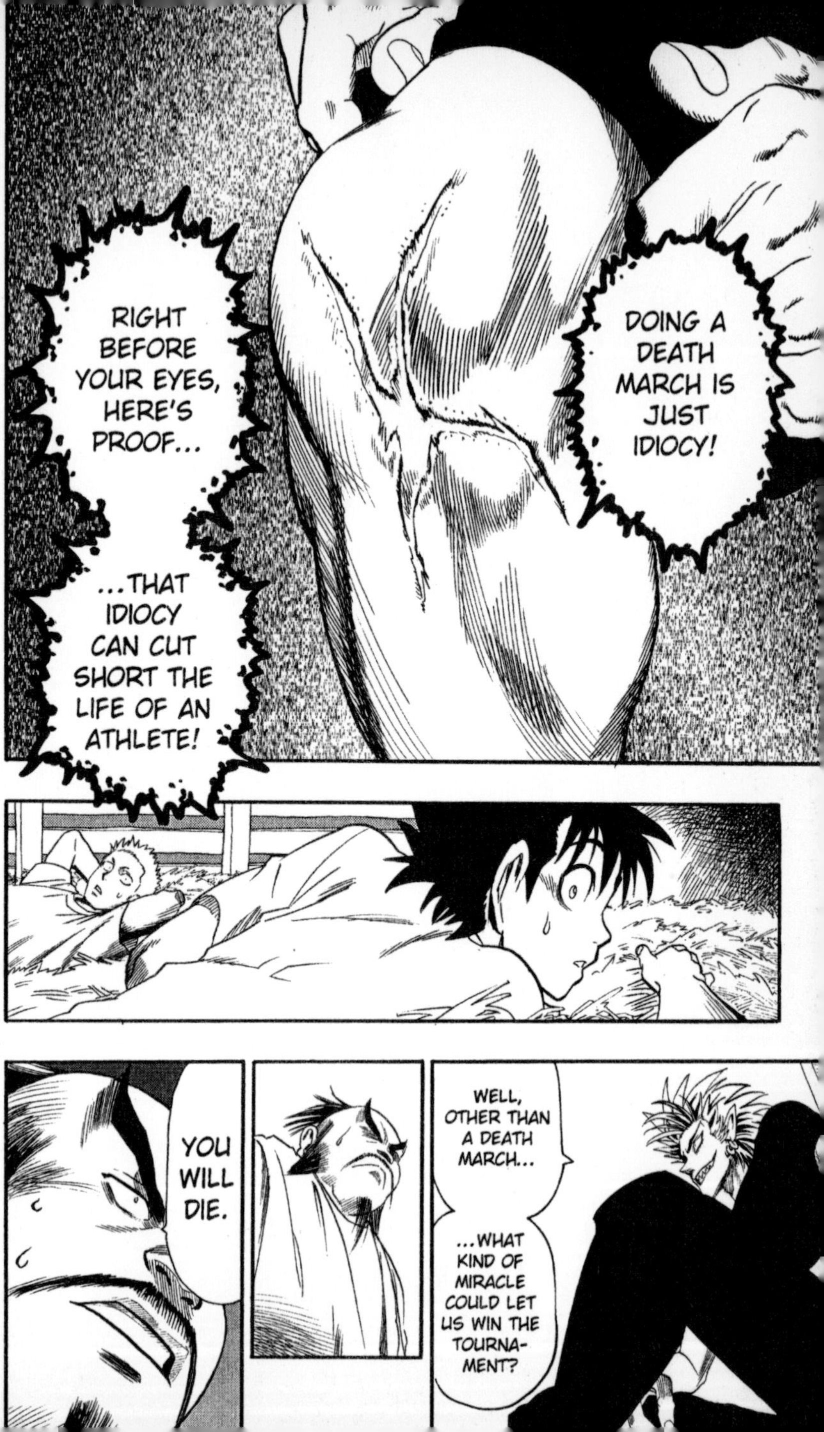
DOING A DEATH MARCH IS JUST IDIOCY!
RIGHT BEFORE YOUR EYES, HERE'S PROOF...
...THAT IDIOCY CAN CUT SHORT THE LIFE OF AN ATHLETE!
WELL, OTHER THAN A DEATH MARCH...
...WHAT KIND OF MIRACLE COULD LET US WIN THE TOURNA-MENT?
YOU WILL DIE.

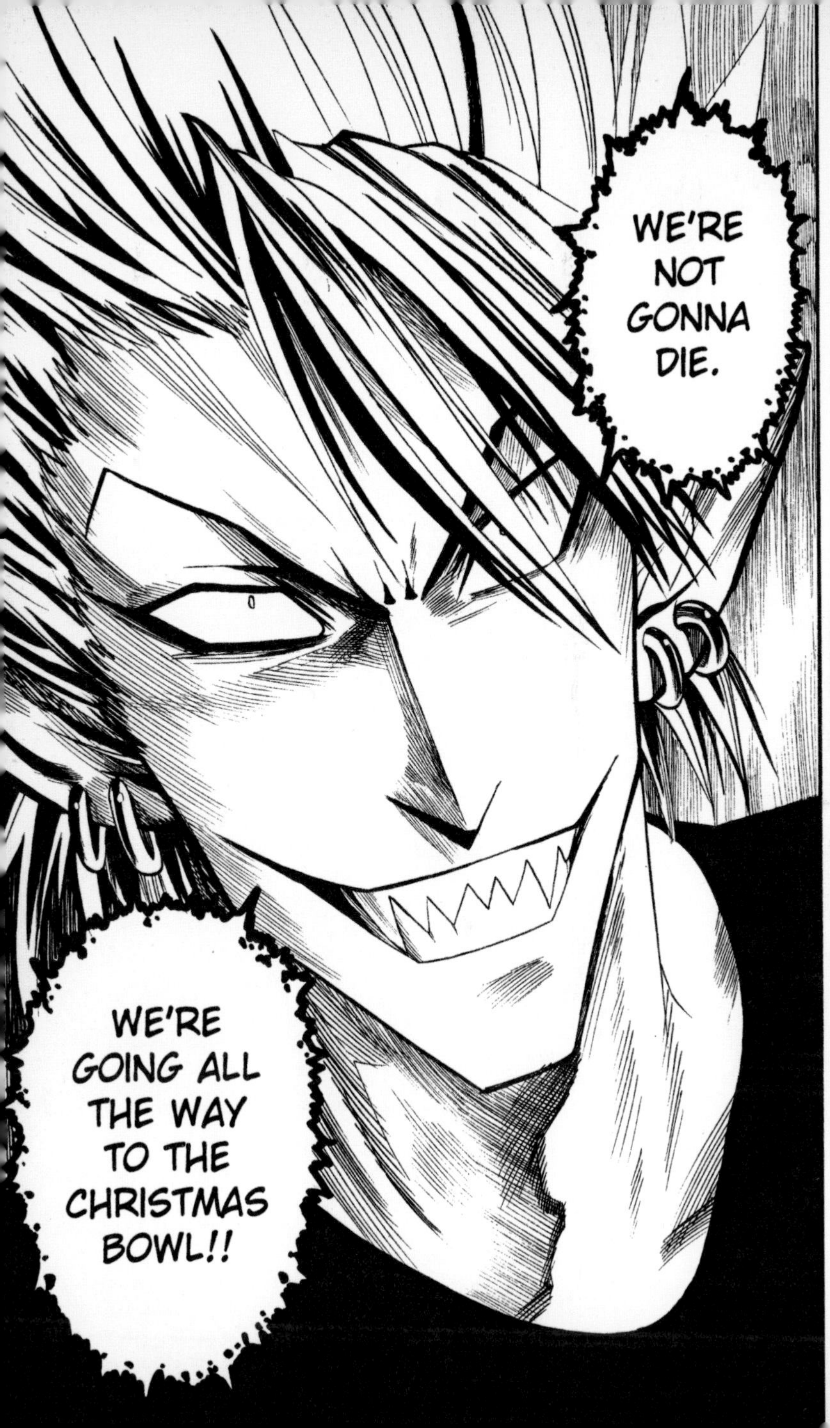
WE'RE NOT GONNA DIE.
WE'RE GOING ALL THE WAY TO THE CHRISTMAS BOWL!!

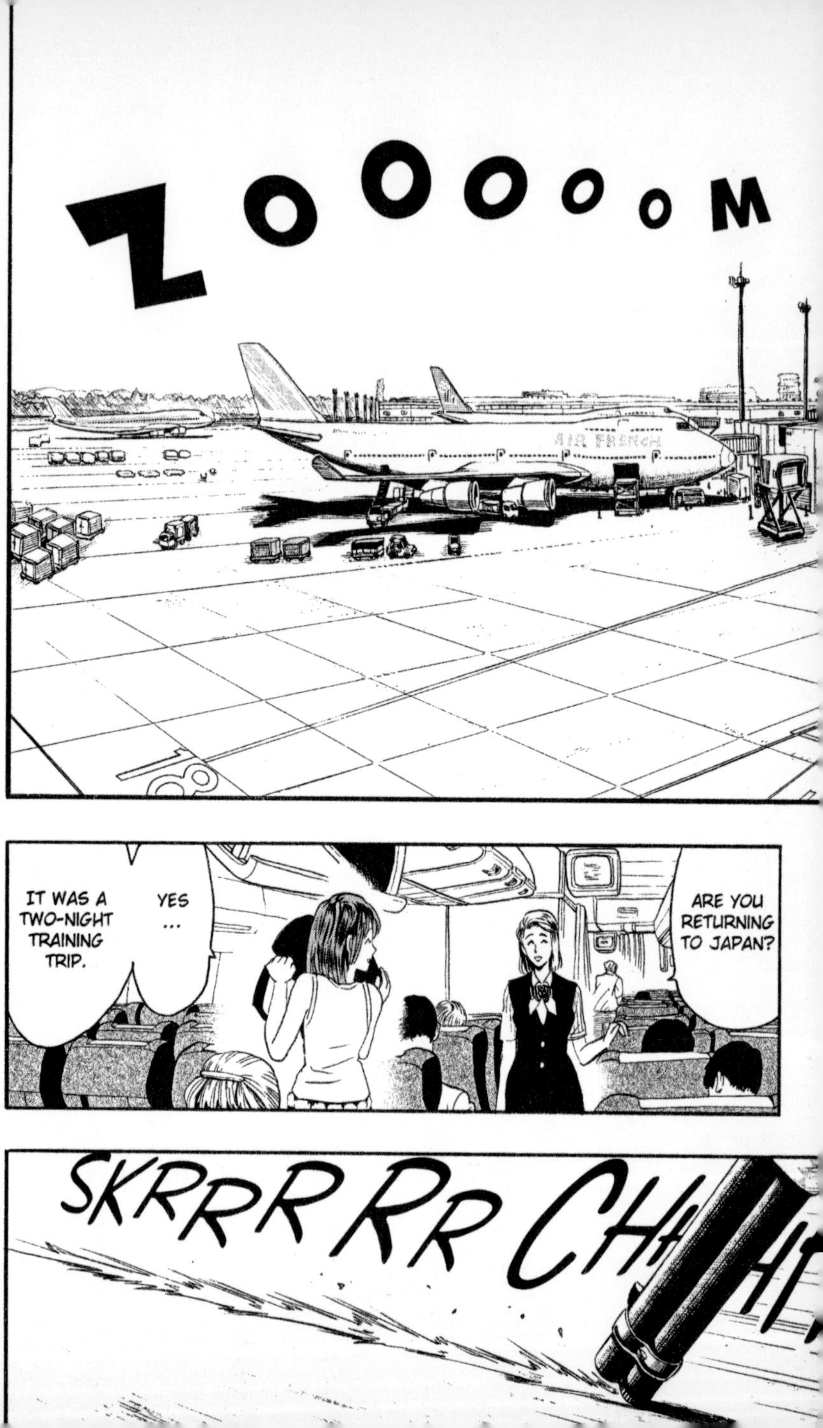
ZOOOOOM
AIR FRENCH
ARE YOU RETURNING TO JAPAN?
YES ...
IT WAS A TWO-NIGHT TRAINING TRIP.
SKRRRRRCH

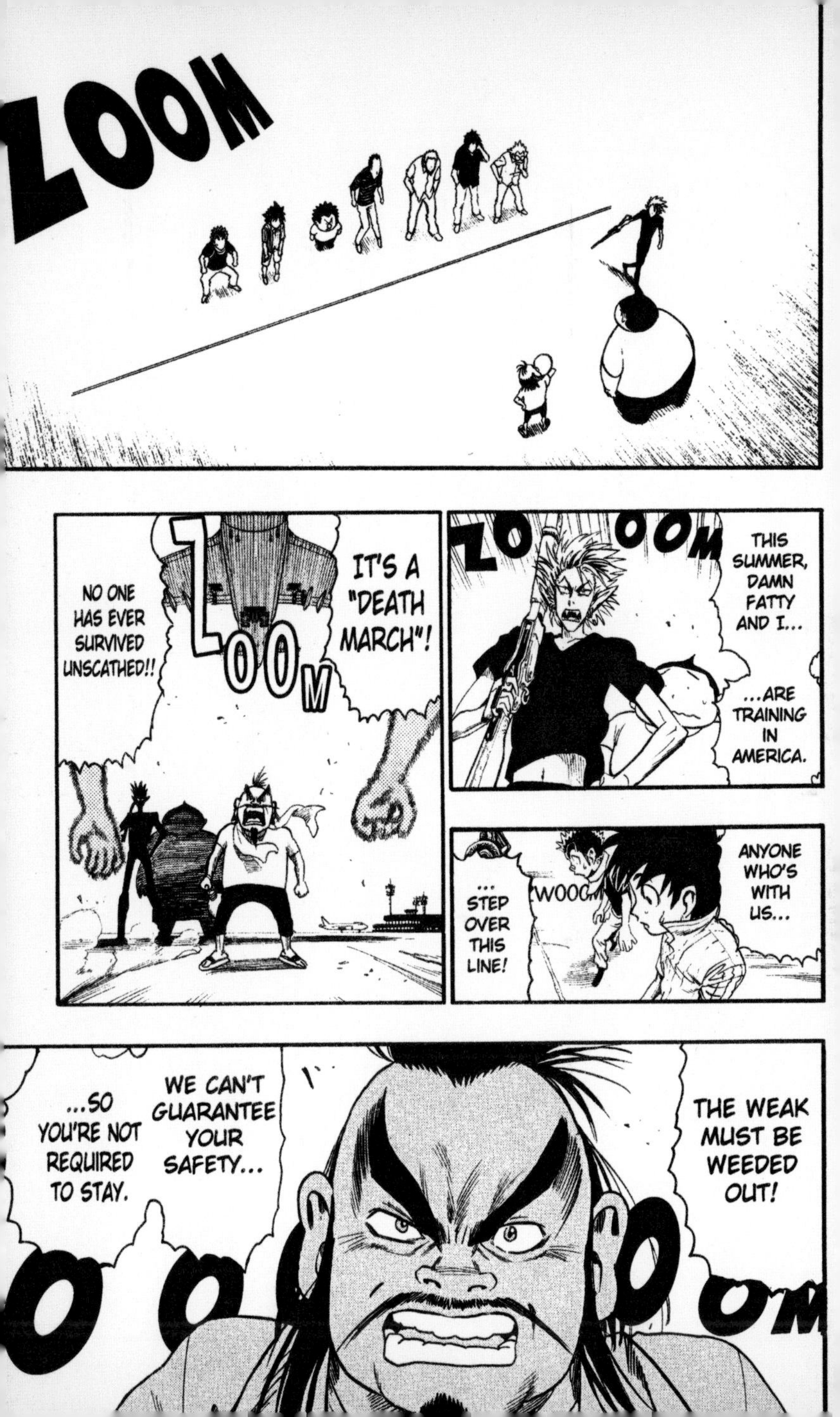
ZOOM
ZO
OOM
THIS SUMMER, DAMN FATTY AND I...
...ARE TRAINING IN AMERICA.
ANYONE WHO'S WITH US...
WOOOM
...STEP OVER THIS LINE!
IT'S A "DEATH MARCH"!
ZOOOM
NO ONE HAS EVER SURVIVED UNSCATHED!!
THE WEAK MUST BE WEEDED OUT!
WE CAN'T GUARANTEE YOUR SAFETY...
...SO YOU'RE NOT REQUIRED TO STAY.

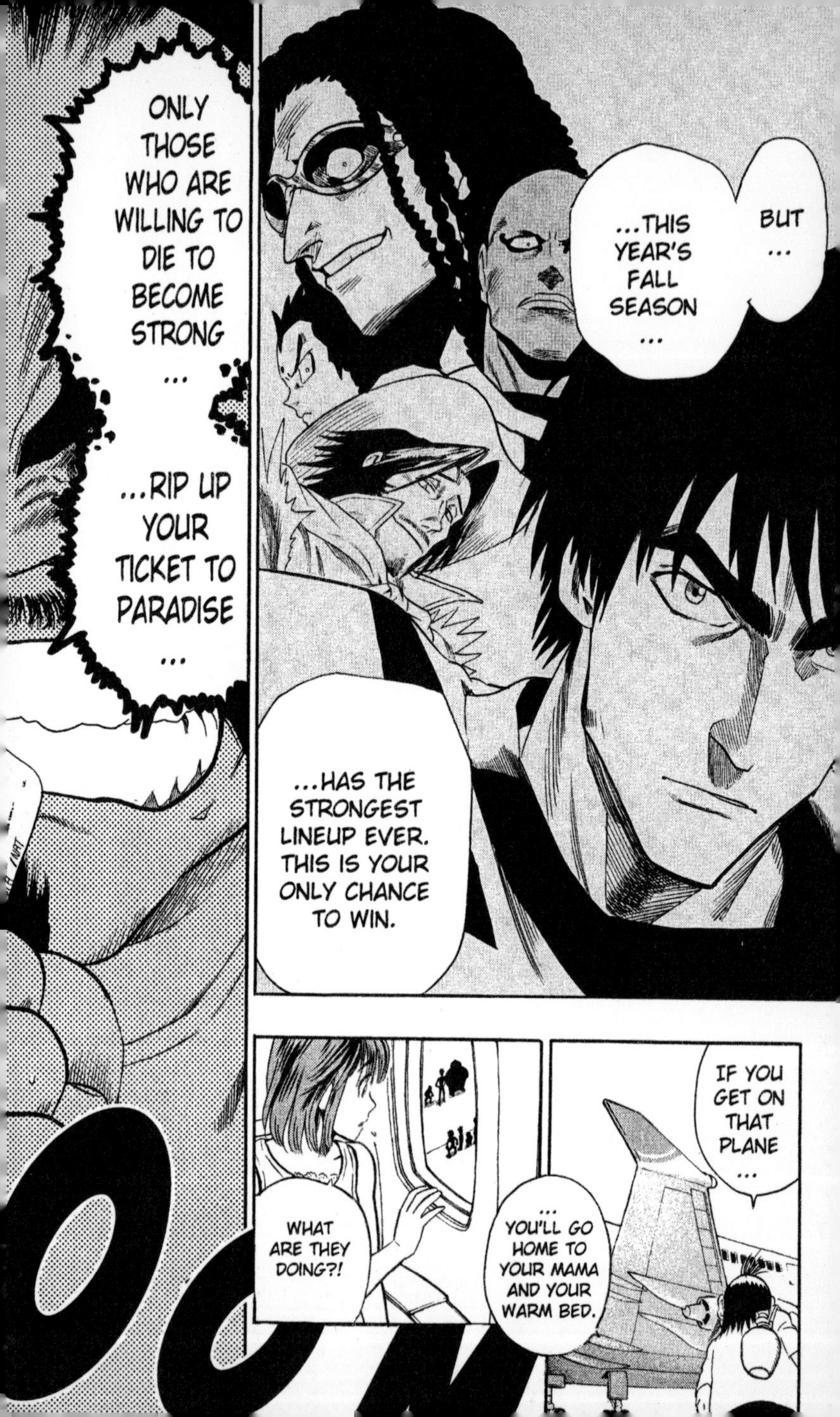
BUT ...
...THIS YEAR'S FALL SEASON ...
...HAS THE STRONGEST LINEUP EVER. THIS IS YOUR ONLY CHANCE TO WIN.
IF YOU GET ON THAT PLANE ...
... YOU'LL GO HOME TO YOUR MAMA AND YOUR WARM BED.
WHAT ARE THEY DOING?!
ONLY THOSE WHO ARE WILLING TO DIE TO BECOME STRONG ...
...RIP UP YOUR TICKET TO PARADISE ...

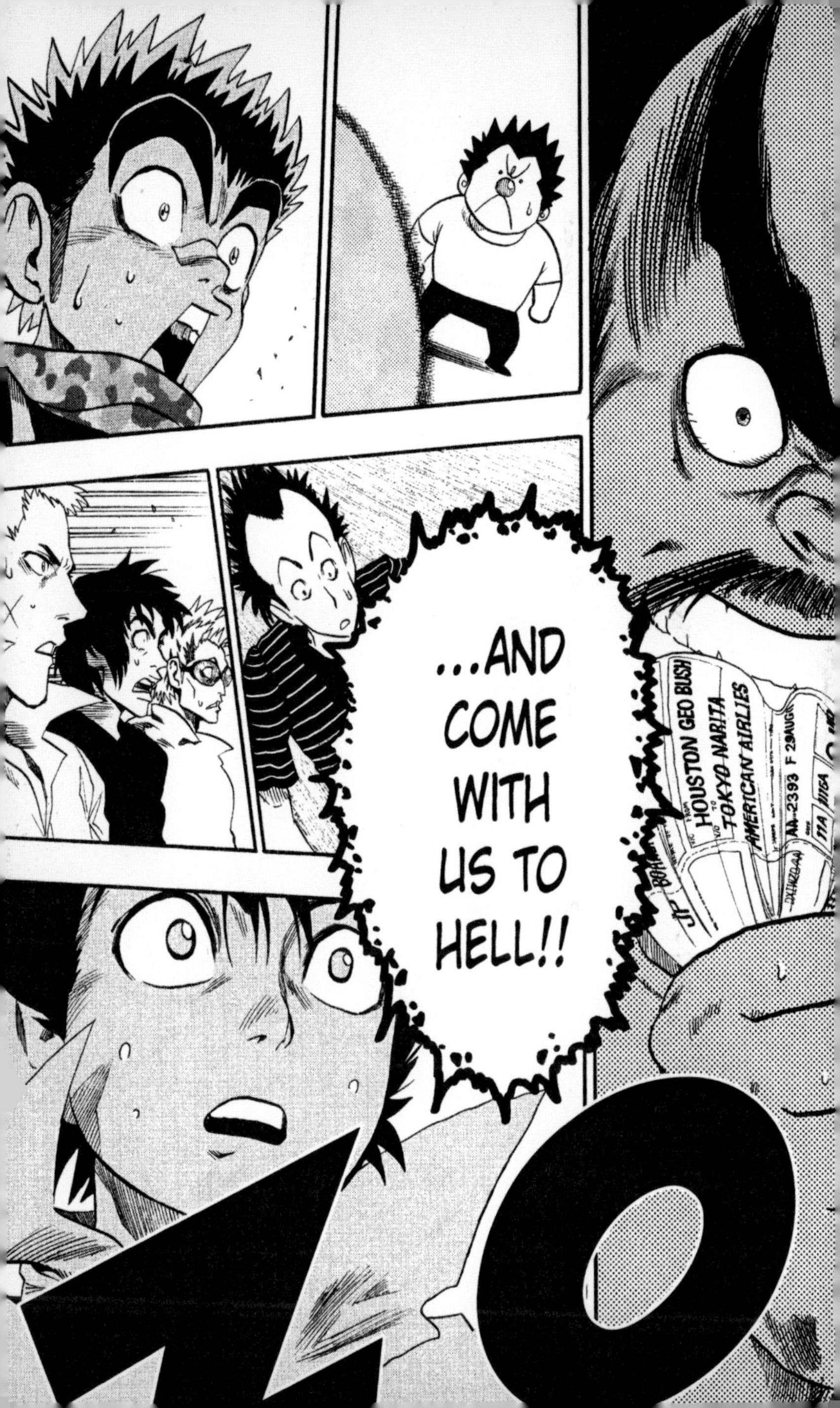
...AND COME WITH US TO HELL!!
HOUSTON GEO BUSH
TOKYO NARITA
AMERICAN AIRLIES
AA-2393 F 29AUG
ZO

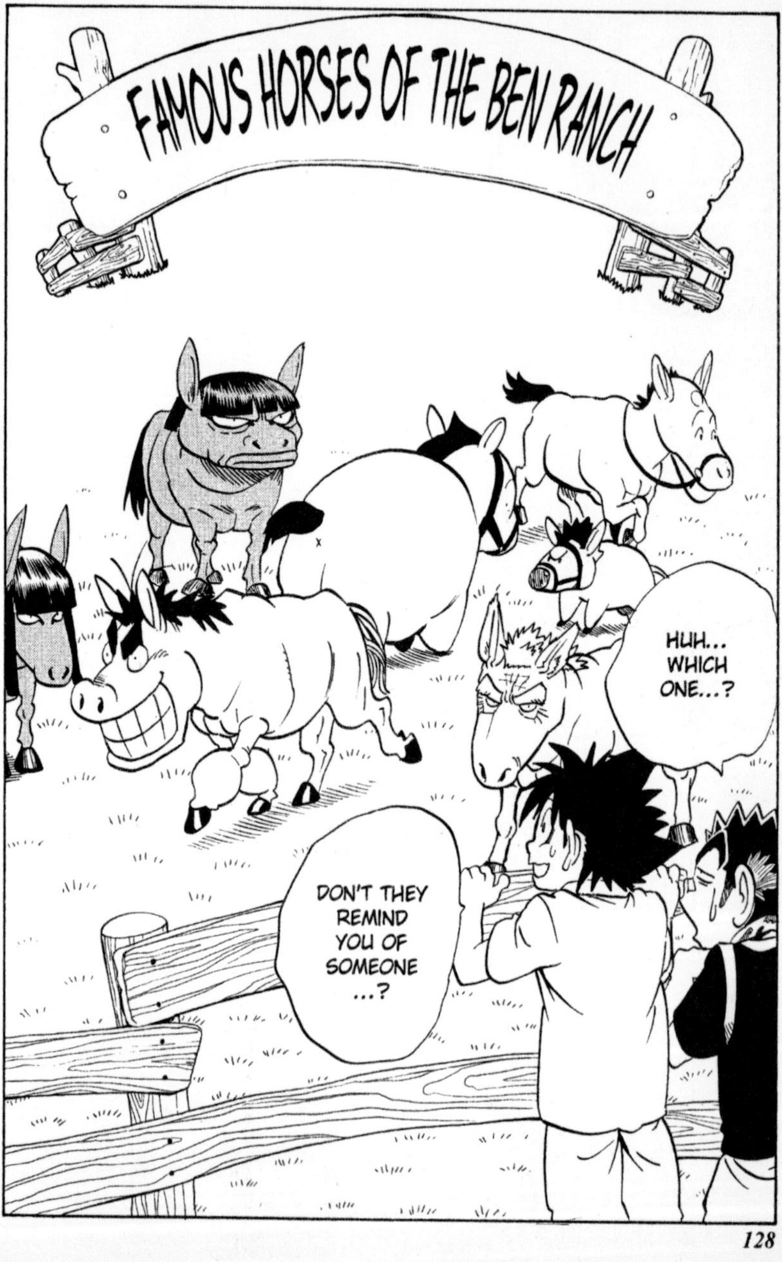
FAMOUS HORSES OF THE BEN RANCH
HUH... WHICH ONE...?
DON'T THEY REMIND YOU OF SOMEONE ...?

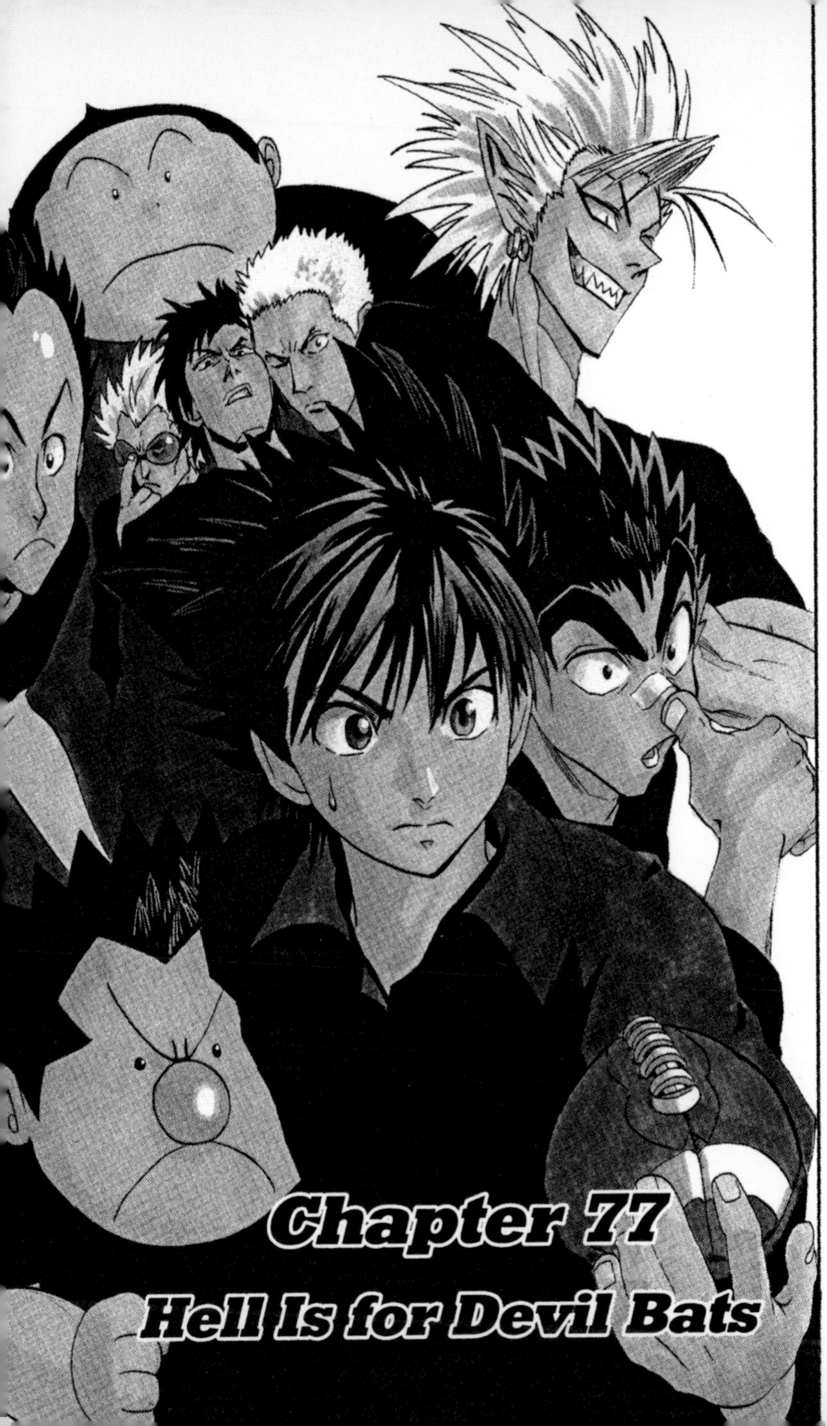

Chapter 77
Hell Is for Devil Bats

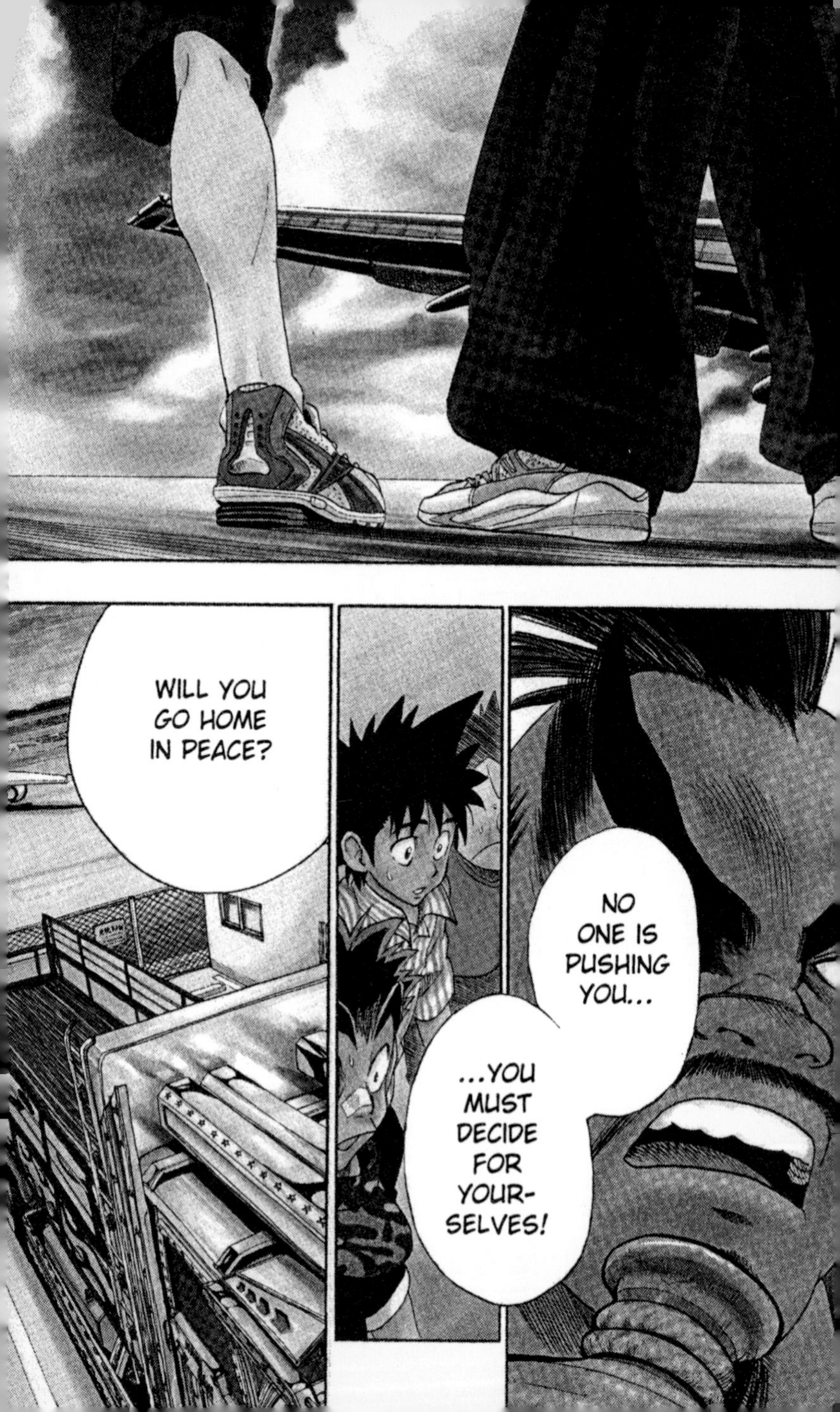
NO ONE IS PUSHING YOU...
...YOU MUST DECIDE FOR YOUR-SELVES!
WILL YOU GO HOME IN PEACE?

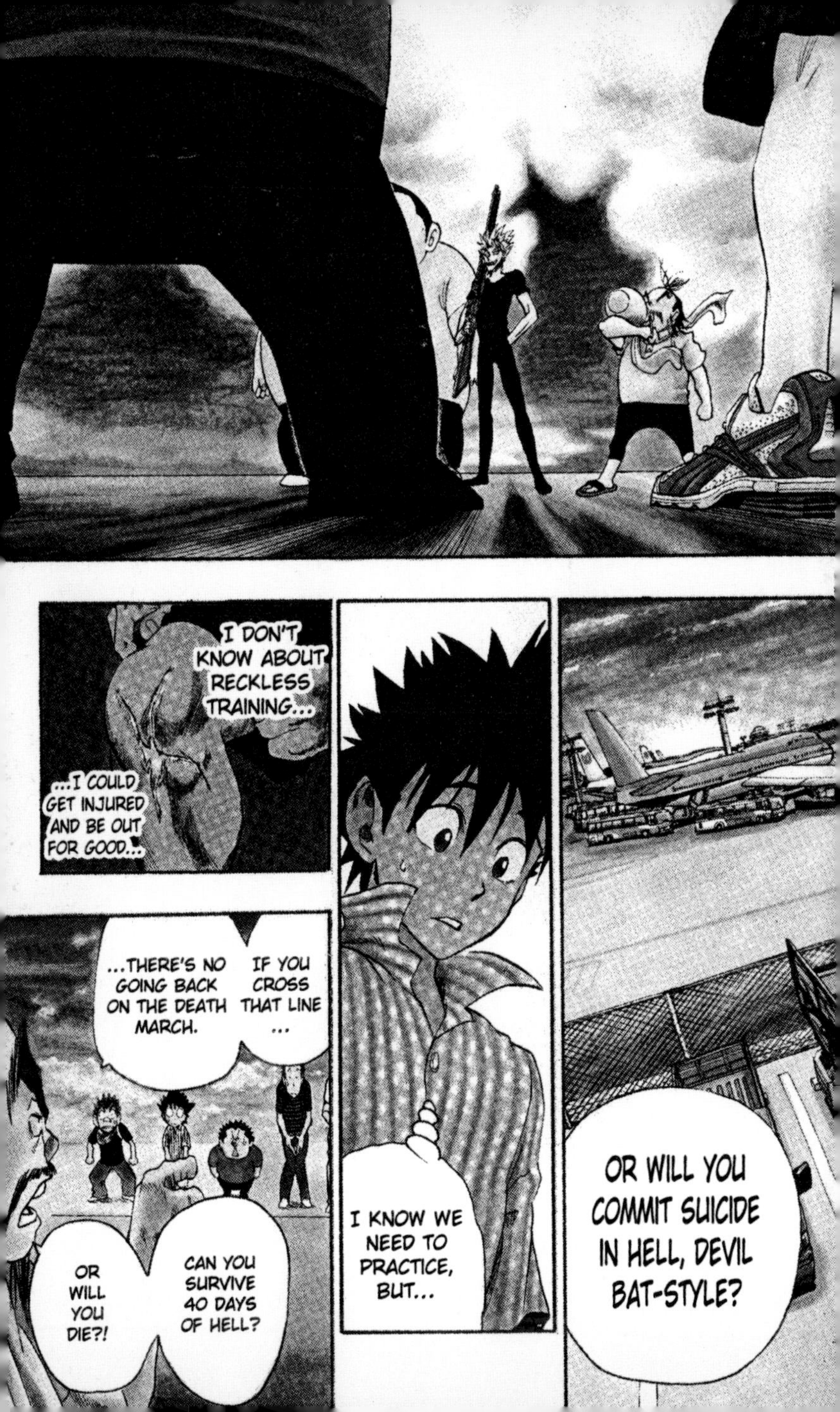
OR WILL YOU COMMIT SUICIDE IN HELL, DEVIL BAT-STYLE?
I KNOW WE NEED TO PRACTICE, BUT...
I DON'T KNOW ABOUT RECKLESS TRAINING...
...I COULD GET INJURED AND BE OUT FOR GOOD...
IF YOU CROSS THAT LINE...
...THERE'S NO GOING BACK ON THE DEATH MARCH.
CAN YOU SURVIVE 40 DAYS OF HELL?
OR WILL YOU DIE?!

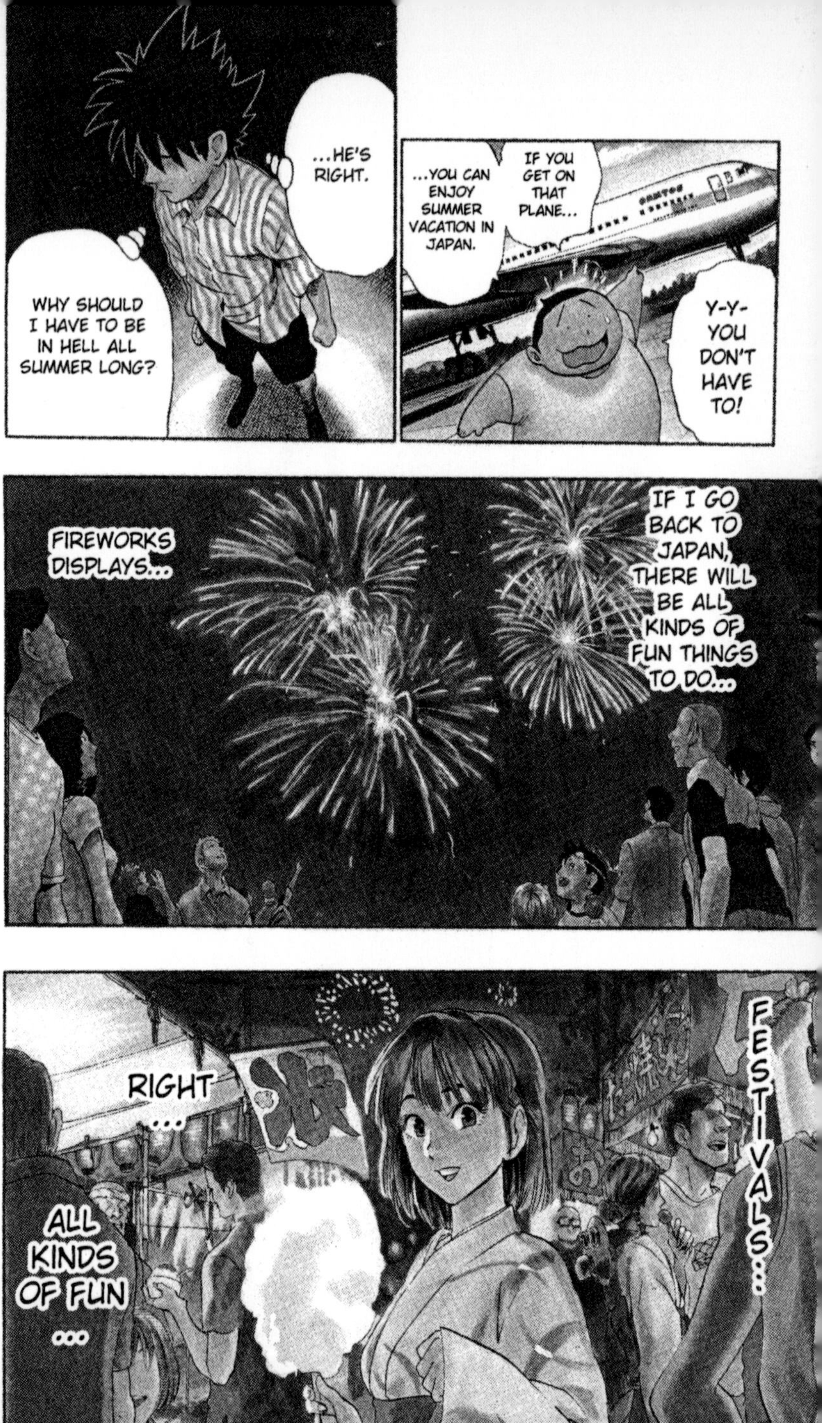
IF YOU GET ON THAT PLANE...
...YOU CAN ENJOY SUMMER VACATION IN JAPAN.
Y-Y-YOU DON'T HAVE TO!
...HE'S RIGHT.
WHY SHOULD I HAVE TO BE IN HELL ALL SUMMER LONG?
IF I GO BACK TO JAPAN, THERE WILL BE ALL KINDS OF FUN THINGS TO DO...
FIREWORKS DISPLAYS...
FESTIVALS...
RIGHT...
ALL KINDS OF FUN...

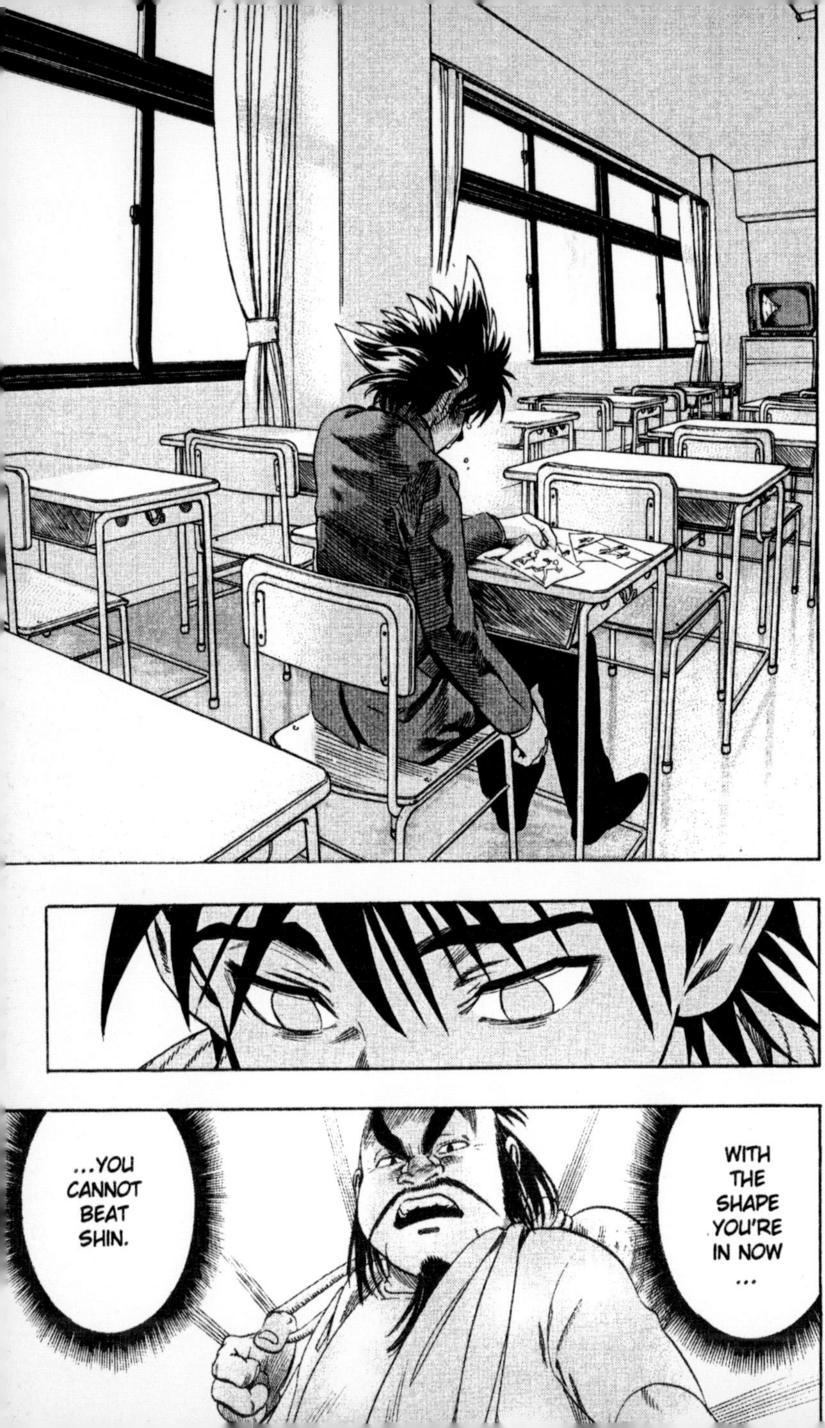
WITH THE SHAPE YOU'RE IN NOW ...
...YOU CANNOT BEAT SHIN.

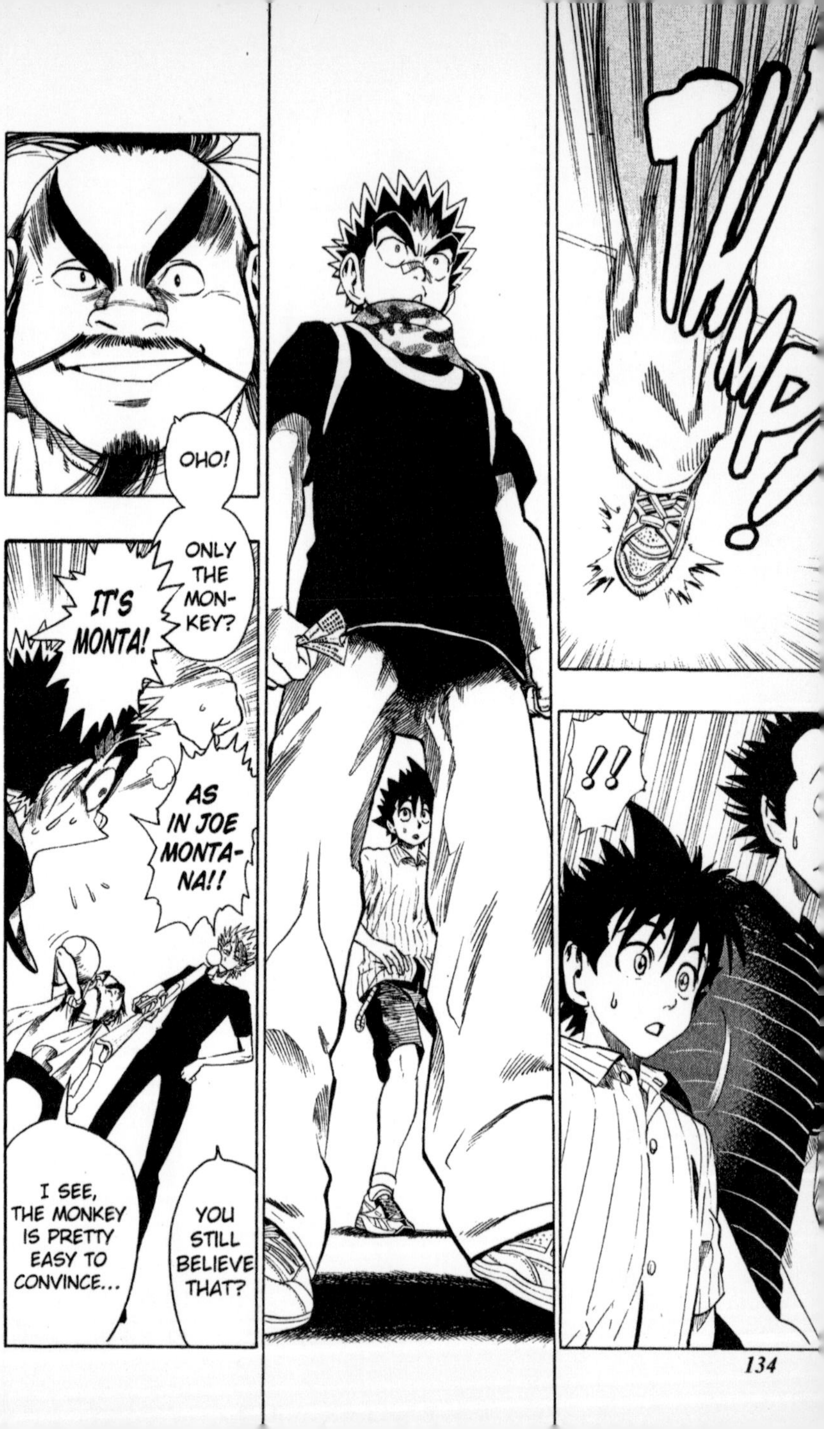
THUMP!
!!
OHO!
ONLY THE MON-KEY?
IT'S MONTA!
AS IN JOE MONTA-NA!!
YOU STILL BELIEVE THAT?
I SEE, THE MONKEY IS PRETTY EASY TO CONVINCE...

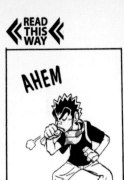

READ THIS WAY
HOW ABOUT THIS...
THOSE OF YOU WHO STEP ACROSS THE LINE...
... INTRODUCE YOURSELVES TO ME...
...BEFORE YOU DIE ON THE "DEATH MARCH"!
AHEM
TARO RAIMON!
NUMBER 80!
SPEED
CATCHING TECHNIQUE
HEIGHT
WEIGHT
POWER
POSITION, WIDE RECEIVER!!
BLOOD TYPE, B!
FAVORITE FOOD, BANANAS!
I LIKE THE WORD "EFFORT"!
THE PERSON I LIKE IS MAMO--...
COUGH
HE'S MAKING A SPEECH ...?
MY FAVORITE SPORT IS...
ALL RIGHT, ALREADY ...!!

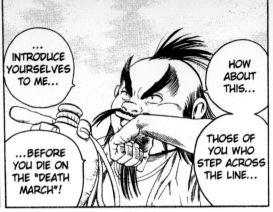

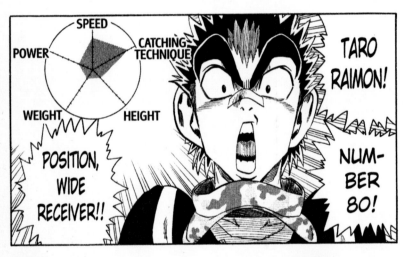

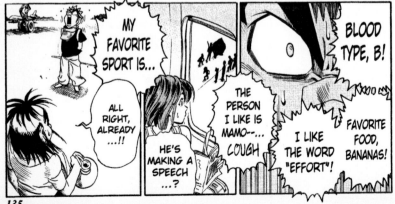

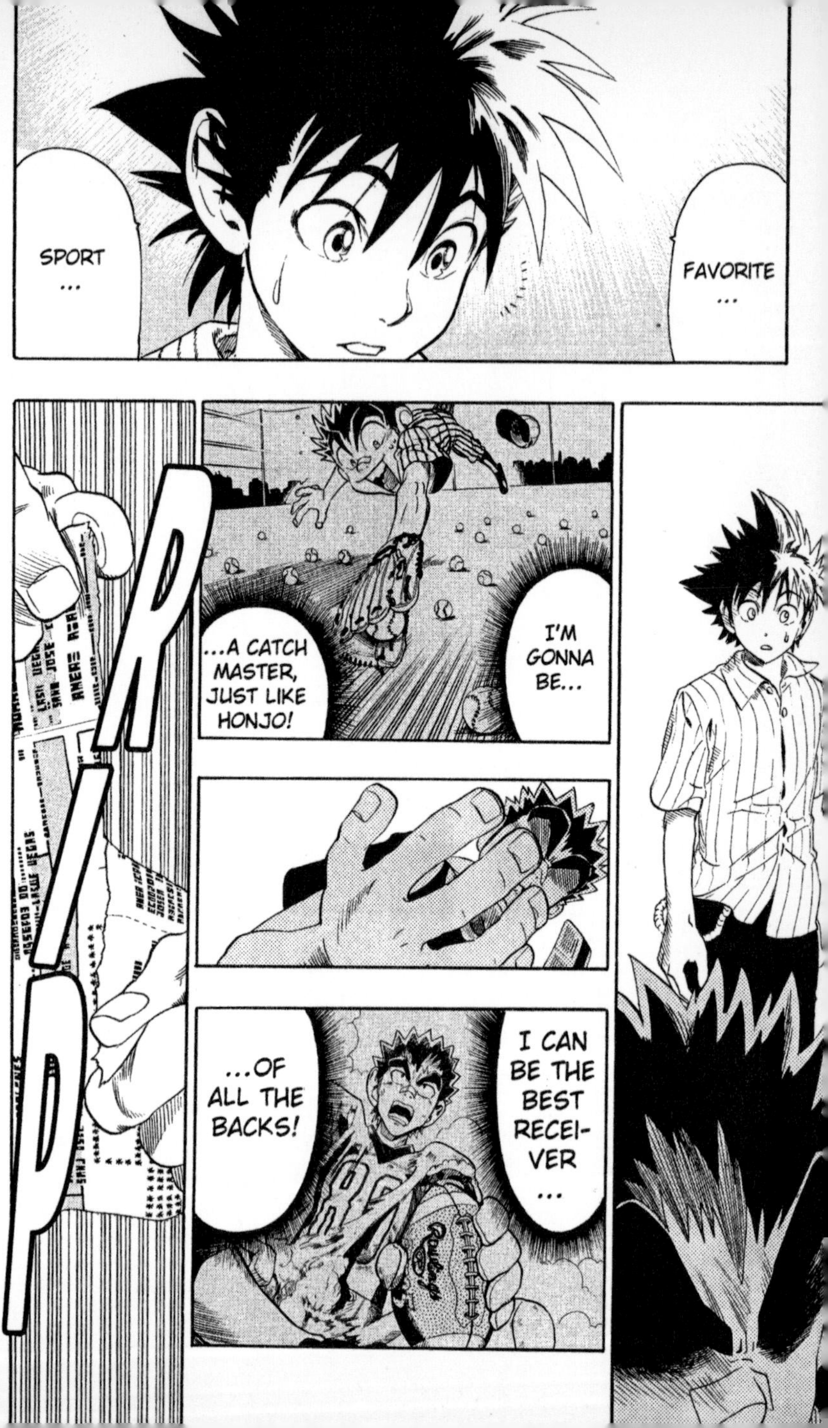
FAVORITE ...
SPORT ...
I'M GONNA BE...
...A CATCH MASTER, JUST LIKE HONJO!
I CAN BE THE BEST RECEI-VER ...
...OF ALL THE BACKS!
RIIP

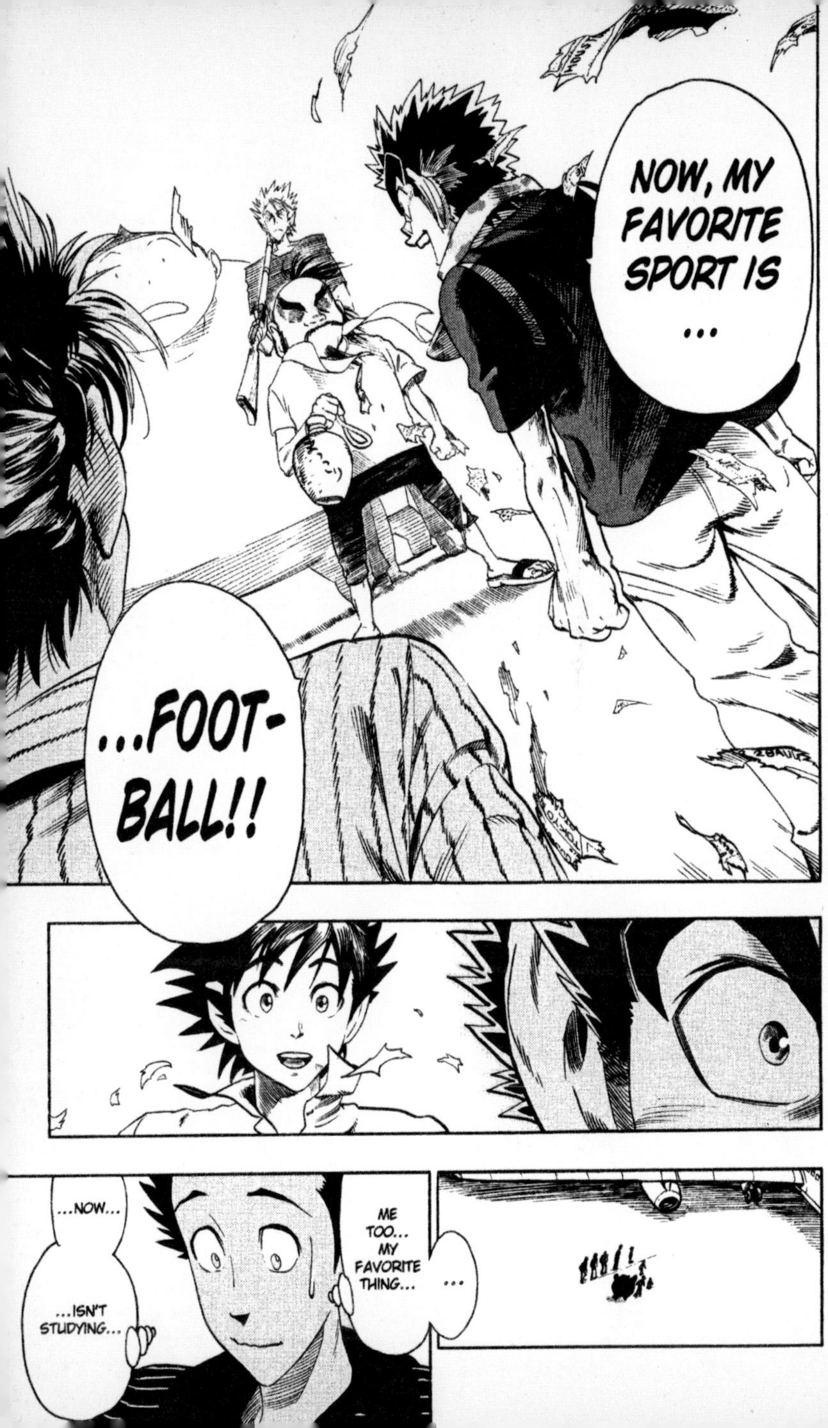
NOW, MY FAVORITE SPORT IS ...
...FOOT-BALL!!
ME TOO... MY FAVORITE THING...
...
...NOW...
...ISN'T STUDYING...

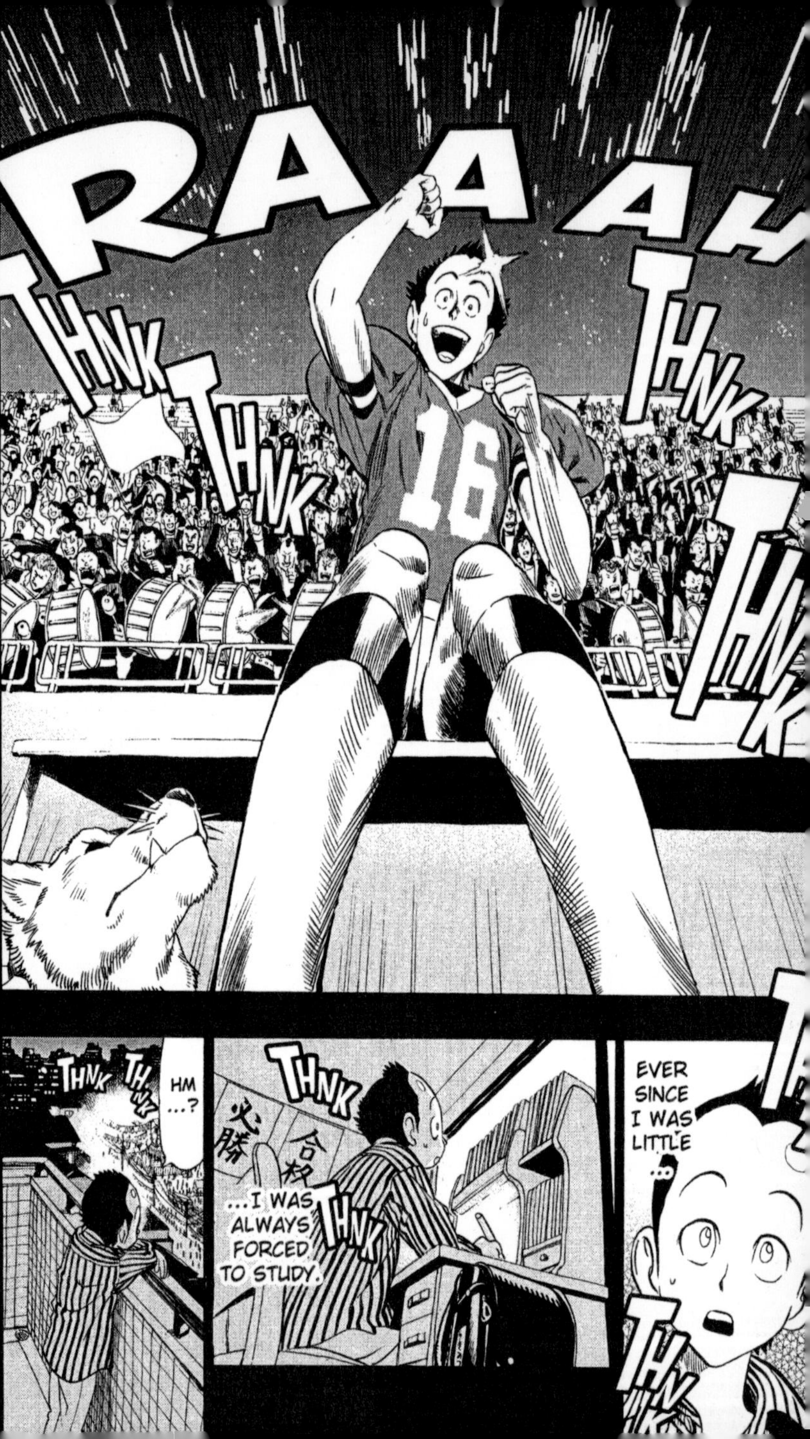
RAAAH
THNK
THNK
THNK
THNK
EVER SINCE I WAS LITTLE...
THNK
THNK
...I WAS ALWAYS FORCED TO STUDY.
THNK
THNK
必勝
合格
THNK
THNK
HM ...?

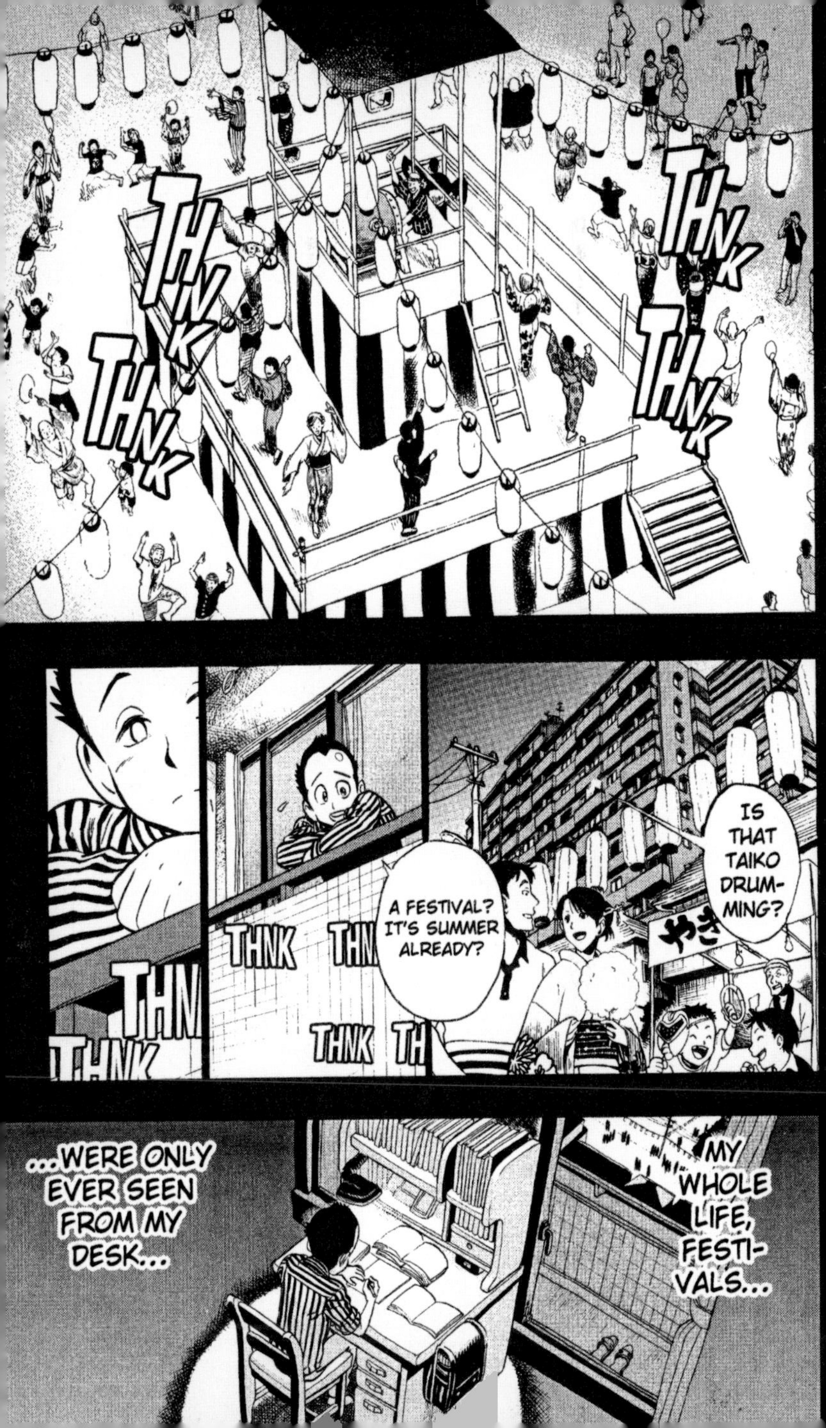
THNK
THNK
THNK
THNK
IS THAT TAIKO DRUMMING?
A FESTIVAL? IT'S SUMMER ALREADY?
やき
THNK THN
THNK TH
THN
THNK
MY WHOLE LIFE, FESTIVALS...
...WERE ONLY EVER SEEN FROM MY DESK...

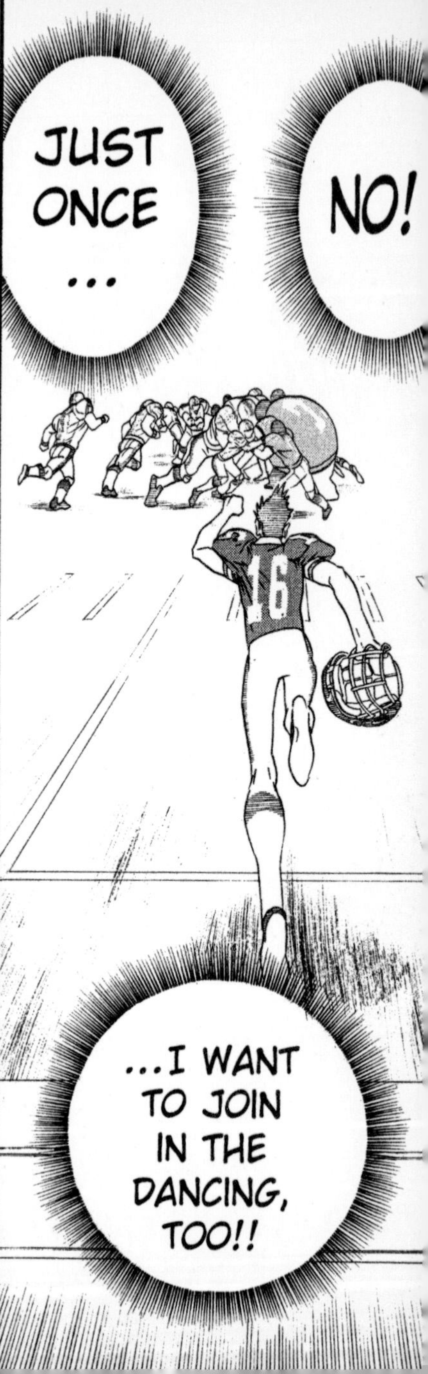

NO!
JUST ONCE ...
...I WANT TO JOIN IN THE DANCING, TOO!!
16

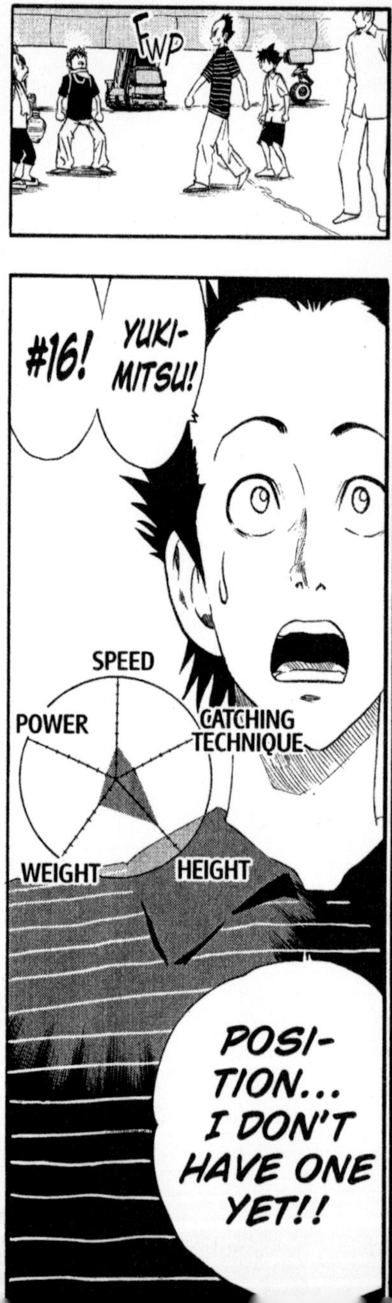

FWP
YUKI-MITSU!
#16!
SPEED
CATCHING TECHNIQUE
POWER
WEIGHT
HEIGHT
POSI-TION... I DON'T HAVE ONE YET!!

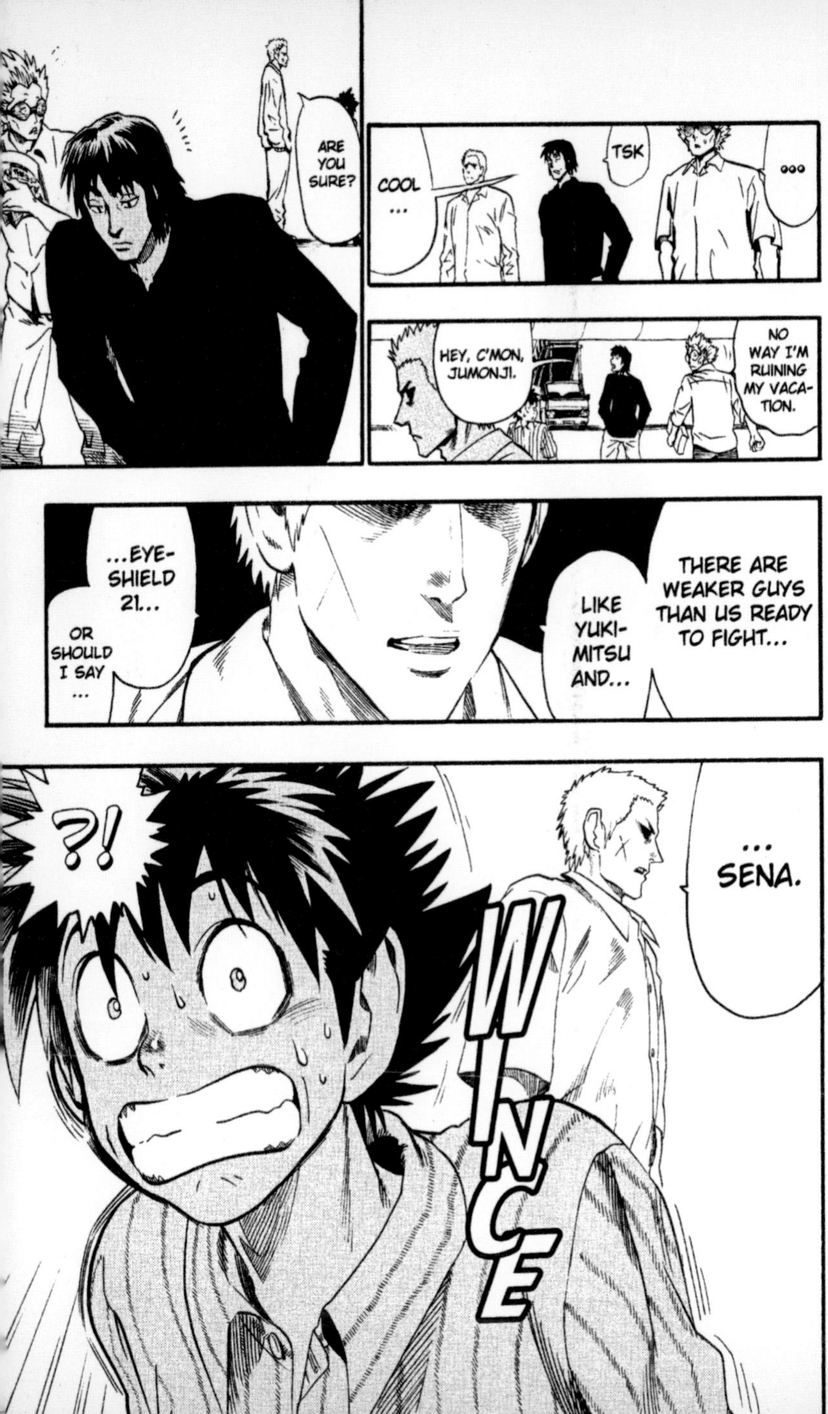
...
TSK
COOL ...
NO WAY I'M RUINING MY VACA-TION.
HEY, C'MON, JUMONJI.
ARE YOU SURE?
THERE ARE WEAKER GUYS THAN US READY TO FIGHT...
LIKE YUKI-MITSU AND...
...EYE-SHIELD 21...
OR SHOULD I SAY ...
... SENA.
?!
WINCE

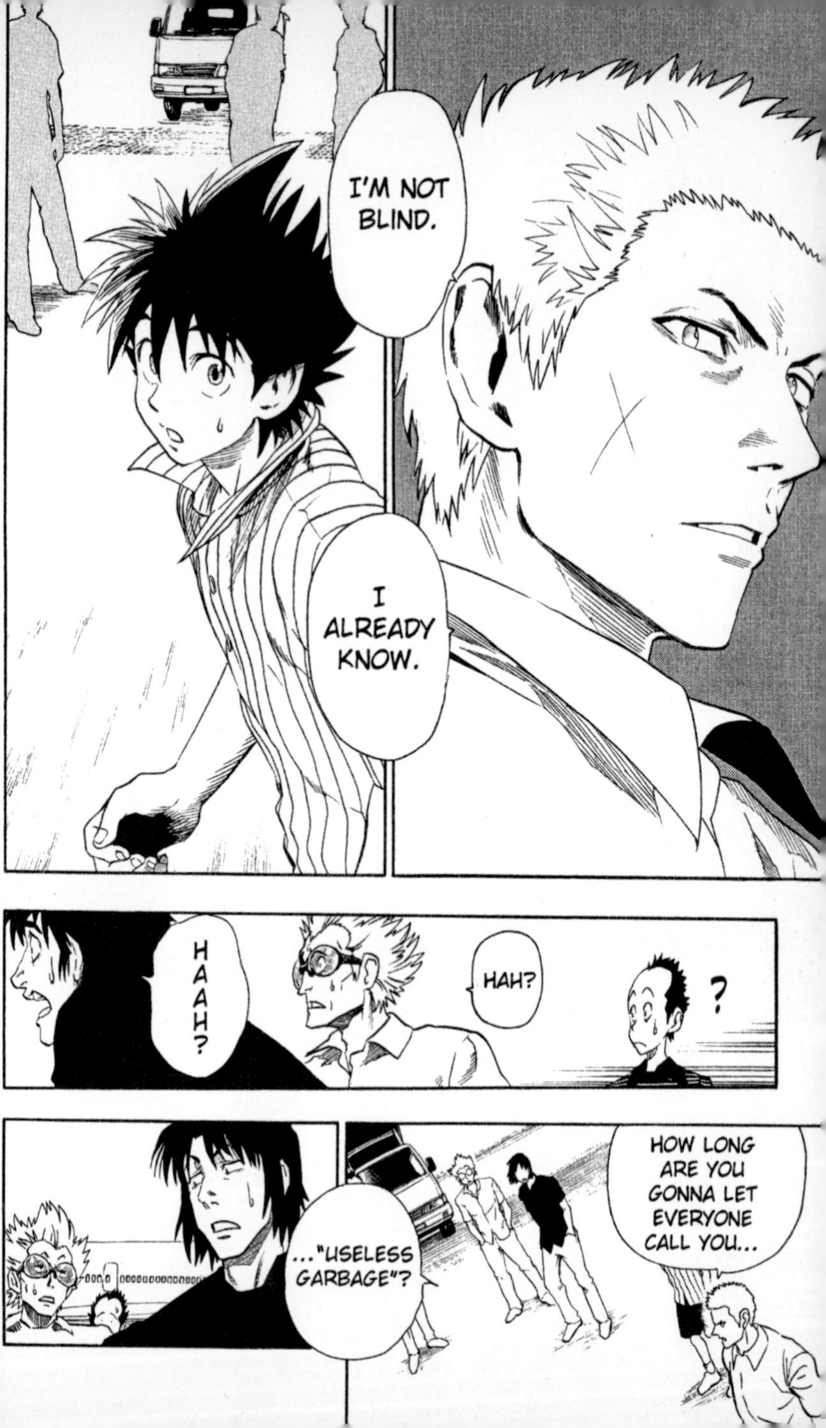
I'M NOT BLIND.
I ALREADY KNOW.
?
HAH?
HAAH?
HOW LONG ARE YOU GONNA LET EVERYONE CALL YOU...
..."USELESS GARBAGE"?

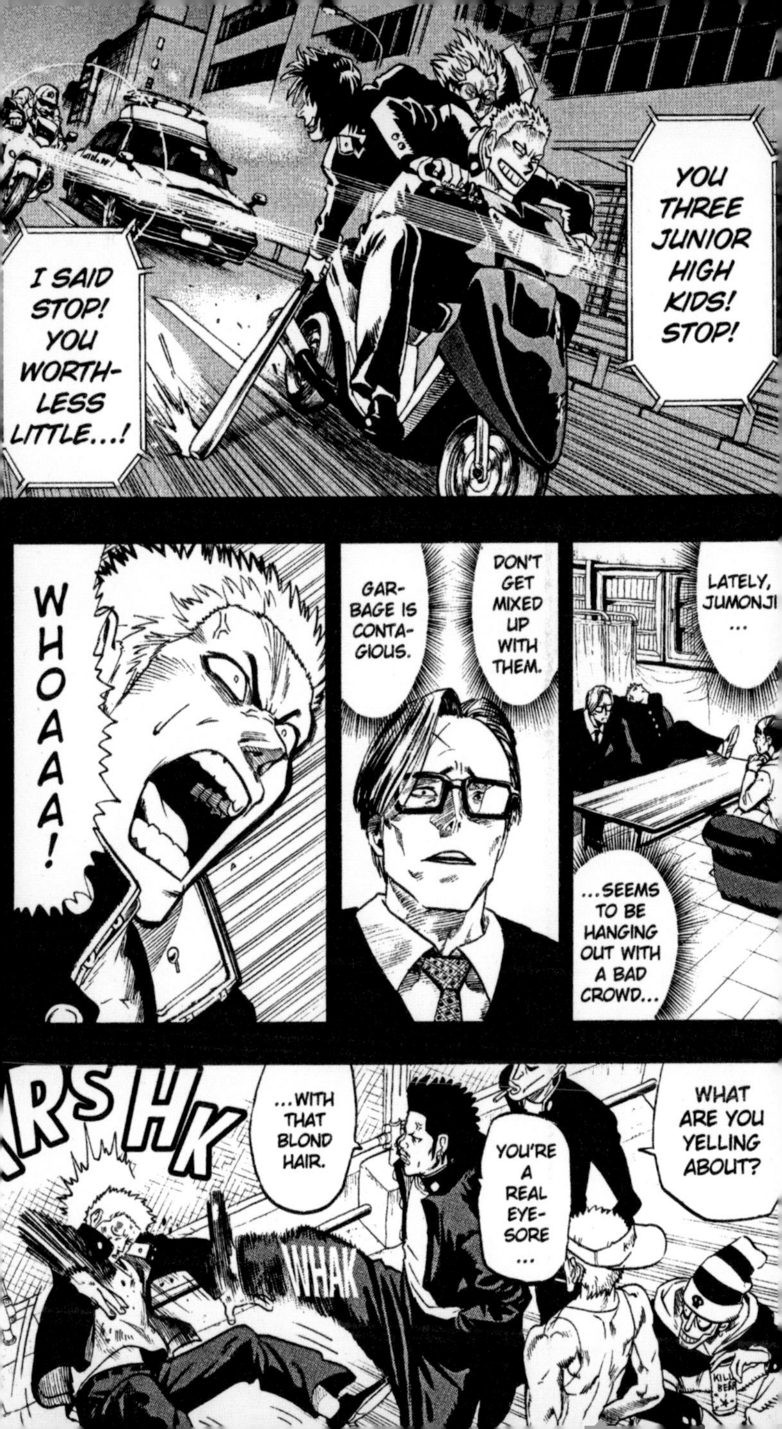
YOU THREE JUNIOR HIGH KIDS! STOP!
I SAID STOP! YOU WORTHLESS LITTLE...!
LATELY, JUMONJI ...
...SEEMS TO BE HANGING OUT WITH A BAD CROWD...
DON'T GET MIXED UP WITH THEM.
GARBAGE IS CONTAGIOUS.
WHOAAAA!
WHAT ARE YOU YELLING ABOUT?
YOU'RE A REAL EYESORE ...
...WITH THAT BLOND HAIR.
RSHK
WHAK
KILL BEER

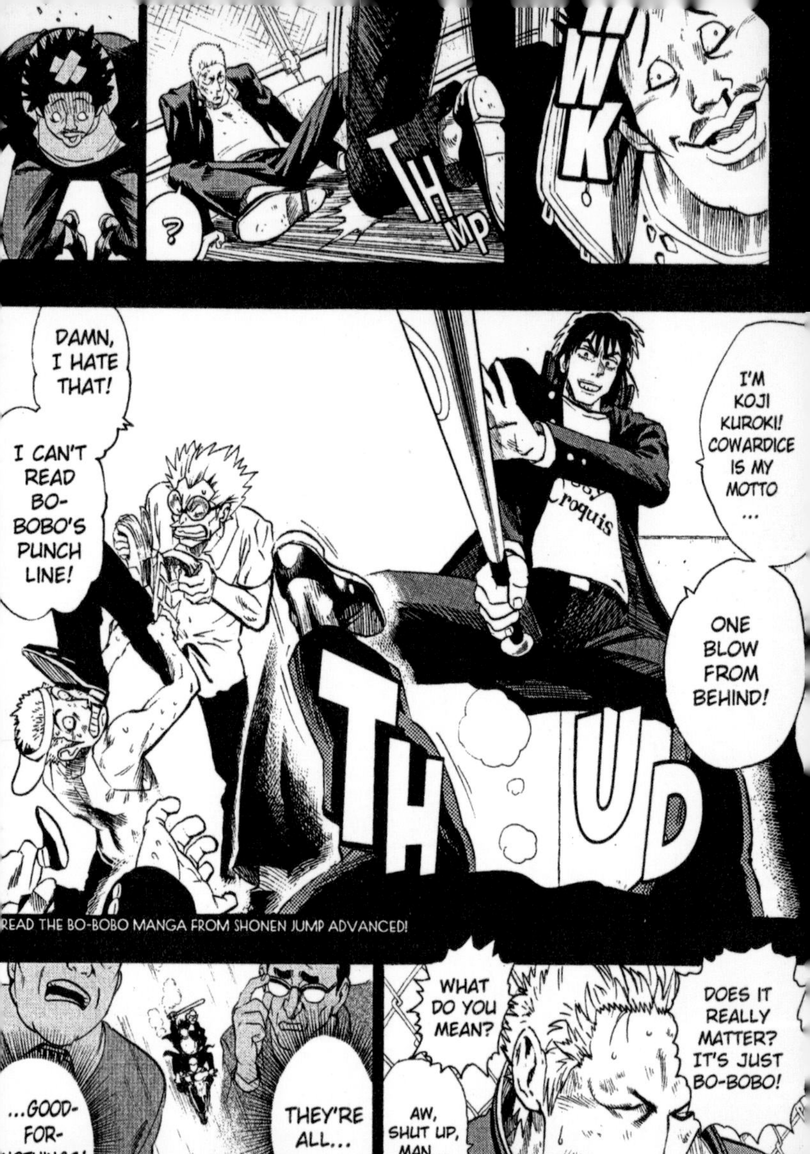
WK
THUMP
?
I'M KOJI KUROKI! COWARDICE IS MY MOTTO...
ONE BLOW FROM BEHIND!
THUD
DAMN, I HATE THAT!
I CAN'T READ BO-BOBO'S PUNCH LINE!
READ THE BO-BOBO MANGA FROM SHONEN JUMP ADVANCED!
DOES IT REALLY MATTER? IT'S JUST BO-BOBO!
WHAT DO YOU MEAN?
AW, SHUT UP, MAN...
THEY'RE ALL...
...GOOD-FOR-NOTHINGS!

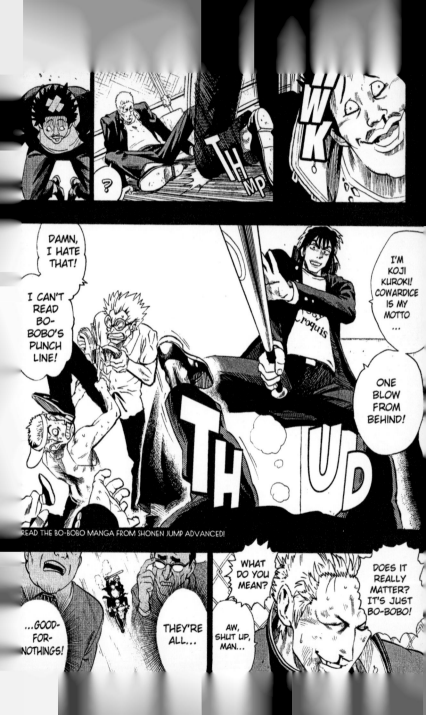

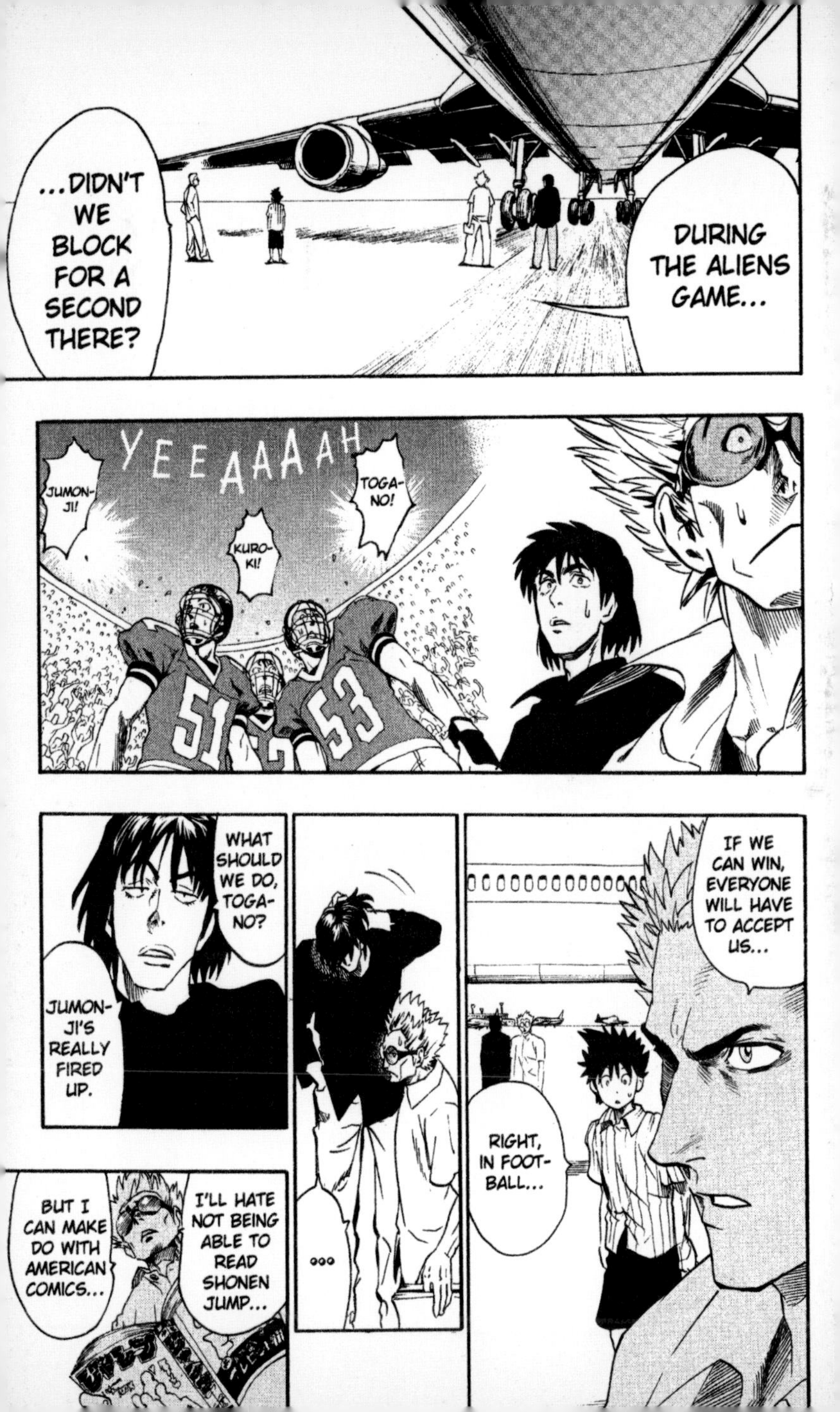
DURING THE ALIENS GAME...
...DIDN'T WE BLOCK FOR A SECOND THERE?
YEEAAAAAH
TOGA-NO!
JUMON-JI!
KURO-KI!
IF WE CAN WIN, EVERYONE WILL HAVE TO ACCEPT US...
RIGHT, IN FOOT-BALL...
...
WHAT SHOULD WE DO, TOGA-NO?
JUMON-JI'S REALLY FIRED UP.
I'LL HATE NOT BEING ABLE TO READ SHONEN JUMP...
BUT I CAN MAKE DO WITH AMERICAN COMICS...

SPEED

CATCHING
TECHNIQUE

POWER

WEIGHT

HEIGHT

KAZUKI JUMONJI!

SPEED

CATCHING
TECHNIQUE

POWER

WEIGHT

HEIGHT

KOJI KUROKI!

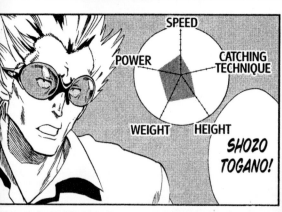

SPEED

CATCHING
TECHNIQUE

POWER

WEIGHT

HEIGHT

SHOZO TOGANO!

FWD

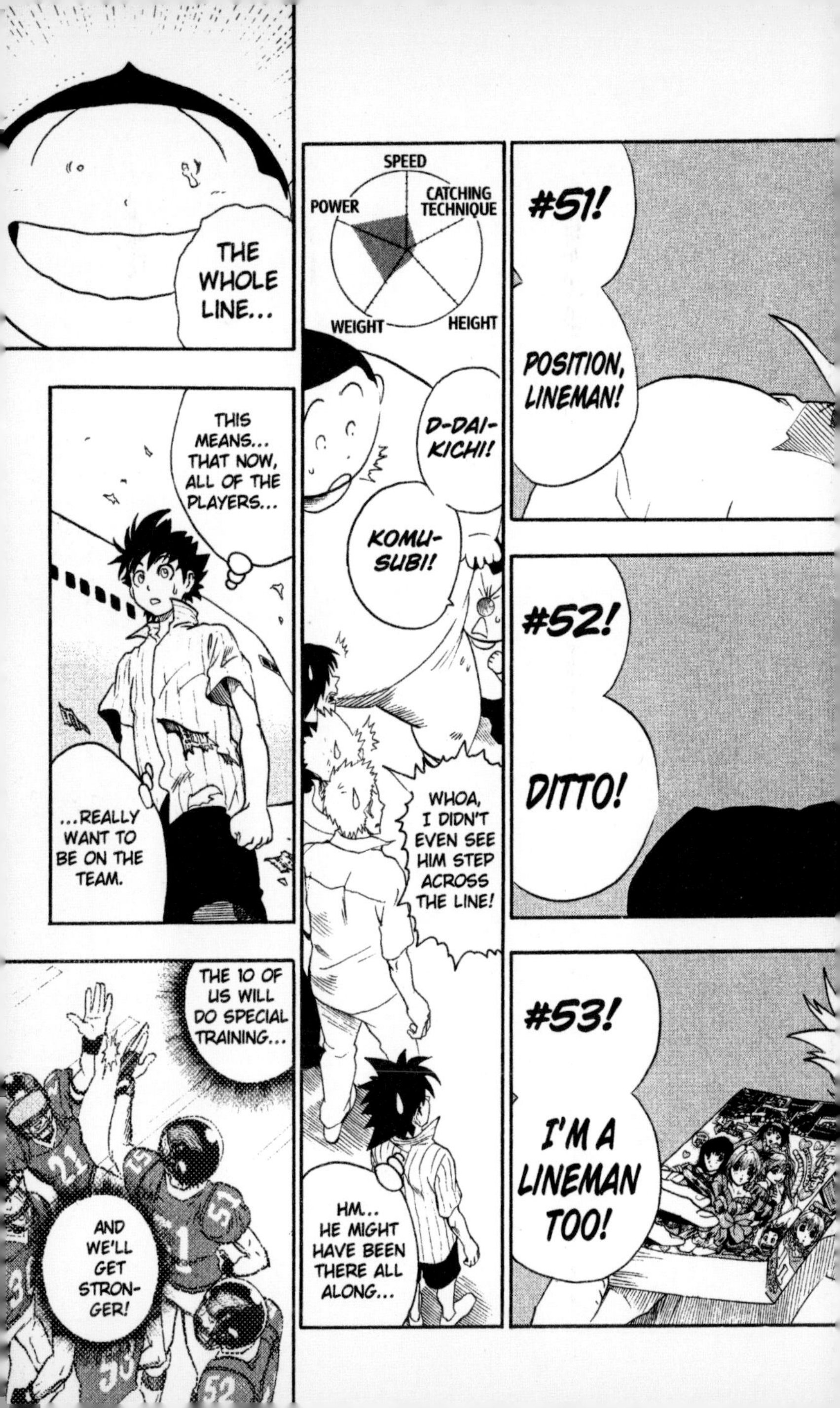
#51!
POSITION, LINEMAN!
#52!
DITTO!
#53!
I'M A LINEMAN TOO!
SPEED
CATCHING TECHNIQUE
HEIGHT
WEIGHT
POWER
D-DAI-KICHI!
KOMU-SUBI!
WHOA, I DIDN'T EVEN SEE HIM STEP ACROSS THE LINE!
HM.. HE MIGHT HAVE BEEN THERE ALL ALONG...
THE WHOLE LINE...
THIS MEANS... THAT NOW, ALL OF THE PLAYERS...
...REALLY WANT TO BE ON THE TEAM.
THE 10 OF US WILL DO SPECIAL TRAINING...
AND WE'LL GET STRON-GER!

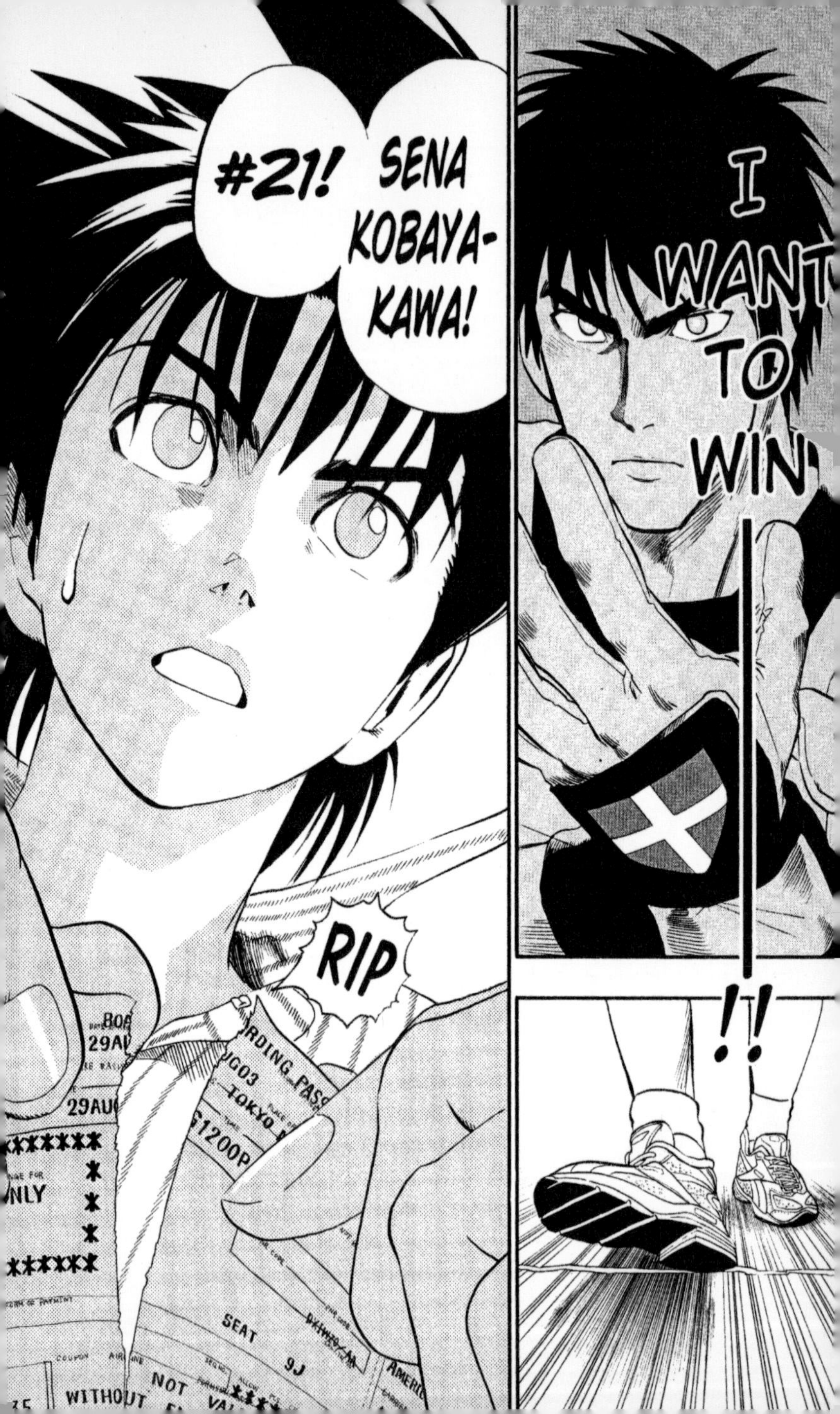
I WANT TO WIN—!!
SENA KOBAYA-KAWA!
#21!
RIP

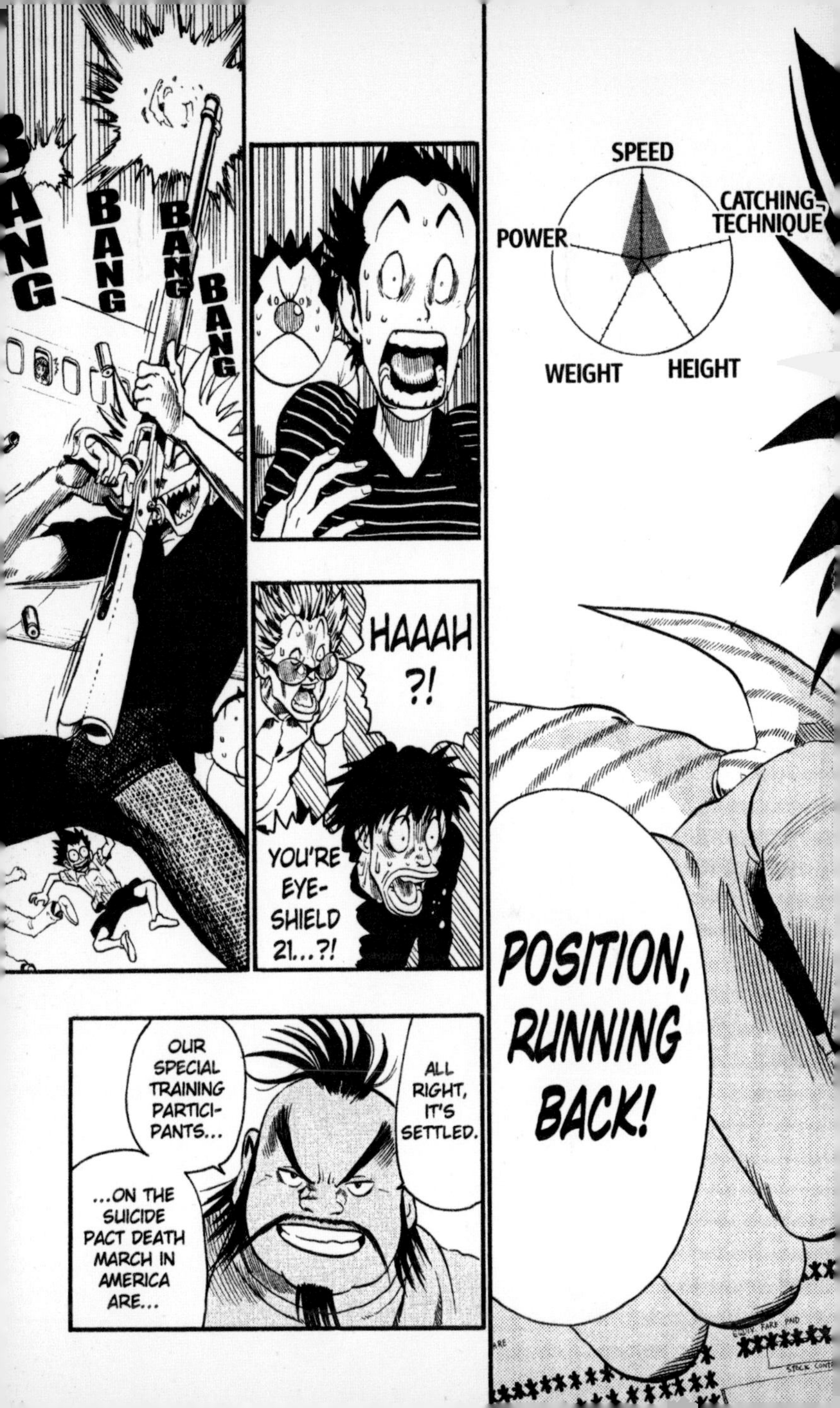
SPEED
CATCHING TECHNIQUE
HEIGHT
WEIGHT
POWER
POSITION, RUNNING BACK!
HAAAH ?!
YOU'RE EYE-SHIELD 21...?!
BANG
BANG
BANG
BANG
ALL RIGHT, IT'S SETTLED.
OUR SPECIAL TRAINING PARTICI-PANTS...
...ON THE SUICIDE PACT DEATH MARCH IN AMERICA ARE...

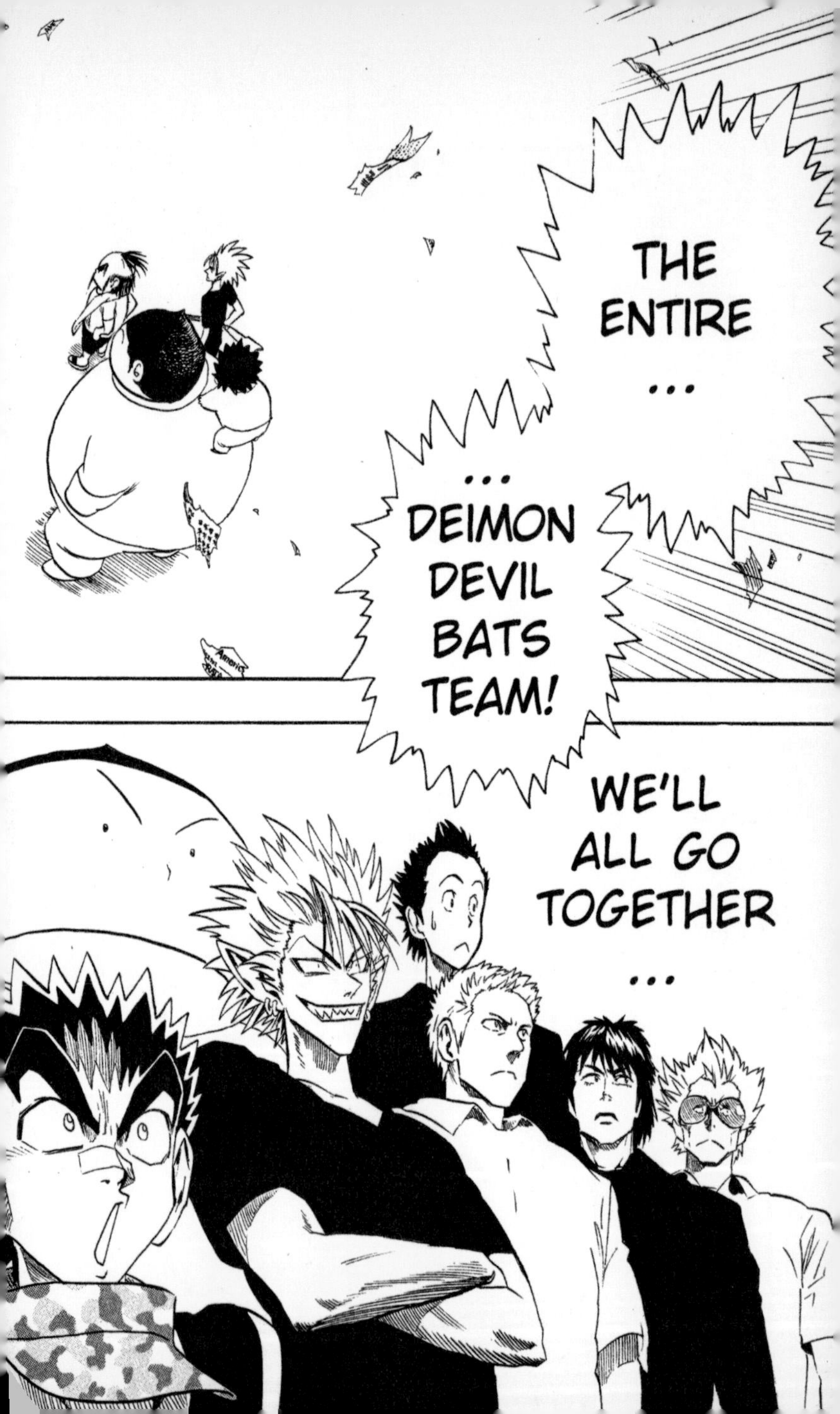
THE ENTIRE ...
... DEIMON DEVIL BATS TEAM!
WE'LL ALL GO TOGETHER ...

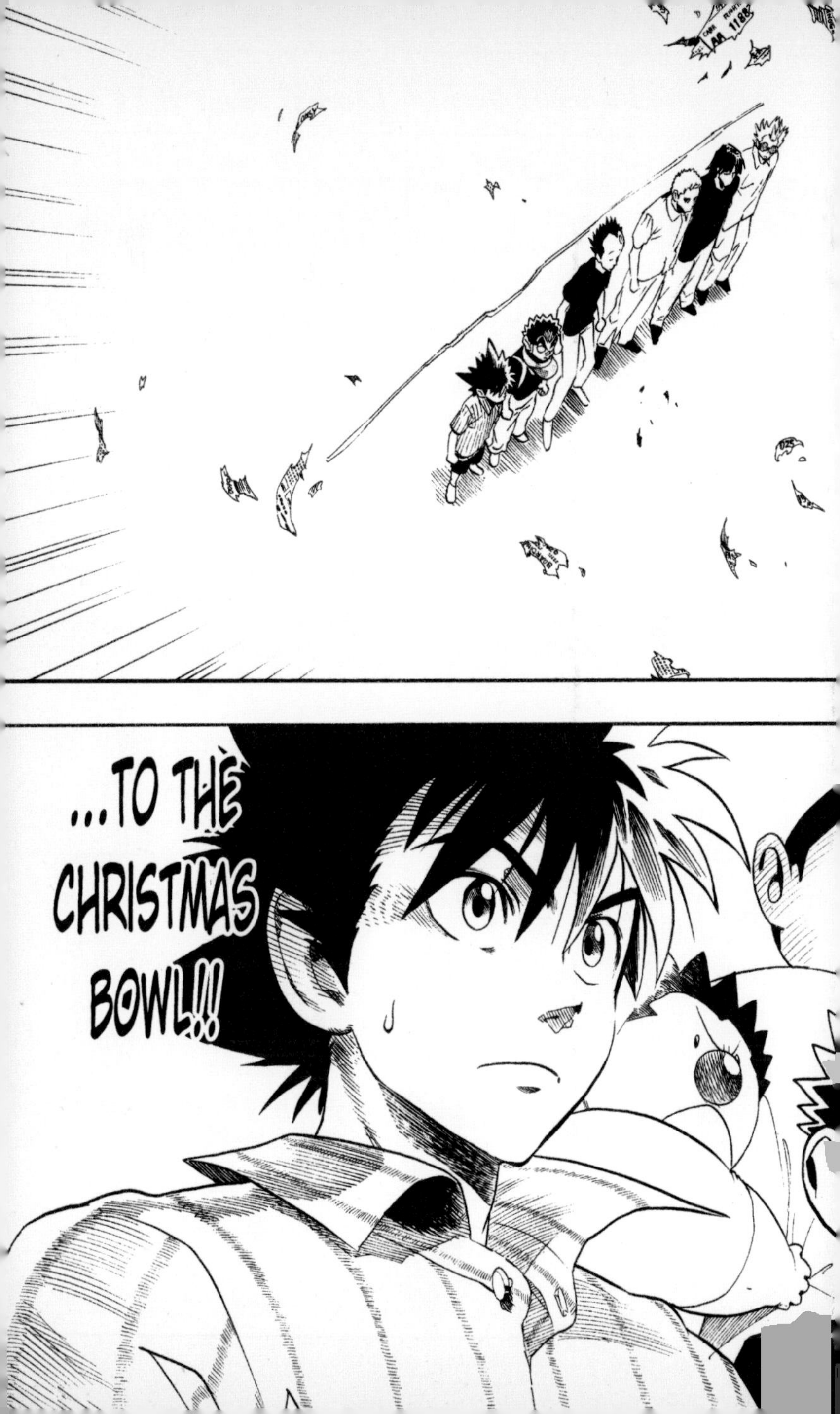
...TO THE CHRISTMAS BOWL!!

Eyeshield 21 Survey Corner **Devil Bat 021**

Investigation File #013

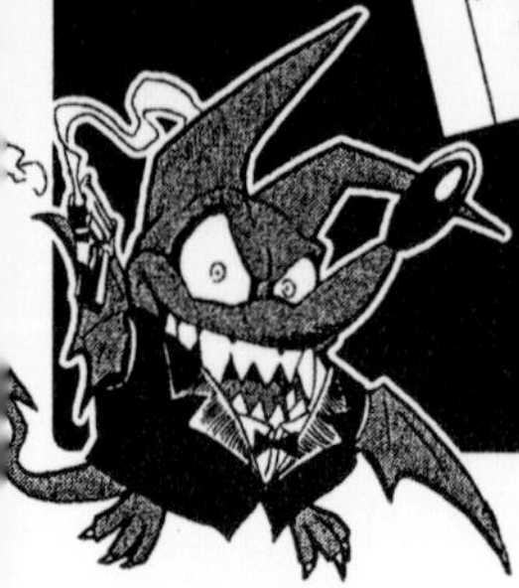

Is there anything that really bothers Ishimaru?

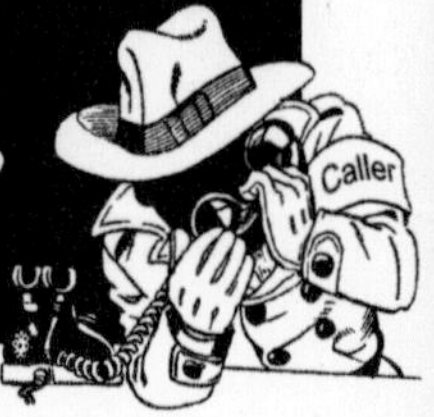
Caller

N.S., Hyogo prefecture

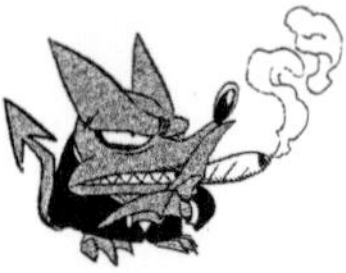

OH, THIS GUY'S GOT GUTS! HE SENT IN A POSTCARD WITH NOTHING BUT THIS QUESTION WRITTEN IN HUGE LETTERS.

HERE'S WHERE HE DRAWS THE LINE!!

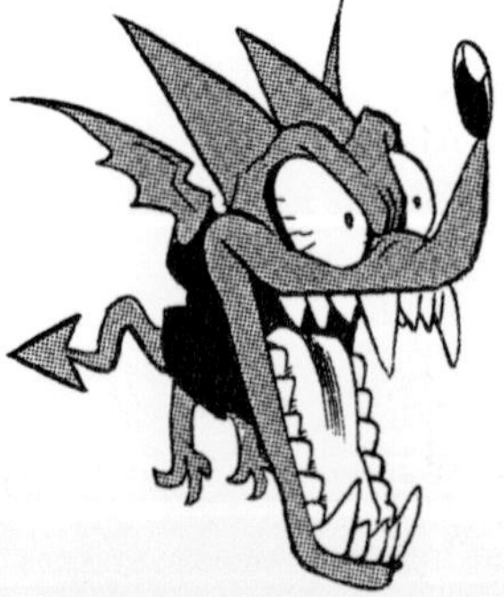

NO PROBLEM

- Completely forgetting he exists
- Throwing a pie in his face
- Recalling all the town flyers after he's finished delivering them

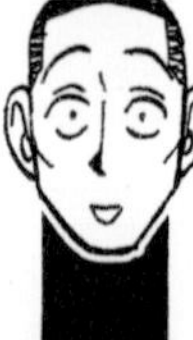

- Permanently removing his eyebrows while he's sleeping
- Kidnapping him and turning him into a cyborg for a black market organization

THAT'S PRETTY BAD...

Chapter 78 Faraway Las Vegas

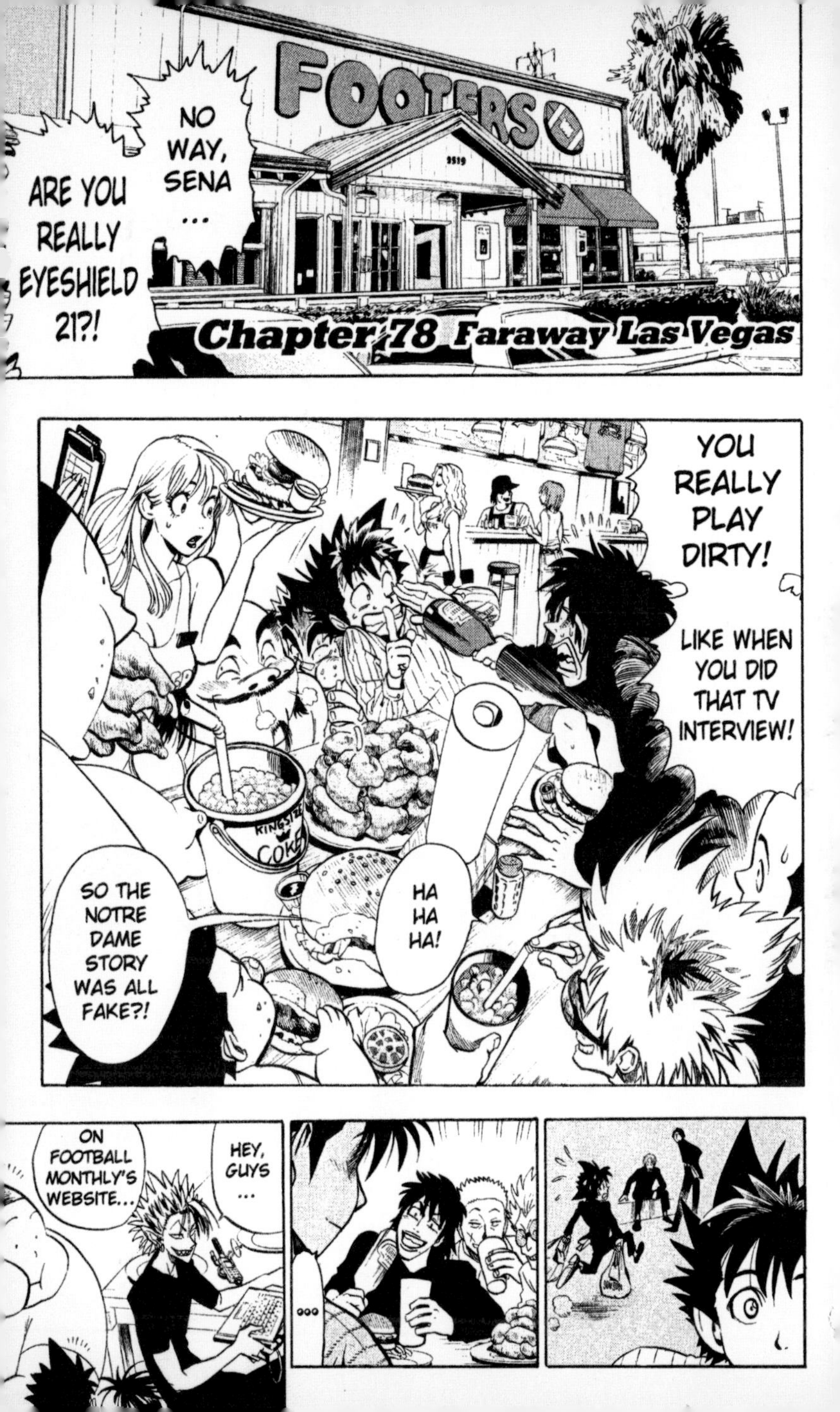
FOOTERS
9519
NO WAY, SENA ...
ARE YOU REALLY EYESHIELD 21?!
YOU REALLY PLAY DIRTY!
LIKE WHEN YOU DID THAT TV INTERVIEW!
KINGSIZE COKE
HA HA HA!
SO THE NOTRE DAME STORY WAS ALL FAKE?!
...
HEY, GUYS ...
ON FOOTBALL MONTHLY'S WEBSITE...

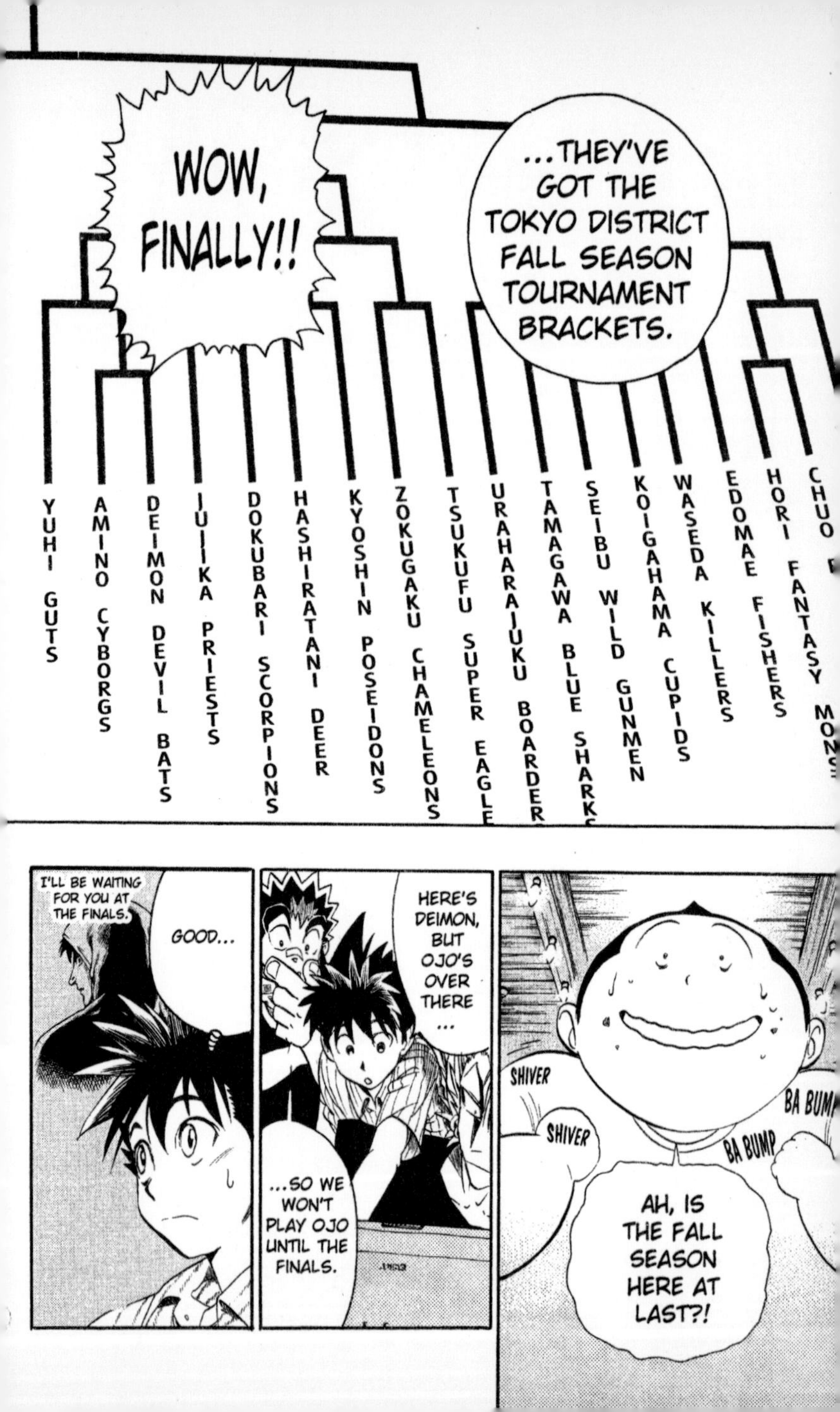
WOW, FINALLY!!
...THEY'VE GOT THE TOKYO DISTRICT FALL SEASON TOURNAMENT BRACKETS.
YUHI GUTS
AMINO CYBORGS
DEIMON DEVIL BATS
JUIIKA PRIESTS
DOKUBARI SCORPIONS
HASHIRATANI DEER
KYOSHIN POSEIDONS
ZOKUGAKU CHAMELEONS
TSUKUFU SUPER EAGLE
URAHARAJUKU BOARDER
TAMAGAWA BLUE SHARK
SEIBU WILD GUNMEN
KOIGAHAMA CUPIDS
WASEDA KILLERS
EDOMAE FISHERS
HORI FANTASY MONS
CHUO
SHIVER
SHIVER
BA BUMP
BA BUMP
AH, IS THE FALL SEASON HERE AT LAST?!
HERE'S DEIMON, BUT OJO'S OVER THERE ...
...SO WE WON'T PLAY OJO UNTIL THE FINALS.
I'LL BE WAITING FOR YOU AT THE FINALS.
GOOD...

Chapter 78
Faraway Las Vegas

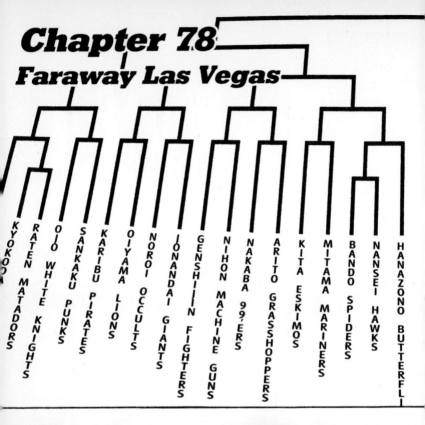

HANAZONO BUTTERFL
NANSEI HAWKS
BANDO SPIDERS
MITAMA MARINERS
KITA ESKIMOS
ARITO GRASSHOPPERS
NAKABA 99'ERS
NIHON MACHINE GUNS
GENSHIJIN FIGHTERS
JONANDAI GIANTS
NOROI OCCULTS
OIYAMA LIONS
KARIBU PIRATES
SANKAKU PUNKS
OJO WHITE
RATEN KNIGHTS
KYOKO MATADORS
WHO DO WE PLAY IN THE FIRST GAME?
THE AMINO CYBORGS!
DEIMON DEVIL BATS
AMINO CYBORGS
CYBORGS ...??

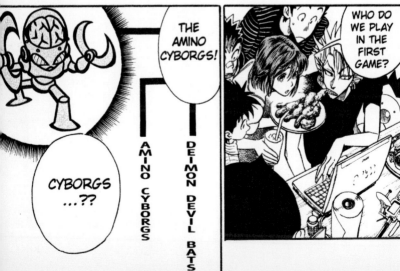

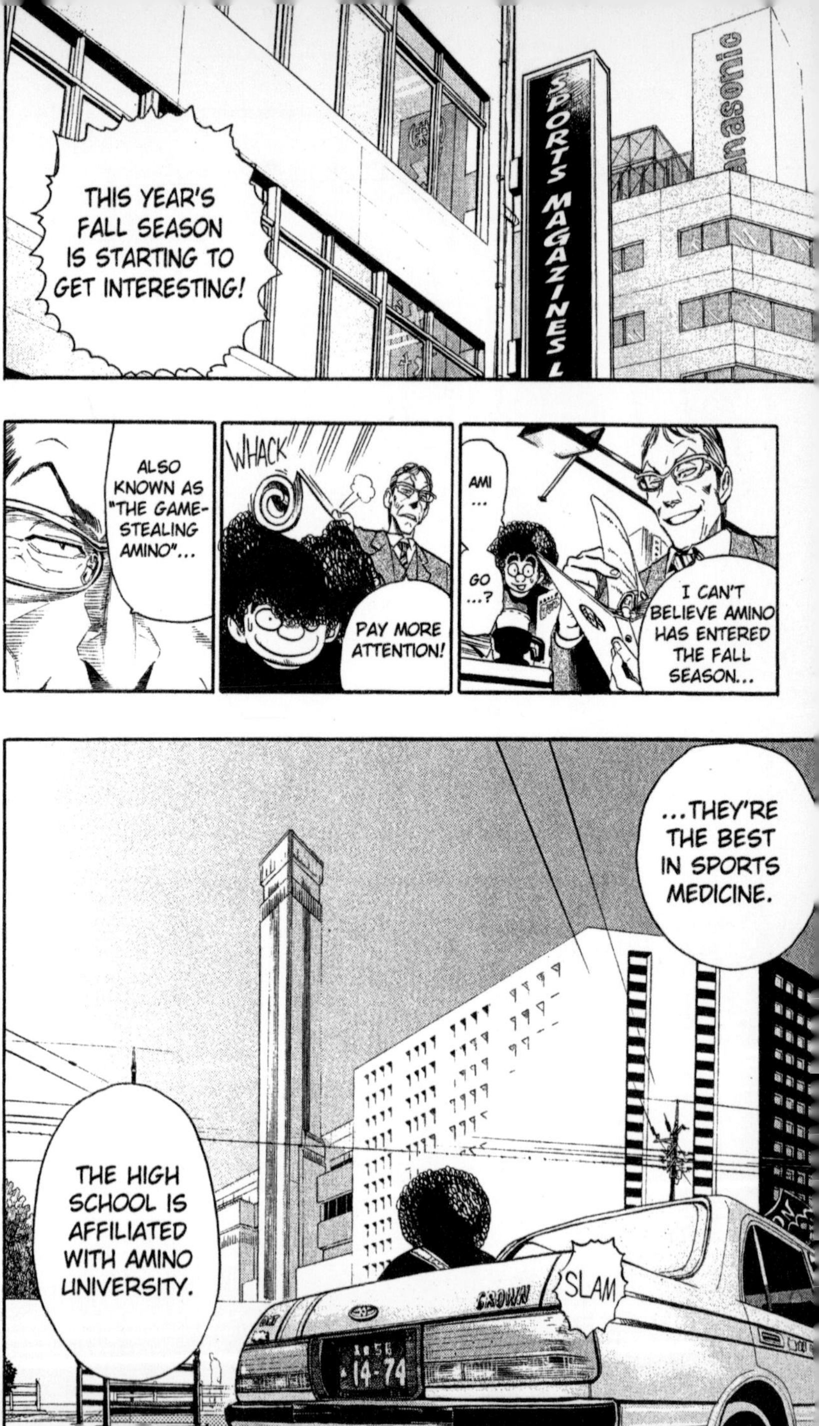
SPORTS MAGAZINES L
THIS YEAR'S FALL SEASON IS STARTING TO GET INTERESTING!
I CAN'T BELIEVE AMINO HAS ENTERED THE FALL SEASON...
AMI ...
GO ...?
WHACK
PAY MORE ATTENTION!
ALSO KNOWN AS "THE GAME-STEALING AMINO"...
...THEY'RE THE BEST IN SPORTS MEDICINE.
THE HIGH SCHOOL IS AFFILIATED WITH AMINO UNIVERSITY.
SLAM
CROWN
14-74

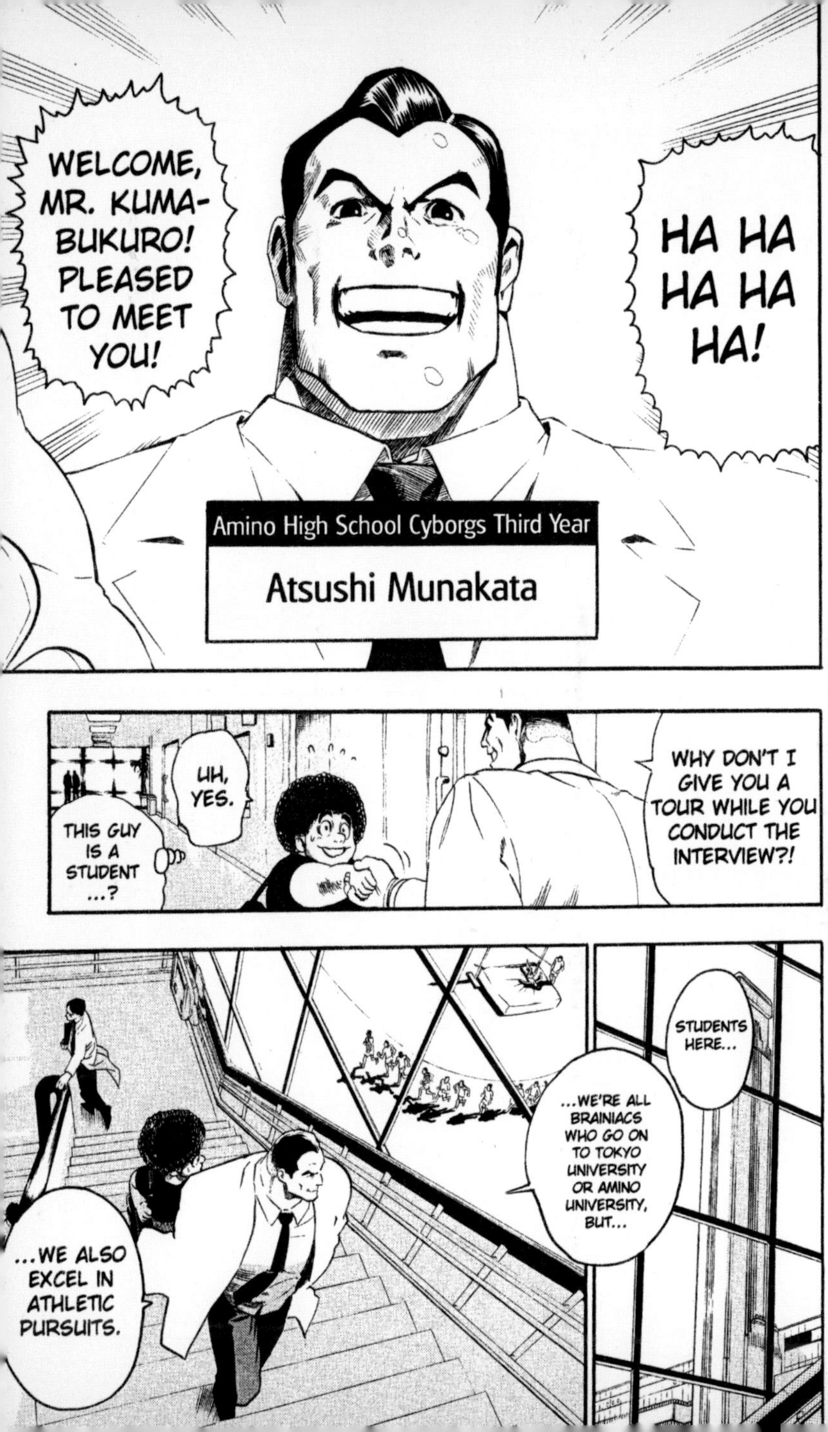
HA HA HA HA HA!
WELCOME, MR. KUMA-BUKURO! PLEASED TO MEET YOU!
Amino High School Cyborgs Third Year
Atsushi Munakata
WHY DON'T I GIVE YOU A TOUR WHILE YOU CONDUCT THE INTERVIEW?!
UH, YES.
THIS GUY IS A STUDENT ...?
STUDENTS HERE...
...WE'RE ALL BRAINIACS WHO GO ON TO TOKYO UNIVERSITY OR AMINO UNIVERSITY, BUT...
...WE ALSO EXCEL IN ATHLETIC PURSUITS.

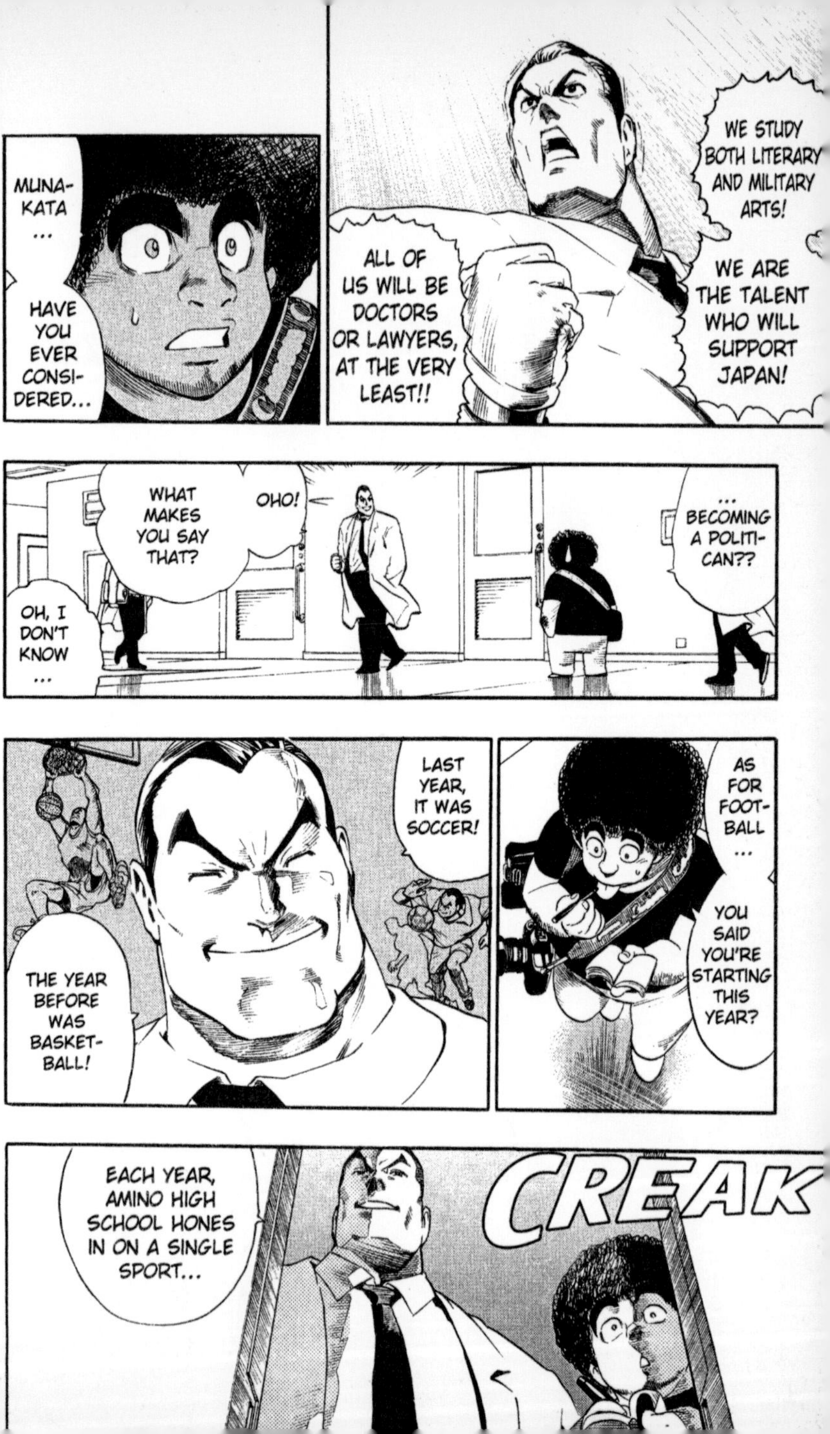
WE STUDY BOTH LITERARY AND MILITARY ARTS!
WE ARE THE TALENT WHO WILL SUPPORT JAPAN!
ALL OF US WILL BE DOCTORS OR LAWYERS, AT THE VERY LEAST!!
MUNA-KATA...
HAVE YOU EVER CONSI-DERED...
...BECOMING A POLITI-CAN??
OHO!
WHAT MAKES YOU SAY THAT?
OH, I DON'T KNOW...
AS FOR FOOT-BALL...
YOU SAID YOU'RE STARTING THIS YEAR?
LAST YEAR, IT WAS SOCCER!
THE YEAR BEFORE WAS BASKET-BALL!
CREAK
EACH YEAR, AMINO HIGH SCHOOL HONES IN ON A SINGLE SPORT...

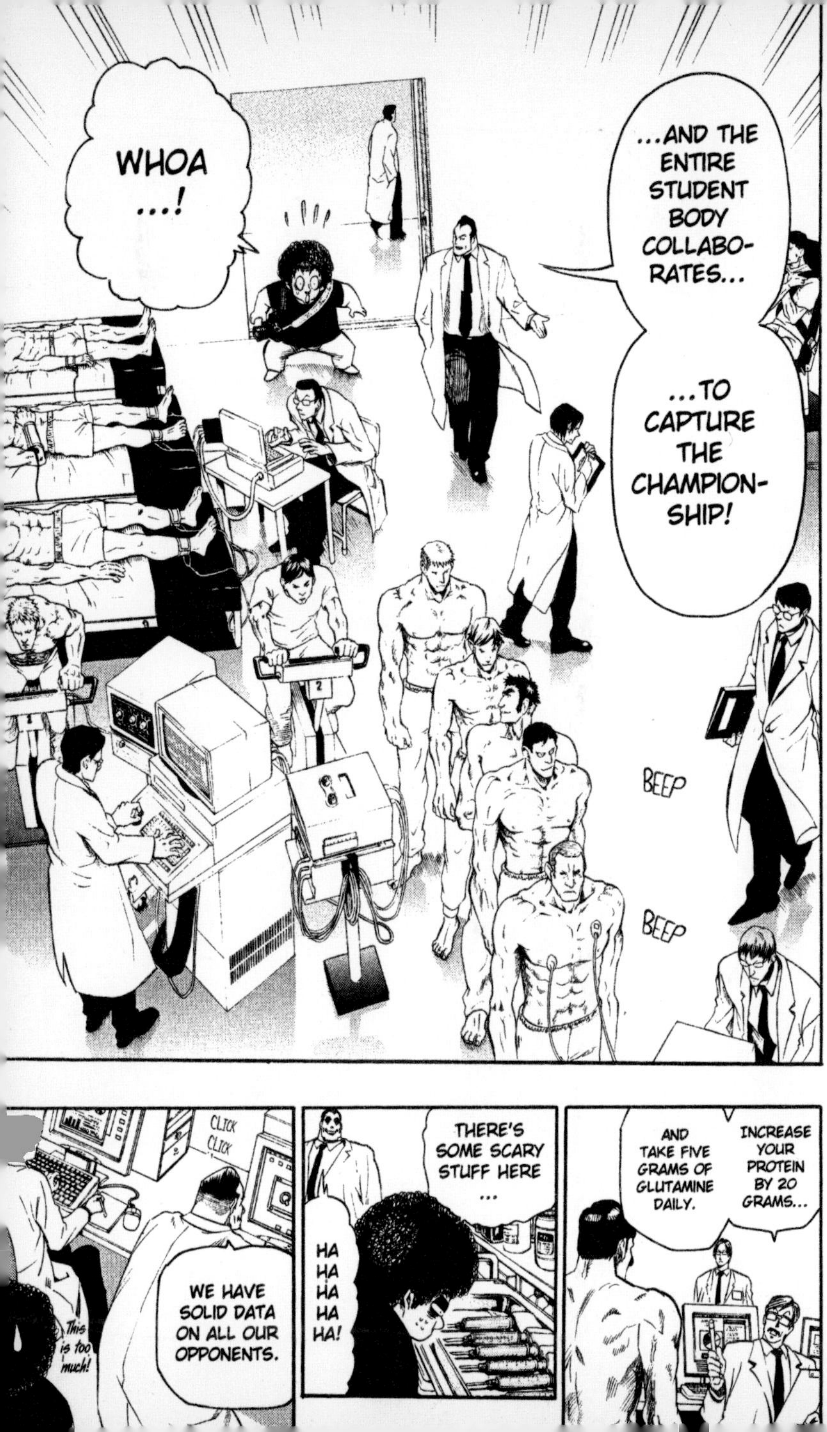
...AND THE ENTIRE STUDENT BODY COLLABORATES...
...TO CAPTURE THE CHAMPIONSHIP!
WHOA ...!
BEEP
BEEP
INCREASE YOUR PROTEIN BY 20 GRAMS...
AND TAKE FIVE GRAMS OF GLUTAMINE DAILY.
THERE'S SOME SCARY STUFF HERE ...
HA HA HA HA HA!
CLICK CLICK
WE HAVE SOLID DATA ON ALL OUR OPPONENTS.
This is too much!

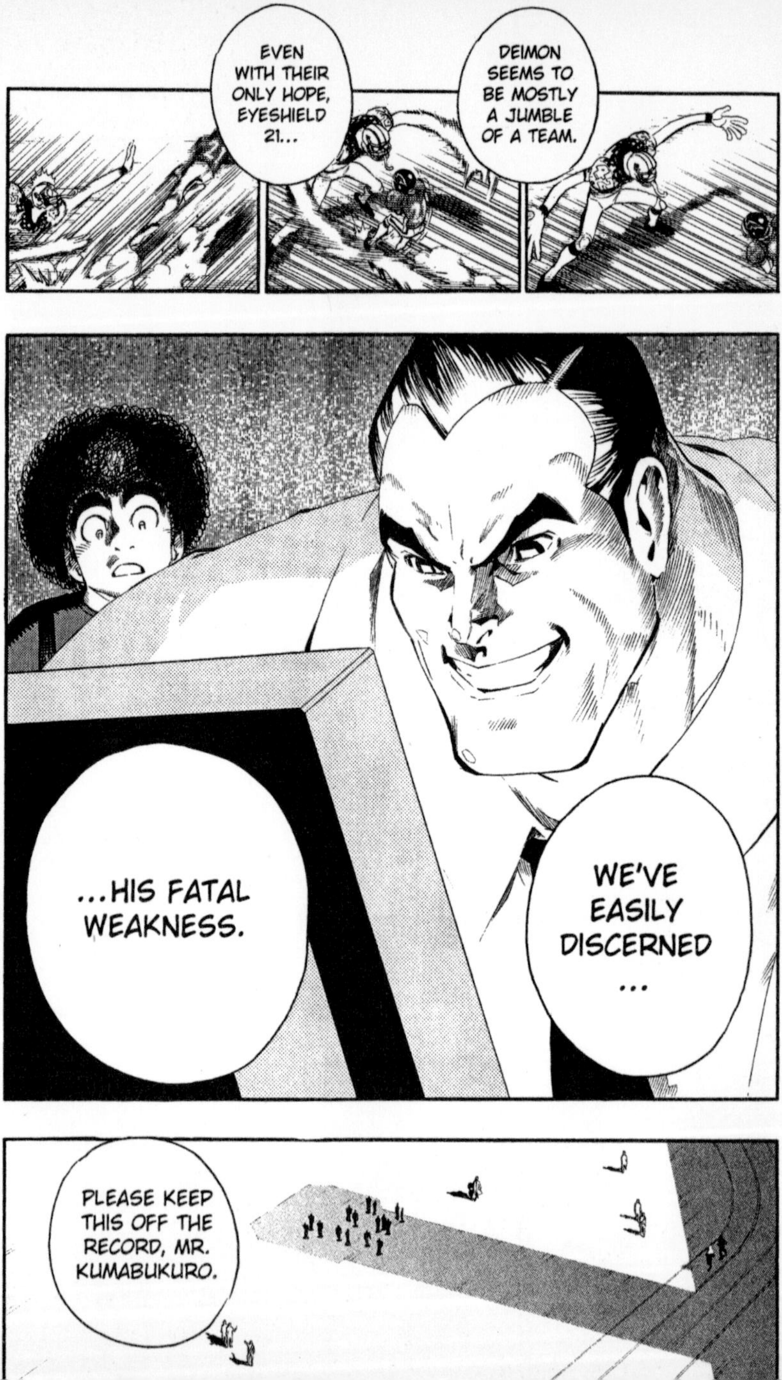
DEIMON SEEMS TO BE MOSTLY A JUMBLE OF A TEAM.
EVEN WITH THEIR ONLY HOPE, EYESHIELD 21...
WE'VE EASILY DISCERNED ...
...HIS FATAL WEAKNESS.
PLEASE KEEP THIS OFF THE RECORD, MR. KUMABUKURO.

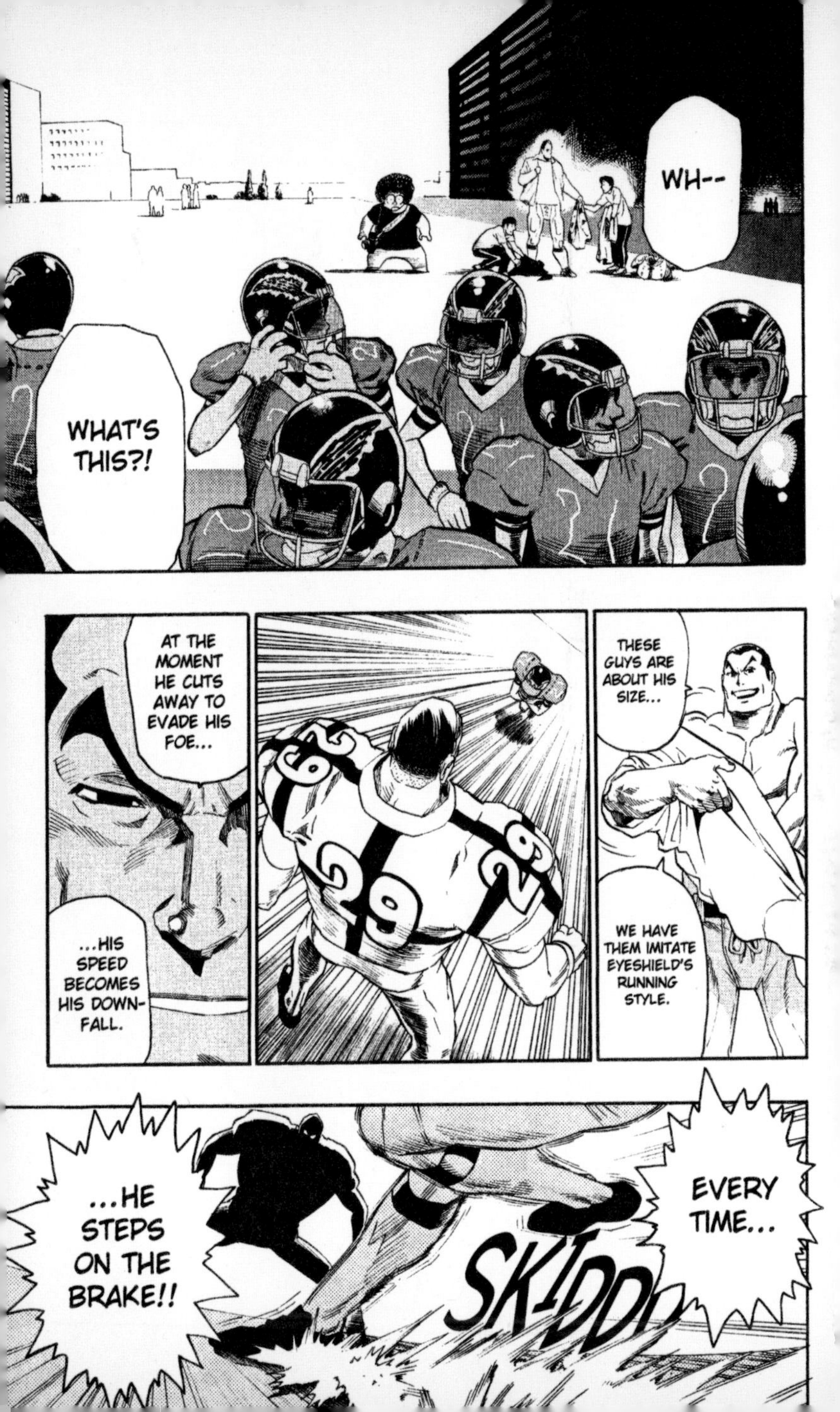
WH--
WHAT'S THIS?!
THESE GUYS ARE ABOUT HIS SIZE...
WE HAVE THEM IMITATE EYESHIELD'S RUNNING STYLE.
AT THE MOMENT HE CUTS AWAY TO EVADE HIS FOE...
...HIS SPEED BECOMES HIS DOWNFALL.
EVERY TIME...
SKIDD
...HE STEPS ON THE BRAKE!!

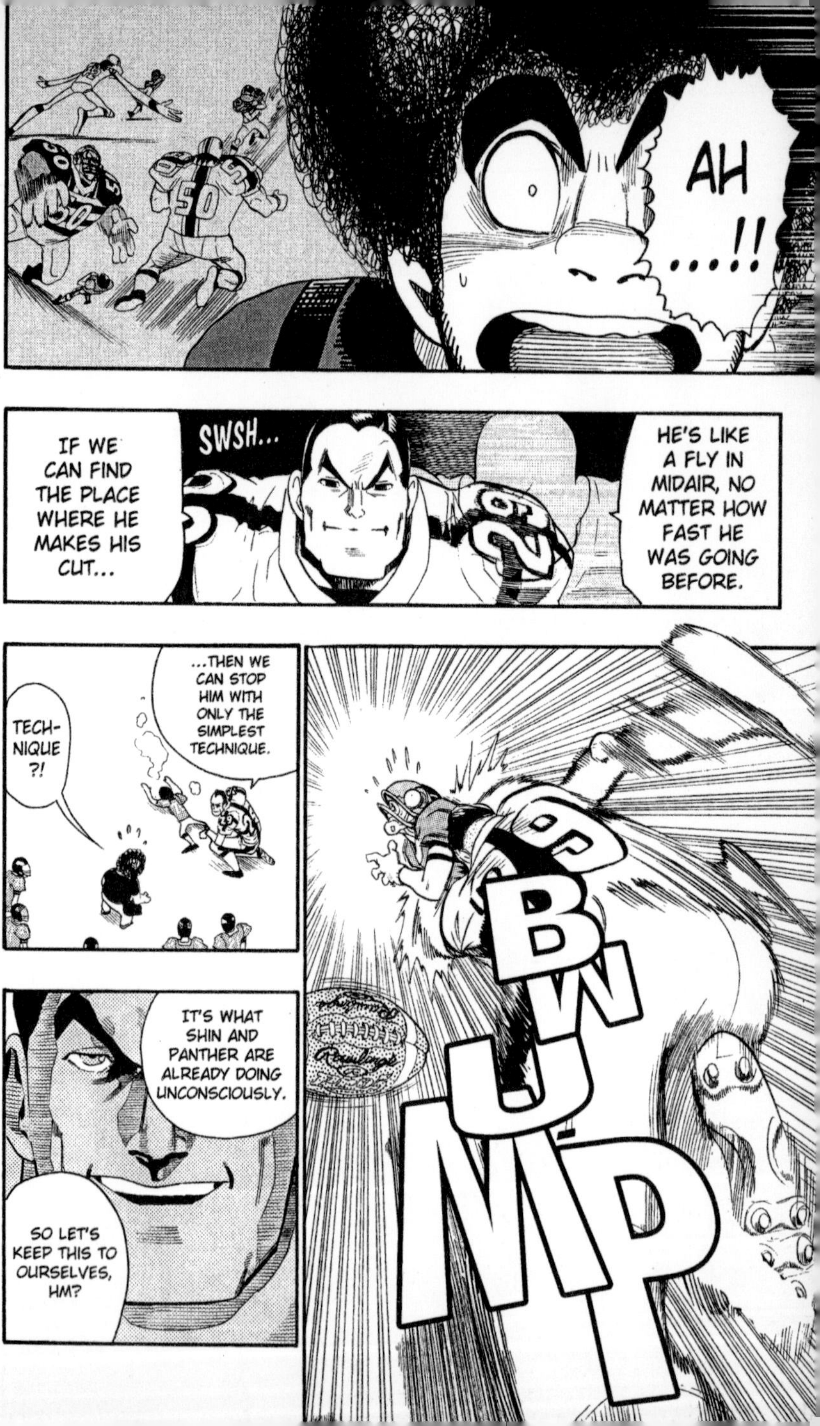
AH ....!!
HE'S LIKE A FLY IN MIDAIR, NO MATTER HOW FAST HE WAS GOING BEFORE.
SWSH...
IF WE CAN FIND THE PLACE WHERE HE MAKES HIS CUT...
BUMP
...THEN WE CAN STOP HIM WITH ONLY THE SIMPLEST TECHNIQUE.
TECHNIQUE ?!
IT'S WHAT SHIN AND PANTHER ARE ALREADY DOING UNCONSCIOUSLY.
SO LET'S KEEP THIS TO OURSELVES, HM?

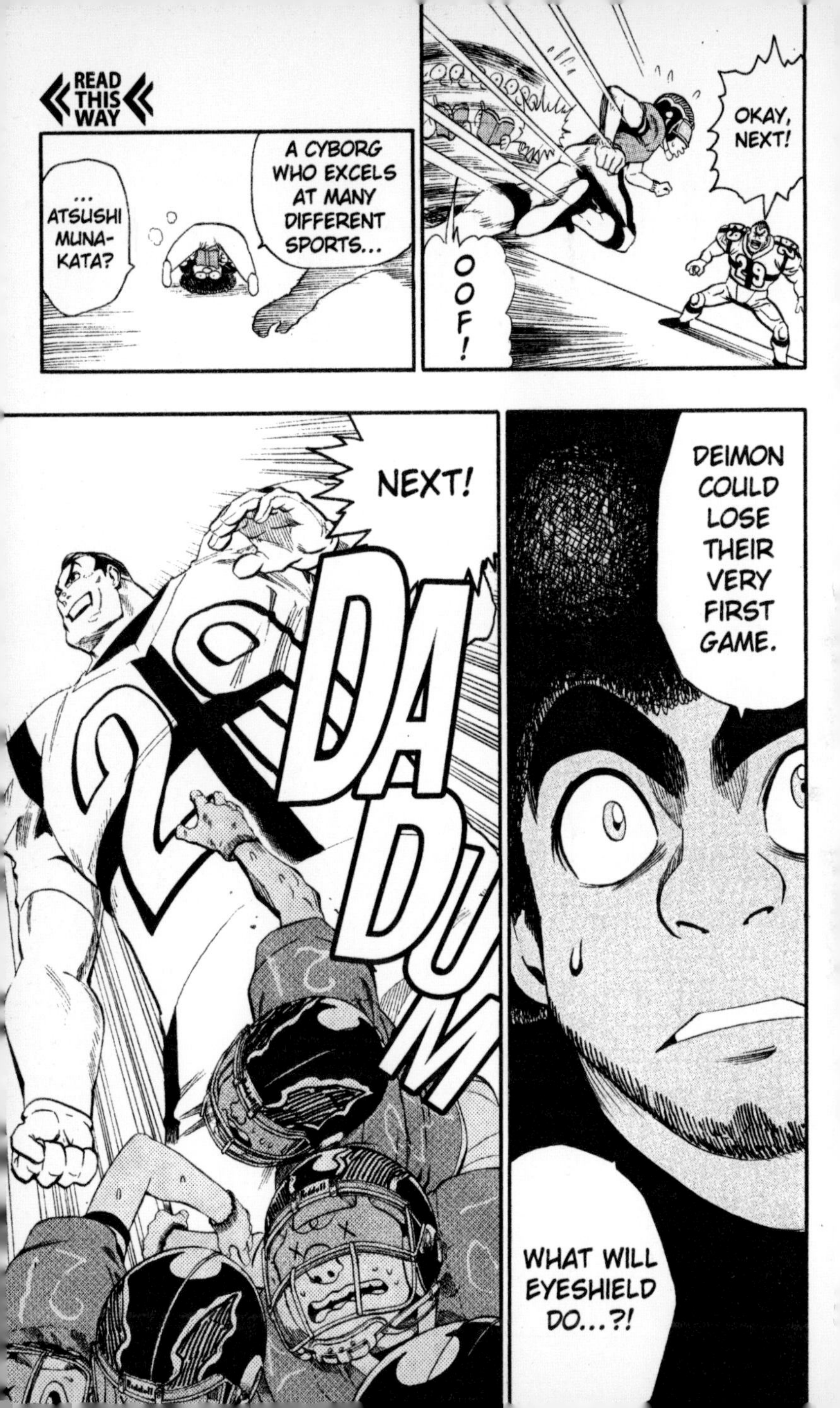
READ THIS WAY
OKAY, NEXT!
OOF!
A CYBORG WHO EXCELS AT MANY DIFFERENT SPORTS...
... ATSUSHI MUNA-KATA?
DEIMON COULD LOSE THEIR VERY FIRST GAME.
WHAT WILL EYESHIELD DO...?!
NEXT!
DADUM

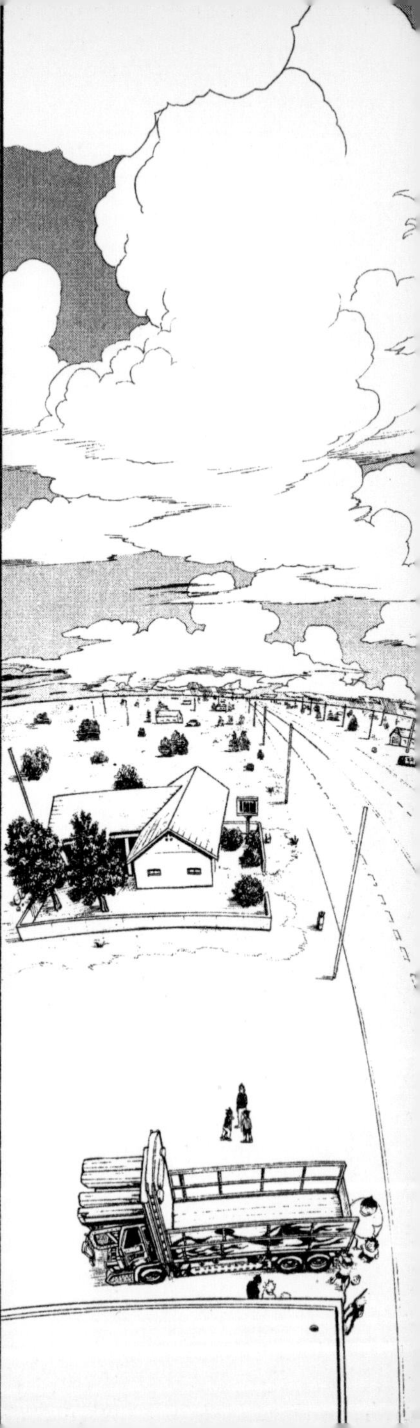

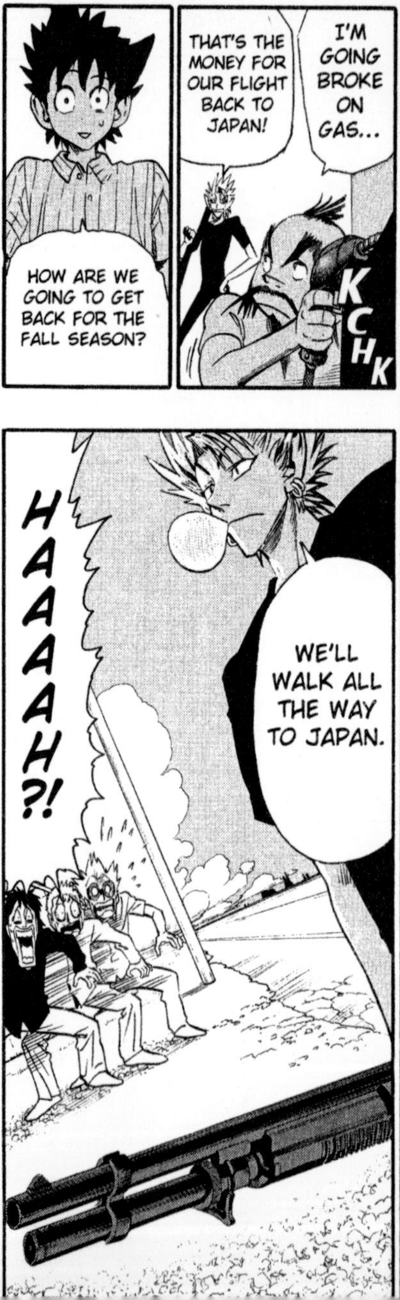
I'M GOING BROKE ON GAS...
THAT'S THE MONEY FOR OUR FLIGHT BACK TO JAPAN!
KCHK
HOW ARE WE GOING TO GET BACK FOR THE FALL SEASON?
WE'LL WALK ALL THE WAY TO JAPAN.
HAAAAAH?!

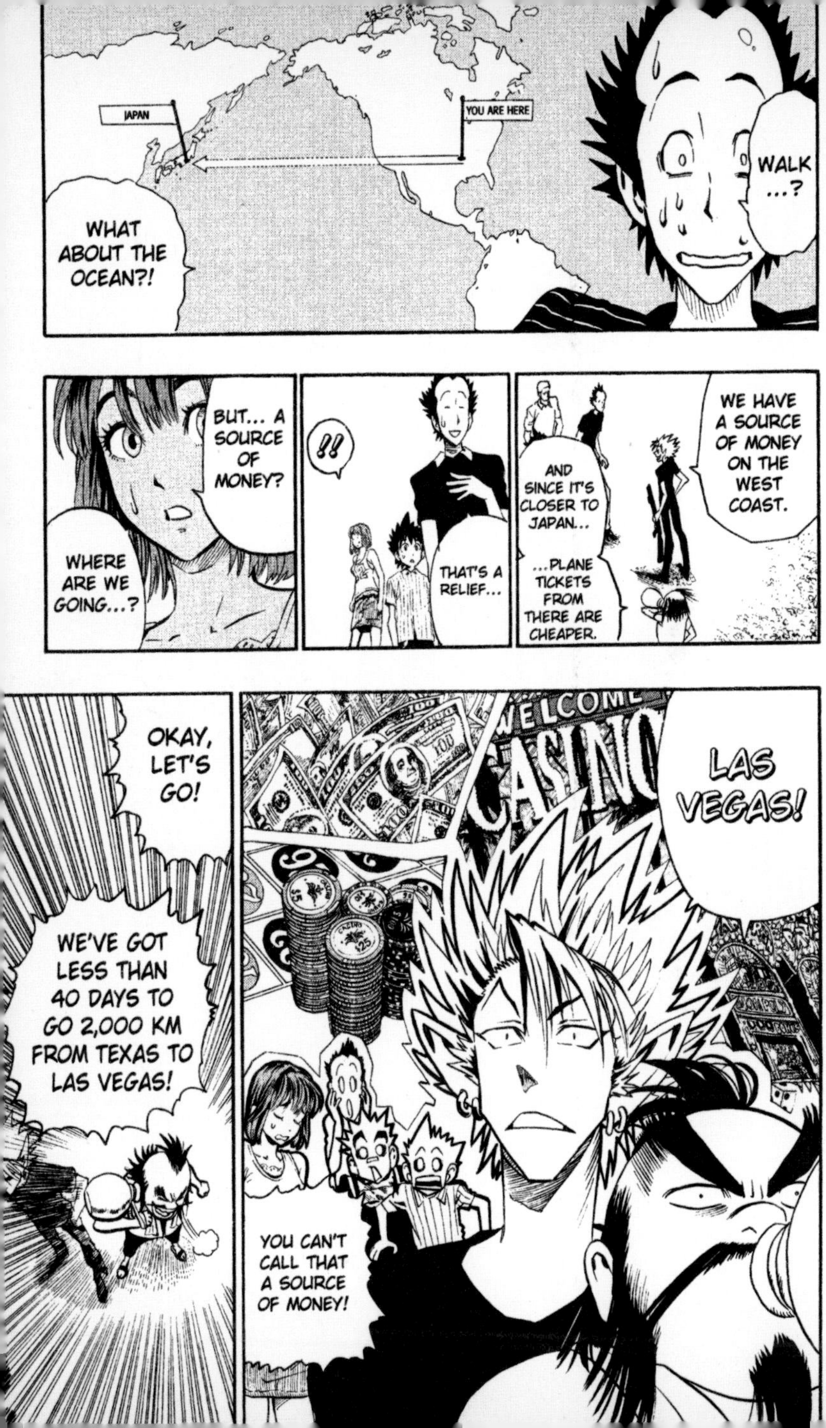
WALK ...?
YOU ARE HERE
JAPAN
WHAT ABOUT THE OCEAN?!
WE HAVE A SOURCE OF MONEY ON THE WEST COAST.
AND SINCE IT'S CLOSER TO JAPAN...
...PLANE TICKETS FROM THERE ARE CHEAPER.
!!
THAT'S A RELIEF...
BUT... A SOURCE OF MONEY?
WHERE ARE WE GOING...?
LAS VEGAS!
WELCOME
CASINO
YOU CAN'T CALL THAT A SOURCE OF MONEY!
OKAY, LET'S GO!
WE'VE GOT LESS THAN 40 DAYS TO GO 2,000 KM FROM TEXAS TO LAS VEGAS!

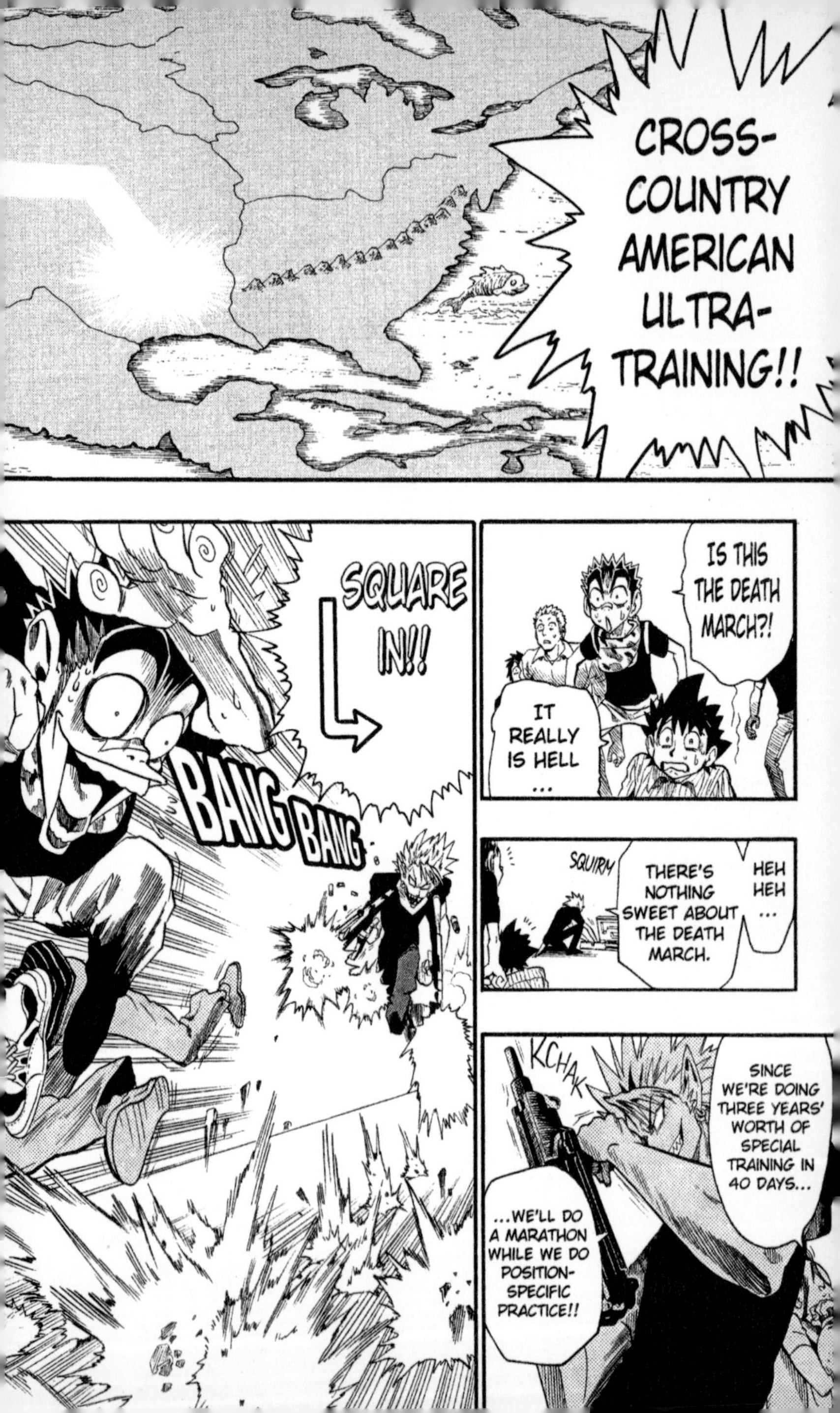
CROSS-COUNTRY AMERICAN ULTRA-TRAINING!!
IS THIS THE DEATH MARCH?!
IT REALLY IS HELL ...
HEH HEH ...
THERE'S NOTHING SWEET ABOUT THE DEATH MARCH.
SQUIRM
KCHAK
SINCE WE'RE DOING THREE YEARS' WORTH OF SPECIAL TRAINING IN 40 DAYS...
...WE'LL DO A MARATHON WHILE WE DO POSITION-SPECIFIC PRACTICE!!
SQUARE IN!!
BANG BANG

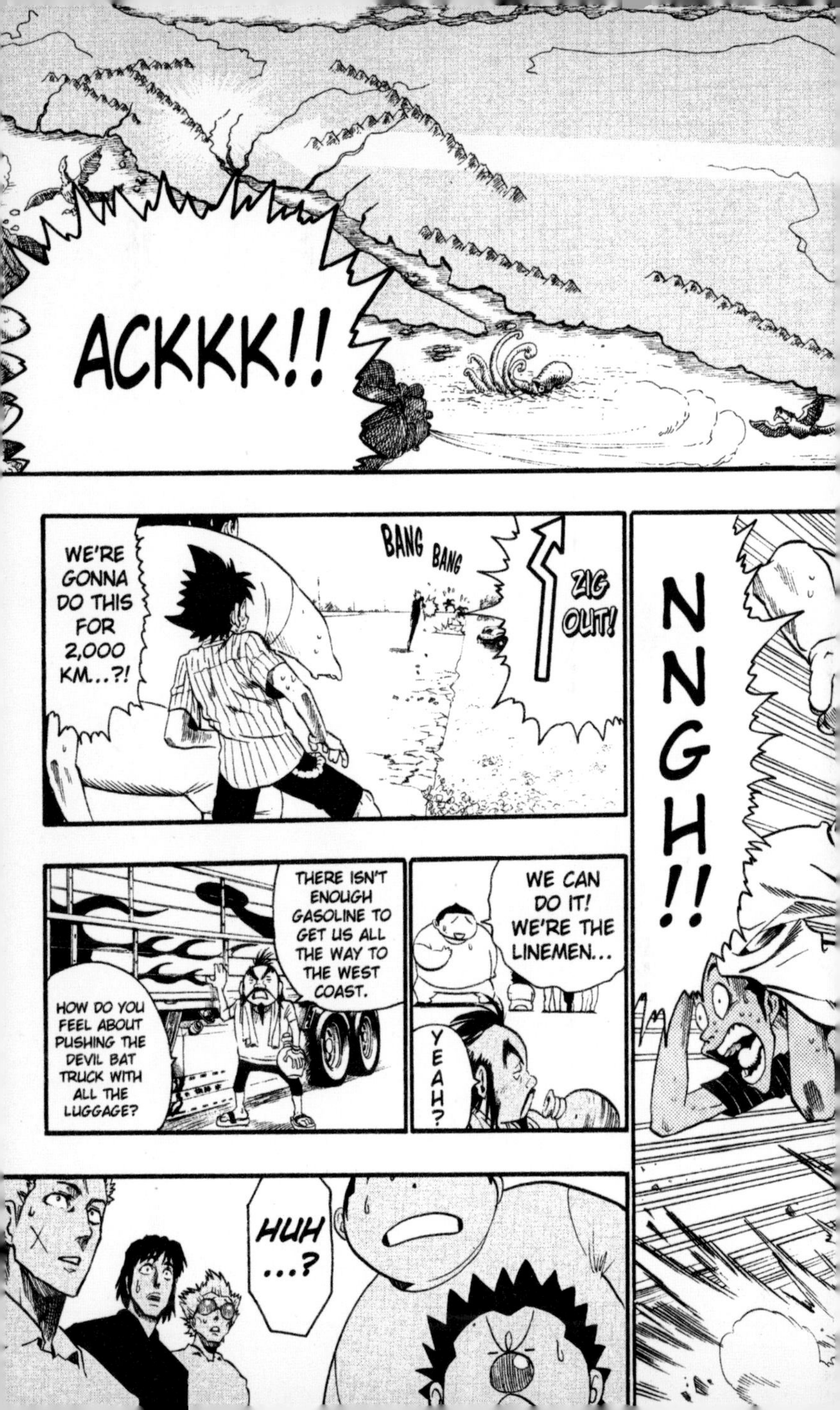
ACKKK!!
NNGH!!
ZIG OUT!
BANG BANG
WE'RE GONNA DO THIS FOR 2,000 KM...?!
WE CAN DO IT! WE'RE THE LINEMEN...
YEAH?
THERE ISN'T ENOUGH GASOLINE TO GET US ALL THE WAY TO THE WEST COAST.
HOW DO YOU FEEL ABOUT PUSHING THE DEVIL BAT TRUCK WITH ALL THE LUGGAGE?
HUH ...?

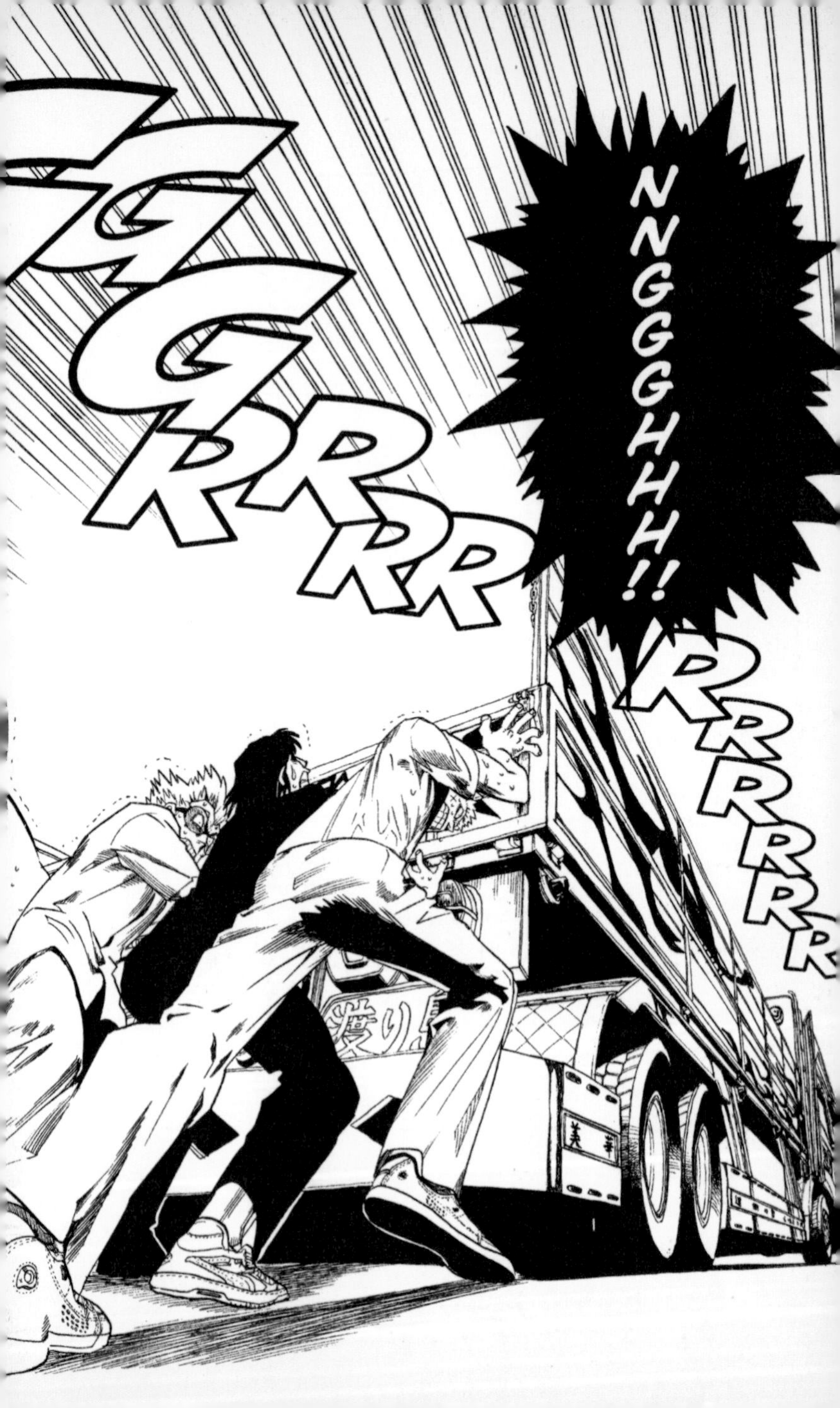
NNGGGHHH!!
RRRRRR
GGGRRRR

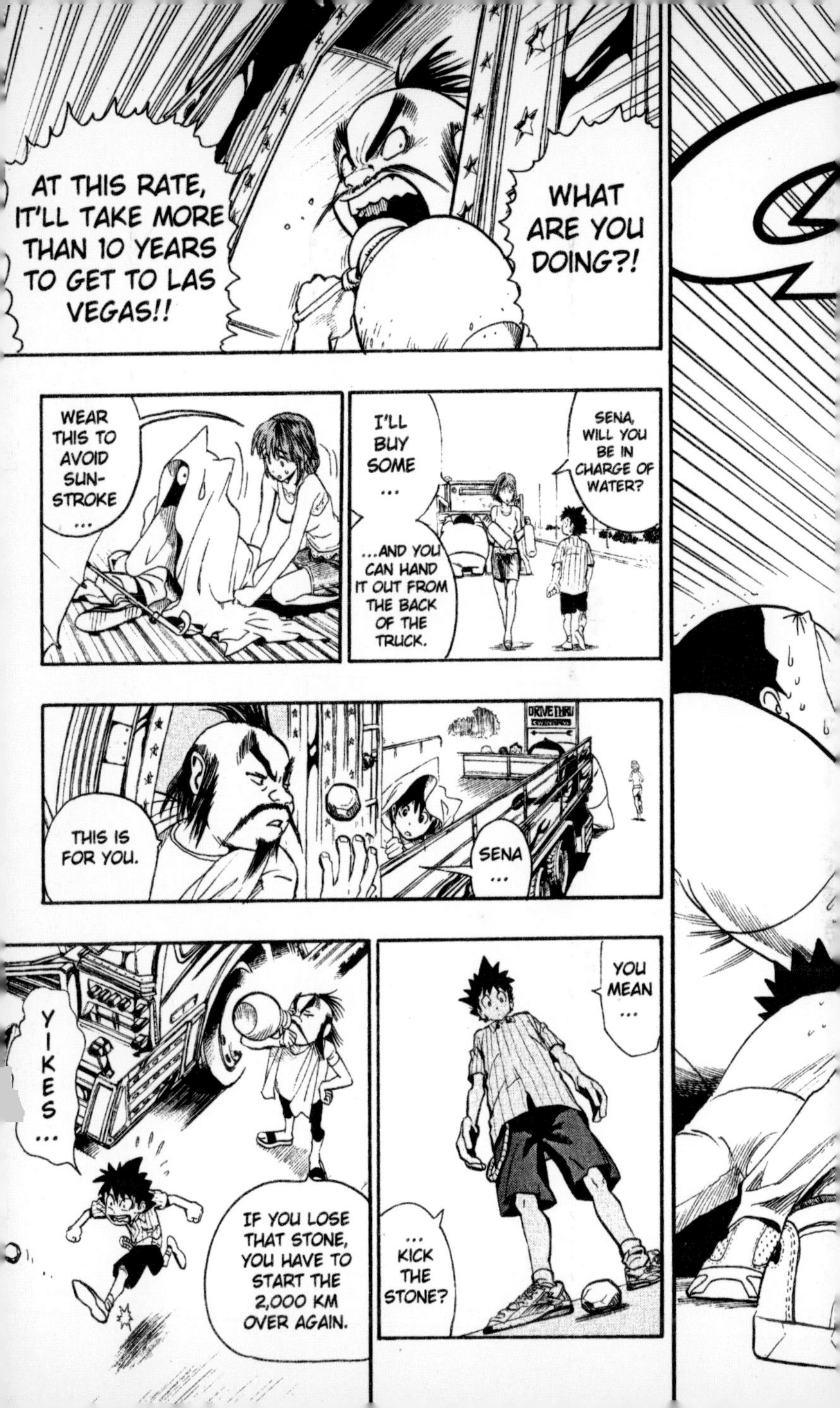
WHAT ARE YOU DOING?!
AT THIS RATE, IT'LL TAKE MORE THAN 10 YEARS TO GET TO LAS VEGAS!!
SENA, WILL YOU BE IN CHARGE OF WATER?
I'LL BUY SOME...
...AND YOU CAN HAND IT OUT FROM THE BACK OF THE TRUCK.
WEAR THIS TO AVOID SUN-STROKE...
DRIVE THRU
SENA...
THIS IS FOR YOU.
YOU MEAN...
...KICK THE STONE?
IF YOU LOSE THAT STONE, YOU HAVE TO START THE 2,000 KM OVER AGAIN.
YIKES...

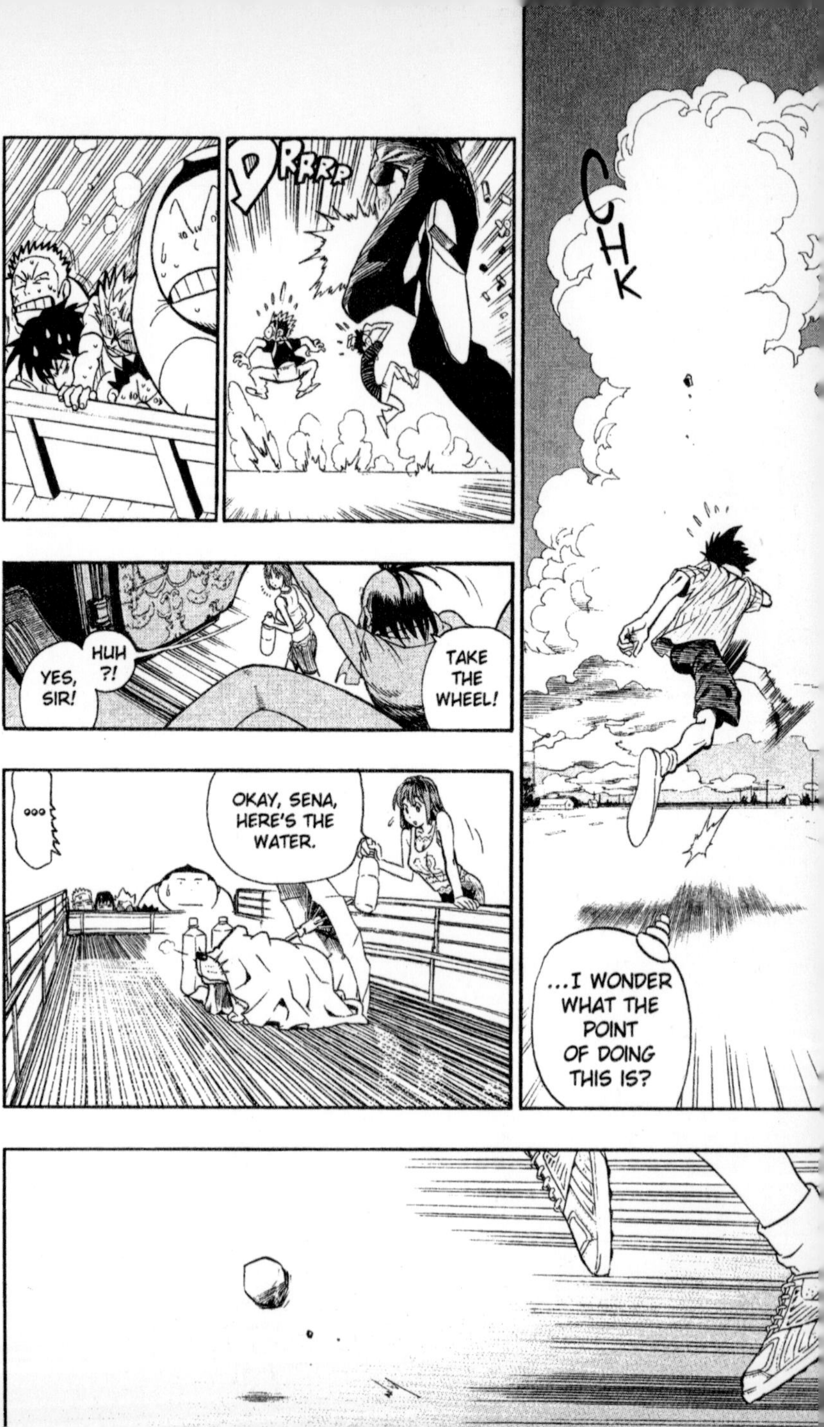
CHK
...I WONDER WHAT THE POINT OF DOING THIS IS?
DRRRRP
TAKE THE WHEEL!
HUH ?!
YES, SIR!
OKAY, SENA, HERE'S THE WATER.
...

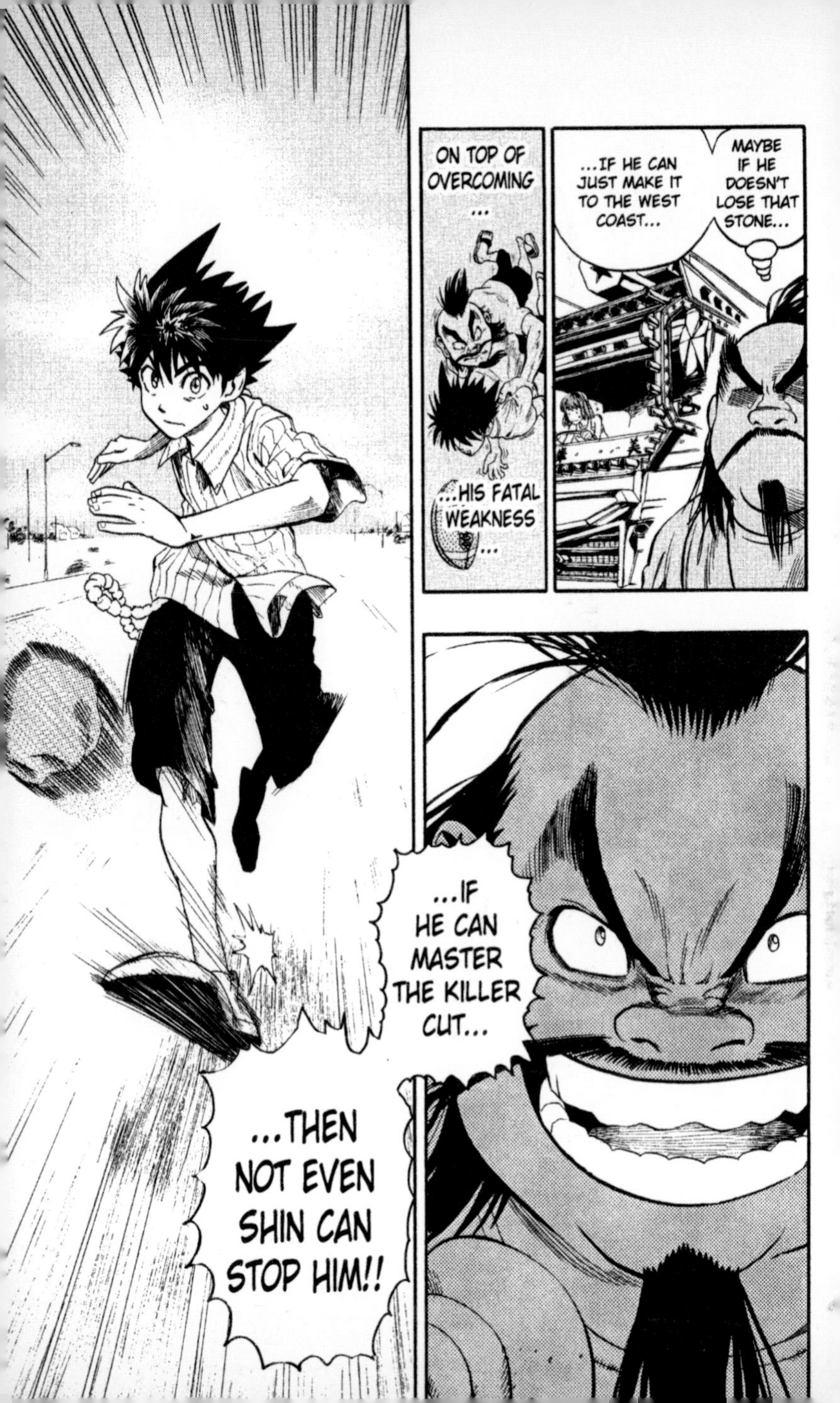
MAYBE IF HE DOESN'T LOSE THAT STONE...
...IF HE CAN JUST MAKE IT TO THE WEST COAST...
ON TOP OF OVERCOMING...
...HIS FATAL WEAKNESS...
...IF HE CAN MASTER THE KILLER CUT...
...THEN NOT EVEN SHIN CAN STOP HIM!!

Eyeshield 21 Survey Corner **Devil Bat 021**

Investigation File #014

If Mamori Anezaki is so smart, what's she doing at a school like Deimon?

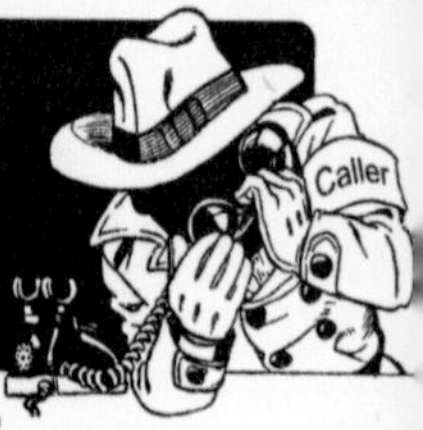
Caller

S.T., Miyagi Prefecture

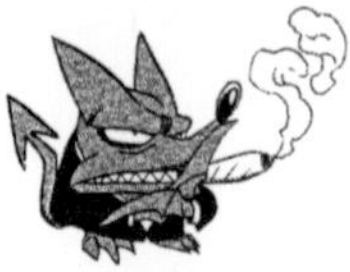

IT'S NOT YOUR SCHOOL THAT DETERMINES YOUR DESTINY... IT'S YOUR OWN ATTITUDE. ANYWAY, IT'S NOT LIKE SHE'S THAT ATTACHED TO DEIMON. I THINK SHE DECIDED TO ATTEND DEIMON BECAUSE HER FRIENDS BEGGED HER, "LET'S ALL GO TO DEIMON TOGETHER."

Investigation File #015

Panther's grandma's oatmeal seems so bad it could kill someone. Please tell me how to make it.

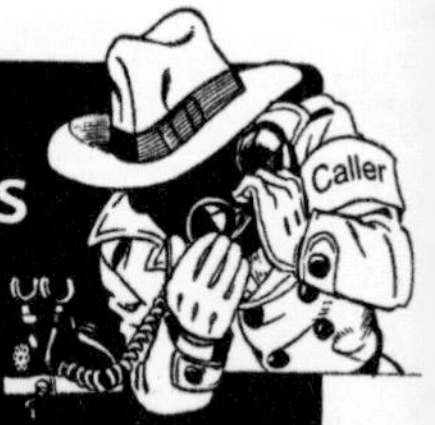
Caller

Guy in a vest, Osaka

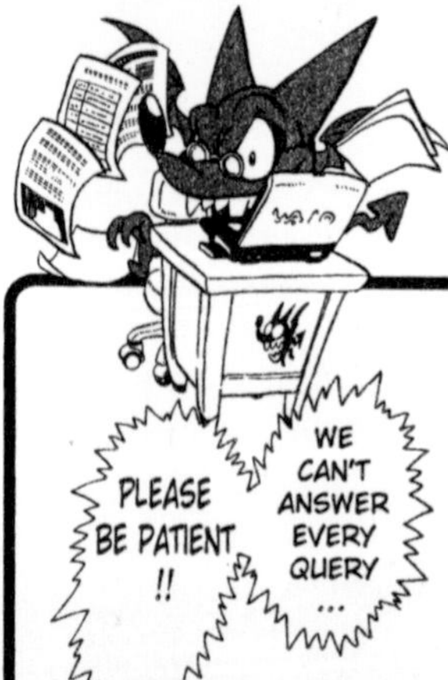
WE CAN'T ANSWER EVERY QUERY ...
PLEASE BE PATIENT !!

AFTER YOU MAKE OATMEAL THE USUAL WAY, ADD ***SPINACH JUICE, GINSENG, ALGAE*** AND WHATEVER OTHER HEALTHY INGREDIENTS YOU CAN FIND. THEN BLEND IT ALL TOGETHER. THAT'S GRANDMA'S RECIPE!

Send your queries for Devil Bat 021 here!!

Devil Bat 021
Shonen Jump Advanced/Eyeshield 21
c/o VIZ Media, LLC
P.O. Box 77010
San Francisco, CA 94107

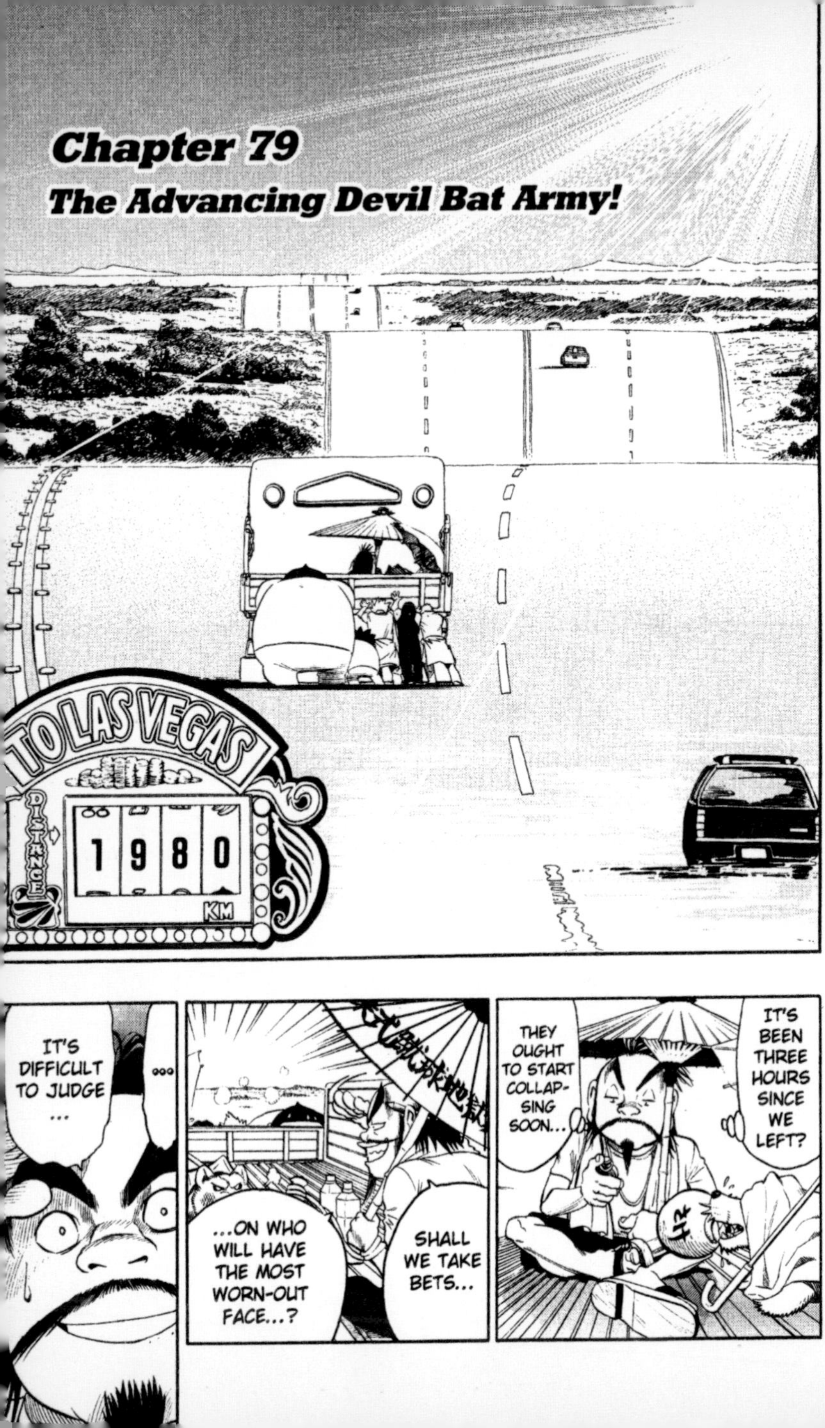
Chapter 79
The Advancing Devil Bat Army!
TO LAS VEGAS
DISTANCE
1980
KM
IT'S BEEN THREE HOURS SINCE WE LEFT?
THEY OUGHT TO START COLLAP-SING SOON...
SHALL WE TAKE BETS...
...ON WHO WILL HAVE THE MOST WORN-OUT FACE...?
...
IT'S DIFFICULT TO JUDGE ...

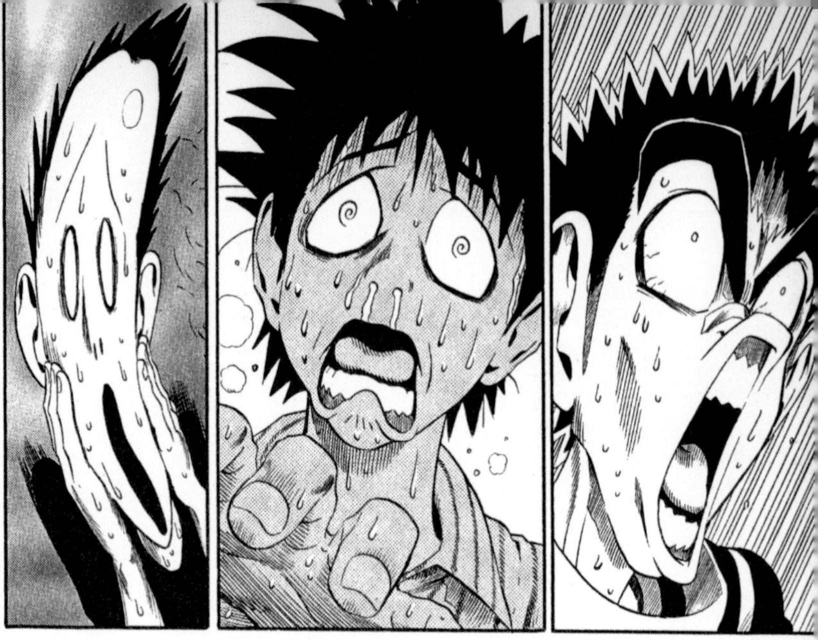

Chapter 79
The Advancing Devil Bat Army!

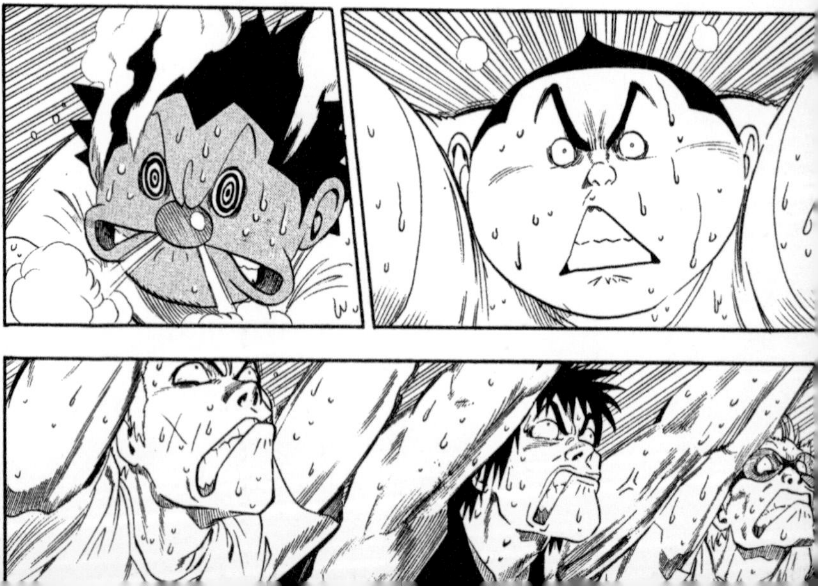

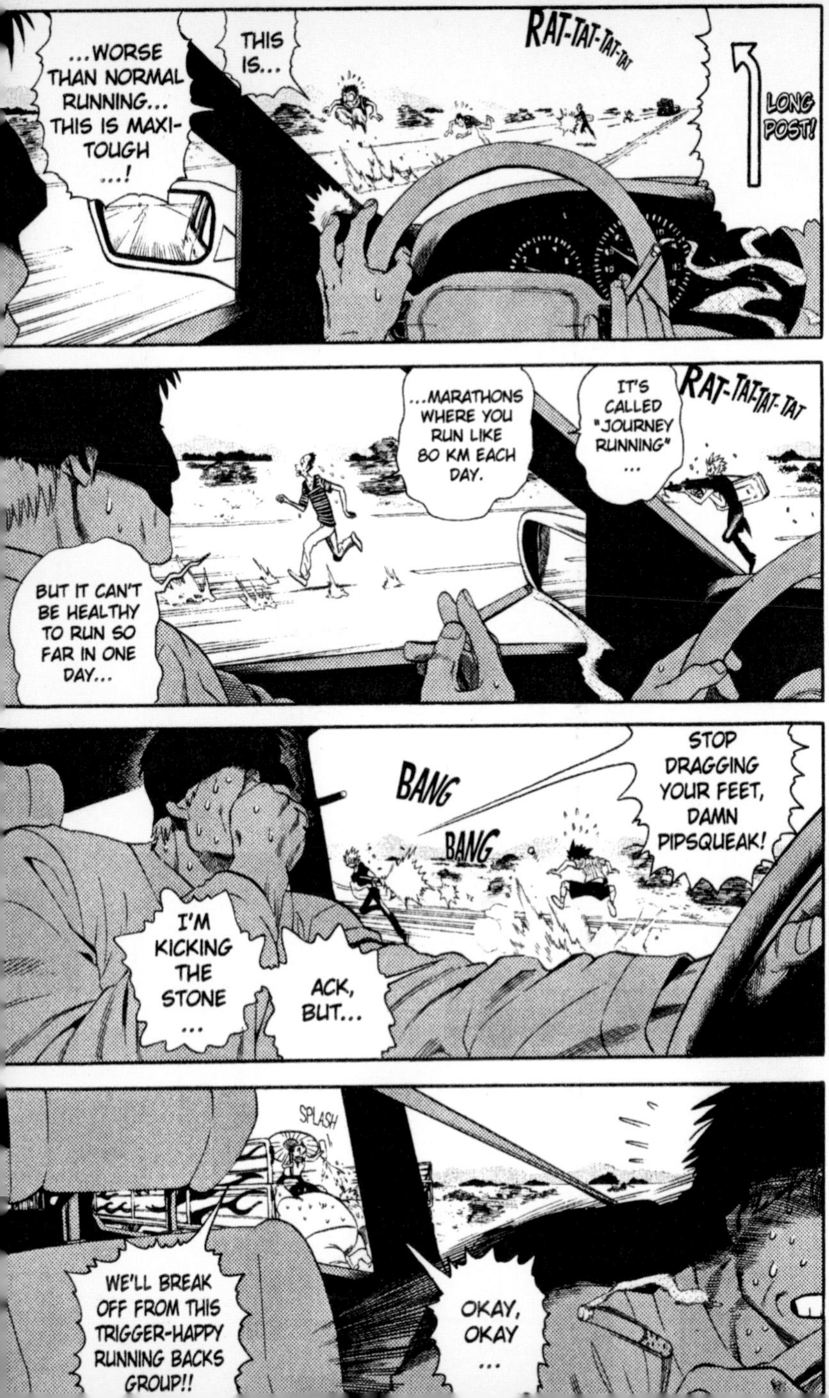
LONG POST!
RAT-TAT-TAT-TAT
THIS IS...
...WORSE THAN NORMAL RUNNING... THIS IS MAXI-TOUGH ...!
RAT-TAT-TAT-TAT
IT'S CALLED "JOURNEY RUNNING" ...
...MARATHONS WHERE YOU RUN LIKE 80 KM EACH DAY.
BUT IT CAN'T BE HEALTHY TO RUN SO FAR IN ONE DAY...
STOP DRAGGING YOUR FEET, DAMN PIPSQUEAK!
BANG
BANG
ACK, BUT...
I'M KICKING THE STONE ...
SPLASH
OKAY, OKAY ...
WE'LL BREAK OFF FROM THIS TRIGGER-HAPPY RUNNING BACKS GROUP!!

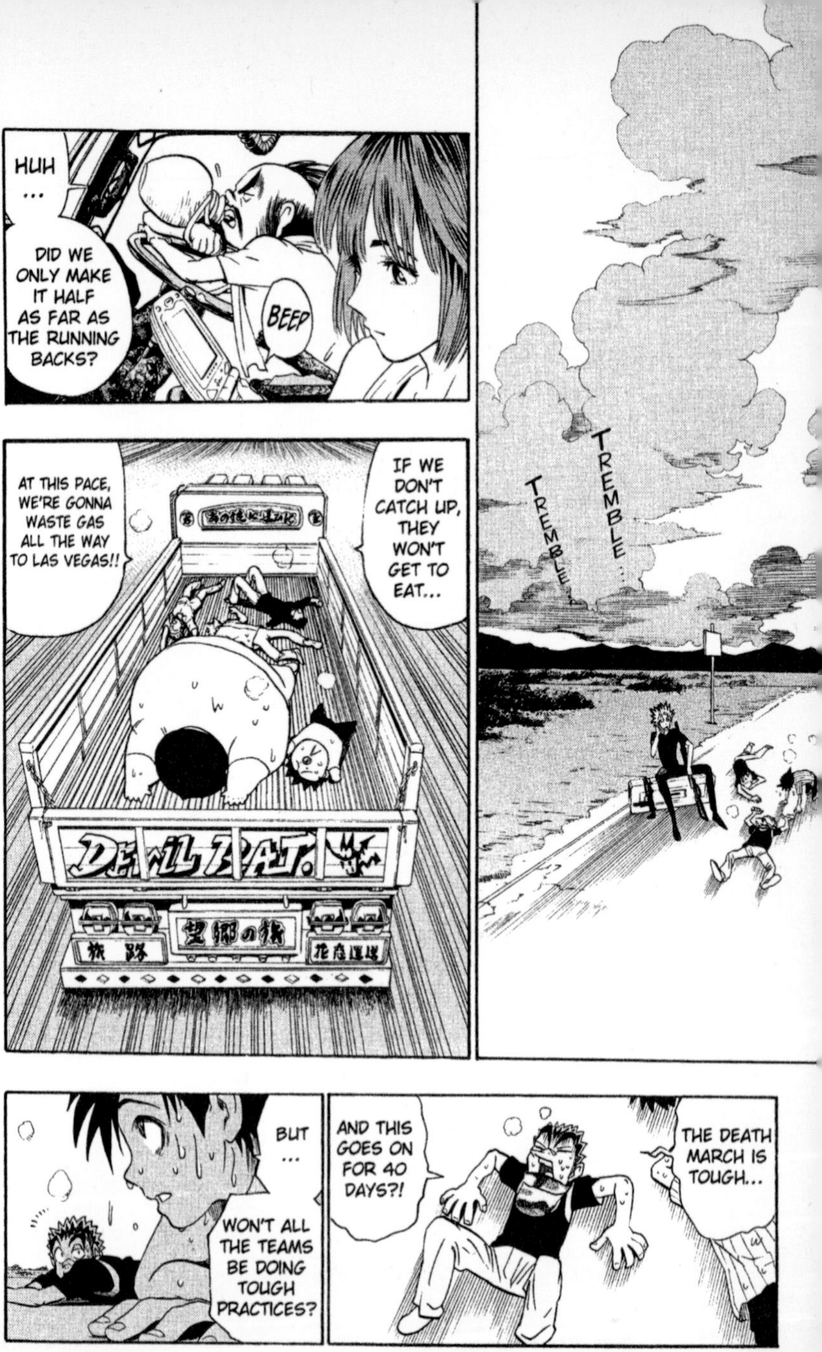
TREMBLE ...
TREMBLE ...
HUH ...
DID WE ONLY MAKE IT HALF AS FAR AS THE RUNNING BACKS?
BEEP
IF WE DON'T CATCH UP, THEY WON'T GET TO EAT...
AT THIS PACE, WE'RE GONNA WASTE GAS ALL THE WAY TO LAS VEGAS!!
望郷の旅
旅路
THE DEATH MARCH IS TOUGH...
AND THIS GOES ON FOR 40 DAYS?!
BUT ...
WON'T ALL THE TEAMS BE DOING TOUGH PRACTICES?

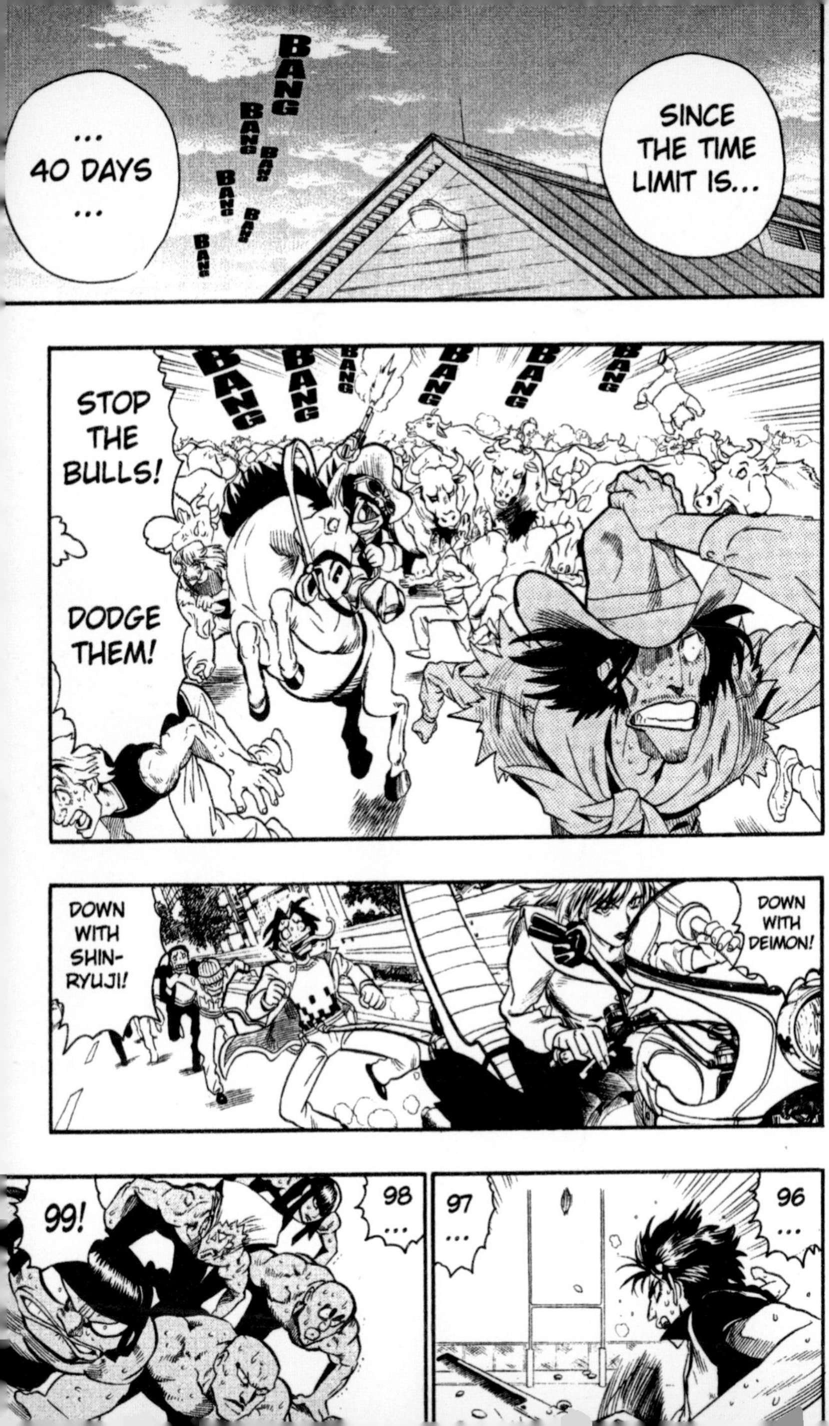
SINCE THE TIME LIMIT IS...
BANG
BANG
BANG
BANG
BANG
BANG
... 40 DAYS ...
BANG
BANG
BANG
BANG
BANG
BANG
STOP THE BULLS!
DODGE THEM!
DOWN WITH DEIMON!
DOWN WITH SHIN-RYUJI!
96 ...
97 ...
98 ...
99!

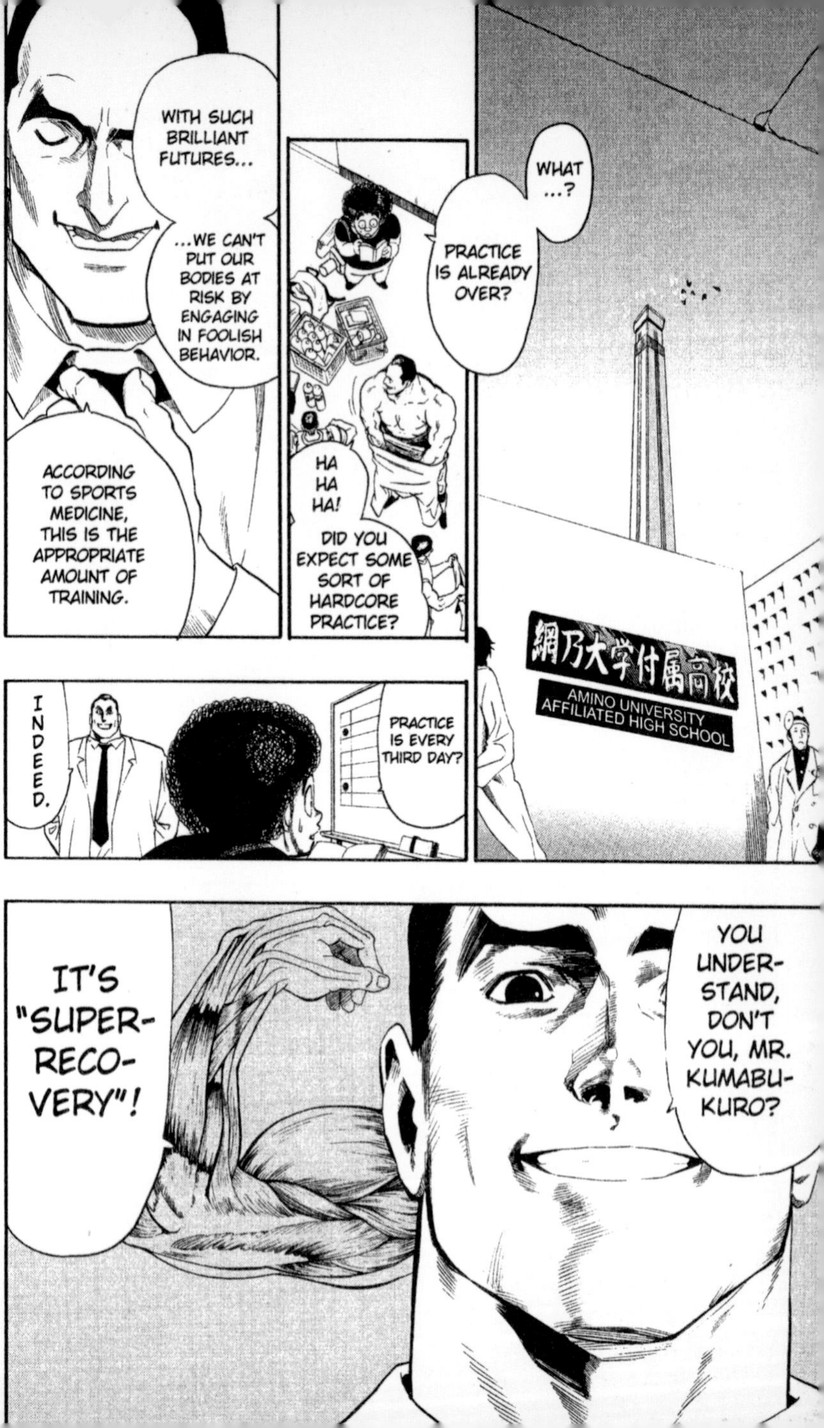
WHAT ...?
PRACTICE IS ALREADY OVER?
網乃大学付属高校
AMINO UNIVERSITY AFFILIATED HIGH SCHOOL
HA HA HA!
DID YOU EXPECT SOME SORT OF HARDCORE PRACTICE?
WITH SUCH BRILLIANT FUTURES...
...WE CAN'T PUT OUR BODIES AT RISK BY ENGAGING IN FOOLISH BEHAVIOR.
ACCORDING TO SPORTS MEDICINE, THIS IS THE APPROPRIATE AMOUNT OF TRAINING.
PRACTICE IS EVERY THIRD DAY?
INDEED.
YOU UNDER-STAND, DON'T YOU, MR. KUMABU-KURO?
IT'S "SUPER-RECO-VERY"!

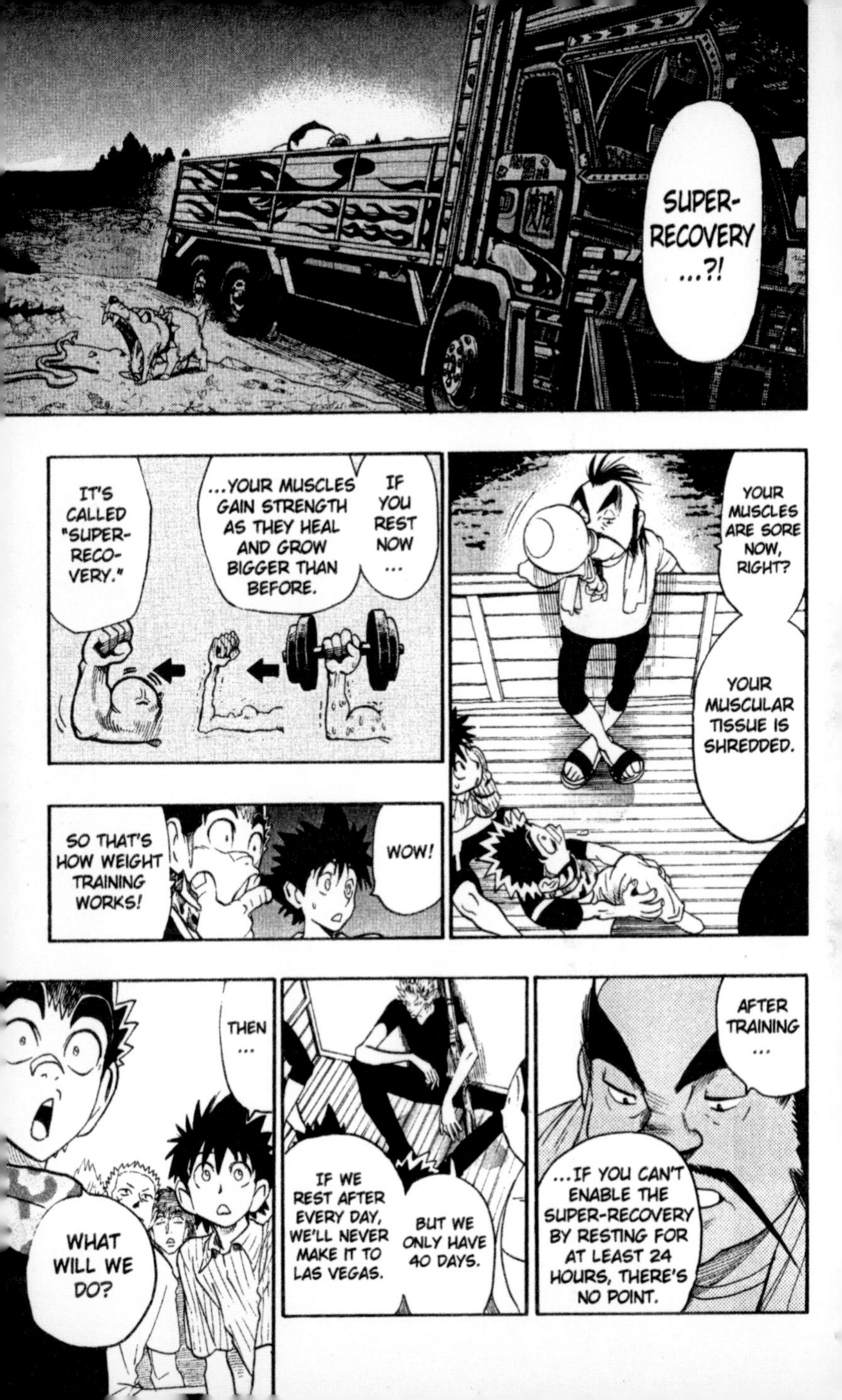
SUPER-RECOVERY ...?!
YOUR MUSCLES ARE SORE NOW, RIGHT?
YOUR MUSCULAR TISSUE IS SHREDDED.
IF YOU REST NOW ...
...YOUR MUSCLES GAIN STRENGTH AS THEY HEAL AND GROW BIGGER THAN BEFORE.
IT'S CALLED "SUPER-RECOVERY."
WOW!
SO THAT'S HOW WEIGHT TRAINING WORKS!
AFTER TRAINING ...
...IF YOU CAN'T ENABLE THE SUPER-RECOVERY BY RESTING FOR AT LEAST 24 HOURS, THERE'S NO POINT.
BUT WE ONLY HAVE 40 DAYS.
IF WE REST AFTER EVERY DAY, WE'LL NEVER MAKE IT TO LAS VEGAS.
THEN ...
WHAT WILL WE DO?

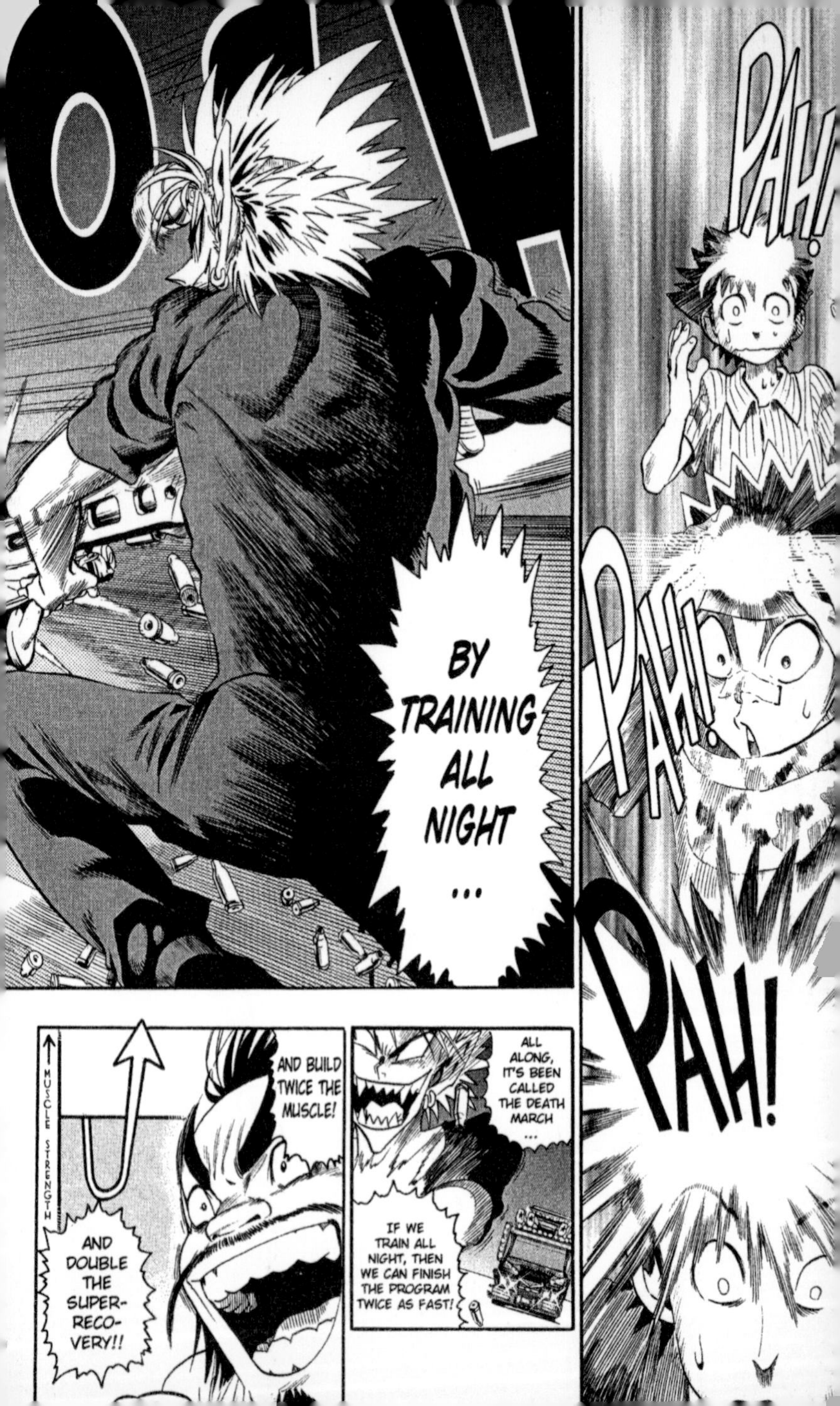

PAH!
PAH!
PAH!
BY TRAINING ALL NIGHT ...
ALL ALONG, IT'S BEEN CALLED THE DEATH MARCH ...
IF WE TRAIN ALL NIGHT, THEN WE CAN FINISH THE PROGRAM TWICE AS FAST!
AND BUILD TWICE THE MUSCLE!
MUSCLE STRENGTH
AND DOUBLE THE SUPER-RECOVERY!!

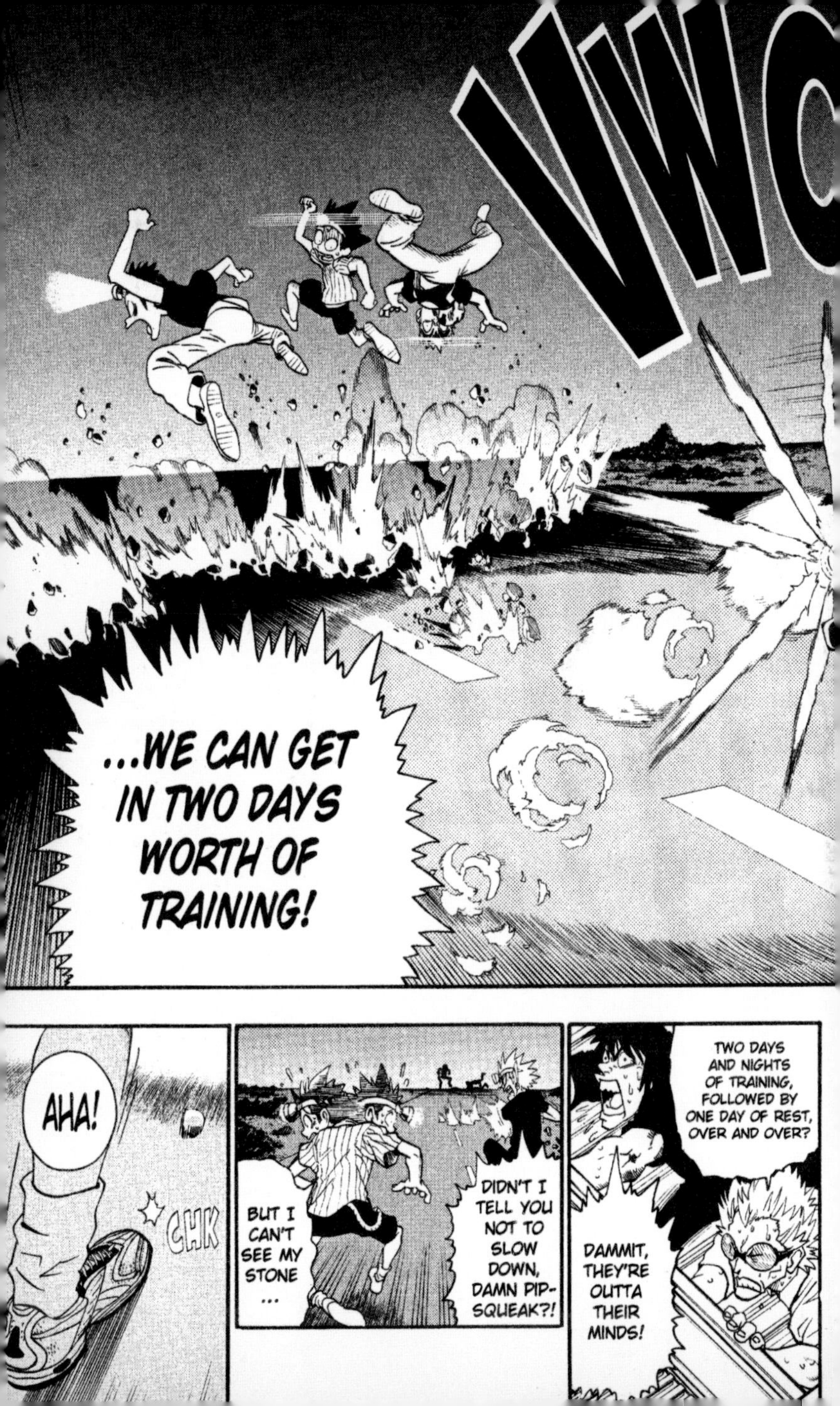
...WE CAN GET IN TWO DAYS WORTH OF TRAINING!
TWO DAYS AND NIGHTS OF TRAINING, FOLLOWED BY ONE DAY OF REST, OVER AND OVER?
DAMMIT, THEY'RE OUTTA THEIR MINDS!
DIDN'T I TELL YOU NOT TO SLOW DOWN, DAMN PIP-SQUEAK?!
BUT I CAN'T SEE MY STONE ...
AHA!
CHK

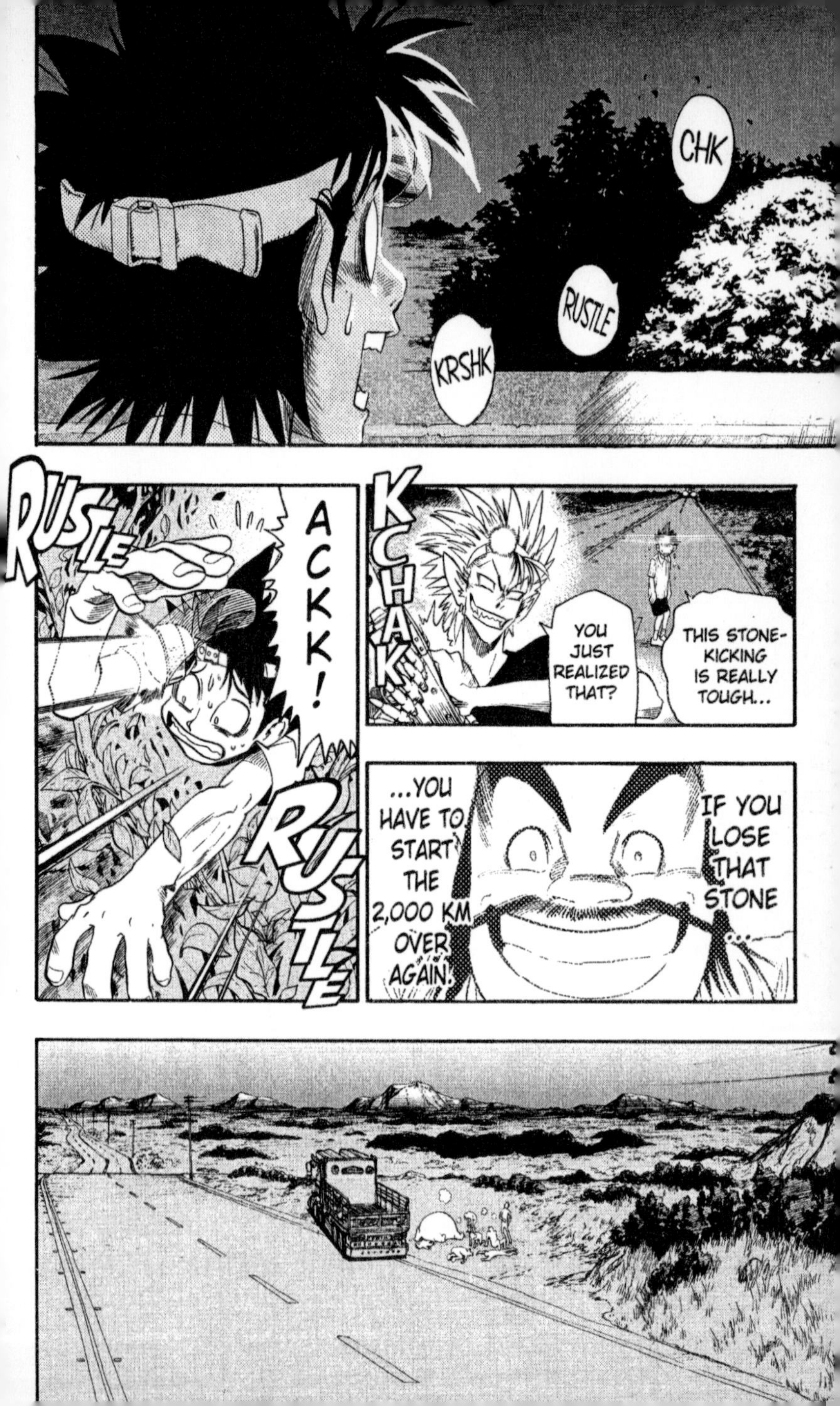
CHK
RUSTLE
KRSHK
THIS STONE-KICKING IS REALLY TOUGH...
YOU JUST REALIZED THAT?
KCHAK
IF YOU LOSE THAT STONE...
...YOU HAVE TO START THE 2,000 KM OVER AGAIN.
ACKK!
RUSTLE
RUSTLE

READ THIS WAY

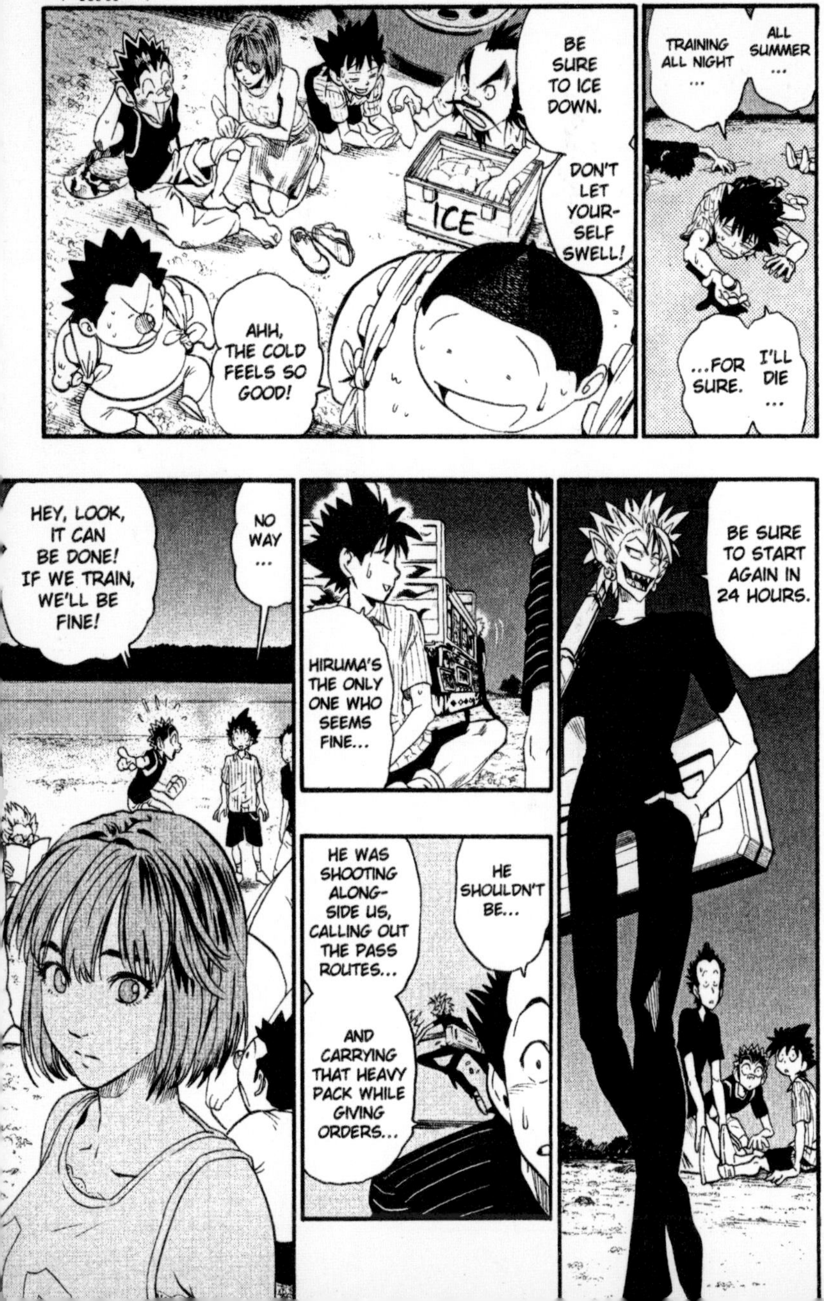
ALL SUMMER ...
TRAINING ALL NIGHT ...
I'LL DIE ...
...FOR SURE.
BE SURE TO ICE DOWN.
DON'T LET YOUR-SELF SWELL!
ICE
AHH, THE COLD FEELS SO GOOD!
BE SURE TO START AGAIN IN 24 HOURS.
HIRUMA'S THE ONLY ONE WHO SEEMS FINE...
HE SHOULDN'T BE...
HE WAS SHOOTING ALONG-SIDE US, CALLING OUT THE PASS ROUTES...
AND CARRYING THAT HEAVY PACK WHILE GIVING ORDERS...
NO WAY ...
HEY, LOOK, IT CAN BE DONE! IF WE TRAIN, WE'LL BE FINE!

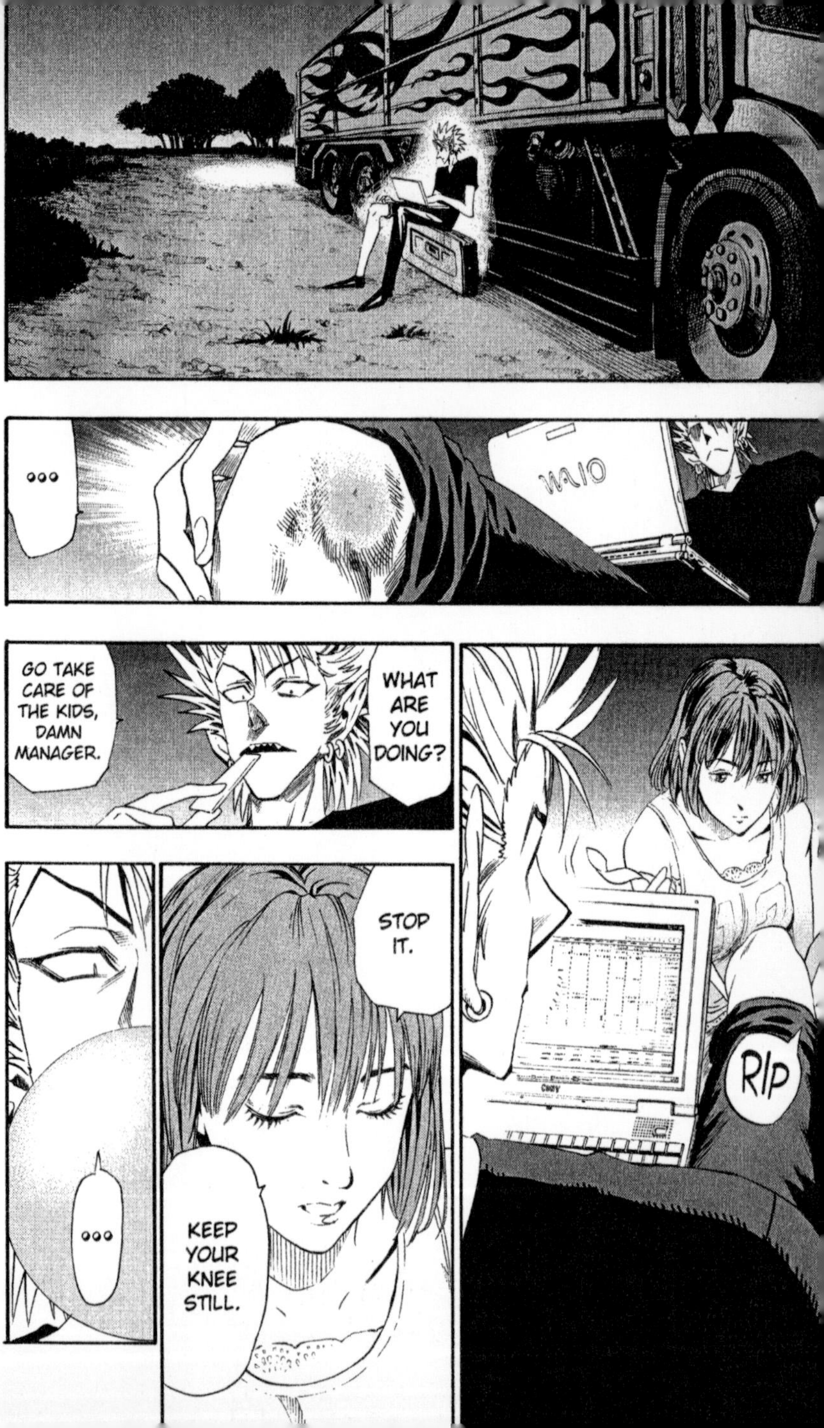
...
RIP
WHAT ARE YOU DOING?
GO TAKE CARE OF THE KIDS, DAMN MANAGER.
STOP IT.
KEEP YOUR KNEE STILL.
...

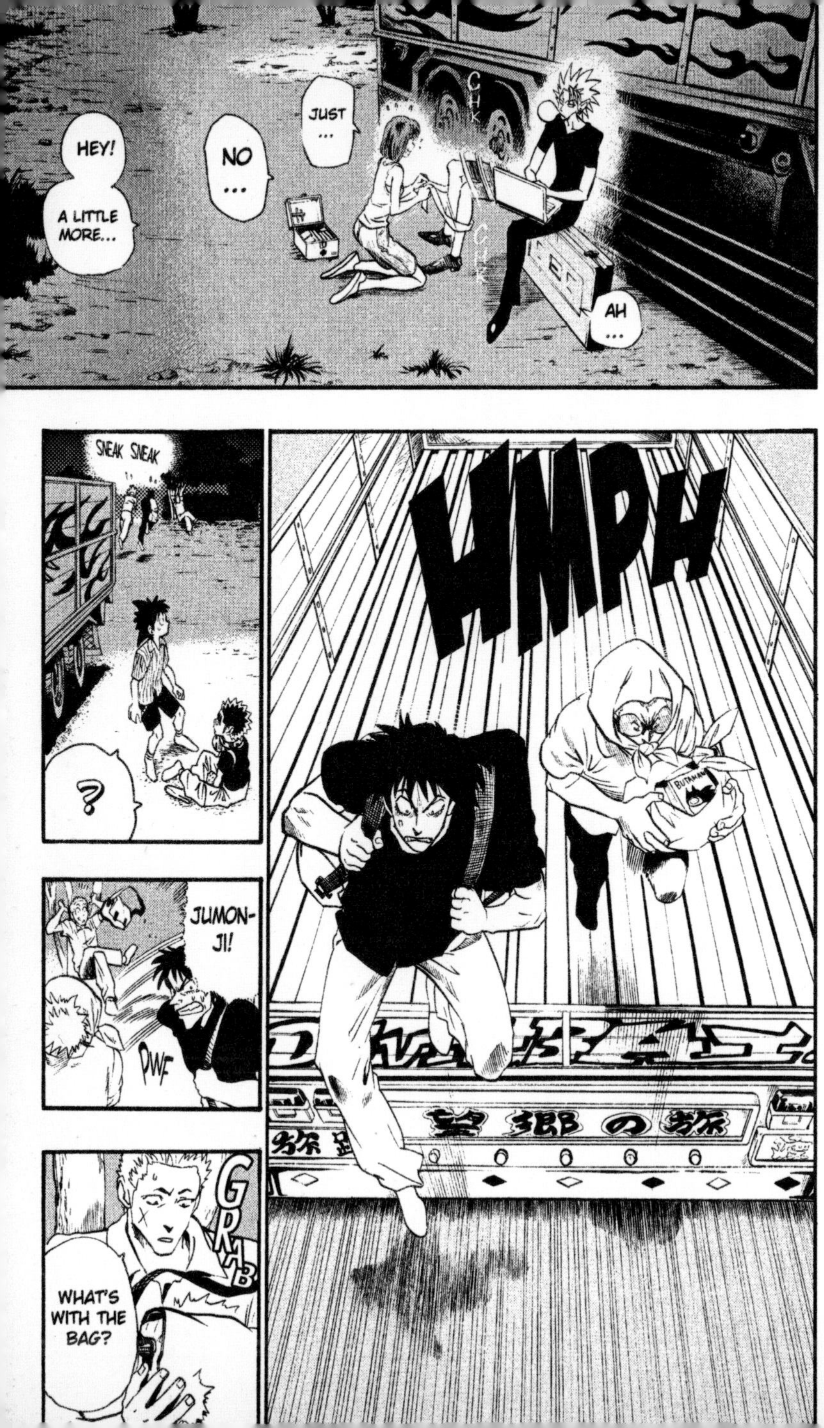
CHK
JUST ...
NO ...
HEY!
A LITTLE MORE...
CHK
AH ...
HMPH
BUTAMAN
SNEAK SNEAK
?
JUMON-JI!
PWF
GRAB
WHAT'S WITH THE BAG?

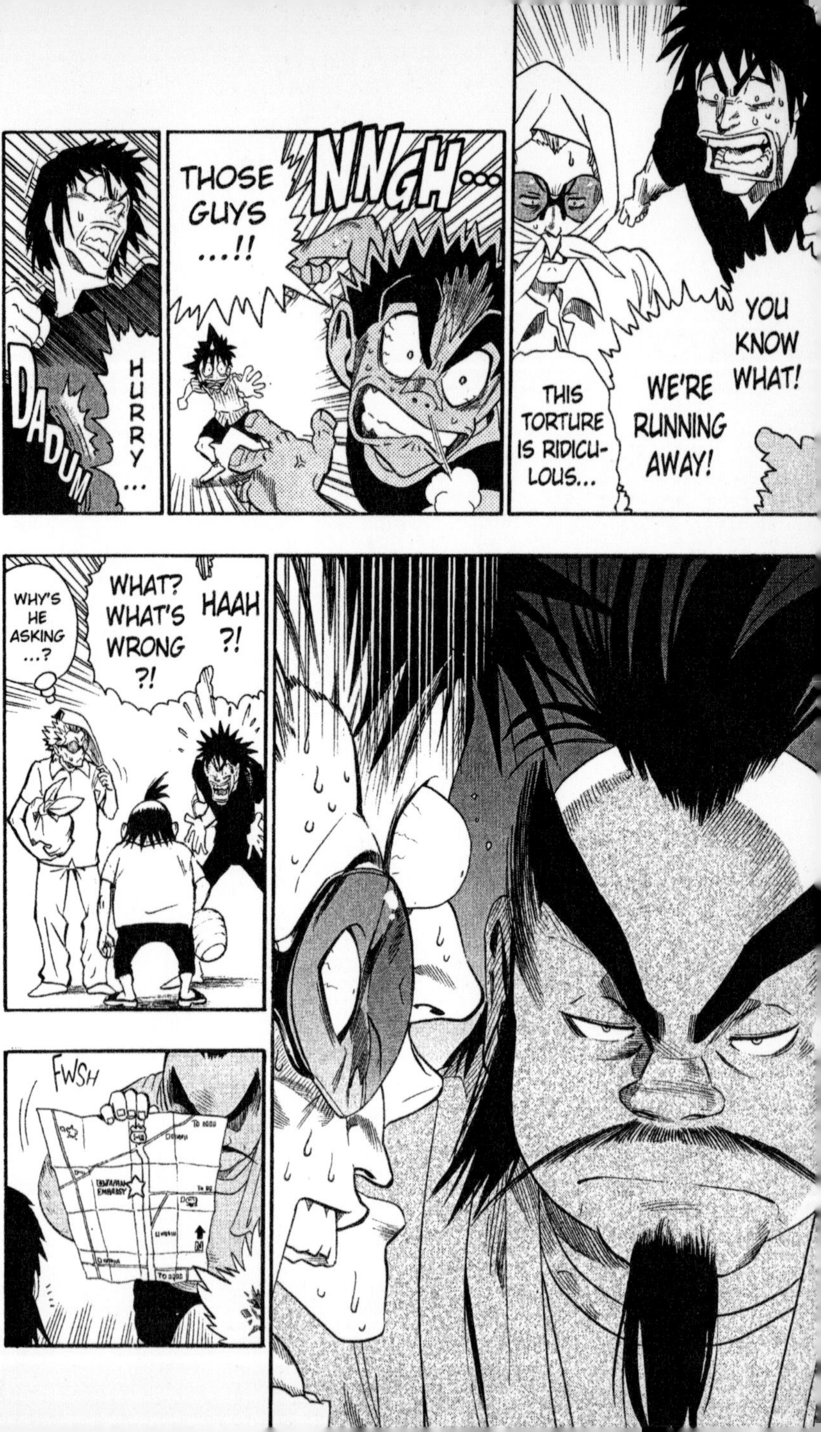
YOU KNOW WHAT!
WE'RE RUNNING AWAY!
THIS TORTURE IS RIDICU-LOUS...
NNGH...
THOSE GUYS ...!!
HURRY...
DADUM
HAAH?!
WHAT? WHAT'S WRONG?!
WHY'S HE ASKING ...?
FWSH
JAPAN EMBASSY
N

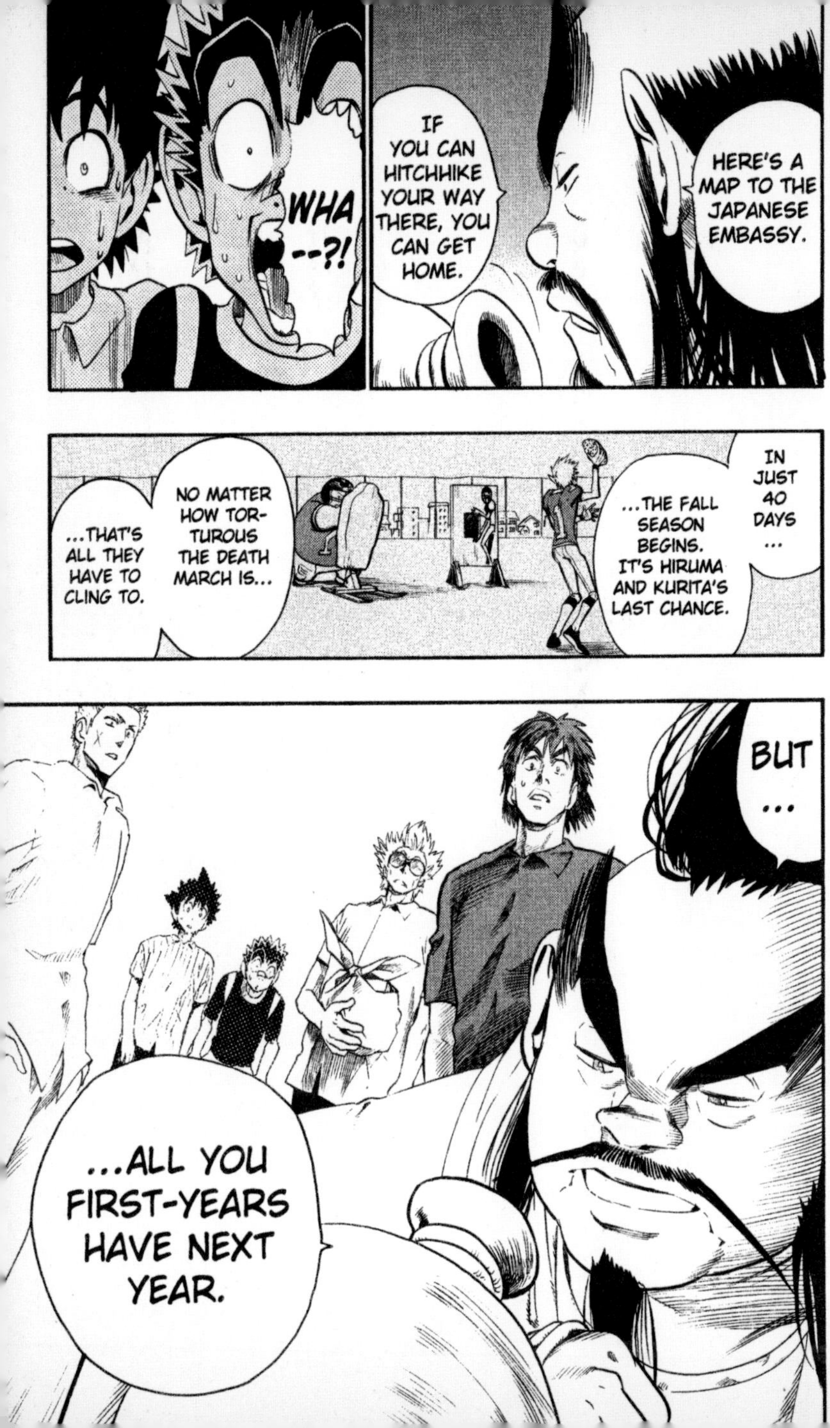
HERE'S A MAP TO THE JAPANESE EMBASSY.
IF YOU CAN HITCHHIKE YOUR WAY THERE, YOU CAN GET HOME.
WHA--?!
IN JUST 40 DAYS...
...THE FALL SEASON BEGINS. IT'S HIRUMA AND KURITA'S LAST CHANCE.
NO MATTER HOW TOR-TUROUS THE DEATH MARCH IS...
...THAT'S ALL THEY HAVE TO CLING TO.
BUT...
...ALL YOU FIRST-YEARS HAVE NEXT YEAR.

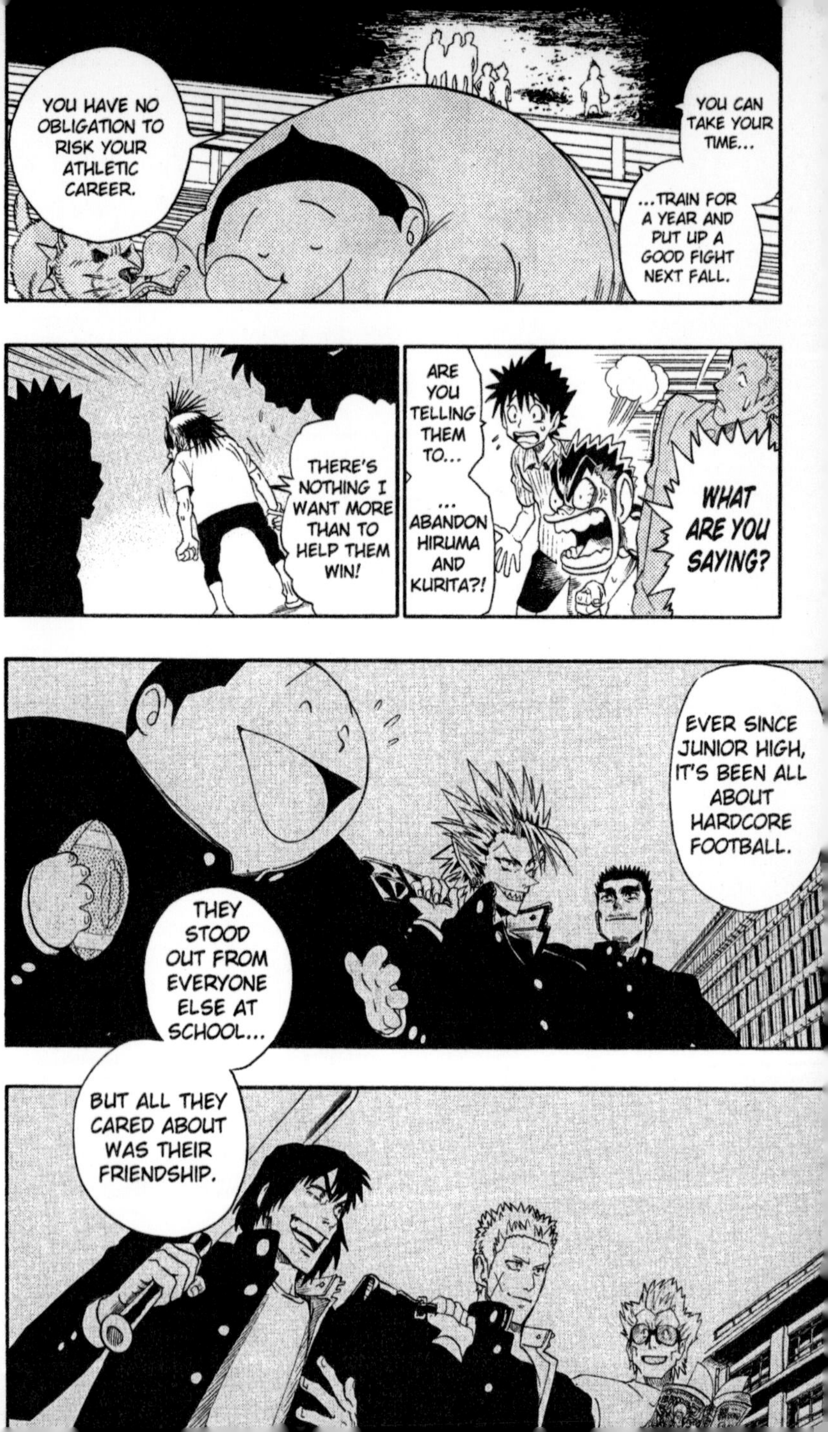
YOU CAN TAKE YOUR TIME...
...TRAIN FOR A YEAR AND PUT UP A GOOD FIGHT NEXT FALL.
YOU HAVE NO OBLIGATION TO RISK YOUR ATHLETIC CAREER.
WHAT ARE YOU SAYING?
ARE YOU TELLING THEM TO...
...ABANDON HIRUMA AND KURITA?!
THERE'S NOTHING I WANT MORE THAN TO HELP THEM WIN!
EVER SINCE JUNIOR HIGH, IT'S BEEN ALL ABOUT HARDCORE FOOTBALL.
THEY STOOD OUT FROM EVERYONE ELSE AT SCHOOL...
BUT ALL THEY CARED ABOUT WAS THEIR FRIENDSHIP.

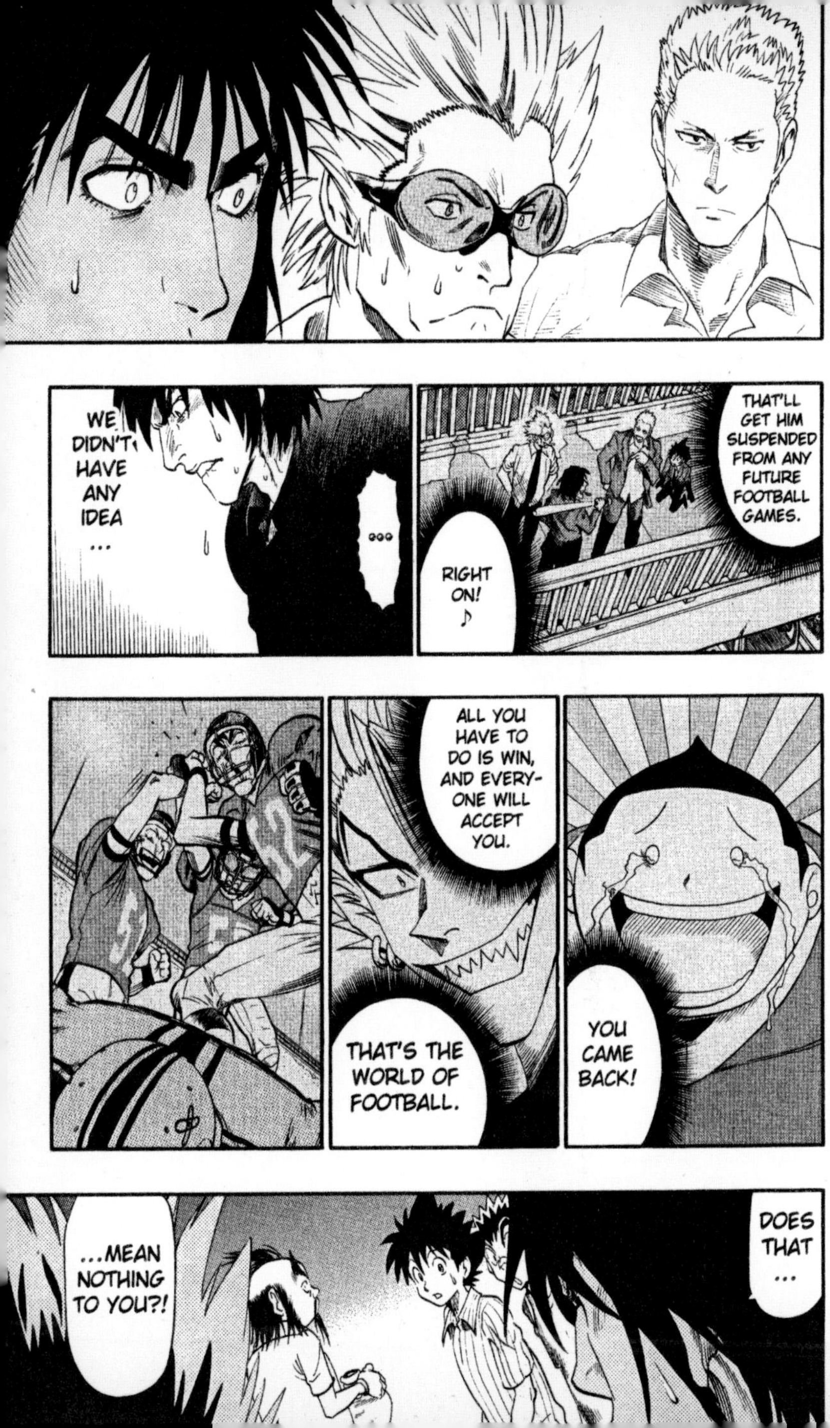
THAT'LL GET HIM SUSPENDED FROM ANY FUTURE FOOTBALL GAMES.
RIGHT ON! ♪
...
WE DIDN'T HAVE ANY IDEA...
YOU CAME BACK!
ALL YOU HAVE TO DO IS WIN, AND EVERY-ONE WILL ACCEPT YOU.
THAT'S THE WORLD OF FOOTBALL.
DOES THAT...
...MEAN NOTHING TO YOU?!

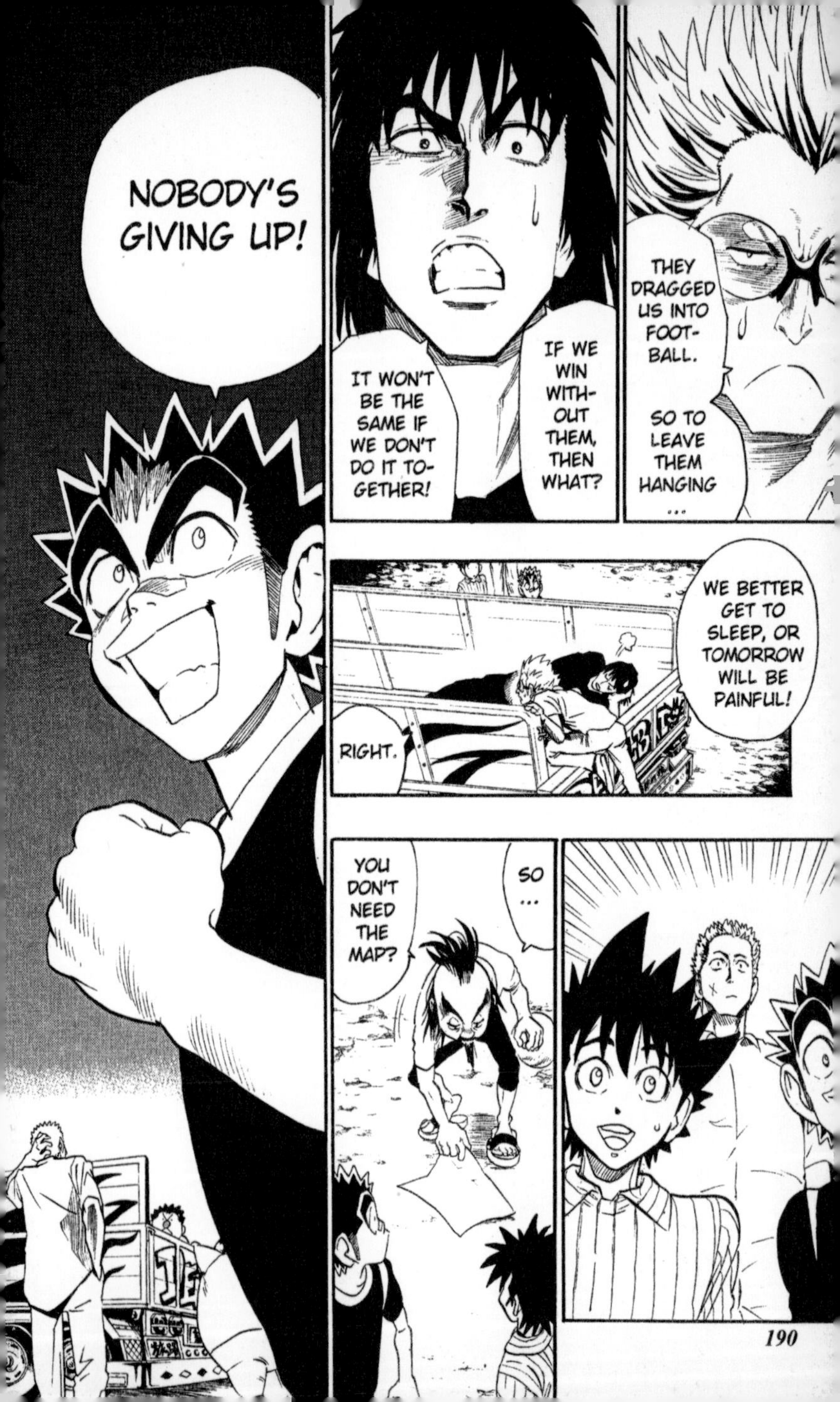
THEY DRAGGED US INTO FOOTBALL.
SO TO LEAVE THEM HANGING ...
IF WE WIN WITHOUT THEM, THEN WHAT?
IT WON'T BE THE SAME IF WE DON'T DO IT TOGETHER!
WE BETTER GET TO SLEEP, OR TOMORROW WILL BE PAINFUL!
RIGHT.
SO ...
YOU DON'T NEED THE MAP?
NOBODY'S GIVING UP!

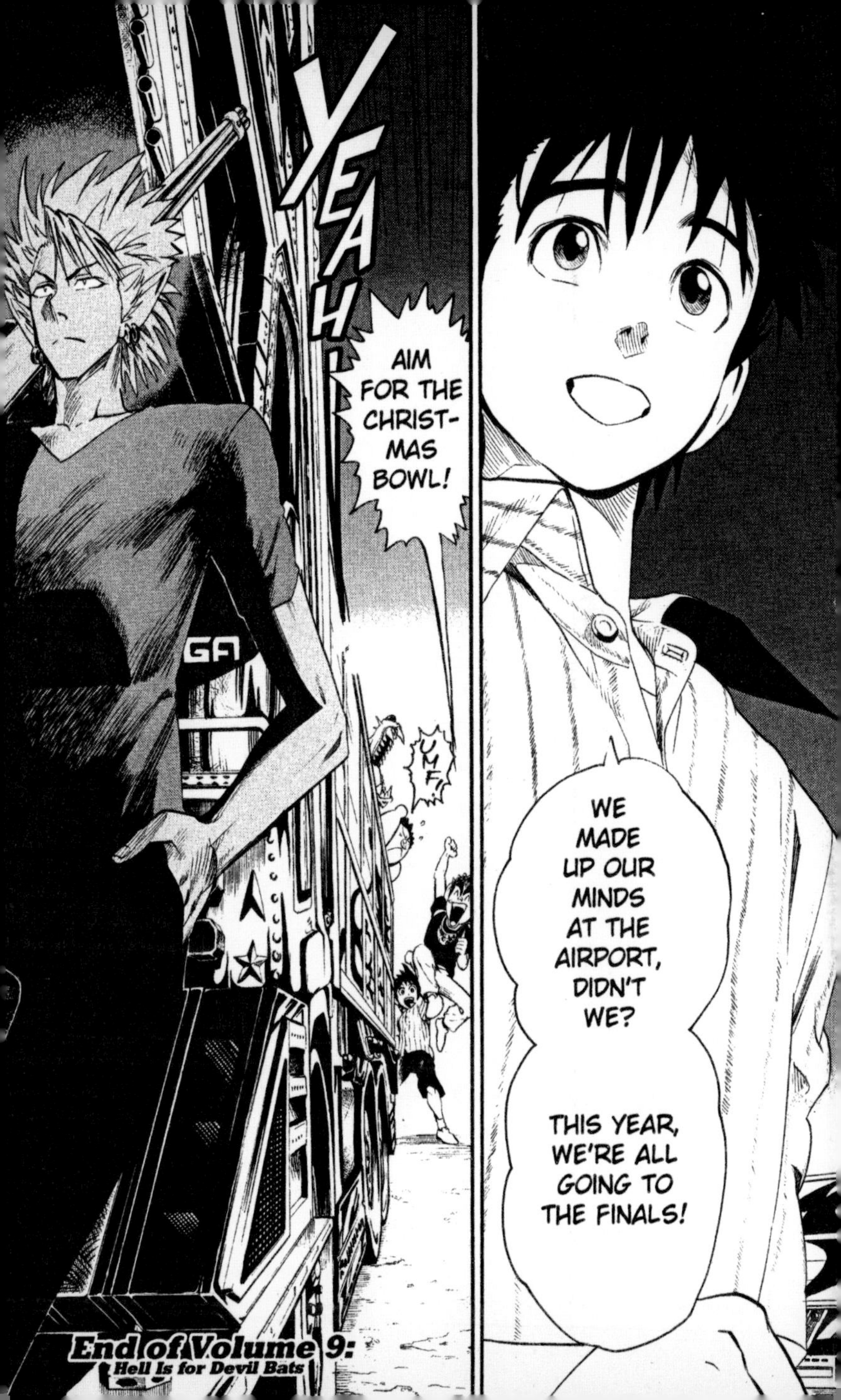
WE MADE UP OUR MINDS AT THE AIRPORT, DIDN'T WE?
THIS YEAR, WE'RE ALL GOING TO THE FINALS!
YEAH!
AIM FOR THE CHRIST-MAS BOWL!
UMF!!
GA

End of Volume 9: Hell Is for Devil Bats

Deluxe Biographies
of the Supporting Cast

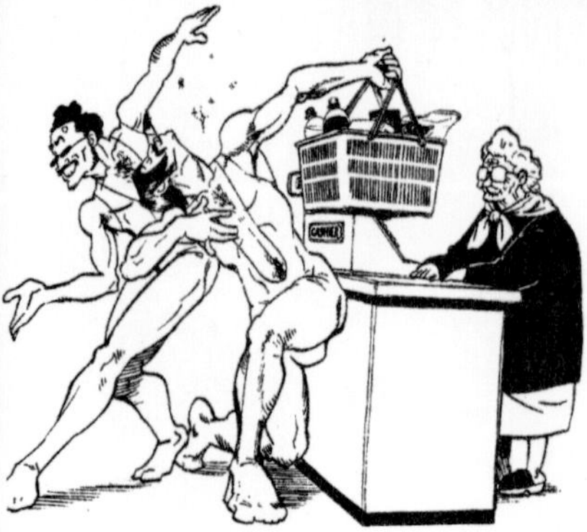

Sexy Queens

This isn't just for beach football. They look like this in everyday life. Their clothing ripped when Tetsuma and Sena ran past them, but it seems like they may have made their uniforms easy to rip on purpose. Oh, sexy!

It will be depressing for their parents when they're still doing this at age 30…

Too Tattooed Team Leader, Simon

When he was 16, he was bored, so he became a drug dealer.

The next day, he learned how to play beach football, which he thought was fun, so he changed his mind.

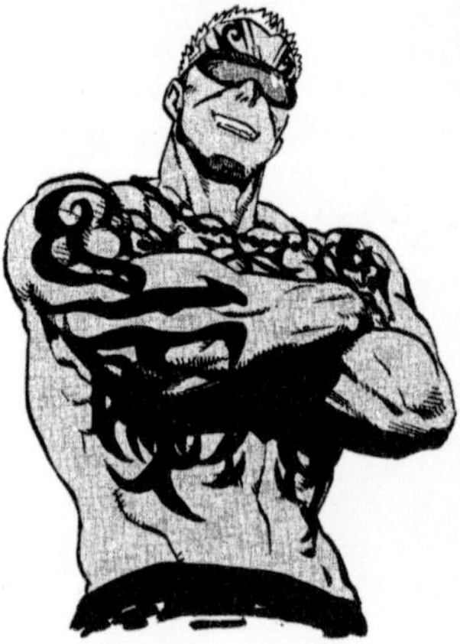

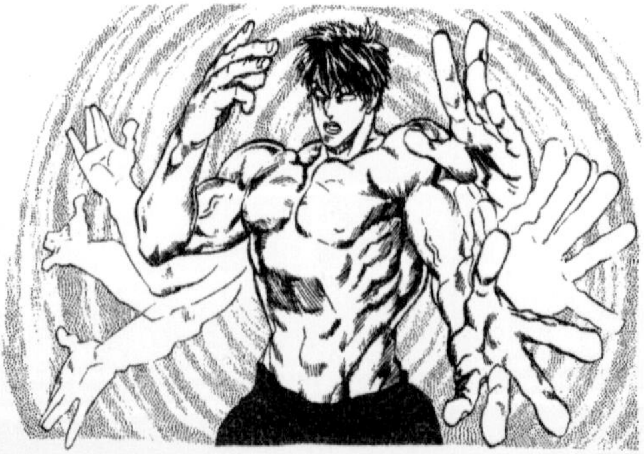

Hallucination Shin

Since he only exists within Sena's hallucinations, he can only change according to Sena's impressions of him. He's probably a master of some martial art like Hokuto Shinken* or Qi Gong.

*The martial art practiced by Kenshiro in "Fist of the North Star."

Gun Shop Manager

He's a strange old man who loves his guns so much he sleeps with them.

According to him, he's a soldier who returned from Vietnam, but he also says that he fought in the Civil War, the French Revolution, and the Battle of Sekigahara, so he must be one of those types...

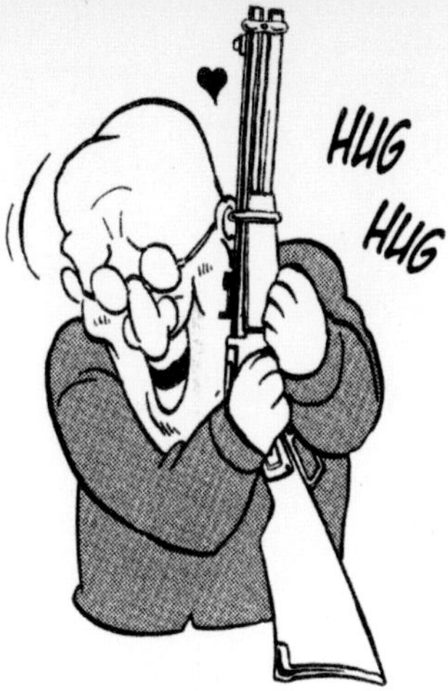
HUG
HUG

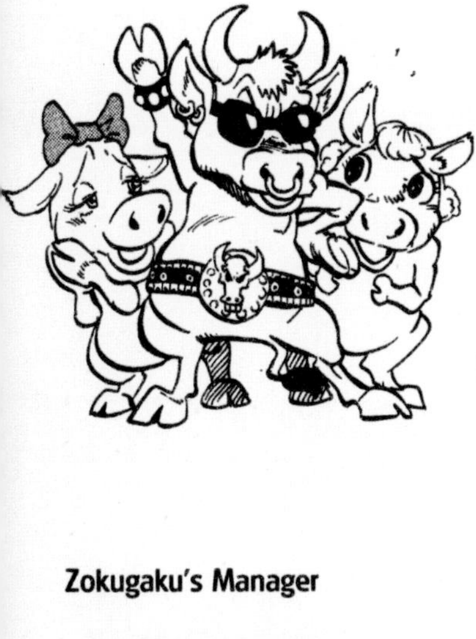

The Bull

He's been a wild bull ever since he was a calf, so he kept getting sold. He was sold so much that it affected the tone of his moo.

But after Sena and the gang rescued him, he became a rodeo star as a wild bull. And then his sound turned to rock-n-roll.
Thank you, thank you very much.

Zokugaku's Manager

Her weapon is a simple bamboo sword, but she's pretty handy with it.

It seems that, as soon a fight starts, she gives a single chop to the crotch. That's all.

Instead of saying that she is cowardly or something, you could say that she's a brisk tactician.

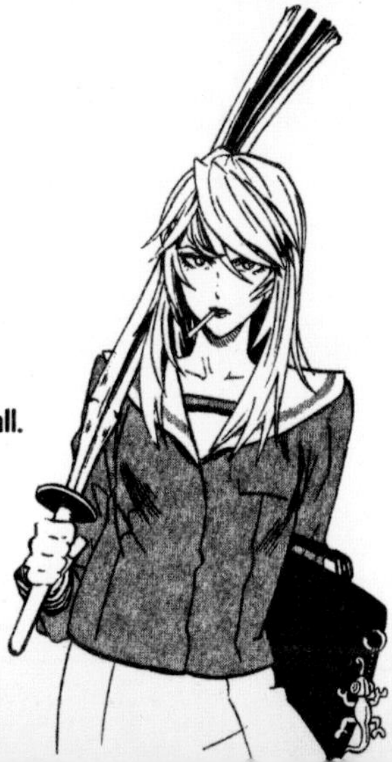
HSK

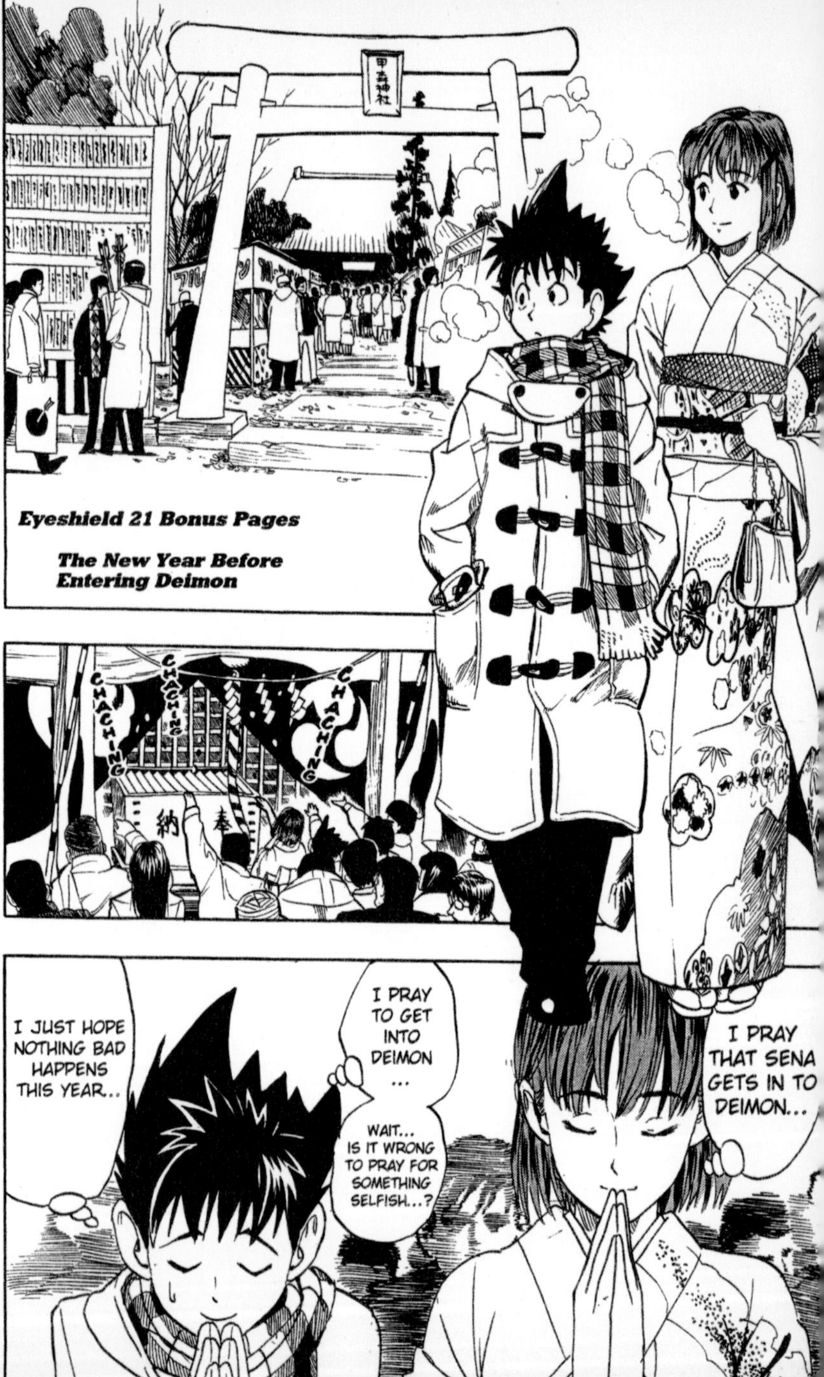

Eyeshield 21 Bonus Pages
The New Year Before Entering Deimon
CHACHING
CHACHING
CHACHING
I PRAY THAT SENA GETS IN TO DEIMON...
I PRAY TO GET INTO DEIMON ...
WAIT... IS IT WRONG TO PRAY FOR SOMETHING SELFISH...?
I JUST HOPE NOTHING BAD HAPPENS THIS YEAR...

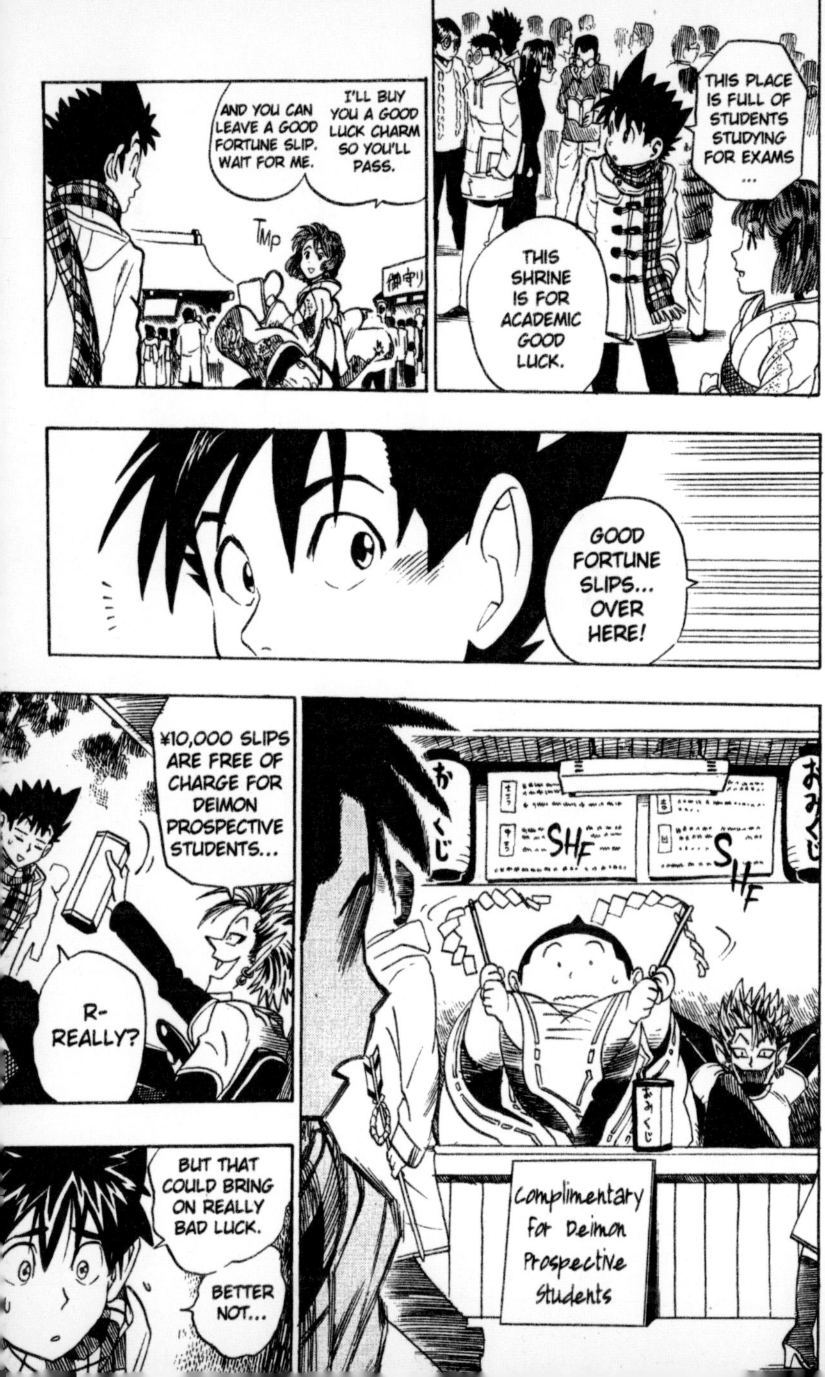
THIS PLACE IS FULL OF STUDENTS STUDYING FOR EXAMS ...
THIS SHRINE IS FOR ACADEMIC GOOD LUCK.
I'LL BUY YOU A GOOD LUCK CHARM SO YOU'LL PASS.
AND YOU CAN LEAVE A GOOD FORTUNE SLIP. WAIT FOR ME.
TMP
御守り
GOOD FORTUNE SLIPS... OVER HERE!
おみくじ
SHF
SHF
おみくじ
Complimentary for Deimon Prospective Students
¥10,000 SLIPS ARE FREE OF CHARGE FOR DEIMON PROSPECTIVE STUDENTS...
R-REALLY?
BUT THAT COULD BRING ON REALLY BAD LUCK.
BETTER NOT...

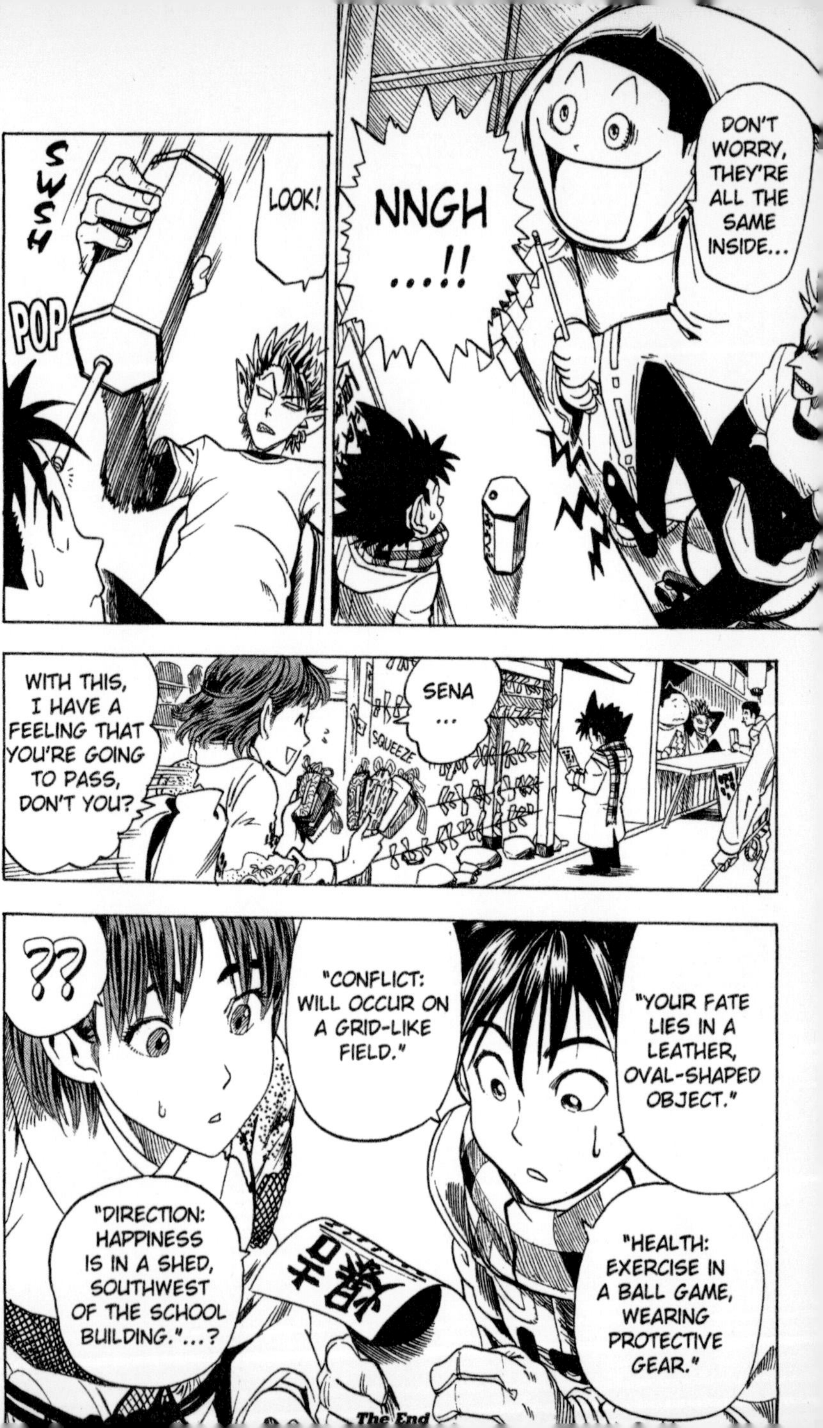
DON'T WORRY, THEY'RE ALL THE SAME INSIDE...
NNGH ...!!
LOOK!
SWSH
POP
SENA ...
SQUEEZE
WITH THIS, I HAVE A FEELING THAT YOU'RE GOING TO PASS, DON'T YOU?
"YOUR FATE LIES IN A LEATHER, OVAL-SHAPED OBJECT."
"CONFLICT: WILL OCCUR ON A GRID-LIKE FIELD."
??
"HEALTH: EXERCISE IN A BALL GAME, WEARING PROTECTIVE GEAR."
"DIRECTION: HAPPINESS IS IN A SHED, SOUTHWEST OF THE SCHOOL BUILDING."...?
The End

Staff

Story: Riichiro Inagaki

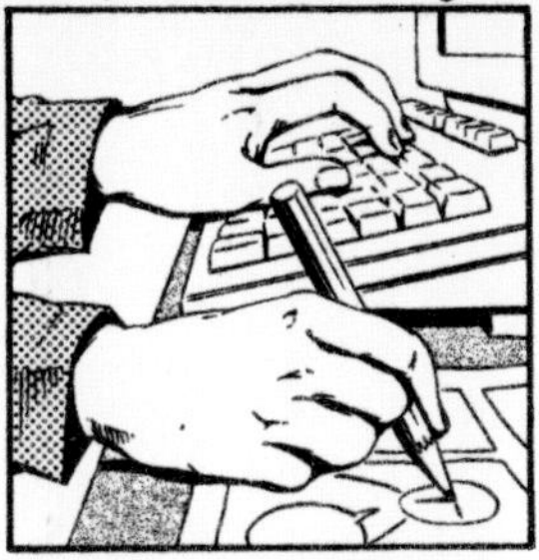

Art: Yusuke Murata

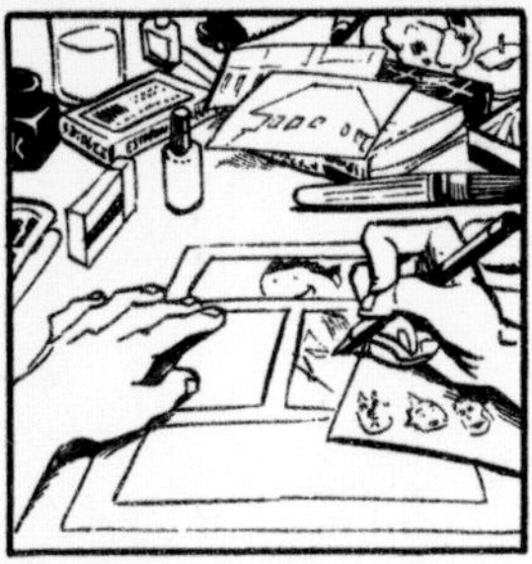

Chief: Akira Tanaka

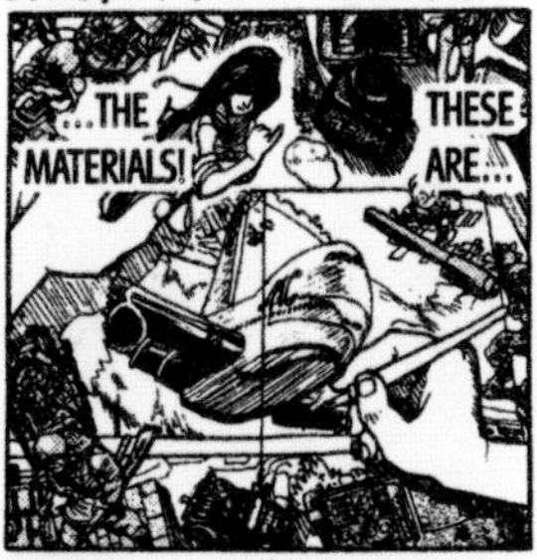
THESE ARE...
...THE MATERIALS!

Takahiro Hiraishi

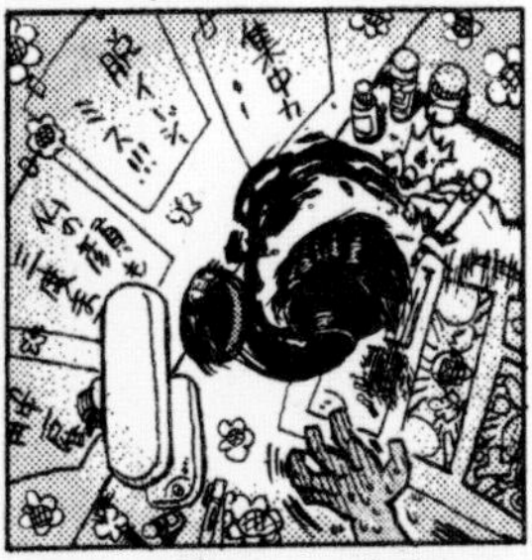

Kentaro Kurimoto

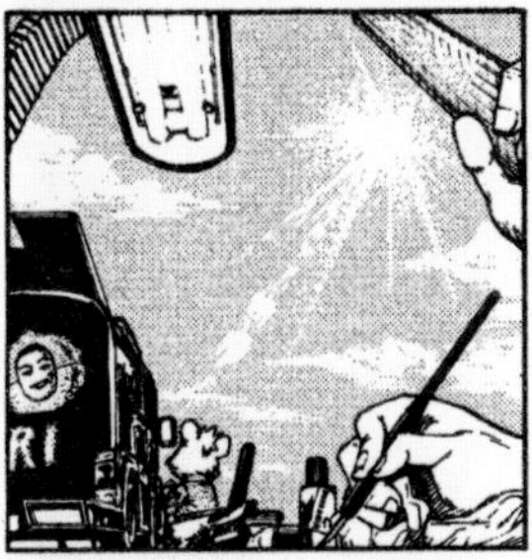

Junko Katsugi

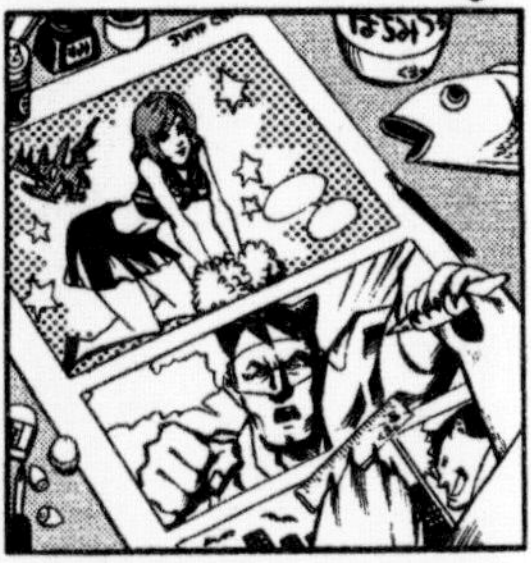

Hiroshi Furuyama

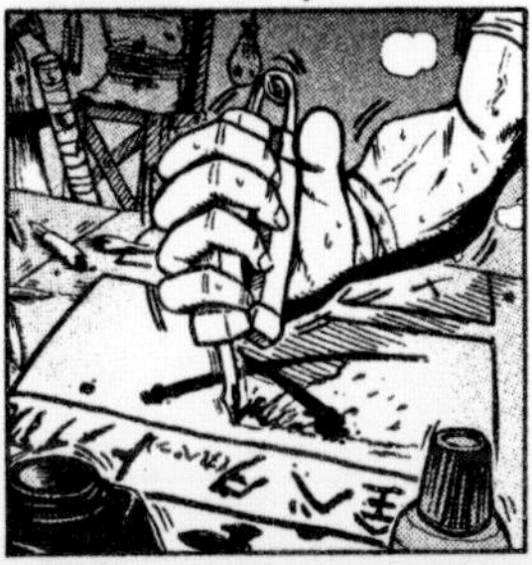

Masayuki Shiomura

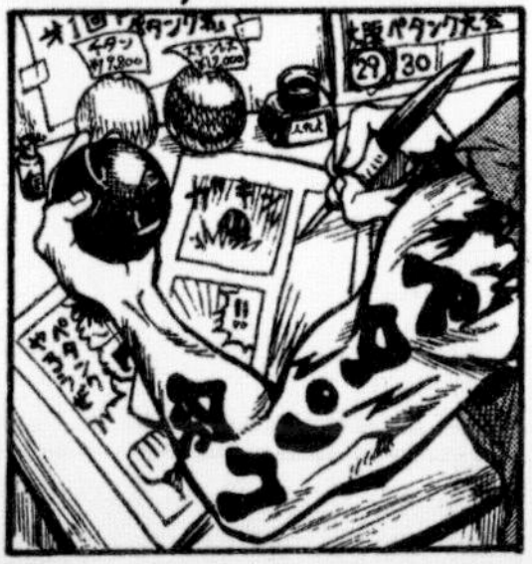

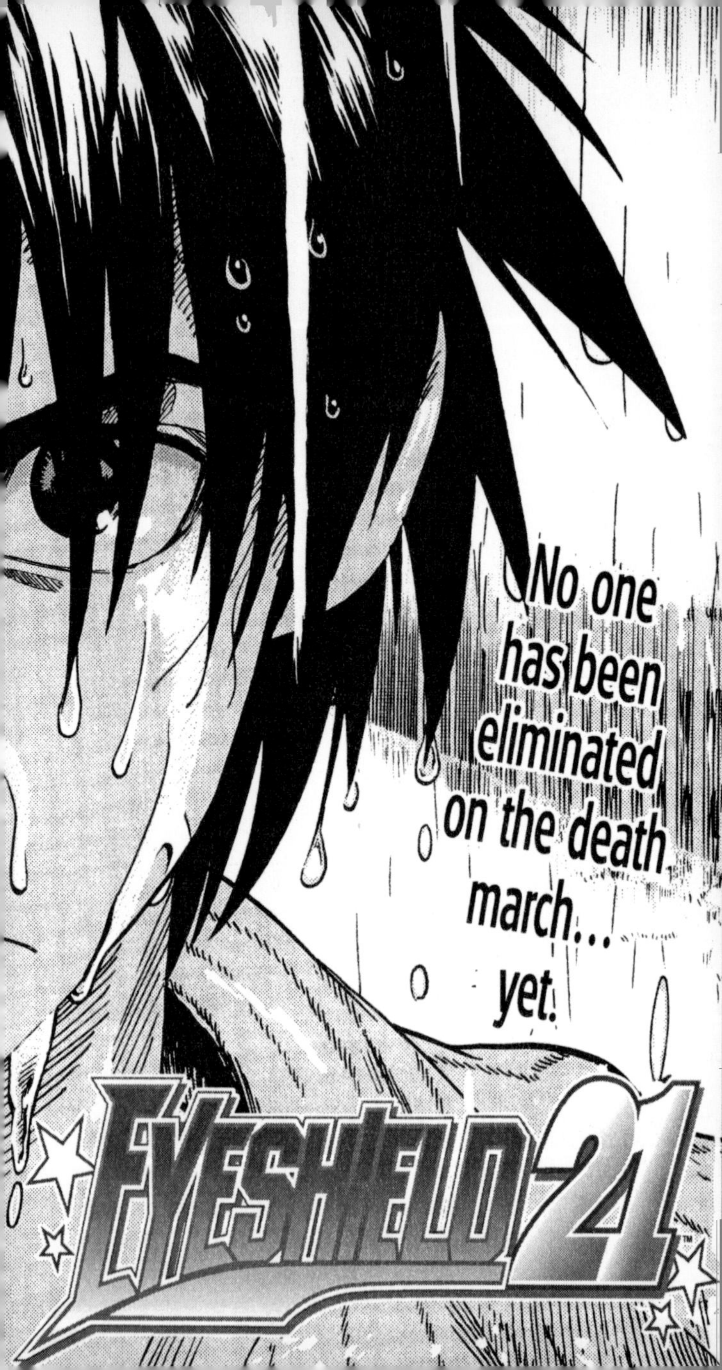
No one has been eliminated on the death march... yet.
EYESHIELD 21

EVEN IF HIS LEGS BREAK HE'LL CRAWL HIS WAY THERE.

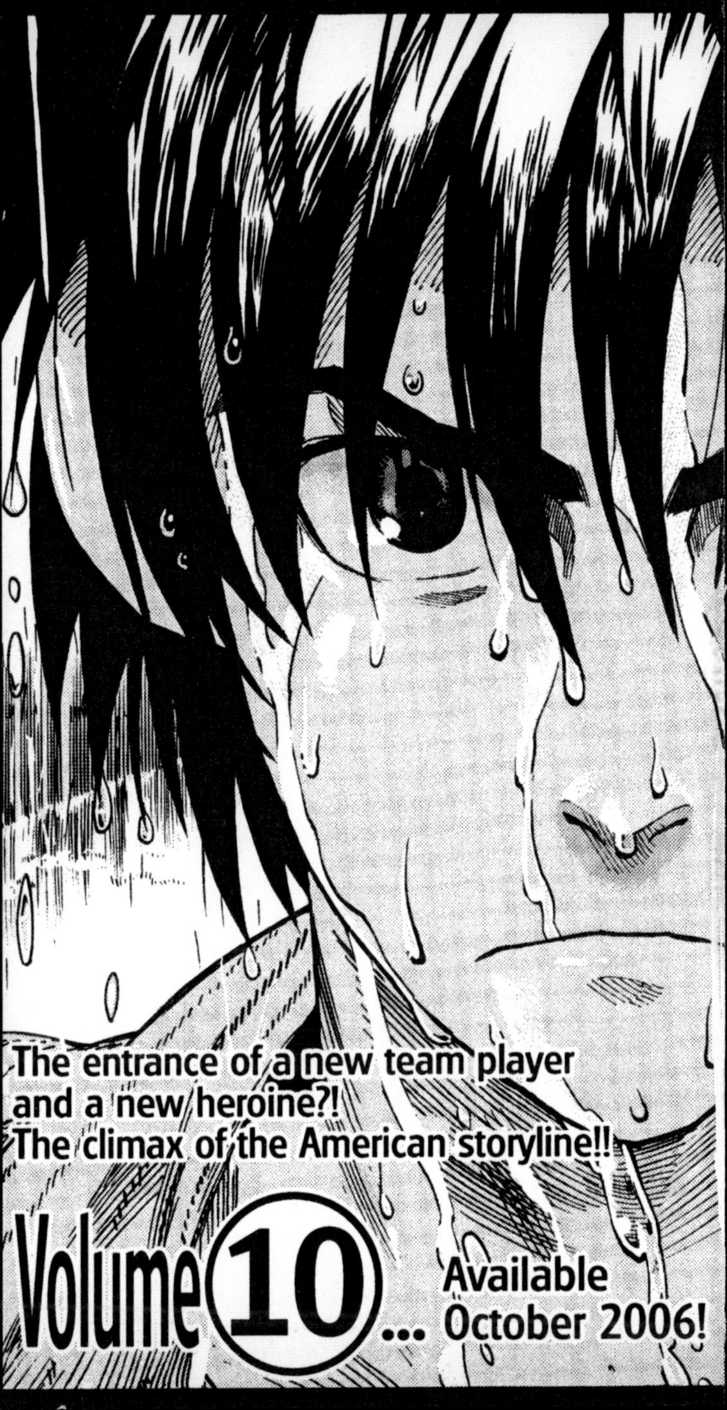
The entrance of a new team player
and a new heroine?!
The climax of the American storyline!!
Volume 10 ... Available
October 2006!

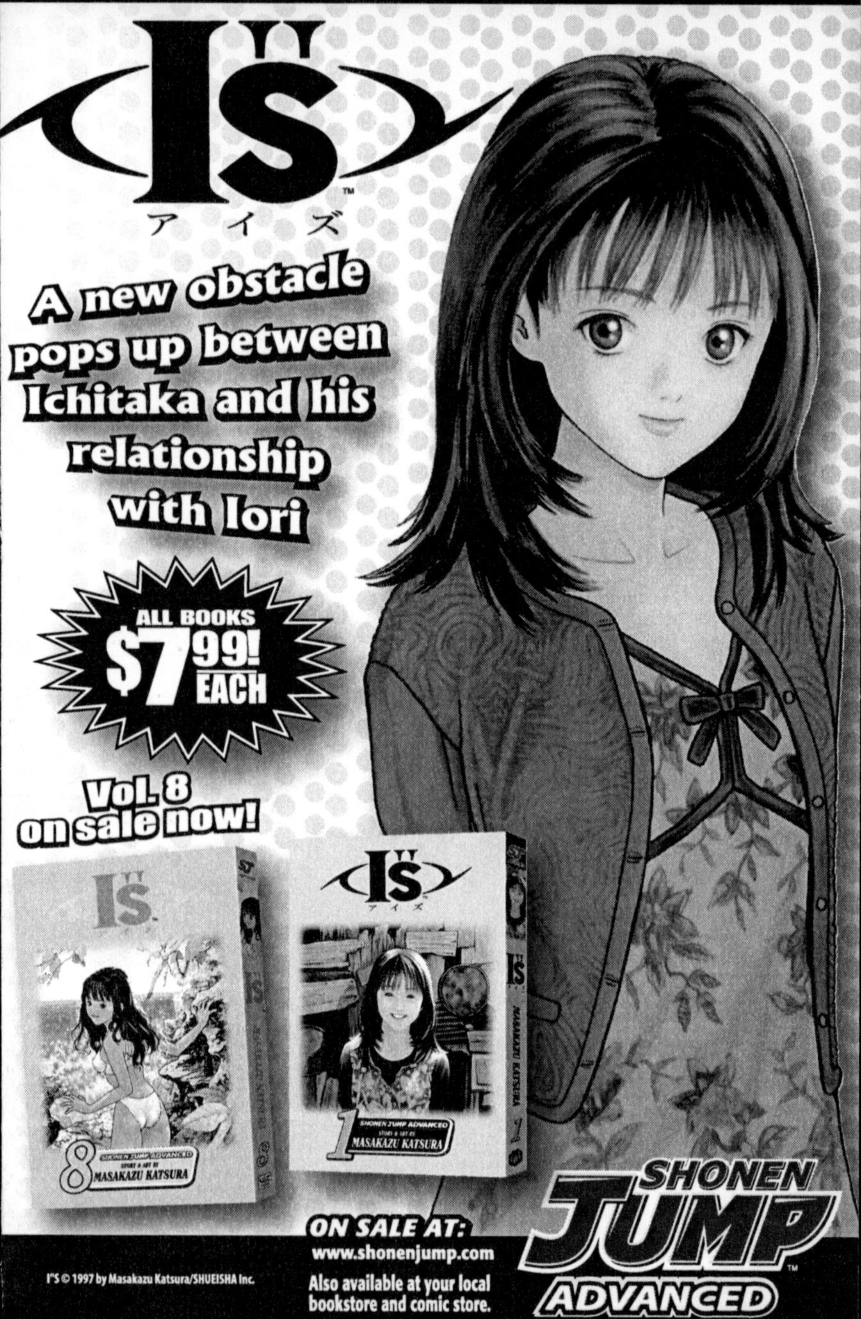
I"S™
アイズ
A new obstacle pops up between Ichitaka and his relationship with Iori
ALL BOOKS $7.99! EACH
Vol. 8 on sale now!
8 SHONEN JUMP ADVANCED MASAKAZU KATSURA
I"S アイズ
1 SHONEN JUMP ADVANCED MASAKAZU KATSURA
ON SALE AT:
www.shonenjump.com
Also available at your local bookstore and comic store.
SHONEN JUMP™ ADVANCED
I"S © 1997 by Masakazu Katsura/SHUEISHA Inc.

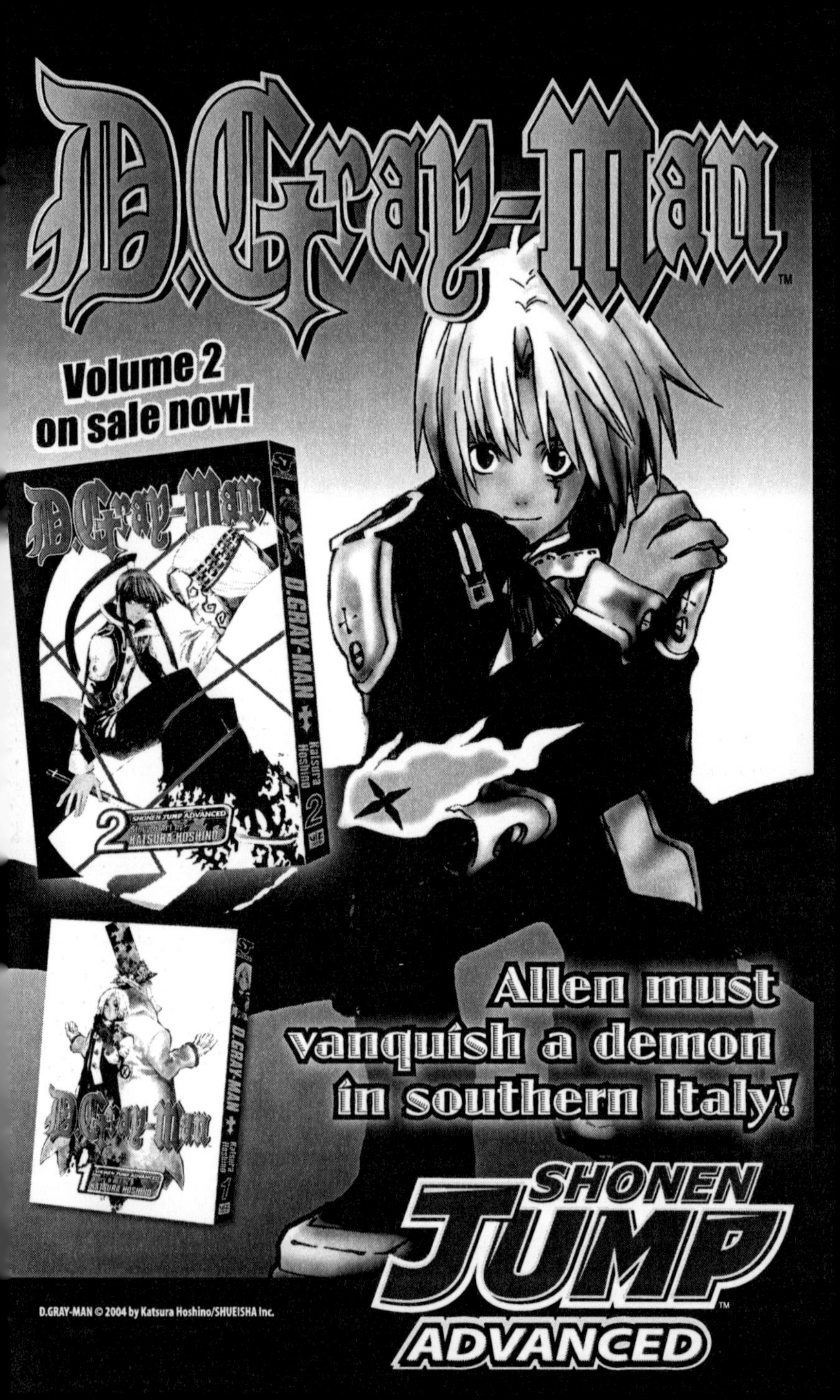
D.Gray-man™
Volume 2 on sale now!
D.Gray-man
2 SHONEN JUMP ADVANCED
Story and Art by KATSURA HOSHINO
D.GRAY-MAN
Katsura Hoshino
2
D.Gray-man
1
D.GRAY-MAN
Katsura Hoshino
Allen must vanquish a demon in southern Italy!
SHONEN JUMP™ ADVANCED
D.GRAY-MAN © 2004 by Katsura Hoshino/SHUEISHA Inc.

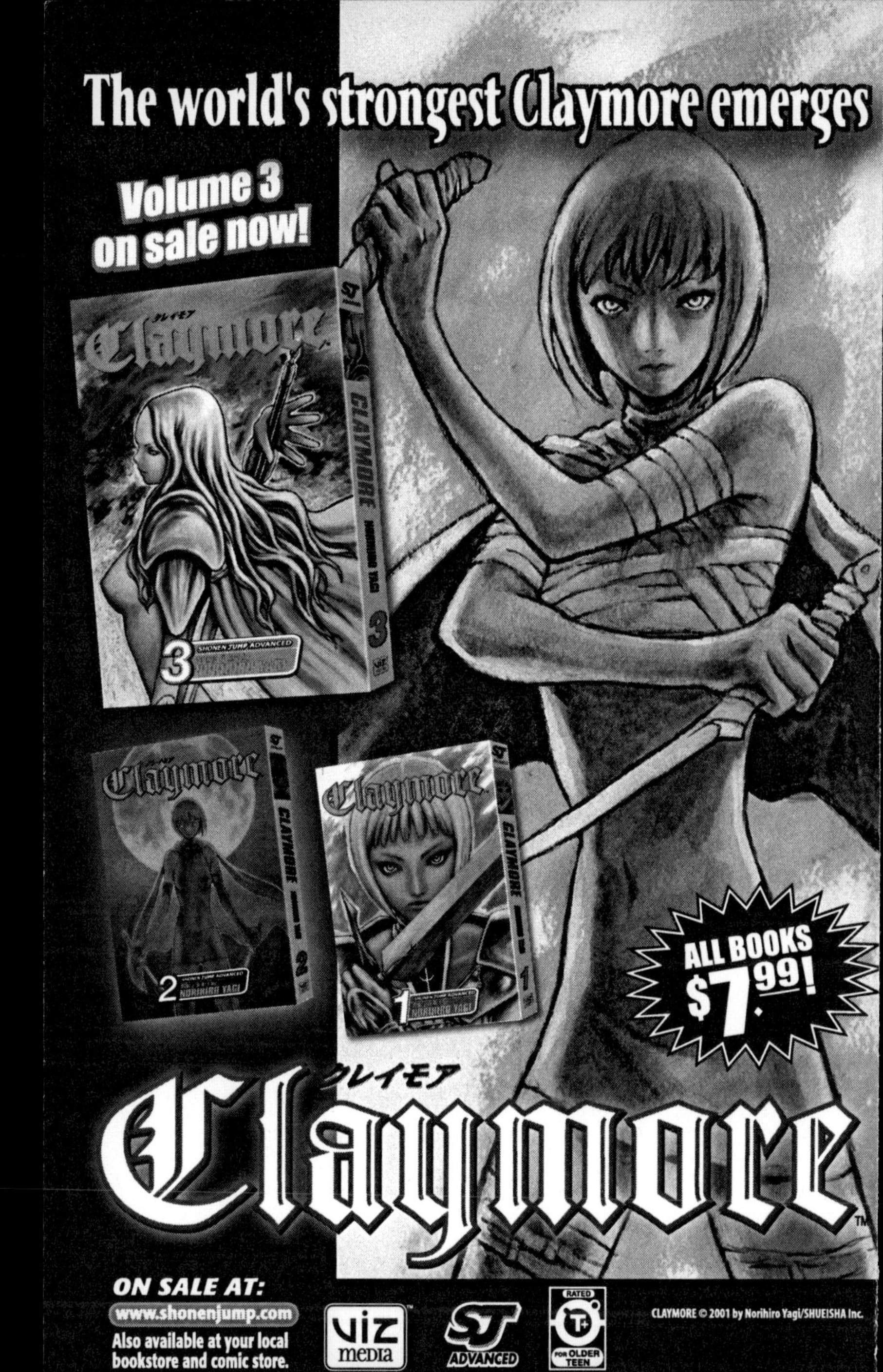
The world's strongest Claymore emerges
Volume 3 on sale now!
ALL BOOKS $7.99!
クレイモア
Claymore™
ON SALE AT:
www.shonenjump.com
Also available at your local bookstore and comic store.
RATED T+ FOR OLDER TEEN
CLAYMORE © 2001 by Norihiro Yagi/SHUEISHA Inc.

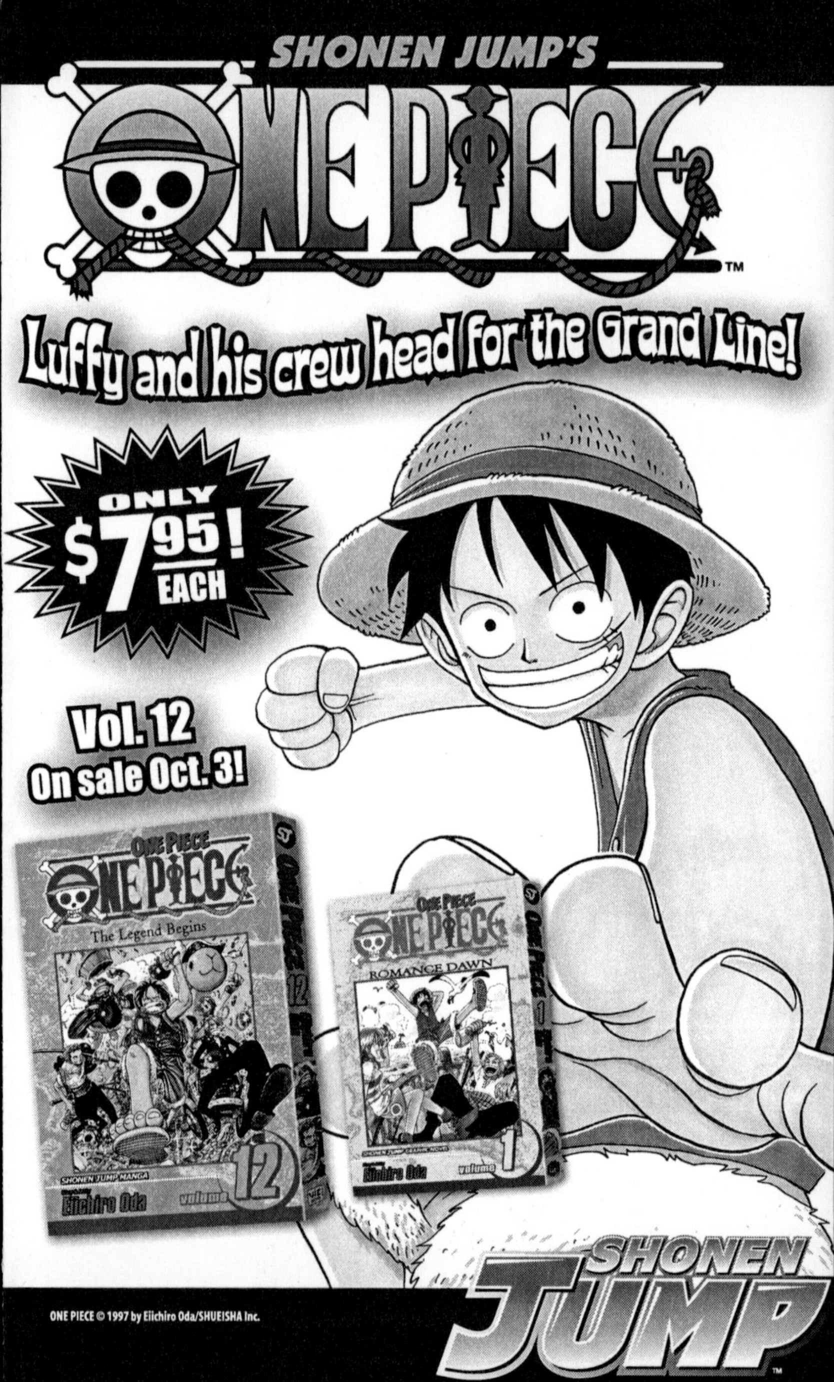
SHONEN JUMP'S
ONE PIECE™
Luffy and his crew head for the Grand Line!
ONLY $7.95! EACH
Vol. 12
On sale Oct. 3!
ONE PIECE
ONE PIECE
The Legend Begins
SHONEN JUMP MANGA
Eiichiro Oda
volume 12
ONE PIECE
ONE PIECE
ROMANCE DAWN
Eiichiro Oda
volume 1
ONE PIECE © 1997 by Eiichiro Oda/SHUEISHA Inc.
SHONEN JUMP™

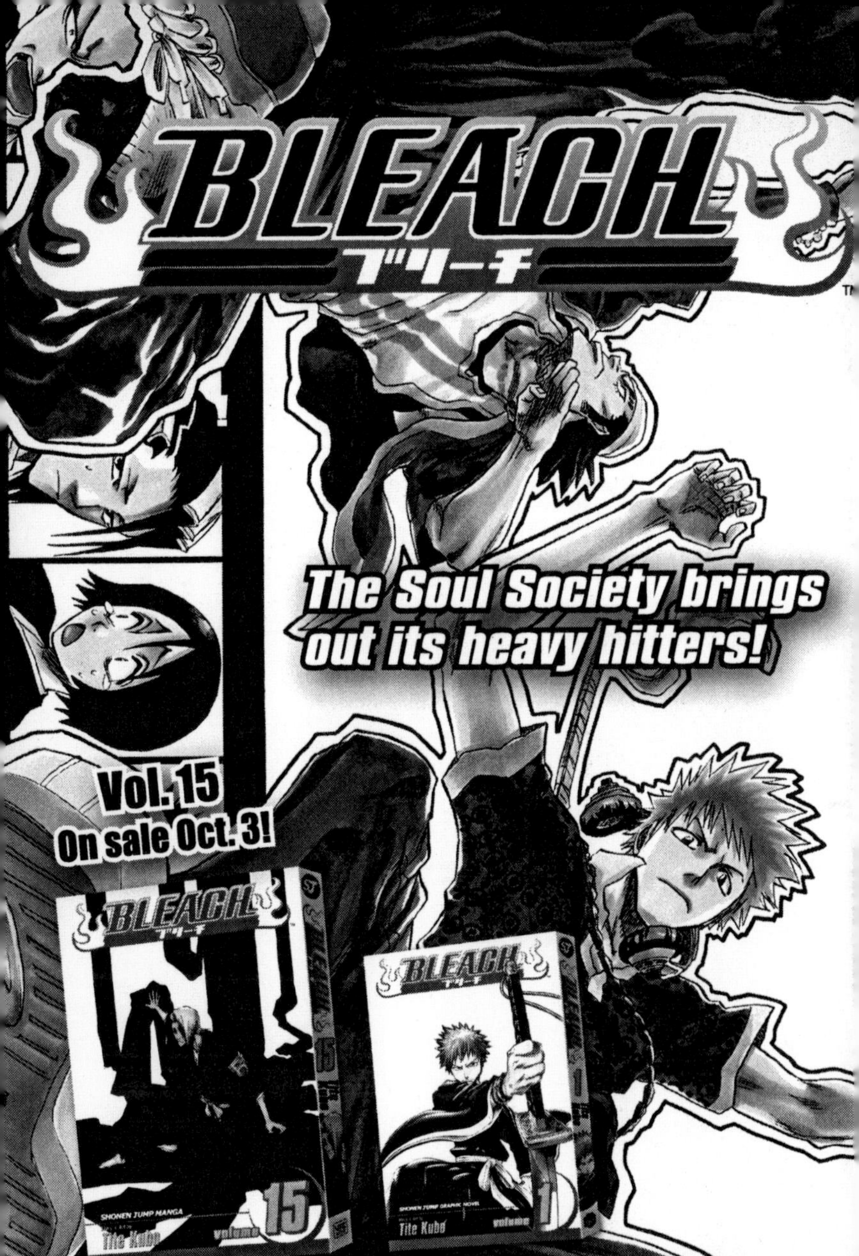
BLEACH
ブリーチ
The Soul Society brings out its heavy hitters!
Vol. 15
On sale Oct. 3!
BLEACH
ブリーチ
SHONEN JUMP MANGA
Tite Kubo
volume 15
BLEACH
ブリーチ
SHONEN JUMP GRAPHIC NOVEL
Tite Kubo
volume 1

Tell us what you think about SHONEN JUMP manga!

Our survey is now available online.
Go to: www.**SHONENJUMP**.com/mangasurvey

THE REAL ACTION
STARTS IN...

SHONEN
JUMP
THE WORLD'S MOST POPULAR MANGA
www.shonenjump.com

ST
ADVANCED

ST

Viz
media

BLEACH © 2001 by Tite Kubo/SHUEISHA Inc. NARUTO © 1999 by Masashi Kishimoto/SHUEISHA Inc.
DEATH NOTE © 2003 by

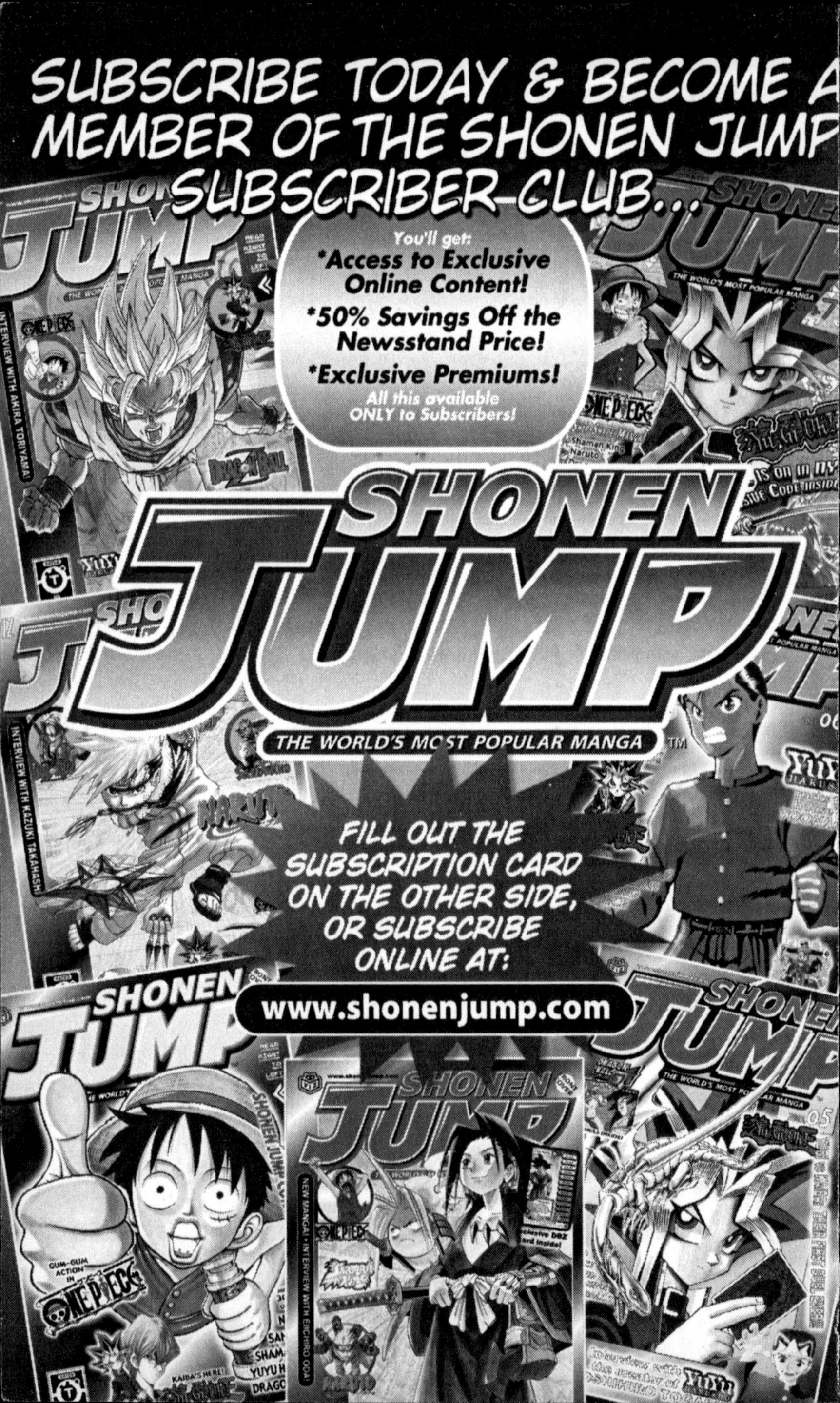
SUBSCRIBE TODAY & BECOME A MEMBER OF THE SHONEN JUMP SUBSCRIBER CLUB...
You'll get:
*Access to Exclusive Online Content!
*50% Savings Off the Newsstand Price!
*Exclusive Premiums!
All this available ONLY to Subscribers!
SHONEN JUMP
THE WORLD'S MOST POPULAR MANGA™
FILL OUT THE SUBSCRIPTION CARD ON THE OTHER SIDE, OR SUBSCRIBE ONLINE AT:
www.shonenjump.com